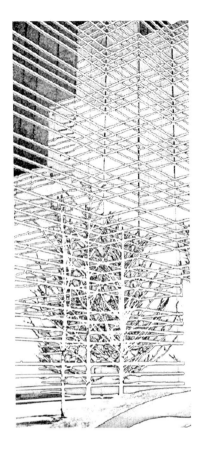

The Practice of

ORGANIZATIONAL COMMUNICATION

Michael Dues

Mary Brown

University of Arizona

McGraw-Hill Primis Custom Publishing

Boston Burr Ridge, IL Dubuque, IA Madison, WI New York San Francisco
St. Louis Bangkok Bogotá Caracas Lisbon London Madrid Mexico City Milan
New Delhi Paris Seoul Singapore Sydney Taipei Toronto

The McGraw·Hill Companies

The Practice of ORGANIZATIONAL COMMUNICATION

McGraw-Hill's Primis Custom Publishing consists of products that are produced from camera-ready copy. Peer review, class testing, and accuracy are primarily the responsibility of the author(s).

4 5 6 7 8 9 0 GDP GDP 0 9 8 7 6 5 4

ISBN 0-07-250860-4

Editor: Nada Mraovic
Cover Design: Maggie Lytle
Printer/Binder: Greyden Press

Acknowledgments

Thanks to the our organizational communication students and teaching staff who helped identify the need and the appropriate content for this book. Thanks to the contributing authors who gave their time, effort, and expertise to make it genuinely useful. And, thanks to Steve Boillot and the McGraw-Hill staff who worked with us patiently on this project.

M. B. & M. D.

Table of Contents

Part III: Specialized Communication Functions

Part IV: Communicating in the 21st Century

Preface

Humans begin learning to communicate at birth, continue learning every day, and develop amazing ability to communicate complex thoughts and emotions. Yet, scholars struggle to agree on the definition of communication, and people are often frustrated by their inability to communicate as effectively as they would like.

Communication is the means by which we create, maintain, and alter our organizations, and the means by which we conduct much of our organizational business. "Poor communication" serves as an almost universal scapegoat, blamed for all manner of organizational failures. "Better communication" tends to be viewed as an almost universal panacea for solving organizational problems, especially when members do not understand the problem, or when they are unwilling to commit real resources to solving it. Communication is neither the cause of nor the solution to all organizational problems, but better communication would certainly reduce the number and magnitude of problems, and help solve existing problems.

We cannot resolve these puzzling paradoxes of communication. What we can do is improve our understanding of communication as it relates to organization and work; and we can improve our communication skills. This book is meant to help the reader build understanding and develop skill in organizational communication.

M. D. and M. B.
Tucson, Arizona
Fall, 2001

Introduction

"What we need is better communication." This phrase is offered every day in organizations as a diagnosis and a prescribed solution for organizational problems. While "better communication" is clearly not a solution to every problem, almost every executive rightly believes that better communication would improve the functioning of her/his organization. Similarly, all professionals working in organizations encounter occasions when they would be individually more effective if they possessed greater skill in communication. Much of what organizations do is accomplished through communication processes that are enacted by individual organization members. To function effectively as a professional member of an organization, one must develop an understanding of organizational communication processes, and the skills required to participate in those processes.

This is a book about organizational communication for communication majors and other students who anticipate careers as managers or professionals working in organizations. Our purposes are to provide introductions to: (1) the concepts that influence communication in organizations; (2) the communication processes by which organizations are formed and maintained, and through which organizational activity is coordinated; (3) the basic communication skills required to participate effectively in those processes; and (4) the emergent conditions that challenge practitioners of organizational communication and require rethinking and adapting of organizational communication processes.

We assume that our reader's primary interest in studying organizational communication is to become a more effective communicator in organizational contexts. Therefore this book emphasizes practical application. Practice, however, is always influenced by ideas and by emergent conditions which require adaptation. To deal with both the conceptual and the practical, we have arranged this book in three parts.

Part I provides a conceptual framework by explaining relevant concepts of communication, organization, and management, by placing these concepts in their historical contexts, and by explaining how concepts of organization influence organizational communication.

Part II offers introductions to core communication skills that are critical to any member's success in an organization. These are listening, self presentation, oral presentations, writing, persuasive argument, conducting useful meetings, group decision-making, team development, conflict management, and leadership. We explain each skill area, identifying general principles which govern effectiveness, and offering specific advice for successful application.

Part III discusses three important organizational communication processes that are usually carried out by specialists: training and development, marketing, and public relations. While it is not necessary that all members possess skill in these areas, it is critical that all managers have a general understanding of these processes, their functions, needs, and limitations.

A concluding chapter addresses organizational communication in the 21st century, pointing to the challenging conditions and processes emerging in today's organizations, and indicating the kinds of communication skills these conditions and processes will demand of organization members.

Both communication and organization are extremely broad subjects encompassing a wide range of human activity. This book was designed as an upper-division level introduction to the basic topics in the practice of organizational communication. It offers a practical, skills-oriented approach. We hope readers will investigate each subject beyond what we have been able to cover in this book. Each chapter ends with suggested further readings.

The scope of this book is too broad to be covered well by a single author. We concluded that to best serve our readers' interests, each chapter should be written by a specialist in its content. We sought writers for specific chapters who could bring both academic credentials and professional experience in organizations to their subject. Their credentials are described prior to each chapter. In a sense, then, this text is more a book of readings than a single text. The styles and approaches of the writers vary, but each communicates clearly. Collectively, we believe their explanations and suggestions offer an excellent practical introduction to organizational communication.

In this text, we attempt to provide a sound conceptual introduction to organizational communication, a practical beginners' manual of important organizational communication skills and specialized processes, and an interesting preview of communication challenges organization members will face during their careers in the 21st century. We hope that readers will find it a valuable basic text, and that they will keep it and use it as a helpful communication manual in their professional careers.

PART 1

Understanding Communication and Organization

Michael Dues holds a Ph.D. in Speech Communication and American Studies from Indiana University, and currently serves as Senior Lecturer in Communication at the University of Arizona. With 35 years' experience in university teaching and administration, and more than 20 years of experience as a successful management communication consultant, he is a recognized expert on organizational change, conflict management, team development, and strategic and action planning. His consulting clients include large and small, public and private organizations of all kinds.

In this chapter, he introduces the complex concept of communication as we know it today, and shows how it applies in organizational contexts.

CHAPTER 1

A Contemporary Understanding of Communication

Michael T. Dues
University of Arizona

Key Terms

Adler-Elmhorst Model
affective
communication
cognitive
context
entertain
feeling
four awful truths
four critical points of view

inform
instrumental
intention
managing
meaning
messages
noise
organization
nonverbal

relate
relational
rhetorical
sense
Shannon-Weaver Model
social reality
tone
verbal symbols

Objectives

This chapter introduces the contemporary concepts of communication, and applies these concepts in organizational contexts. The chapter objectives are to:

1. Show that communication and organization are not fixed realities, but evolving ideas that interact with one another.
2. Offer three useful definitions of communication.
3. Consider two models of communication to illustrate key aspects of the communication process.

4. List four "awful truths" about human communication.
5. Describe five additional characteristics of communication that are especially relevant in understanding organizational communication.
6. Identify three common wrong ideas about communication that tend to interfere with effectively communicating.

Because it is almost as common as the air we breathe, most people assume that communication just *is*. We take communication for granted; we just do it automatically. We think about communication only when it fails. In a way living in organizations is almost as common and automatic as communicating. Organizations provide the jobs and careers at which we spend our days and by which we earn our living. We belong to clubs, churches, fraternities, all of which are organizations. Our governments are organizations. Our families are organizations. Because we live in and through organizations, we tend to take their existence and their nature for granted too.

Communication and organizations are all around us, but it is a mistake to take either for granted. Both communication and organizations are human creations. Our *ideas* about both have been evolving for centuries. The basic concept of **communication** we use today did not exist during most of human history. John Locke coined the term *communication* in 1690 to refer to the sharing of information, ideas, feelings, and intentions, that is necessary to achieve cooperative interaction and, in turn, enjoy the benefits of living among other humans (Locke, 1690/1979). Locke's idea of communication has been refined considerably during the last century, and our concept of communication continues to evolve, especially in the last several decades.

Like our concepts of communication, our ideas about what **organizations** are and how organizations are managed are evolving. In the late nineteenth century Max Weber, a German sociologist, developed the basic concept of an organization as a kind of hierarchical structure made up of interrelated compartments, each with a specialized set of tasks. Over the course of the twentieth century human resources theorists, systems theorists, and communication theorists have not only added to Weber's ideas, but also have generated fundamentally new ways of thinking about organizations.

To become a competent organizational communicator, then, the first thing one needs to understand is that neither communication nor organization is a fixed reality that will stay as it is. What we have are *ideas* about communication and organization that are constantly changing as emerging conditions and new information stimulate new research and thought. The second fundamental thing to understand is that our ideas about communication and organization are always connected; they interact with one another. It is important to recognize that:

Our ideas about communication affect the ways we organize, and our ideas about organization affect the ways we communicate . . . both within organizations and between organizations and their external environments.

A competent organizational communicator needs to understand contemporary ideas about communication, and to recognize how they relate to interactions among members of organizations. And a competent organizational communicator needs to understand contemporary concepts of organizational structure and management and to recognize how they affect organizational communication. Part I of this book provides a foundation for these basic understandings. Chapter 1 concerns communication as a universal human process, and Chapter 2 explains the evolution of ideas about organization and their impact on organizational communication.

We begin with the concept of communication as it stands at the beginning of the 21st century, considering aspects of communication that are especially important for members of organizations to understand. This chapter describes what communication is, what communication does, and what communication is not. In it we will approach a contemporary understanding of the nature of communication by considering some useful definitions, some visual models of the communication process, and several key characteristics of communication.

What Communication Is

As we use it today, the term communication encompasses a highly complex set of interactive human processes and behaviors. The practice of human communication changes with new technologies, and with new economic and social conditions. Our understanding of communication shifts with new information and new theories. The subject of communication, then, is a kind of moving target; it keeps changing and we must keep adapting our understanding accordingly.

Like love, communication is a common phenomenon that is easy to recognize but very difficult to define. Communication scholars have proposed hundreds of definitions over the years, none of which is able to include all that communication is. Perhaps communication defies adequate definition because it is not one, but a family of concepts (Dance, 1970).

The word "communication" has a rich and complex history. It first appeared in the English language in the fourteenth century, taken from the Latin word *communicare*, which meant to impart, share, or make common. Over the course of the 20th century, the term *has been used with a broad variety of meanings ranging from the simple transfer of information to the utopian ideal of a place where "nothing is misunderstood, hearts are open, and expression is uninhibited" (Peters, 1999).*

Definitions

Bearing in mind that definitions are only starting points for understanding, and that various definitions serve to highlight differing aspects of the phenomenon of **communication,** let's consider three useful definitions.

(1) Drawing upon Locke's thought, communication can be defined as *the sharing of information, ideas, feelings, and intentions among humans.*

    The concept of sharing is especially important in this definition. Locke recognized that humans must achieve shared meanings in order to gain the benefits of living together in society.

(2) A more contemporary and precise definition focuses on three basic terms that are fundamental to the communication process. Frey, Botan, and Kreps (2000) define communication as **managing messages for the purpose of creating meaning.** The term **managing** includes all the activities of creating, encoding, sending, receiving, interpreting, and giving feedback. **Messages** are what humans send and receive when we communicate. **Meanings** are carried in messages. They are what we intend to share when we communicate.

(3) Organizational communication, the term in the title of this book, can be defined as **the exchange of information and the transmission of meaning and the lifeblood of the organization** (Dessler, 1982). A key point in this definition is that without communication organizations cannot exist.

Like all the other definitions of communication, these fall short of accomplishing what good definitions are supposed to do. They fail to clearly mark the boundaries between what communication is and what communication is not. Nevertheless, they provide a viable starting point for understanding communication. Communication includes all the activities involved in managing the creation, sending, receiving, and interpreting of messages. Its general purpose is to achieve shared meanings. And in organizations communication is so essential that it can rightly be called their lifeblood.

Two Models of the Communication Process

Models help us to conceptualize communication by visualizing the process by which it occurs. Communication scholars have developed a variety of communication models, each of which offers some insight into the nature of the process. Like definitions of communication, all models are imperfect. Each relies on a visual metaphor. Each depicts a simplified version of the communication process. Each highlights certain important aspects of communication while omitting others; none offers a complete description. Let's consider an old model that is still useful, and a more contemporary model that better illustrates the complexity of communication.

A Linear Model of Communication

An early model of the communication process was developed by Shannon and Weaver (1949). Because their model was intended for use by the telephone company, Shannon and Weaver were primarily concerned with the accurate transmission of messages over the telephone. Their model envisions a source who encodes or creates a message and transmits it through a channel to a receiver who decodes it, recreating the meaning of the message (see Figure 1.1).

The Shannon-Weaver Model illustrates how ideas are encoded as symbols so that they can be transmitted via some physical medium to the receiver, and shows that the receiver must decode the symbols once they are received in order the determine the meaning of what has been communicated. An important concept introduced in the Shannon-

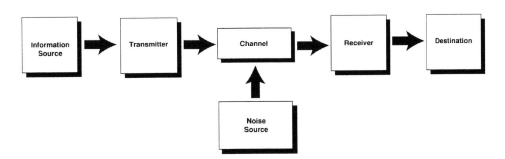

Figure 1.1   The Shannon-Weaver Model

Weaver model is *noise.* Virtually all communication occurs in contexts where there are stimuli that can disrupt the accuracy of the message being transmitted. There is always some background noise. For Shannon and Weaver noise represented static interference on a phone call. For us noise can represent another person talking, background music, a siren outside the window, or any other random sound or sight that competes with an intended message for the receiver's attention. Noise can be physical or psychological. Psychological noise refers to a person's thoughts, feelings, or stresses. Worry, or anticipation about an upcoming event can interfere with hearing, interpretation, and understanding of messages. Daydreaming can cause us to miss a message completely.

This model provides a simple snapshot of the steps in the sending and receiving of a single message. As a *linear* model of communication it visualizes communication as a sequential, one-way process. It does not illustrate the on-going, interactive nature of communication. It views communication only as transfer of information, but communication involves much more than information transfer. Thinking of communication in terms of single messages from senders to receivers is sometimes useful for strategic or analytic purposes. However, a single-message view is comparable to using a still picture to describe a basketball game. The picture captures one instant of the action, but it does not represent the *game*, which is ongoing and interactive. Despite these limitations, the Shannon-Weaver Model serves to illustrate the use of symbols to encode and decode messages, the function of the physical channels that carry messages between people, and the impact of background noise on message reception.

An Interactive Model of Communication

In recent years various communication scholars have sought to improve existing models of communication in order to more accurately reflect the communication process and place it in its social context. Writing for business and the professions, Adler and Elmhorst (1996) elaborated the Shannon and Weaver model to better illustrate the on-going, interactive **nature of communication and the pervasiveness of noise in a business environment. The** Adler and Elmhorst Model (Figure 1.2) describes two communicators who are each simultaneously sending and receiving messages through multiple channels, while physical noise in their communication channels impedes transmission of messages, and psychological noise in the form of competing thoughts and concerns impedes encoding and decoding messages. This model helps us appreciate the complexity and difficulty of communication in an organizational setting.

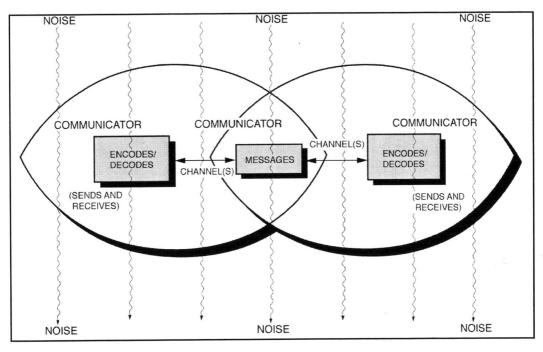

Figure 1.2 The Adler-Elmhorst Model of Communication in Business

Characteristics of Human Communication

In addition to definitions and models, studies of the communication process allow us to describe some of its characteristics that are especially important to bear in mind as we try to communicate as professionals in organizational settings. The Adler-Elmhorst Model helps us see the complexity of human communication. The daunting challenge humans face when we try to communicate begins to become clear when we consider four basic characteristics that I call the *Four Awful Truths About Communication.* These are:

1. Communication is inevitable. (You can't avoid communicating.)
2. Communication has consequences. (Whenever you communicate, something changes.)
3. All communication involves error. (You can't get it perfectly right.)
4. Communication is irreversible. (You can't take it back.)

Let's briefly consider each of these awful truths.

1. Communication is inevitable.

It became clear over the course of the 20th century that communication in organizations is best understood not as the sending and receiving of single messages, but as a continuous interactive process in which all the participating parties are constantly sending and receiving multiple messages. Since the 1960s scholars have applied systems theory to depict the systemic nature of communication processes. From the perspective of systems theory, human relationships (including organizational relationships) are seen as *open systems* that are comparable to living organisms in which all the parts are interdependent, constantly interacting and influencing one another. Communication *is the interaction. Because any action or inaction, whether intentional or not, may affect others in the system and may be assigned meaning by others in the system (Watzlawick, Beavin & Jackson, 1967), it is virtually impossible to* not communicate. Communication is an inherent, necessary aspect of participating in a relational system. As such, it is inevitable.

2. Communication has consequences.

An old saying often taught to children says, "Sticks and stones may break my bones, but words can never hurt me." But every child *knows* this saying is not true. Words can and do hurt. And words can and do soothe, delight, teach, or persuade. There is rarely such a thing as "just talk." Whenever people communicate, there are consequences. By its very nature, communication elicits a response in the receiver. Consequences may be large or small, intended or unintended, direct or indirect, temporary or permanent, immediate or delayed; but communication always has some impact.

3. All Communication Involves Error.

Most people assume when they communicate that the recipient received and accurately understood their message. That assumption represents a terribly unrealistic expectation. In reality, what the receiver thinks a message means is *never* exactly what the sender meant. All communication involves error. Why? Each person brings to each communicative act a different set of experiences, varying mental abilities and habits, different levels of interest and attention, a different set of needs, and a different array of competing concerns. All of these variables can affect the way senders choose words to convey messages and the way receivers interpret them. Given these differences, therefore, the match between the sender's intended meaning and the receiver's assigned meaning of a message will never be perfect. There will always be a meaning gap between sender and receiver. The gap will be greater when we communicate about complex or abstract concepts. Most people have a pretty clear idea of what "justice" means, for example, but justice means very different things to different people in different contexts. If we accept the fact that all communication involves error, we can work with more realistic expectations when we communicate, and take steps to identify and deal constructively with the inevitable communication errors.

4. Communication is Irreversible.

The fourth awful truth about communication is one that virtually everyone has experienced with regret. We have all said things and then wished we hadn't said them. Once something is said, it cannot be unsaid. We can apologize, or explain, but we can't take it back. When we consider this irreversible quality of communication in light of the facts that communication cannot be avoided, all communication has consequences, and all communication involves error, we can begin to gain a healthy respect for the daunting challenge that human communication represents.

When combined, these truths portray the dilemma we face as communicators: we can't avoid communicating; it always has consequences; we can't ever get it perfectly right; and we can't take it back. It's a wonder we communicate as well as we do.

Other Key Characteristics of Communication

In addition to the four awful truths, there are five other communication characteristics that are important to recognize when communicating in organizations. These are:

1. Human communication is *symbolic*. It employs symbols in addition to, and in combination with, sounds and behaviors.
2. Communication is *contextual*. It always occurs in a specific context, and the context influences meaning.
3. Messages are *complex*. They have cognitive, affective, relational, and instrumental dimensions.
4. Meanings are always *personal*. Words are assigned meaning in the minds of the communicators.
5. Communication is *rhetorical*. It is used strategically to achieve goals.

Each of these characteristics is explained below.

1. Human Communication is Symbolic.

Most animals convey messages to other living creatures by means of natural sounds and behavior. Dogs bark and assume threatening postures to warn off potential opponents. The rattlesnake's rattle sends a clear and strong message. Some animals signal surrender by lying on their backs and exposing their bellies. Humans, too, communicate by means of behavior and natural sound. In fact, nonverbal signals carry most of the meaning when humans communicate face to face with one another. However, humans also employ words, or **verbal symbols,** to communicate. The use of language to communicate distinguishes humans from lower animals, permits us to represent and share complex and abstract ideas. Language makes complex organization, civilization, and culture possible.

Use of language to communicate also has a down side. For language to be efficient and manageable words often have more than one meaning; otherwise one would need a vocabulary of hundreds of thousands of words to communicate. Furthermore, because words "stand for" the things or ideas they represent, there is much room for variation in the meanings we learn to associate with them. The problem of multiple meanings of symbols creates opportunities for equivocation, ambiguity and misunderstanding. Use of words to convey abstract ideas that have no concrete reference in the material world adds to the potential for misunderstanding. There is no ambiguity or uncertainty about the meaning of a rattlesnake's rattle; there is a great deal of ambiguity and uncertainty in linguistic communication. When humans use language to communicate we often think we have communicated successfully when we have not.

2. Communication is contextual.

Communication always takes place in the context of existing ideas, in a particular place, and in a specific set of circumstances. The **context** shapes the meaning of what is communicated. In fact, it would be extremely difficult to understand the meaning of a message without knowing its context. Thus, we say that communication is contextual: it cannot be understood separate from its context. Communication scholars refer to several different types of contexts. Cultural contexts of communication include the broad cultures that give us our languages, our fundamental beliefs, customs, and primary institutions. Cultural contexts also include the more specific cultures developed by organizations that provide some linguistic jargon, group norms and values, social settings, and prescriptions about human relationships. Physical contexts are the places where we communicate. Situational contexts include previous interactions, the status of the relationship between the communicators, events leading up to the current communication exchange, and conditions surrounding the current communication exchange. Some scholars have also described psychological contexts, including past experiences, temperament, emotions and goals, that individuals carry with them when they communicate (Cupach & Canary, 1997; Lewin, 1948; Pearce, 1994).

It is important to recognize that contexts influence meaning. In some cultures to look another person in the eye sends a message saying "I am being honest with you; you can trust me." In other cultures to look a person other than one's spouse or immediate family in the eye is an insult that says "I don't respect you." Standing beside a swimming pool and saying "jump in" means something very different from standing on a bridge high above a river and saying "jump in." Contexts also influence meaning over time. The outcomes of past interactions become the context for today's interaction. Likewise, the results of today's interaction becomes the context for future communication events. People who attempt to communicate without being sensitive to context often send messages they didn't intend.

3. Messages are Complex and Multi-dimensional.

Every act of communication is complex in that it involves *thought, feeling, relating,* and *purpose.* Communication scholars refer to these aspects of messages as **cognitive, affective, relational,** and **instrumental** dimensions. One useful way to conceptualize these dimensions is based on the work of the British communication theorist I. A. Richards. Richards observed that in order to fully comprehend the meaning of a statement, one must consider it from **four critical points of view** (Richards, 1936). He labeled these sense, feeling, tone, and intention. Let's briefly consider each, and then look at an example.

> **Sense** refers to the meaning directly conveyed by the words. It is the surface content of the message. Sense represents the cognitive dimension, which is predominantly carried in verbal form.

> **Feeling** refers to the sender's feeling toward the content of her/his message. Whenever humans make a statement we also, necessarily, communicate something about how we feel about whatever we are saying. We may communicate that we passionately care about what we are saying, or that we feel objectively distant from

our subject, or that we are tentative or uncertain about it, or any number of other complex feelings. Feeling represents the affective dimension of a message. The affective dimension modifies and supports the cognitive dimension. It can also cancel out the cognitive dimension. The affective dimension of a message is often carried in nonverbal codes. Tone of voice, posture, timing, and gestures are nonverbal codes that serve to communicate how we feel about what we are saying.

Tone refers to the **relational** dimension of the message. Any time a person sends a message to another person she/he must do so in a way that makes a claim about the relationship between them. We make relational claims through the manner in which we address one another, our tone of voice, the physical distance from which we speak, our choice of words, and the content of what we say.

Intention refers to the message the receiver receives about the sender's intention in communicating. Any time we receive a message, it comes with some cues about why the sender sent it. This is the instrumental dimension of the message. The understanding between the sender and receiver about the *reason* for any communication is part of the meaning of that communication. Like tone, intention is communicated both verbally and nonverbally. Often, the context in which communication occurs, especially in work settings, carries the instrumental dimension of a message.

It is important to understand that communication is not simply a matter of sending single cognitive messages, or conveying information. What the receiver of a message receives is a complex mixture of the four dimensions described above—*four messages in one communication.* If the four are commensurate with one another, and all four are acceptable to the receiver, the communication effort has a good chance of succeeding. Often, however, the message dimensions appear to contradict one another, and sometimes receivers do not find the tone or intention dimension acceptable. Inconsistencies among message dimensions can lead to considerable confusion. When receivers reject the tone or intention dimension of a message, they typically refuse to process the sense and affect dimensions. The relationship between the four dimensions of a message, and the receiver's willingness to accept the tone and intention dimensions greatly affect the outcomes of communication efforts.

Here is an example of how inconsistencies among the message dimensions can interfere with effective communication. The supervisor says, "we really need to get this shipment out by four o'clock." However, he roles his eyes as he says this, and smiles. His crew may interpret his nonverbal cues as a feeling message saying he doesn't really want to get the job done by 4:00, and they may slow down in their work. Of course, if they are suspicious of his intentions, and believe he may be deliberately attempting to confuse them, they may work even harder to get the shipment out. However the crew interprets his message, they are confronted with the task of discerning the meaning of a complex message in which some of the dimensions appear to contradict others.

The fact that messages include four dimensions of meaning creates opportunities for subtlety and sophistication in human communication. This complexity also creates opportunities of equivocation, obfuscation, and confusion.

4. Meanings are Always Personal.

The words and other symbols we use to communicate are tools that serve to convey meaning. Meanings, however, are not contained in words; meanings are formed in people's minds. Communication is about sharing meaning between people. Words and symbols are tools we use to convey meaning. The only places meanings actually reside are the minds of senders and receivers. The meaning of any message is the meaning in the mind of the communicator. The extent to which the meaning in the receiver's mind matches the meaning intended by the sender is the measure of the accuracy of the communication. What counts is *what the sender meant to say* and *what the receiver thinks she/he heard*, which may be two very different things. For example, a technologically savvy young man said to his mother, "I'm going to burn a couple of CDs." "Oh, don't do that," she countered, "Even if you don't like them, they're valuable." From a communication standpoint the dictionary definition of "burn" doesn't really matter. The message the young man sent was not the message his mother received. When we understand that meanings are personal, we can better see communication as a cooperative effort among two or more people to achieve a matching of meanings.

5. Communication is Rhetorical.

Humans are constantly using communication strategically to influence one another. Long ago, Aristotle defined *rhetoric* as "the art of discovering all the available means of persuasion in a given situation." For more than 2,400 years people have studied rhetoric—the art of persuasion—because success in persuading others affects the material and personal quality of one's life. Success in persuasion certainly affects one's status and effectiveness in any organization. It is useful to recognize that rhetoric is an art, not a science, because every specific communication effort is unique, occurring in a specific situation between specific people. A **rhetorical** understanding of communication in-cludes recognition of the need to adapt a message to its intended audience and to the specific context in which it occurs. Rhetorical understanding includes knowing that persuasion involves a combination of rational, emotional, and personal appeals to the receiver. Rhetorical understanding includes awareness of the fact that others are at-tempting to persuade us, and an ability to recognize and evaluate their strategies and tactics. Rhetorical understanding includes awareness of the fact that our messages may have unintended influence on their receivers. Good communicators are constantly sen-sitive to the rhetorical the rhetorical aspects of communication.

Functions: What Communication Does

The definitions, models, and characteristics discussed above serve to describe the process of communication. Next we focus on what communication *does*. Whether or not we are communicating deliberately or consciously, communication is a strategic activity by which humans achieve cooperation with one another, and influence our social environment. Hu-man communication serves five important functions: to inform, to influence, to relate, to entertain, and to create and maintain social realities. Let's consider these one at a time.

1. To Inform.

One basic function of communication is to allow humans to share information and ideas with one another. This function vastly extends to total of human knowledge and ability. We need information and ideas in order to make choices and to carry out certain tasks, and communication allows us to provide these for one another.

2. To Influence

Humans engage in efforts to influence one another in order to have their personal needs and wishes met, and to coordinate their efforts to meet mutual goals. Social influence is the second key function of communication. In addition to advancing the individual in-terests of communicators, the social influence function of communication serves the common good. The effectiveness of organizations, communities, and whole societies de-pends on people being able to persuade one another to work cooperatively toward com-mon goals.

3. To Relate

Humans use communication to develop, maintain, and manage their relationships with one another (Duck & Pittman, 1994). Humans have what Schutz called three interpersonal needs: inclusion, affection, and control (Schutz, 1958). We need to feel a sense of belonging, of being with others, and we meet this need by communicating. We need affection, and we seek it, give it, and receive it by communicating. And we need to maintain a level of independence and self-control while relating to others, and we achieve this by communicating. Thus, a third basic function of communication is the management of our relationships. The building and maintaining of supportive relationships is critical to individual and collective success in organizations.

4. To Entertain or Express Ourselves

Often we communicate for the sheer enjoyment of communicating. Entertainment and self expression may seem less important than sharing information or managing relationships, but the fact is that humans need and seek self expression and entertainment. Expressing ourselves and entertaining one another are fundamental human social activities, even in organizations. Entertainment and self expression are the fourth function of communication.

5. To Create and Maintain Social Realities

Sociologists have distinguished between two kinds of reality: hard realities and social realities (Berger & Luckmann, 1966). Hard realities are physical things, such as buildings, desks, chairs, human bodies. Hard realities would exist, and be what they are whether or not people recognized them or agreed about their nature. Social realities are every bit as real as hard realities, but their existence and their nature depend upon people's agreement about their existence and their nature. Nations are social realities, as are universities. Human bodies are hard realities, but what it means to be human is a **social reality.** All organizations are social realities. They are quite real, but if people stop agreeing about their nature, they will stop being what they are.

Social realities make up much of the environment in which individuals live. The mechanism by which humans develop and maintain social realities is communication, and this is communication's fifth fundamental function. This function of communication is certainly vital for organizations. It is the fundamental process by which organizations are developed, defined, and maintained.

Three Wrong Ideas: What Communication is Not

In addition to describing what communication is and what communication does, it may be useful to briefly consider what communication is not. There are three common beliefs about communication that are simply wrong, and that hinder effective organizational communication as well as effective problem solving. These are:

1. Most problems are caused by communication failures, and can be solved by better communication.
2. Communication is free.
3. Sending the message is sufficient to accomplish communication.

Let's consider these misconceptions in more detail.

1. Most problems are caused by communication failures, and can be solved by better communication

Among the most pernicious myths in modern society is the idea that if people could just communicate effectively enough to really understand one another all conflicts and most problems would simply disappear. Because we prefer to think of ourselves and our colleagues as good people with good intentions, we tend to think that if we could just express ourselves well enough, others would understand and appreciate us. We tend to think that if we could just find the right thing to say and the right way to say it we could persuade a person whose behavior we wish would change. These are hopeful, but wrong ideas. There are real differences among people and real problems that no amount of perfect communication can resolve. Sometimes, the better we are understood, the *less* we are appreciated. And sometimes there is nothing we can say, no matter how well we say it, that will bring about the change we hope for.

It has become common in our organizations and personal relationships to blame problems on communication failures, or breakdowns. Sometimes communication failure is to blame, but more often the problem consists of real differences, behavior patterns, or unmet needs. Blaming our problems on lack of communication leads to the naive belief that we can readily solve our problems by resolving to improve communication. Such resolutions usually leave the problem unsolved. *Some* problems are communication problems, and can be solved by improving communication. Most problems, however, are matters that require changes in behavior, work processes, organizational structure, or resource distribution. Communication is almost always a necessary tool for diagnosing problems and identifying solutions. Rarely is communication, alone, a solution.

2. Communication is Free

One reason organizational professionals and managers look to communication to solve an unrealistically long list of problems may be that they think of communication as having no cost. The idea that communication is free literally *prevents* effective communication in organizations because it prevents assignment of the time and resources necessary for communication to succeed. Communication requires time and attention and it requires facilities and equipment. It also requires conducive structures, grouping, and processes. It is quite common for members of organizations to decide to solve a problem by communicating more, or more promptly, or more accurately. If they fail to consider and provide for the time, attention, and resources required to accomplish the intended communication improvement, however, communication does not improve and their problem is not solved.

3. Sending the Message is Sufficient to Accomplish Communication.

Because we are most aware of communication when we are intentionally sending a message to another person or persons, we tend to equate communicating with sending messages—with talking, or writing, or making a presentation. Constructing and sending messages, however, are only the beginning steps in the communication process. Communication has not occurred until the message has been received, decoded, and placed in the cognitive system of a receiver. The tendency to equate communication, or communication skills, with speaking, writing, and presenting, interferes with effectively completing the communication process. Listening, for example, is a far more common communication activity than speaking, and every bit as important as speaking in determining whether a communication effort succeeds. If we fail to attend to the conditions that promote effective listening because we are totally focused on the sending of messages, we diminish the likelihood of successful communication.

Summary

A contemporary understanding of communication begins with recognizing that communication is a broad concept we use to label a complex array of related human behaviors and that those behaviors and our ideas about them keep changing. Contemporary understanding will stay contemporary only if we keep learning. It is also important to remember that our ideas about communicate affect the ways we communicate and the ways we organize.

We discussed the phenomenon of human communication as contemporary communication scholars understand it. From definitions of communication we observed that it is an ongoing, interactive process of sending and receiving messages to achieve shared meanings. Visual models help us conceptualize the process of communication, highlighting and illustrating specific aspects of the process. However, no definition or model provides a perfect description of the subject.

Nine characteristics of communication are important for members of organizations to remember. The first four, the awful truths that communication is inevitable, consequential, never perfect, and irreversible, make it clear that communication represents a profoundly difficult challenge. The remaining five help us see attributes of the communication process that are especially important to recognize in organizations: that humans communicate both verbally and nonverbally, that context influences meaning, that messages are multiple and complex, that meanings are in people and not in words, and that communication tends to be rhetorical.

Communication has five general functions. It serves to inform, to influence, to relate, to entertain, and to create and maintain the social realities that make up much of our human environment. Lastly, three common misconceptions interfere with effective communication. These are the notions that most problems are caused by communication failures, that communication is free, and that sending messages is sufficient to accomplish communication.

A sound contemporary understanding of the nature and functions of communication is a necessary foundation for effective communication in organizations. Our ideas about communication influence the ways we set up our organizations, and wrong ideas about communication can lead to inefficient and dysfunctional organizations.

References

Adler, R. B. & Elmhorst, J. M. (1996). *Communicating at work: Principles and practices for business and the professions*, 5th Ed. New York: McGraw-Hill.

Berger, P. L. & Luckmann, T. (1966). *The social construction of reality*. New York: Doubleday.

Cupach, W. R., & Canary, D. G. (1997). *Competence in interpersonal conflict*. New York: McGraw-Hill.

Dance, F. E. (1970). The 'concept' of communication. *Journal of Communication, 20,* 201–210.

Dessler, G. (1982). *Organization and management*. Reston, VA: Reston.

Duck, S., & Pittman, G. (1994). Social and personal relationships. In M. L. Knapp & G. R. Miller (Eds.), *Handbook of Interpersonal Communication*, 2nd ed. (Pp. 676–695). Thousand Oaks: Sage.

Frey, L. R., Botan, C. H., & Kreps, G. L. (2000). *Investigating communication: An introduction to research methods*. Boston: Allyn & Bacon.

Lewin, K. (1948). *Resolving social conflicts: Selected papers on group dynamics*. New York: Harper, Row.

Locke, J. (1979). *An essay on human understanding* (P. Nidditch, Ed.). Oxford, UK: Clarendon Press. (Original work published in 1690).

Pearce, W. B. (1994). *Interpersonal Communication: Making social worlds*. New York: Harper Collins.

Peters, J. D., (1999). *Speaking into the air: A history of the idea of communication*. Chicago: University of Chicago.

Richards, I. A. (1936). *The philosophy of rhetoric*. London: Oxford University Press.

Schutz, W. C. (1958). *The interpersonal underworld*. Palo Alto, CA: Science and Behavior Books, Inc.

Shannon, C. E., & Weaver, W. (1949). *The mathematical theory of communication*. Urbana IL: University of Illinois Press.

Watzlawick, P., Beavin, J., and Jackson, D. (1967) *Pragmatics of human communication*. New York: W. W. Norton.

Communication and organizational theory are closely linked. In this chapter, Michael Dues summarizes the development of organizational theory in the 20th century, and relates each new theoretical approach to its historical context and to its impact on organizational communication.

CHAPTER 2

Evolving Concepts of Organization: Their Influence on Organizational Communication

Michael T. Dues
University of Arizona

Key Terms

organizations	Human Resources approach	Total Quality Management
Classical Management	Systems approach	Fifth Discipline
bureaucracy	General Systems Theory	social realities
Scientific Management	Organizational Cultures	dialogic competence
Human Relations approach	approach	core communication skills

Objectives

This chapter presents the ideas about organizations that have influenced management and organizational communication in the twentieth century. In this chapter we:

1. Point out the events and conditions that led to development of Western ideas about organization.
2. Describe the major approaches in organizational theory that have affected communication in organizations during the 20th century.
3. Identify the effects of each organizational approach on communication in organizations.
4. Point out the communication processes occurring in contemporary organizations, and the communication skills organization members need for success.

Organizing is a daily human activity. Every day we engage in arranging and maintaining relationships in which we cooperate with one another to better satisfy our material and psychological needs. We often institutionalize these cooperative relationships so that we can count on them to serve us consistently over time. We institutionalize them by defining membership, assigning roles, establishing communication patterns, stating rules, and giving them names and legal status. We call our institutionalized cooperative relationships *organizations.*

An organization can be defined as "an ongoing, cooperative relationship between three or more persons who share a common purpose." Organizations are the companies where we work, the schools where we learn, the charitable institutions through which we give and receive, the clubs through which train and play, the hospitals where we try to get well, the stores where we buy what we need and want. Almost everyone participates as a member of a number of organizations. To a great extent, we live our lives in and through our organizations.

Communication is the means by which we accomplish organization, and the means by which we coordinate all our efforts in organizational settings. When communication is used for these purposes, we call it *organizational communication.* Chapter 1 describes contemporary concepts of communication, and illustrates how ideas about communication can influence the ways we attempt to organize. This chapter describes how ideas about organization influence the ways we communicate in organizations. It presents the ideas about organization that have guided management and influenced organizational communication in the twentieth century.

Like communication, organizations are *contextual.* They occur in the contexts of their times and places. They are influenced by surrounding events and conditions. They occur, in part, as responses to surrounding events and conditions. So, it is also important to recognize the surrounding events that have given rise to our ideas about organization. And it is important to recognize that, since context is always changing, our concepts of organization will continue to change.

This chapter covers six major approaches to conceptualizing and theorizing about organizations: the Classical Management Approach, the Human Relations Approach, the Human Resources Approach, the Systems Approach, the Organizational Cultures Approach, and the Integrative Approach. For each of these, I note the influencing contextual developments, the major theorists, the key assumptions and concepts, and the implications of each approach for communication in organizations.

Ideas about organization directly influence the communication processes employed, and the communication skills required of members to participate successfully. I conclude by listing communication processes that enact organizational communication today, and the skills organization members will need to communicate effectively as they enter the twenty-first century. These processes and skills will be the subjects of Part II.

Classical Management

Context

The beginning of the 20th century was a time of considerable hardship and economic uncertainty for most people in Europe and North America. Nevertheless, it was a time of great optimism, especially for those who had achieved middle class or wealthy status. Four major developments during the second half of the 19th century had generated conditions in which many believed that humans were on the verge of truly mastering their world. These developments were: (1) The invention of powered machines, (2) the invention of mass production, (3) major population growth, and (4) faith in the power of science.

(1) Powered Machines: Three developments massively increased the power of humans to move around in, and to control their environment. The invention of the steam engine enabled humans to manufacture things on a scale larger than ever before, and to transport themselves and almost anything else over great distances relatively quickly (Van Doren, 1991). Large scale manufacturing, combined with rail and steam boat transportation, led to an exponential increase in commerce and knowledge. The inventions of electricity and the internal combustion engine multiplied this increase in the power of humans relative to their natural environment. With powered machines, humans could, for good or ill, conquer nature.

(2) Mass Production: The impact of powered machines on manufacturing was greatly increased by the invention of a new way to organize manufacturing work. The *assembly line* provided a way to produce large quantities of a product, with consistent quality, at a relatively low cost (Van Doren, 1991). The assembly line was a refinement of the idea of a *factory* in which a large number of people would produce products by working cooperatively, selling their labor as a commodity to a factory owner. Employing powered machinery, the assembly line generated "mass production" of manufactured goods. Com-

bined with use of steam engines to transport raw materials to factories, and manufactured products to distant markets, mass production amounted to what we call the *Industrial Revolution* (Van Doren, 1991).

(3) Major Population Growth: Due partly to advances in medicine and agriculture, and to the increased prosperity and optimism made possible by the Industrial Revolution, people lived longer and produced more children. During the nineteenth century world population doubled (Van Doren, 1991). More people meant more need for products, services, homes, more workers, and more consumers. "Growth, more, and bigger" became values in themselves.

An abundance of people, many of whom were newly arrived in cities from farms, or as immigrants from other countries, meant that human labor was a plentiful commodity, and people could therefore be required to deliver a lot of labor in return for very little pay or security. This condition produced great wealth for a few, and brutally difficult working and living conditions for many.

(4) Faith in Science: Given the astounding effects of the steam engine, internal combustion, electricity, railroad transportation, mass production, "wireless" communication, and the steady stream of other new discoveries, it is understandable that people might come to believe they would soon solve all their problems by applying science and effort. The early 20th century was thus a time of grandiose optimism about what humans would accomplish. Typifying this faith, the builders and owners of the Titanic truly believed their claim that the "world's largest ocean liner" was "unsinkable." What was unbounded confidence among the industrial and political elite was at least hopefulness among the thousands of people who crowded into growing industrial cities seeking employment.

Need for a New Theory of Organization

As a result of these developments, beginning in the nineteenth century, and accelerating in the twentieth century, large, complex organizations formed. Organizational "empires" were built. But how could such large organizations be arranged and managed to assure their survival and success? The shear scale and power of early 20th century organizational efforts required development of new concepts and theories of how to organize. This was the context, and these were the needs addressed by the two great theorists of what is now called the **Classical Approach** to organizational management, Max Weber and Frederick Taylor.

Max Weber and the Theory of Bureaucracy

The German sociologist, Max Weber, developed a theory of **bureaucracy** during the 1880's which provided a useful way to conceptualize and structure large organizations. His work was translated into English and other languages in the early twentieth century, and became a central element of organizational theory (Gerth and Mills, 1947). Weber focused on the design of an organization's structure—on the formal relationships of authority and responsibility among members. Weber gave us both the term and the theory of *bureaucracy*. He observed that two conditions appeared essential for an organization to succeed: efficiency, and stability. To discover how organizations could achieve these conditions, he studied the structures of two large organizations. One organization, selected because it appeared to be the most efficient of its time, was the Prussian Army. The other organization, selected because it had simply survived longer than any other, was the Roman Catholic Church. Weber identified the structural characteristics shared by these two organizations to develop a set of seven principles for successful organization. These principles were (Gerth and Mills, 1947):

1. A clear hierarchy of authority.
2. Standardized and stated procedures and rules.
3. Clear division of labor according to assigned tasks.
4. Placement of individuals in roles for which they were suited by traits, talents, and training.
5. Formal communication along clear lines of authority, and maintenance of records. (He also adopted the Prussian Army term for this principle, *chain of command.*)
6. Definitions of expectations, responsibilities, and authority for each job role.
7. Maintenance of an objective, impersonal organizational environment in which organizational goals are primary, and individual goals are secondary.

Weber adopted the Prussian Army's "line and box" chart for graphically depicting organizational structure because it accurately and efficiently described an organization's specific hierarchy, division of labor, and chain of command. As a result of Weber's work, the line and box organizational chart, and the concept of chain of command serve almost universally to describe the structure of Western organizations. Figure 2.1 shows a typical "line and box" organization chart.

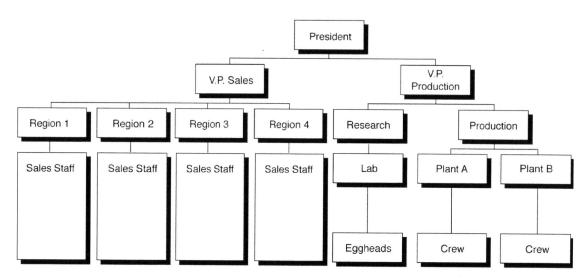

Figure 2.1   Line and Box Organization Chart

Frederick Taylor and "Scientific Management"

Educated as an engineer, Frederick Taylor saw the need to bring order and efficiency to the processes of management. He believed this could be accomplished by applying what he called "scientific principles" to the management of production. In his classic work, ***Principles of Scientific Management*** (1913), Taylor laid out an approach to designing and building an organization much as one would design and build a bridge or a highway (Shafritz and Whitbeck, 1978). While Weber had focused primarily on the structure of organizations, Taylor focused on the tasks organizations must accomplish.

It was Taylor who said "Time is money." And the principle of efficient production embodied in this slogan guided his design concepts. He originated the "time and motion" study as a way to design tasks for maximum efficiency. To design and build organizations for carrying out and coordinating multiple tasks, Taylor advocated the following (Shafritz and Whitbeck, 1978):

1. Design carefully limited tasks for individual workers, and a sequence of tasks to complete production of the product.
2. Design an organizational structure to fit the sequence of tasks needed for production.
3. Select employees whose talents are suited to specific tasks.
4. Train employees to do the specific task to which each is assigned.

Taylor approached the subject of organizational design from a management perspective, but he was also genuinely concerned about the moral issues of fair treatment and the well being of employees. He believed that his "scientific" approach would produce objective decisions about work and tasks that would be equally fair to all. Unfortunately, this belief proved to be naive.

Taken together, the ideas about organization provided by Taylor and Weber and their followers constitute the *Classical* approach to management.

Key Metaphors of Classical Management

Four metaphors captured the vision of the Classical Approach. One was the *"well oiled machine."* With this phrase managers aimed to have their organizations operate with the coordinated efficiency and controlled impact of the machines that had multiplied the power of humans, and so captured their imaginations. A second metaphor was the *"bureau."* Weber named his set of principles for dividing labor and hierarchical organization "bureaucracy," because, on paper, an organization so designed resembled a large French bureau that stood in his room, with one large drawer at the top and smaller drawers below. A third metaphor was the *"chain of command"* which described the relationships of authority and accountability between superiors and subordinates. The fourth powerful metaphor embedded in the Classical Approach, was *"hierarchy."* In a hierarchy, a few people are *"superior;"* have more power, more freedom, more security, more wealth, and higher social status; and members agree that this represents an appropriate order. Most members in a *hierarchy* are *subordinates;* they have less power, less freedom, less security, less wealth, and lower social status; and members agree that this is an appropriate order. The metaphor of *hierarchy* defined the social order of organizations in terms of military authority structures and governments of monarchy and aristocracy during the twentieth century, while Western nations moved in philosophy and political practice toward democracy and equality.

Classical Assumptions About Communication

Embedded in the Classical Approach are five important assumptions about communication in organizations. These assumptions exert a major influence on organizational communication. Taylor, Weber, and their followers assumed that:

1. The person at the top of the organization's hierarchy knows whatever he/she needs to know to make decisions and give orders.
2. Organization employees are motivated by desire to acquire money, and by safety and security needs.

3. Communication is a matter of giving orders and instructions to employees.
4. Communication is formal, flowing along the organization's lines of authority.
5. The direction of communication flow is downward. Bosses tell; employees listen and act.

How Classical Management Affects Communication

The ideas provided by Taylor and Weber were extremely useful. The Classical Approach served for most of the 20th century as the basic conceptual framework for organizing and managing. Effective communication in this approach is concerned with four major functions: (1) giving clear orders and instructions, (2) accurate transmittal, storage and retrieval of information, (3) control of information flow by gatekeepers, and (4) receiving and following orders (Eisenberg and Goodall, 1993). In general, under the Classical Approach, these communication functions are adequately accomplished.

Classical Management affects organizational communication, however, in seven significant ways, some of which were neither intended nor foreseen. These effects are:

1) Downward communication is condensed and distorted. Limited to flowing along formal lines, and controlled by gatekeepers, information and orders are slowed and altered on their way to employees.

2) Informal communication about relationships and relevant information other than orders and instructions is inhibited. Informal communication is confined to the "grapevine," or "rumor mill." Differences in social status among organization members tend to restrict informal communication across the lines of status difference.

3) Information and ideas which employees possess about problems and solutions rarely reaches managers who make decisions.

4) Conflicts are resolved on the basis of who has authority to make decisions and give orders, not on the basis of mutual discussion and agreement. Status differences inhibit successful conflict resolution; disagreement by a subordinate tends to be viewed as "insubordination."

5) Minimum performance standards are clearly communicated to employees, who are motivated by fear to meet them. Little communication occurs that would help motivate employees to exceed minimum standards.

6) Leadership is viewed as a matter of making decisions and giving orders. Leadership ability is viewed as a set of personal traits possessed by the manager who

belongs to the higher status group; leadership is seen as both a responsibility and a privilege of the higher status group. Leadership is not viewed or practiced as a communication process.

7) Employees who value consistency and security are satisfied. They are valued for their reliability and their willing subordination. Employees who think independently and creatively are discouraged from speaking up. Creative, independent, or outspokenly honest employees may be viewed as troublesome and "insubordinate." They are not valued and are not satisfied.

Shortcomings of Classical Management

Classical Management worked. It served to organize large-scale work. It produced large quantities of products with regularity and a predictable (not necessarily high) standard of quality. Employees made a living, and owners got rich. In practice, however, Classical Management never achieved the utopian vision of Frederick Taylor, or the impartial fairness for which Max Weber hoped. Underpayment and mistreatment of workers led to the development of labor unions. Throughout the twentieth century, there were strikes, often accompanied by violence. There was work sabotage. There were major production inefficiencies, and large-scale failures of organizations. As early as 1928, it was clear that Classical Management did not offer flawless solutions to the problem of how to structure and run a large organization. Beginning in 1929 and extending through most of the 1930's severe economic depression throughout the Western World closed thousands of companies and caused massive unemployment. After World War II, rapid technological changes affected the very nature of production and work. Between 1945 and 1960, the developed world moved from the Industrial Age into the Information Age. In the face of these changes, the shortcomings of Classical Management became more clear and more problematic. New concepts of organization and management were needed.

The Human Relations Approach
Elton Mayo and Chester Barnard

Approaching the study of organizations and management from the perspective of social psychology, Elton Mayo (1927) suggested that such factors as working conditions and work relationships could affect motivation and productivity. In an effort to discover ways to increase worker productivity at the Hawthorne Plant of the Western Electric Company he conducted a series of experiments, testing whether certain changes in working conditions might reduce employee turn-over and increase productivity (Eisenberg and Goodall, 1993). His results were puzzling. He found that when he increased lighting in the plant, worker satisfaction and productivity improved; he also found that when he decreased lighting, satisfaction and productivity improved. He even found that when he moved workers to a different room, but kept the same lighting conditions, worker satisfaction and productivity improved. Similar results with changes in various other working conditions led Mayo to conclude that something other than the conditions themselves was influencing productivity. Noting that each of his experiments involved giving attention to the workers, he concluded that attention itself was the variable enhancing productivity. Attention was a matter of relationships. This marked the beginning of what came to be called the Human Relations School of management. Mayo and his followers advocated the view that good management included not only the aspects identified by Taylor and Weber, but also the tasks of developing and maintaining good human relationships with employees.

Chester Barnard(1938), an innovative corporate executive, added several important concepts to the Human Relations approach (Goldhaber and Barnett, 1988). Barnard focused on the role of the manager as a leader of people, and on the role of communication in management. Noting that organizations are about coordinating work, he observed that communication systems were required. He suggested that the role of executive management was to formulate and maintain the communication system, and set abstract goals. The roles of middle managers and supervisors, he said, were to translate those abstract goals into concrete objectives and communicate them to workers. He viewed communication as the primary tool for employee selection, placement, and training, as well as for giving instructions and orders. To accomplish all their functions, he suggested, organizational communication systems should consciously include both formal and informal communication channels.

The Human Relations Metaphor

The Human Relations School of management theory added a new metaphor for conceptualizing organizations. An organization, they said, is like a "family." "Family" evokes images that are quite different from "well oiled machines," or "bureaus," or "chains of command." Ideally, family is about human relationships that are both functional and emotional, relationships that include identity and belonging. In a family, the "boss" is (or should be) a loving parent, and all members are valued. The nature and content of communication in a family differ greatly from communication in a machine. The family metaphor was compatible, however, with the concept of hierarchy; bosses were comparable to parents, with unquestioned authority and more freedom than employees who were likened the children.

Human Relations Assumptions About Communication

Not surprisingly, Human Relations theorists made assumptions about communication in organizations that were different from those of the Classical School. The Human Relations assumptions were:

1) Communication is not only a matter of giving orders and instructions, but also a matter of building and maintaining friendly, supportive relationships.
2) Information about what needs to be done is distributed among executives, managers, supervisors, and workers. This information must be shared as needed.
3) Communication must flow, down, up, and across the different parts of the organization. The boss must listen as well as tell.
4) Top executives must design and implement the organization's communication system.
5) Executives know what needs to be done at the abstract, global level. Middle managers and supervisors must translate abstract ideas into concrete ones, and communicate them to workers.
6) Solutions to problems are created by executives, managers, and supervisors on the basis of shared information, some of which comes from workers.

Human Relations Approach Effects on Communication

Human Relations concepts had a major impact on patterns of communication in organizations. Communication was no longer limited to formal channels; Informal communication (the "grapevine") was recognized as an existing and useful aspect of organizational communication. Communication flowed upward and across as well as downward, although downward continued to be the dominant direction. Information and ideas were sometimes sought from workers. More members, especially managers and supervisors were included in decision making processes. And communication included deliberate (sometimes embarrassingly transparent) efforts to develop friendly, supportive relationships between managers and workers.

Harmony between management and labor improved, as did worker satisfaction, but measurable gains in productivity were not dramatic. Better understanding of motivation and human productivity were clearly needed. By the 1950's, however, the social science perspective was well established in management theory, and a larger group of researchers and theorists was prepared to offer more complete answers. This group is generally referred to as the Human Resources School of management.

The Human Resources Approach

Context

The world emerged from World War II with a whole new set of conditions, which provided a far more complex and challenging context in which organizations would function. Communication and transportation technology (radio, television, and jet airplanes) made possible instant communication with people anywhere on the planet; most places in the world could be reached in a matter of hours. World War II had introduced North Americans to people, cultures, and markets across the globe. This was the nuclear age. By the 1960's it was the age of space travel. Driven in part by the scientific competition associated with the Cold War, technology advanced rapidly. International trade and international business competition grew in intensity. Work required more technical knowledge; "specialization" became the by-word as individuals strove to become experts.

As organizations scrambled to keep up with technology and global competition, they found themselves facing challenges of a different kind. In the 1960's and 70's three major movements altered values in the United States, and significantly affected organizational life:

1) The *Civil Rights movement* demanded for minorities equal rights to jobs and advancement.
2) The *Feminist movement* demanded for women equal rights to jobs and advancement.
3) The *Environmental movement* challenged the right of organizations to pursue profit in ways that damage, destroy, or place at risk the natural environment.

Government efforts to ensure equal access to jobs and advancement for minority and women citizens brought increased and more complex regulation of organizations. Equal access to work and promotion for all citizens led to an increasingly diverse work force. This more diverse work force was also more highly educated as many more people went to college. And, given the prosperity of the 60's, this more highly educated work force also had higher expectations for monetary rewards and job security. At the same time, government efforts to protect the natural environment added regulatory complexity and, in some industries, limited the ways organizations could pursue their goals. Due in part to their history of behaving irresponsibly and harmfully toward their own employees and toward their social and natural environments, organizations came under government regulation which required them to behave as good citizens.

In this complex competitive and social context the concepts of Classical and Human Relations management were inadequate. At the least, major refinements in organizational theory were needed. A number of management theorists and social psychologists took up the effort. Although each of these theorists brought his/her own ideas to the endeavor, and each contributed independently valuable insights, they generally shared **five central premises** which make up what we call the Human Resources Approach. These premises were (Eisenberg and Goodall, 1993):

1) Organizations are collections of human beings with a set of tasks to perform. Therefore, theorists should integrate the useful ideas of the task oriented Scientific Approach with the ideas of the human relationships-oriented Human Relations Approach.
2) Humans are the primary resource to be applied to the tasks.
3) Both the task and the resource must be managed well to sustain high productivity and quality work over time.
4) The objective of management is to secure maximum effort from the resources (humans), applied appropriately and efficiently to the tasks.
5) The fundamental strategy for accomplishing this objective is to match the goals of the organization with the goals of the individual.

Some of the important theorists in this group are Douglas McGregor, Rensis Likert, Abraham Maslow, and B. F. Skinner. Below, we list some of their major ideas and contributions to organizational theory.

Douglas McGregor (1960) challenged the assumptions about human motivation made by the Scientific School of management. In discussing motivation, he invented the terms *Theory* X and *Theory* Y. Identifying the Scientific School with *Theory* X, he noted that it assumed people did not want to work, that work could not be enjoyable, that people needed to be controlled, and that fear and monetary rewards were management's only tools for motivating employees. In place of *Theory* X, he offered *Theory* Y, which assumed people *do* want to work, that work can be enjoyed, that people can be self-disciplining, and that motivation is complex, even including such factors as enjoyment of work. McGregor argued that application of *Theory* Y would bring about greater productivity than application of *Theory* X. McGregor's approach was widely cited and applied in many organizations.

Rensis Likert (1961) observed that human resources not only work, they also can think and creatively solve problems. Likert coined the term *participative management*. By *participative management*, he meant that workers with information about, or a major stake in, a decision should participate in making that decision. Such participation, he argued, would not only produce more and better solutions to problems, but would also increase worker motivation, since workers would feel a sense of ownership about decisions. Likert carefully studied group dynamics and described the characteristics of members, leadership and processes that lead to group effectiveness. His work brought into focus the concept of interactive teams as ideal work units.

B. F. Skinner (1969) offered a narrower view, but one better supported by empirical evidence. He originated the concept of *positive reinforcement*. Skinner's research demonstrated that humans tend to repeat behavior when that behavior is followed by positive reinforcement, and that humans are more likely to continue performing the desired behavior if the reinforcement is intermittent, that is, if it usually, but not always follows the desired behavior. He advocated what he called "behavioral engineering," which could be accomplished by rewarding workers intermittently for work well done. Such reinforcement would not, of course, replace regular pay. Skinner noted that once workers had become dependent on their regular pay, it no longer served as reinforcement; rather the threat of losing the job, and therefore the pay was a way to motivate through fear. He also noted that rewards need not be material; compliments expressing appreciation for work well done constituted positive reinforcement. Skinner's positive reinforcement approach to "engineering" desired employee behavior has been credited with remarkable improvements in the functioning of some companies. In one widely publicized case, application of Skinner's approach to positive reinforcement is credited with bringing the Emery Air Freight Company from a condition of near bankruptcy, to one of organizational and financial health in the early 1970's (Organ, 1978, p. 251).

A more complex theory of motivation was provided by **Abraham Maslow** in *Eupsychian Management* (1965). Maslow posited what he called the *Hierarchy of Human Needs*. At the lowest level are physiological needs, such as food and clothing. Humans will focus on these needs until they are met. Once they are met, however, focus will shift to a higher level; safety needs, such as shelter, security, and having a job, will become the primary motivators. Once safety needs are met, higher needs for love, belonging, affection and respect will become motivators. When these needs are met, self-esteem needs, such as rank and status, will become important motivators. At the highest level, Maslow placed the need for what he called "self-actualization," which he described as the need to fully reach one's potential. The Hierarchy (Figure 2.2) is often diagramed as follows (Eisenberg and Goodall, 1993)

Maslow's Hierarchy of Needs contributed the important insight that motivation varies, depending upon conditions. And managers have widely adopted his view to more effectively address the issue of employee motivation.

The above theorists are only a few of the most notable in the Human Resources School. This school produced a considerable body of research and theory which itself became an area of specialization. It had, and continues to have, a major impact on organizational management.

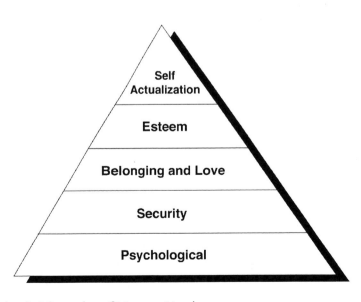

Figure 2.2   Maslow's Hierarchy of Human Needs

The Human Resources Metaphor

The key word and central metaphor for Human Resources management was the *team*. The "team" concept embodies both the interpersonal connection of "family," and the commitment to task accomplishment of the "machine." A strong team can be both a "family" and a "well oiled machine."

Human Resources Assumptions About Communication

Human Resources theorists shared the following assumptions about communication in organizations:

1) Communication has multiple purposes: Instructions, orders, information sharing, decision-making, training, relationship building and management, and motivation.
2) Communication is multidirectional: it moves up, down, and across, and is interactive.
3) Information about tasks, problems, and solutions is distributed across all levels and divisions of the organization, and the central function of communication is to bring people together to share relevant information.
4) The synergy of interacting groups offers the best potential for problem solving.
5) Human motivation is varied and complex.
6) Communication must be dually focused on both tasks and people.

Effects of Human Resources Management on Communication

Given that the Human Resources Approach embodies a variety of ideas, introduced in an extremely complex, rapidly changing organizational environment, it is difficult to assess the actual impact of Human Resources ideas on organizational communication. One can say with reasonable confidence that Human Resources theorists helped organizations stay afloat in an increasingly challenging environment. Clearly, this approach added new and useful ideas and processes. The general impact of Human Resources ideas on communication was to increase effects begun by the Human Relations movement.

Use of informal communication channels increased. Upward and horizontal communication were enhanced. Consultation of employees about conditions and decisions increased. More decisions were made by groups of employees acting as a team. Use of communication to help motivate employees became more sophisticated. More attention was given to communicating successfully, and this attention included establishing new job roles focused on communication. Among the new job roles were coordinators, ombudspersons, labor relations officers, trainers, facilitators, and counselors. Some organizations established whole work units called "Human Resources" offices.

Two important limitations of the Human Relations Approach constrained its impact, however.

(1) Human Resources theorists sought to build upon the Classical and Human Relations approaches by focusing on the relationships between tasks and people, and also on the relationships between people. They did not fundamentally challenge classical assumptions about organizational structure. Thus, the Human Resources practitioners found themselves attempting to insert new ideas about flexible, egalitarian teamwork into organizations that remained committed to the principles of hierarchy, bureaucracy, and stability. Top managers often talked in Human Resources language, but made important decisions and resolved conflicts employing secrecy and hierarchy (Morrill, 1995). Organization members generally noticed the "mixed message." There was one way to talk, and another way to act, and action spoke louder.

(2) Human Resources theorists developed efficient, useful interactive group processes for problem-solving, decision-making, and planning, but did not question classical modes of analysis. In classical analysis, one seeks to diagnose a problem by identifying a single cause that accounts for the problem, and then making a single change to solve the problem. In other words, one locates the problem, then applies a specific change at that location. This approach dates all the way back to Aristotle, and, for some problems, it works very well. In complex organizations, however, every problem has multiple causes, and every change has multiple effects. So, despite the advances in group processes, old assumptions about analytic processes constrained the thought and communication of interacting groups, and limited their value as creative problem-solvers.

The Systems Approach to Management

The existing ways of structuring organizations and analyzing problems, which the Human Resources theorists did not challenge, are representative of a way of analyzing and conceptualizing inherited from the ancient Greeks that had guided thought in Western Civilization for 2500 years. In the Western mode of analysis, objects and processes were conceptualized as structures composed of related parts. Analysis was a matter of discovering what all the parts were, then identifying how they fit together. Diagnosis was a matter of identifying which part was malfunctioning, and fixing or replacing that part. This way of thinking had produced remarkable results over the centuries. It had become so central in the thought processes of Western Civilization, that it had ceased to be questioned. It was *the* way of thinking, not *a way* of thinking. Human Resources theorists were scholars well trained in Western thought; they applied Western modes of thought to improve organizational theory; they did not challenge Western thought itself.

Ludwig Von Bertalanffy was not an organizational theorist; he was a biologist who did his major work during the 1930's. Biology, with its endless efforts to classify all living things by genus and species, had for centuries been the quintessential model of Western analytic method. Bertalanffy challenged this approach to understanding living beings at its core. In its place he offered General Systems Theory (1969). Whatever lives, he said, must be understood not as a thing, but as a "system" which is made up of interacting parts, each of which is itself a system, and each of which affects all the other parts. Each system is part of a larger system, which it affects. In this view, any action has multiple consequences, many of which are unintended.

Bertalanffy said that each system exists in an environment, and interacts with that environment. Each is an "open" system in that it draws "input" from its environment, which it processes internally ("through-put"), and delivers "output" back to the environment. An "ecological system" is a collection of systems, which is itself an environment, all interacting with one another in a mutually sustaining way. Changes in any one part can affect any or all other parts, and affect the whole system.

Bertalanffy's theory revolutionized the field of biology, and affected the very way we think of our environment and our role within it. It launched the field of ecology. But what does all this biology have to do with organizations?

The answer to this question was suggested by Kenneth Boulding (1956), and provided in detail by **Daniel Katz** and **Robert Kahn** (1966). These theorists applied General Systems Theory to organizations and to organizational management. Organizations, they said, are "open systems" which take in input "energies" from their environment and convert them to "output" (Rogers and Rogers, 1976). In this view the organization is not an entity unto itself, but a system that is part of an ecological system. And every organization was a "nesting of systems" composed of interacting systems (Rogers & Rogers, 1976).

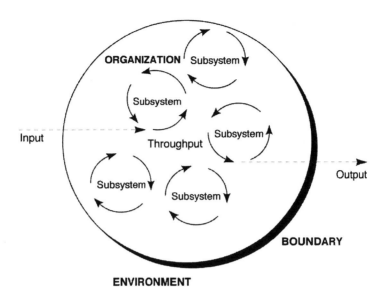

Figure 2.3   Systems Model of an Organization
(Source: Rogers & Rogers, 1976)

In place of the static structure represented in the line and box chart, the Systems Approach (Figure 2.3) offered a dynamic, interactive model.

Systems Metaphors for Organizations

With the Systems Approach came a fundamentally new metaphor for conceptualizing organizations, the *living organism*, and a new concept for conceptualizing the organization's environment, *the ecological system*. This way of thinking about organizations provides for richer complexity, and for evaluating the relationship of the organization to its environment as well as to its individual parts. Embedded in these metaphors are new assumptions and new values for organizational life. Success in the Classical Approach had been viewed as a matter of "doing things right;" success resulted from efficiency. Success in the Systems view was also a matter of "doing the right thing;" success was about effectiveness. Moreover, effectiveness was measured not only in terms of meeting the organization's stated goals, but also in terms of the organization's total impact on its environment, and its ability to remain "in balance" with its environment.

Systems Assumptions About Communication

Systems theorists assume that:

1) Communication is the basic process facilitating interaction between the various parts of the organization. It is through communication that organization members control, coordinate, provide information to decision-makers, and adjust the organization to its changing environment.
2) Information itself is an essential resource upon which organizations depend for their life.
3) Information processing is the main function performed by the organization.
4) Communication must flow up, down, across, *and in an out of* the organization.
5) Communication is itself a system, and is subject to problems of distortion, overload, and unresponsiveness.

Systems Approach Effects on Organizational Communication

The Systems approach recognizes communication as the central aspect of organizational operations, and employs the contemporary concepts of communication discussed in Chapter 1. The Systems approach gives increased attention to improving the speed, accuracy, and relevance of communication, and to the capacities of communication systems. Problems of information overload are identified and addressed. Large scale and technical issues with communication systems can be addressed without ignoring human and personal aspects; all are seen as systems interacting with systems. Systems thinking provides a way of analyzing organizational processes that can accommodate the rich complexity of organizational life.

With the Systems approach communication is understood to be constantly interactive, flowing in all directions. All members participate. Leadership is exercised through process management; not content decisions. The primary purpose of control is to ensure an open, flowing communication system (Rogers and Rogers, 1976).

Organizational Cultures

During the 1970's business organizations in the United States gradually woke up to the fact that Japanese businesses were surpassing them in quality of products, production efficiency, trade strategies, and profits. One result of this awakening was that North American organizations attempted to improve their operations by adopting methods of managing, motivating, and communicating with employees that characterized Japanese organizations. Efforts to import Japanese management methods caused theorists to focus on the cultural contexts in which organizations operate and on the organizational cultures in which organization members function. William Ouchi, in his best selling book, *Theory Z* (1981), explained that ways of interacting with employees must be compatible with their culture to be effective. In so doing, he focused attention on the relationship between culture and organization.

Terrence Deal and Arthur Kennedy (1982) added the concept of "organizational cultures," to organizational theory in another best selling book, *Corporate Cultures*. Deal and Kennedy suggested that, over time, organizations develop informal symbols, beliefs, languages, norms, ways of behaving, and roles. These, they observed, constitute the organization's culture. They argued that an organization's continued success depends to a significant extent upon whether it develops and sustains a strong culture that is consistent with its mission and suitable in its environment.

The **Organizational Cultures** approach broadened the Systems view, and provided a somewhat systematic way to consider informal roles and informal aspects of organizational communication. It provides for a broader understanding of leadership, and for appreciation of some communication behaviors that were not previously valued in organizational theory. The Cultures approach reinforces the Systems view that communication is the central aspect of organizing to be understood and managed; communication is the means by which cultures are formed and maintained. In this view, a "culture" is not merely something an organization *has*; a culture is what an organization *is*.

Cultures Approach Metaphors

With the Cultures approach came new metaphors for conceptualizing the organization. In this view, organizations are seen not only as *organisms*, but also as *communities* and as *tribes*. Communities are living institutions that are something more than the total of their individual parts. The concept of community is a natural extension of the ideas of family and team. Members of communities are truly interdependent, with each affecting the others, but members are also complete individuals in themselves, and are able to enter and leave, belong to or not belong to their communities. Tribes have shared values, beliefs, norms, expectations, language, and rituals. In communities and tribes, certain members hold designated positions and roles; various members take on informal roles as well, such as hero, priest, gossip, clown. In enacting such informal roles, members serve important organizational communication functions.

Cultures Approach Assumptions About Communication

Organizational cultures theorists have incorporated the assumptions of the Human Resources and Systems theorists about communication in organizations (Pepper, 1995). To these, they have added the assumptions that:

1) Groups of people working together invent or discover ideas and techniques informally, as they learn to cope with both their internal and external environments. (Schein, 1991)
2) When these ideas and techniques work well enough to be considered "valid," they are communicated to new members of the group as correct ways to think, perceive, feel, and act. (Schein, 1991)
3) Organizational culture is communicated through symbols, special language, informal behavior patterns, and informal communication patterns. Generally, it is not expressed through official communication channels. (Schein, 1991)
4) Organization members assume various informal roles in the culture which are not the same as members' officially designated organizational roles. Through these roles, they teach the culture to new members, and enact and sustain the organization's culture. (Deal and Kennedy, 1982)

Cultures Approach Effects on Organizational Communication

During the 1980's a great deal of attention was given to the question of whether organizational cultures were strong and appropriate to an organization's work and environment. Cultures, however, as Edgar Schein points out, belong collectively to the group; they are not the property of management alone, and they are not readily amenable to "management. (Schein, 1991). Cultures are developed and maintained by the complex, informal dialogue of members; so it is difficult to deliberately implement, control, or measure cultural change (Eisenberg & Goodall, 1993).

Although it is difficult to identify specific effects of the Cultures approach on organizational communication, we believe effects can be seen in greater attention to organizational symbols and language, greater emphasis on informal gatherings and communication not directly related to specific work, and greater valuing of informal roles and functions of specific members.

Integrative Approaches

Contemporary efforts of organizational theorists focus not on developing new approaches, but on integrating the useful elements of existing approaches into a useful set of management principles. The strategy of these theorists is to provide managers with a system of managing that makes good use of all the twentieth century organizational research and theory. Two of the most influential among these **integrated approaches** are *Total Quality Management (TQM),* and *"Fifth Discipline" Management.*

Total Quality Management

Total Quality Management (TQM) is an integrated system of management developed by W. Edwards Deming (Berk and Berk, 1993). Deming was an important organizational theorist throughout the second half of the twentieth century who served as consultant to Japanese organizations during the 1960's. Deming (1969) incorporated Human Resources concepts and methods, Systems methods of analysis, understanding of organizational cultures, appreciation of the management opportunities afforded by new information technology, and the Japanese philosophy and methods for pursuing "Continuous Quality Improvement" (CQI). The core of Deming's approach, however, was that of Classical Management; it was squarely focused on task, and committed measuring the efficiency and effects of all processes. All decisions, he said, should be based on objective data.

Viewing organizations from a Systems perspective, Deming observed that piecemeal changes in management techniques tend to have minimal impact. He argued that what is needed is an integrated system of management based on a clear philosophy. He established the goal of Continuous Quality Improvement as the core philosophical value. In TQM task accomplishment and quality improvement are continuously pursued, and are constantly measured and reported to managers using information technology. Problem solving and process improvement are continuously addressed through teams.

TQM has been widely implemented in both public and private organizations during the 1990's. Ford Motor Company has been perhaps the most visible in its TQM effort, and claims remarkable success as a result. Other organizations have attempted to implement TQM with little success. Deming insisted that attempting to implement TQM piecemeal, and/or expecting quick results is a formula for failure. TQM, he said, must be implemented as a complete system, with a philosophy at its core, and given enough time to produce results (Berk and Berk, 1993).

The Fifth Discipline and the Learning Organization

Peter Senge, Director of the Center of Organizational Learning at Massachusetts Institute of Technology, developed an integrated approach that rests upon two key concepts, *learning* and *discipline* (1990). He argues that five "disciplines" are essential to build and maintain a "Learning Organization." Since organizations' environments are constantly changing, continuous adaptation is essential for an organization to survive and thrive over time. Adaptation is a matter of "learning" which, Senge suggests, is the "only perpetually renewable resource" (Senge, 1990).

Learning is perpetually renewable because it does not depend upon resources which can be consumed. Instead, it depends on five "disciplines." A discipline is a "combination of a way of thinking and development of skill in acting and communicating based on that way of thinking" (Senge, 1990). Each of the five disciplines he describes incorporates one or more of the organizational approaches we have discussed in this chapter. The **five disciplines** are (Senge, 1990):

1. **Systems Thinking.** Applying the systems approach to analyze organizational conditions and problems.
2. **Personal Mastery.** Continually clarifying and deepening one's personal vision, focusing energies, developing patience, and seeing reality objectively. This discipline is essentially spiritual in nature, and Senge draws from Eastern philosophies in discussing it. It applies the Systems perspective in that it views each individual member as a system which must be continually learning for the organization to be continually learning.
3. **Mental Models.** Learning begins with identifying the fundamental models with which we think about the organization, its work and its environment. These translate into language for thinking and communicating—learning and sharing learning. This discipline incorporates the Cultures approach.
4. **Building Shared Vision.** Creating a shared vision of the desired future; shared commitment to goals, values, missions, and objectives. These cannot be dictated from the top; they must be built together. This discipline incorporates both the Systems and Human Resources approaches.
5. **Team Learning.** This discipline involves suspending individual members' assumptions, engaging in genuine dialogue, and thinking together, to discover new solutions. In incorporates Human Resources concepts and the "team" metaphor, as well as the Cultures concept of dialogue.

Senge's book, *The Fifth Discipline: The Art and Practice of the Learning Organization*, has been a standing best seller among trade publications, and a number of large organizations, Procter and Gamble, Digital, and AT&T have embraced his approach. As with TQM, some, but not all, report remarkable success. Implementing major systemic change, as is required in TQM or Learning Organizations involves fundamentally altering an organization's culture; it is extremely difficult. It requires resources, time, and faith; the beneficial results may not be evident for several years (Kanter, 1983).

An Environment of Ideas and Terms:

Core Skills for Participating in the Organizational Dialogue

Organizations are *social realities.* That is, they are created, sustained, and adjusted by people through a *dialogic* process of thinking and communicating. The dialogue about organizations is ongoing. New thought generates new terms; new terms become part of the language for communicating in and about organizations; new ideas are sometimes implemented; some ideas have lasting impact; many are temporary fads. To be an effective communicator in an organization, one must first be competent to participate in this dialogic process.

What Does Dialogic Competence Require?

1) Recognize the dialogue.   It is essential to understand that organizations are not fixed, hard realities like buildings or rocks. Organizations are literally "made up" by their members, and the process of making them up is an ongoing dialogue. Ideas and terms are elements of the dialogue; they are never final or complete. One can participate in this organizational dialogue only if s/he recognizes it as a dialogue. Any member who confuses ideas with fixed realities, or believes that only one correct answer exists for her/his organization is unable to participate. One who confuses an idea with a fixed reality is a *prisoner of that idea, and an impediment to the organizational dialogue.*

2) Recognize and use established ideas and terms.   The Classical, Human Relations, Human Resources, Systems, and Cultures approaches to conceptualizing and managing organizations, which we have described in this chapter, are firmly established. TQM and Learning Organizations appear to be moderately well established. These sets of ideas and terms are likely to continue to be used in the organizational dialogue. To be a competent organizational communicator, one will need to recognize and understand both the ideas and the terms.

3) Recognize and use current ideas and terms.   The organizational dialogue is ongoing, and new ideas and terms are constantly being introduced. A competent organizational communicator must keep up with new ideas and terms. Here are some examples: (1) Peter Drucker introduced the idea of *Management by Objectives* (MBO) in the 1950's (1957). MBO became and remains a concept and a term with which one must be familiar; to communicate in many organizational conversations. (2) The concepts and terms of strategic planning, including "vision, mission, goals, stakeholders, and clients" have become widely used in organizations; one must know them to participate in the conversation (Bryson, 1991). (3) More recently, Peters and Waterman introduced terms and ideas in their book, *In Search of Excellence* (1982). Their work has been influential, introducing new vocabulary into the dialogue. The term "excellence" in the context of organizational management now has added meaning. And phrases like "stick to the knitting," and "management by walking around" (MBWA) have acquired specific meanings. Even the term "customer" is now used with a wider meaning than previously as a result of Peters and Waterman's work. One who is not familiar with Peters and Waterman's work, and with these terms is handicapped in discussions where they are used. (4) Similarly, Kenneth Blanchard and Spencer Johnson introduced terms and phrases in *The One Minute Manager* which became part of the vocabulary of organizational communication (1982). Competent organizational communicators now must know, for example, what a "one minute reprimand" is. (5) During the 1990's, organizational terms such as "reengineering, reinventing, downsizing, and rightsizing" have entered the dialogue (Osborne and Gaebler, 1993). Today's competent communicator must be familiar with these terms as well.

The established and new concepts and terms which constitute the vocabulary of the organizational dialogue are tools by which members make, sustain, and shape their organizations. To effectively participate in this dialogue, one must know these tools and be capable of using them.

4) Relate ideas to actions and outcomes.   Competent organizational communicators must be able to recognize ideas in their enacted form, that is, in behaviors, processes, and structures. They must be able to associate, for example, giving orders with Classical Management, or group problem solving with the Human Resources approach. In addition, they must be able to recognize the outcomes of enacting ideas. If the relationships between ideas, actions, and outcomes are not recognized, the organizational dialogue is not relevant, and is of little use.

5) Assess context: recognize operant ideas and terms.   In most large organizations today, the basic structure is still based upon Classical Management concepts. Human Relations and Human Resources concepts are visible in many of the communication processes; Systems and Cultures terms are used in the organizational dialogue. In some organizations current terms and concepts, such as TQM, or ideas from Peters and Waterman's work are in use. Various members of each organization hold different beliefs about the value of the concepts currently being enacted. Some members rigidly attach themselves to certain organizational ideas, and are unable to participate in the dialogue. An important component of communication competence in organizations is the ability to assess the ideas and abilities of other members. Assessing context is essential to accurately judging what to say and what not to say to any given member at any given time.

These "core" organizational communication competencies are requisite to participation in the process of making, shaping, and sustaining an organization. Acquiring these skills begins with understanding this chapter. Real competence will require building on this beginning. It will be necessary to study the major approaches to organizational theory in some detail, and then to read about new ideas, theories and processes as they are introduced.

Core Communication Competencies for Organizational Life

In the era when Classical Management was the sole source of organizational concepts and practices, relatively few communication skills were regularly needed to conduct business. Today, however, a complex set of core communication abilities is needed to participate effectively in the organization. Critical among these competencies are:

1. **Listening.** Every member, including the boss, must be able to listen well.
2. **Self Presentation.** To be accepted and given credibility, every member must be able to present an appropriate, positive image of herself/himself.
3. **Oral Presentations.** Every member should be able to effectively present ideas orally to groups of colleagues.

4. **Writing.** Every member should be able to express herself/himself clearly, efficiently, and effectively in writing.

5. **Persuasive Argument.** To be effective in influencing decisions, every member should be able to construct persuasive, rational arguments in support of her/his views.

6. **Leading and Participating in Meetings.** Communication in the context of the Human Resources and Systems approaches requires frequent meetings of organization members. Every organization needs members who are able to lead meetings effectively, providing appropriate group processes and guiding members in making group decisions. And every member must be able to function as a contributing participant in meetings.

7. **Making Group Decisions.** Participative management involves group decision-making. So, every member should be able to participate effectively in group decision-making processes. Groups must be able to function as teams in decision-making processes, and must be adept at reaching consensus whenever possible.

8. **Developing Productive Relationships and Teams.** Since the team approach, introduced by the Human Resources theorists, will continue to be applied in the foreseeable future, the communication skills involved in building relationships and maintaining strong teams will continue to be essential. It is important to know how to function as a member of a team.

9. **Managing Conflict.** In the era of Classical Management, conflicts were suppressed and, when they arose, were "resolved" by authority. Human Relations and Human Resources approaches made it clear that conflicts are better handled by mutual discussion and agreement. Today, every member must be able to participate constructively in efforts to resolve conflicts. These efforts involve an important set of communication skills.

10. **Leadership.** In contemporary organizations leadership is a vital and complex skill. No participative process and no amount of teamwork can replace the essential factor of individual leadership. Managers, supervisors, and often other organization members are called upon to exercise individual leadership.

We introduce these core communication skills in Part 2.

Summary

This chapter described six major approaches to the study of organizations and management, the Classical approach, The Human Relations approach, The Human Resources approach, The Systems approach, the Cultures approach, and the Integrative approach. For each approach, I identified historical context, major contributors of ideas, key metaphors, assumptions about communication, impacts on organizational communication.

I then identified core communication competencies members must develop to participate effectively in the dialogue by which organizations are formed, adjusted, and sustained. These are abilities to (1) recognize the dialogue, (2) recognize and use established ideas and terms, (3) recognize and use current ideas and terms, (4) relate ideas to actions and outcomes, and (5) assess context, recognizing operant ideas and terms.

Finally, I identified ten fundamental communication processes in which persons must be competent to work effectively and cooperatively in organizations. These are listening, presenting yourself, oral presentations, writing, persuasive argument, facilitating and participating in meetings, group decision-making, relationship and team development, leadership, and conflict management.

Part II provides beginning instruction in each of these ten core communication processes.

References

Berk, Joseph, and Berk, Susan, *Total Quality Management: Implementing Continuous Improvement*. New York: Sterling Publishing Co., 1993.

Bertalanffy, Ludwig Von, *General Systems Theory: Foundations, Development, and Applications*. New York: G. Brazillier, 1969.

Blanchard, Kenneth, and Johnson, Spencer, *The One Minute Manager*. New York: Morrow, 1982.

Bryson, John, *Strategic Planning for Public Service and Non Profit Organizations*. San Francisco: Jossey-Bass, 1991.

Drucker, Peter, *The Landmarks of Tomorrow*. New York: Harper and Row, 1957.

Eisenberg, Eric M., and Goodall, H. L., *Organizational Communication: Balancing Creativity and Constraint*. New York: St. Martin's Press, 1993.

Gerth, Hans, and Mills, C. Wright, *Essays in Sociology*. London: Oxford University Press, Inc., 1946.

Goldhaber, Gerald M., and Barnett, George A., *Handbook of organizational communication*. Norwood, New Jersey: Ablex Publishing Corporation, 1988.

Kanter, Rosabeth Moss, *The change masters: Innovation and entrepreneurship in the American corporation*. New York: Simon & Schuster, 1983.

Katz, Daniel, and Kahn, Robert, *The Social Psychology of Organizations*. New York: John Wiley and Sons, 1966.

Kolb, David A., Rubin, Irwin M., and McIntyre, James M., *Organizational Psychology: Readings on Human Behavior in Organizations* (4th ed.): Englewood Cliffs: Prentice-Hall, Inc., 1984.

Likert, Rensis, *New Patterns of Management*. New York: McGraw-Hill, 1961.

McGregor, Douglas, *The Human Side of Enterprise*. New York: McGraw-Hill, 1960.

Morrill, Calvin, *The executive way: Conflict management in organizations*. Chicago: University of Chicago Press, 1995.

Organ, Dennis W., *The Applied Psychology of Work Behavior*. Dallas, Texas: Business Publications, Inc., 1978.

Osborne, David, and Gaebler, Ted, *Reinventing Government: How the Entrepreneurial Spirit in Transforming the Public Sector*. New York: Penguin Books, 1993.

Pepper, Gerald L., *Communicating in organizations: A cultural approach*. New York: McGraw-Hill, 1995.

Peters, Tom, and Waterman, R., *In search of excellence*. New York: Random House, 1982.

Rogers, Everett M., and Agarwala-Rogers, Rekha, *Communication in Organizations*. New York: Macmillan Publishing Co., Inc., 1976.

Schein, Edgar, *Organizational culture and leadership*. San Francisco: Josses-Bass, 1988.

Senge, Peter M., *The fifth discipline: The art & practice of the learning organization*. New York: Doubleday, 1994.

Shafritz, Jay M. and Whitbeck, Philip H., *Classics of organizational theory.* Oak Park, Illinois: Moore Publishing Company, 1978.

Skinner, B. F., *Contingencies of Reinforcement: A Theoretical Analysis.* New York: Appleton-Century-Crofts, 1969.

Van Doren, Charles, A *History of Knowledge.* New York: Ballantine Books, 1991.

PART II

Core Communication Skills

The first and most essential communication skill is *listening*. An enormous problem in most organizations is that too many messages go unheard and unheeded. Skillful listening is important in performing virtually every role in an organization. So we begin our discussion of communication skills with listening.

Michael Dues co-authors this chapter with Dr. Powena Sirimangkala. She holds a Ph.D. in Speech Communication from Kent State University, and is currently Assistant Professor of Communication at Barry University, teaching courses in organizational, interpersonal and intercultural communication. A native of Thailand, she brings a valuable intercultural perspective to the subject of listening.

CHAPTER 3

Listening: The Cornerstone Communication Skill

Pawena Sirimangkala
Barry University
and
Michael Dues
University of Arizona

Key Terms

listening process
listening effectiveness
other orientation
listening to learn
listening to evaluate
listening to help
listening barriers

conductive communication
   environment
psychological interfence
physical interference
verbal listening skills
nonverbal listening skills
cross-cultural communication

high context cultures
low context cultures
positive reinforcement
respond
reciprocate

Objectives

The goals of this chapter are to motivate and enable students to practice listening as a vital skill at work. The chapter objectives are to:

1. Identify the relationship between effective listening and better personal relationships, more successful careers, and organizational success.
2. Show that listening *begins* then communication process.
3. Identify barriers that prevent effective listening
4. Help you improve your listening skills

"The key to success is to get out into the store
and listen to what the associates have to say."

Sam Walton

In Chapter 1 we observed that communication is an ongoing, interactive process with no clear beginning or ending. Attempting to determine the beginning point of any communication is like asking whether the chicken or the egg came first: chickens lay eggs, but eggs bring forth chickens. Listening is like the egg in this comparison. Effective listening enables communication. People communicate when they have reason to believe someone will listen well. In this sense we can say that effective communication begins with listening. Good listening provides the environment needed for accurate information flow. Conversely, poor listening damages both individual and organizational productivity. So, we begin our discussion of core communication skills with listening.

We hope this chapter motivates you to take listening more seriously and to listen more actively. Improved listening skills will help you establish and maintain successful relationships, climb the organizational ladder, and interact effectively with people from cultures and subcultures different from your own. Our intent is to deepen your understanding of the value of listening in organizations, to describe the reasons for listening, and to offer ways to improve listening in today's multi-cultural workplace.

The Process of Listening

Listening is more than just hearing. It requires focused effort. Wolvin and Coakley (1996) define listening as a process of receiving, attending to, and assigning meaning to aural and visual stimuli. According to this definition, beyond hearing spoken words, listening includes attending to the nonverbal and visual aspects of messages and their contexts. Listening is thus a multi-sensory experience: we listen with our ears, eyes, minds, and other senses. . .even our intuition. Verderber and Verderber (2001) take a somewhat broader view, suggesting the listening process includes attending, understanding, evaluating, and responding. In this chapter we offer a still broader and more active view of listening, suggesting that good listeners invite others to communicate openly, and that they not only respond, but also promote ongoing communication by reciprocating.

People speak and listen to others because of what they want to achieve through the interaction (Canary & Cody, 1994). A sales associate listens to a customer because she wants to make a sale; a boss praises staff members because she wants to motivate them to work effectively; and a mechanic tells you your car is worth fixing because he wants your business. Although specific goals vary, in general, people engage in communication because they want to learn, to relate, to influence, and to help (DeVito, 1995). Listening is essential for meeting all these goals, and this chapter offers practical tools for becoming a good listener.

Assessing Your Level of Listening Effectiveness

Before reading the rest of the chapter, evaluate your own listening habits by taking the self-evaluation test on the following page.

The test focuses directly on the skills you need to be a good listener. To score your listening skills, add the numbers you assigned to the seventeen items. The average total score is 61. Is your score higher or lower than the average? By itself, your total score is less important than your responses to the individual items. Items on which you rated yourself 1, 2, or 3 indicate areas in which you need to improve.

The Value of Listening in Organizations

Listening well enhances our lives at work in several ways. Effective listeners are more likely to be employed, and to occupy higher positions in organizations. They are promoted more often, and enjoy deeper, more satisfying relationships with others (Borisoff & Purdy, 1991; Guffey, 1997; Sypher, Bostrom, & Siebert, 1989). Despite the advantages of listening well, the quality of listening is generally poor in most organizations (Adler & Elmhorst, 1996). As a result, people often find themselves in situations where misunderstandings due to poor listening lead to conflicts or escalation of conflicts, and additional problems that take time to fix. Such listening errors can be costly to organizations. Imagine a shipping clerk is told to expedite a package to a distributor in Portland, Maine, but only hears "Portland," and sends it to Oregon. At the very least, the shipper has cost the company money and time to correct the error. When you add in the additional consequences, such as an irate distributor, a dissatisfied customer and a damaged customer service reputation, the costs increase.

Effective listening is not a talent with which we are born; rather **listening effectiveness** comes through learning and practice. Researchers and practitioners alike indicate that listening is a skill acquired through learning (e.g., Berko, Rosenfeld, Samovar, 1997; Brownell, 1990). Why should we invest our time and energy learning

Listening Self-Evaluation Test
(Berko, Rosenfeld, & Samovar, 1997)

How often do you find yourself engaging in the following listening patterns? Use the following scale to indicate your response to each item on the next page.

1   you engage in the behavior ***almost always***   (91–100 percent of the time).
2   you engage in the behavior ***usually***   (71–90 percent of the time).
3   you engage in the behavior ***sometimes***   (31–70 percent of the time).
4   you engage in the behavior ***seldom***   (11–30 percent of the time).
5   you engage in the behavior almost never   (0–10 percent of the time).

_____   1. When someone has just told me a dramatic or humorous story about herself or himself, I say, "That's nothing. Let me tell you what happened to me."
_____   2. I let a lack of organization get in the way of my listening.
_____   3. I interrupt if I have something I want to say.
_____   4. When someone is telling me a story or making a point about something, as soon as I realize what he or she is driving at I let my mind wander until it's my turn to talk since I know what is going to be said.
_____   5. I fail to repeat what is said before I react.
_____   6. I give little verbal or nonverbal feedback to the other person.
_____   7. I pay attention only to the words and ignore the tone and pitch being used.
_____   8. I let emotionally charged words make me angry.
_____   9. In a brief social conversation I use the other person's name rarely.
_____   10. If I consider the subject boring, I stop paying attention.
_____   11. I criticize the other person's delivery or mannerisms.
_____   12. I do not take notes during lectures and phone calls.
_____   13. I let distractions interfere with my concentration.
_____   14. When someone is explaining something technical or complicated, I act as if I am following what she or he says, even if I am not, so I won't look or sound stupid.
_____   15. I do not recognize when I am too upset or tired to listen.
_____   16. I try to give advice when someone is telling me his or her problems.
_____   17. I slump in my chair when listening in class.

_____   **TOTAL SCORE**

and practicing to improve our listening skills? First, because information is essential to functioning in organizations, and listening is a primary means of gaining information. As we learned in Chapter 2, organizations are becoming more and more information-driven. In fact, information is the strongest source of power in any organization, so listening is a primary avenue to power. The more effectively we listen, the more power we acquire, and the better we are able to function in organizations.

Second, the functional advantages of good listening are especially apparent in today's global economy. The world market brings together organizations, employees, and clients who bring with them their cultural, ethnic, and racial backgrounds into the marketplace and the workplace. To survive in this highly competitive global economy, businesses strive for maximum efficiency. Employers seek to hire qualified individuals who also have the ability to communicate with different kinds of people in a variety of situations. Such communication skills have become important considerations in hiring and promoting (Arnold, 1992). Moreover, current workplace trends demand team efforts where team members work together to identify problems, analyze alternatives, and recommend solutions. We must listen to each other well if we are to become effective business communicators. Effective listening is essential in working with others to solve problems, negotiate differences, and manage conflicts.

Of the basic communication skills, listening is used the most. Listening occurs more frequently than speaking, reading, or writing. Most North Americans spend from 42 to 80 percent of their communication time listening; only about 9 percent of their time is spent writing, 16 percent reading, and 35 percent speaking (Barker, Edwards, Gaines et al., 1981; Wolvin & Coakley, 1995; Purdy, 1996). Considering how important it is, and how much we take it for granted, listening may be the most underrated communication skill (Verderber & Verderber, 2001), particularly in organizational settings. Despite its obvious value, listening as a communication skill tends to be overlooked both in the classroom and in the workplace. For our most used skill, we receive the least training. Chances are you probably received less than half a year of formal listening training in all of your elementary and secondary schooling. Compare that short time to the usual six to eight years devoted to formal reading instruction, twelve years to writing, and one year to speaking (Wolvin & Coakley, 1995). We can, however, still turn the situation around, so that it's not too late to learn more about ourselves, others, and situations through listening.

Reasons to Listen

We listen in different ways, depending on our reasons to listen. We listen for a variety of reasons; however, when we think about communication in the workplace, there are three major reasons why organizational members listen. They listen **to learn, to evaluate,** and **to help.**

Listening to Learn

When you **listen to learn,** your purpose is to acquire knowledge from others. The benefits of this type of listening are many, including profiting from the insights of others who have learned, done, lived, or seen what you have not. Listening to learn enables you to profit from other's experience, learning from them how to respond to situations before problems develop, escalate, or become impossible to control. Listening to learn enables you to make reasonable choices based on the acquired information.

Listening to learn is the most common type of listening in most occupations (Adler & Elmhorst, 1996). One important reason we engage in this listening strategy is to understand others' messages accurately. For example, we listen to learn about a supervisor's instruction, a subordinate's complaints, or a customer's need. Instead of making hasty conclusions by suggesting that you know exactly how to do your job, that other people were not trying hard enough, or that you know what the customer is about to tell you, you might very well be learning something new from the situation by listening to others.

When listening to learn, it is important to listen thoroughly and completely before responding or acting. This can be difficult. We usually get no where in a dialogue when we make hasty judgments of what is right or wrong, or when we insist on our own way to do things. Instead, we are better off to listen first and withhold our thoughts and opinions until they are sought. When we genuinely listen to learn, we gain much more than we lose.

Without a clear reason to listen and a clear goal in mind, people are likely to make mistakes by using a listening strategy in the wrong place and at the wrong time. Having unclear goals can lead to misunderstanding, defensiveness, destructive conflict, and making judgment of the speaker and the situation. For example, a co-worker may be telling another co-worker about an incident that happened to her. Instead of listening to learn more about the incident and the impact that it has on the speaker, the listener assumes a role of listening to help by mistakenly interpreting the message as a request for advice. As it turns out, the listener has offended the speaker by giving unsolicited advice. When we are critical and mindful about what we want and how to behave in a situation, we can be quite accurate in determining our reason to listen and communicative goals.

When you have chosen to listen to learn, remind yourself to withhold judgment and evaluation until you have heard the complete message. Although some of the things you hear may tax your listening skills, always keep two basic things in mind when listening to learn: (1) yours and the speaker's roles (e.g., your role is to listen to be informed and the speaker's role is speaking to inform) and (2) the goals of the parties involved (e.g., your goal is to listen to satisfy a customer's needs and the customer's goal is to find answers to the questions).

Successful business people are *other-oriented*. **Other orientation** simply means considering the rights and needs of others and giving others freedom of choice. By acknowledging the fact that people think, behave, and react to situations differently due to their individual circumstances, you have respected them as unique individuals who may have something to say that may be an eye-opener and beneficial to you. By being other-oriented, you are constantly and critically adjusting and adapting when dealing with different people in different situations.

So when you listen to learn, you should walk into a situation with a clear goal in mind. For example, when meeting with your supervisor, your goal is to find out how the supervisor feels about a project that you're working on. With this goal in mind, you are likely to be open-minded in hearing the supervisor's comments and expectations and be logical in explaining your plans for the proposal. As a result, you discover not only how your supervisor feels about the project but also ways to improve the proposal so that it is likely to be approved when submitted.

Listening to Evaluate

When you **listen to evaluate,** your goal is to listen to acquire information that you can then use to solve problems and to make critical decisions and judgments. This critical thinking process allows us to evaluate others' messages reasonably accurately. Examples for this type of listening include listening to (a) make a decision to hire or accept employment during a job interview, (b) handle a complaint from a customer, (c) evaluate a proposal for a new project, (d) respond to comments from your supervisor, or (e) help resolve disputes between subordinates. Effective listeners make evaluations based on the following factors: the speaker's main points, supporting evidence, credentials, motives, and emotional appeal. When listeners overlook any of these factors, they rely only on partial information to make an evaluation. In addition, listeners make poor evaluations when they let their own prejudices and biases interfere, when they are close-minded, or have unclear goals get in listening. Listening to evaluate requires a great deal of attention and critical thinking.

There are several ways you can improve your ability in evaluative listening. One way is to put yourself in situations where you get to observe others' listening behavior and learn from their success and failure. Another way is to build your skill in critical thinking. Chapter 7, on persuasive argument, will help in this effort. Still another way is to increase interaction with others to give yourself opportunities to practice your listening skills. Through trial and error, you will be able to decide what works and what does not.

Listening to Help

When we listen to help in an organizational setting, the outcomes are likely to meet both the personal needs and the organizational needs. When the organizational climate is good, people not only look forward to going to work but they are likely to perform their job effectively (see the discussion of "communication climate" in Chapter 10). **Listening to help** has many benefits. First, when you listen to help, you are also forming and maintaining friendships with someone at work. When people feel your genuine concern for them, this mutual influence becomes a meaningful experience that we share with another human being. More importantly, shared experience through listening is vital to our well-being. While listening to help others makes you feel good, your attentive and supportive listening will also allow you to build network among colleagues and associates (again, see Chapter 10). This network will also likely provide future opportunities for your career growth.

Second, helping to meet the personal needs is consistent with meeting organizational need. Good relationships generate effective good team work. In addition, when people ask to be listened to (e.g., asking you to offer your advice), you have an opportunity to share with them your knowledge, expertise, and experience., which benefits the organization.

Key things to remember when listening to help include (a) make sure that help is actually being sought; (b) maintain a balance between your needs and the speaker's needs; (c) have clear communicative goals in mind in your interaction with others; and (d) remember that listening to others creates an image of how you want others to perceive you.

When deadlines are near and your time is limited, the challenge is often on maintaining a balance between your needs and the speaker's needs. In carefully assessing the situation, you should be able to select a listening strategy that is likely to result in desirable outcomes for both you and the speaker.

Listening Barriers

There are many barriers to effective listening in the workplace. These barriers act as "noise" in the communication process: they have the potential to reduce the accuracy of messages sent. Listening barriers can be grouped into five general categories (DeFleur, Kearney & Plax, 1998).

1. **Differences in meaning.** As we learned in Chapter 1, each of us assigns or attaches different meanings to words. Denotative meanings of abstract terms can be a problem. But connotative meanings those personal, subjective interpretations for verbal and nonverbal symbols and signs which are *not part of the message intended by the sender can seriously impair our listening.*

2. *Personal circumstances.* Conditions that affect us physically, like illness, exhaustion, hunger, pain, and intoxication can interfere with our capacity to listen. Psychological distractions and worries such as problems with finances, work, a sick child, or a relationship in distress can interfere with listening. Emotions such as anger, sadness and fear can get in the way of listening well.

3. **Physical conditions** in the listening environment can interfere with our concentration. Background noise from lawn mowers, leaf blowers, air conditioning, aircraft, office equipment, others' voices, even music be listening barriers. Other environmental conditions also affect our capacity to listen: temperature, time limits, placement of furniture, and level of privacy.

4. **Cultural differences.** People of different cultures and subcultures can have trouble listening due to differences in cultural beliefs, norms, attitudes, expectations, language use and behaviors. These differences can make listening extremely difficult for persons of different cultural backgrounds, especially if they are unaccustomed to cultural diversity.

5. **Bias.** Personal prejudices against groups of people of different race or ethnicity, sex or sexual orientation, age, religion, political or economic status, ways of thinking, or behavior can get in the way of listening. In addition, listening

can be impeded by more subtle prejudices concerning appearance, such as physical attractiveness, weight, baldness, etc. Our stereotypical beliefs about the categories people belong to can speak louder than words and overpower the message.

Keys to Effective Listening

Most people are relatively poor listeners and their listening behavior could be much improved. People can improve their listening skills in nine ways:

- Establish a conducive environment for speaking.
- Assume equal responsibility with the speaker for communication.
- Focus your attention *fully* on the task of listening.
- Seek to comprehend what the *speaker* means.
- Use verbal listening skills to check perceptions and clarify meanings.
- Use nonverbal listening skills to read nonverbal cues and to provide feedback.
- Take notes to help ensure accurate recall.
- Increase intercultural communication competence.
- Respond and reciprocate. Give back appropriately in return for the messages you receive.

Each of these keys to improvement is described below.

Establish a Conducive Environment for Speaking.

Effective listening begins with creating an environment that invites, promotes, and rewards open and honest communication. Good listeners invite others to speak by showing interest in what they might have to say, and making it clear that honest communication is valued, even when messages carry bad news. We all know people with whom we feel free to communicate openly, and with whom we sense that our ideas and feelings are respected. We talk more, and talk more openly, with these people. We also know people around whom we tend to say very little, and to be careful about what we say. The difference is that some create an environment conducive to communication, and some don't.

A conducive environment for communication is one in which people are genuinely interested in one another's ideas, information, and feelings. A conducive environment is one in which the consequences of speaking up honestly are affirming. In conducive environments, "bad news messengers" are never punished for delivering bad news. Prompt, honest, complete sharing of relevant ideas and information is highly valued. To create such an environment, one must not only claim to have these values, but must live them and communicate them.

Assume Equal Responsibility with the Speaker for Communication.

The Shannon-Weaver Model of communication described in Chapter 1 clearly illustrates that for a message to be transmitted successfully, *half* of the action and effort must be expended by the receiver. And, *half* of the failures that can cause of communication effort to misfire can occur on the part of the listener. So, it is fair to say that half of the responsibility for the success or failure of a communication effort belongs to the listener. One reason many people listen poorly is that they assume that the *work* of communicating is mostly to be done by the speaker. A useful place to begin improving our listening skills, then, is to consciously take 50% of the responsibility for the communication, and accepting the fact that listening requires effort. Adopt a mind-set of working with the speaker to complete the communication successfully.

Focus Your Attention Fully on the Communication Effort.

Good listeners focus their attention fully on their listening task. They eliminate competition from other thoughts and tasks while listening. We may very well be able to do more than one thing at a time, but listening is a complex and difficult task; it cannot be done well unless we give it our full attention. When you listen, shift your self-focus to other-focus, quieting your inner dialog so that you can fully attend to the speaker.

Before listening takes place, assess yourself and the situation to make sure that distractions and other listening barriers are kept to a minimum. **Psychological interference** (thoughts or feelings in the listener which interfere with receiving the message) can reduce your listening competence. If you are preoccupied with another matter or thought, it might be best to postpone a conversation until you can devote full attention to listening. Also, the environment should promote listening by minimizing **physical interference.** Ask yourself questions such as: should the conversation take place in a public area or in private? Should we meet in my office, the other person's office, or neutral territory? Should we sit side-by-side, or across the desk? Realize that when physical or psychological noise interferes, messages may not be accurately delivered, heard or understood.

Listen to Comprehend What the Speaker Means.

We pointed out in Chapter 1 that "meanings are in people, not in words." We can do a better job of listening, if we carefully bear this truth in mind. Listen to comprehend what the speaker *means* to say, not just for what the words themselves mean. In this way, you will be working with the speaker to accomplish the communication; you will more easily recognize what needs to be clarified; and you will encounter less misunderstanding.

Use Verbal Listening Skills to Check Perceptions and Clarify Meanings.

Recall from Chapter 1 that, when communicating, both speaker and listener encode and decode messages simultaneously. So while you listen you also engage in both verbal and nonverbal communication, providing responses to your communicative partner. Remember that communication is a collaborative effort in which speaker and listeners work together to achieve accurate transmission of messages. Effective listening includes talking to clarify the other persons's perceptions and meanings. Some **verbal listening skills** for effectively carrying out the listener's role are identified below.

1. Identify areas of agreement or share common experience with the speaker to demonstrate your understanding of the topic. By creating common ground with the speaker, without dominating the conversation, you are also communicating a level of maturity and receptivity to the speaker, creating a leveled ground for the conversation.
2. Ask direct questions, without interrupting the conversation, to encourage the other person to continue the conversation. Questions are useful when you are not sure whether you should engage in either listening to learn, to evaluate, or to help. By asking for clarification or additional information, you will become more aware of the speaker's needs and therefore, be able to select an appropriate listening strategy for the situation.
3. Restate the content of the speaker's message by repeating key words and phrases, and ideas to indicate your understanding of the speaker's issue. Restating what you heard allows the speaker to check your understanding, and increases your accuracy in interpreting the message. Since our different frames of mind and circumstances may act as listening barriers, it is useful to make sure that you hear and understand the message content accurately.

4. Paraphrase both the content and the intent of the speaker's message without disagreeing or evaluating the message. This practice ensures that you understand both the content and the intent of the message prior to making a judgment. Sometimes listeners rely on past information to interpret the speaker's current statements. Using old information is problematic because the speaker's intent may have changed and/or moved away from past positions. In relying on past statements and intentions, the listener may be making incorrect assumptions about the speaker's current state of mind. Remember that people have reasons for making statements, and that they change their minds and behaviors due to circumstances that may be unknown to others. Make sure you understand the speaker's *current* frame of mind before reaching a conclusion.

5. Use words that are calm, rational, fair, logical and open-minded. It is best to refrain from using emotionally loaded language in the organizational setting. Even if the speaker is upset, when you paraphrase and respond you can choose words that reduce emotionality without changing or discounting the speaker's meaning and intent. In this way you may help the speaker reframe the issue in more rational, manageable terms.

Use Nonverbal Listening Skills to Carefully Read Nonverbal Cues, and to Provide Feedback to the Speaker.

Not all the skills required to listen well are verbal. It is also essential to accurately read a speaker's nonverbal signals and consider these cues in relation to the words he or she is speaking. Nonverbal cues include gestures, eye contact, facial expressions, postures, positions, timing, and nonverbal uses of the voice, all of which are combined with the words being spoken to produce the total message. **Nonverbal listening skills** are probably more culture-specific than the verbal skills discussed above. Be aware that there are many different cultural factors involved in interpreting nonverbal behaviors. For examples, eye contact, personal distance, body movements and hand gestures, and voice volume have different meanings in different cultures. Moreover, degrees of expressiveness and formality vary greatly from culture to culture. While some cultures allow for higher degrees of facial and vocal expressiveness, other cultures may value a lower degree of expressiveness and voice volume. The best advice when communicating with someone who is from a culture or subculture with which you are not familiar is to observe the behavior of the person and allow extra time for effective listening and relational development. Some of the universal nonverbal skills that are useful in listening situations include:

1. Demonstrate bodily responsiveness by showing your interest in the conversation. This type of responsiveness refers to the state of being alert and attentive while listening.
2. Use positive facial expressions such as smiling appropriately to indicate your pleasant feelings in the conversation.
3. Use eye contact to communicate your interest. A Thai proverb that says eyes are windows of the soul is applicable here. The key is to display liveliness through the eyes while listening to others. However, keep in mind that some cultures interpret direct eye contact or avoidance of eye contact differently. Again the best thing to do when unsure of how to behave nonverbally is to observe how others communicate with their nonverbal behaviors.
4. Read speakers' nonverbal cues to help assess the feeling, tone, and intention dimensions of messages. Recall that in Chapter 1 we discussed these four dimensions of each message. Sense, the surface content dimension, is communicated primarily through verbal symbols. The other dimensions—feeling, which conveys how the speaker feels about the message; tone, which reveals the relationship between speaker and listener; and intention, which shows the speaker's purpose in communicating—all tend to be expressed nonverbally. It is important to attend to all these dimensions in order to understand the full meaning of the message.

Take Notes.

Research suggests that misunderstandings are extremely common (Cupach & Spitzberg, 1994). Conversational partners typically achieve no more than 25 to 50 percent accuracy in interpreting each other's remarks. Multiply this percentage by the number of organizational members you interact with daily and the results could be overwhelming. To increase the rate of accuracy, listeners need to first find out the causes of the inaccuracy. If the cause has to do with an inability to remember important things you hear, you are not alone. One researcher found that immediately after a ten-minute presentation, a normal listener can recall only 50 percent of the information presented. After forty-eight hours, the recall level drops to 25 percent (Nichols, 1987). A way to improve our listening skills so that we retain important messages is to develop the note taking habit by putting important topics in writing. Just like students taking notes to recall important information for an exam, business professionals can also adopt this valuable note taking technique. Note taking does not require writing down every detail in every setting but when the topic is important, it is best to put it in writing.

Increase Intercultural Communication Competence.

One of the new challenges facing the American workforce is to increase our effectiveness when communicating with people who come from different cultural, ethnic, and racial backgrounds. We need to understand how cultures affect the way people communicate. There are two assumptions to keep in mind about **cross-cultural communication:** (a) communication is *rule governed*, and (b) rules are *culturally diverse*. Because communication is governed by rules, each culture has different sets of rules of how to behave verbally and nonverbally. For example, people who come from cultures where they believe that "silence is golden" have a tendency to take a role of listener and believe that they will learn more from listening to others than being the speakers themselves. On the other hand, if you come from a culture that believes that "only the squeaky wheels get the grease," you will be more likely to verbalize your needs and concerns to make sure that they are heard.

Differences between high-context and low-context cultures also affect how one listens and speaks. In **high context cultures** such as Japan, the rule is that most of the meaning is carried in the *context* in which something is said. Based on their belief that meanings are embedded within the context, members from high-context cultures naturally value silence and only speak when necessary. Therefore, when members from high-context cultures communicate, their words and meanings are often indirect, implicit, and vague. For them, nonverbal behavior is louder than verbal messages. As a result, they tend to speak less and listen more. On the other hand, the rule in **low context cultures** is that the message *content* carries most of the meaning. Members of low-context cultures such as the United States pay less attention to the contextual meaning and focus more on the spoken words. Therefore, members from low-context cultures tend to use words and meanings more directly and explicitly. As a result, they convey meanings verbally and tend to speak more and listen less.

Obviously, when members of two different cultures interact, misunderstanding is likely. The question is can we successfully avoid misunderstandings based on cultural differences? The answer is yes, but it requires a great deal of willingness to understand how significantly culture has an impact on all of us. Rather than making judgment of another person based on their cultural belief system, it is best to try to understand the person's cultural background and realize that communication and culture are often inseparable. When two people from two different cultural systems interact, understanding, open-mindedness, and withholding judgment are keys to communication success.

Respond and Reciprocate. Give Back Appropriately in Return for the Messages You Receive.

Psychologists tell us that **"positive reinforcement"** motivates people to repeat or continue behaviors. The surest way to induce people to continue communicating honestly and openly with us is to reward the desired communication behavior. Conversely, lack of reinforcement will "extinguish" behavior. That is, behavior that appears not to have any impact tends not to be repeated. The surest way to cause people to stop communicating with you is to not respond at all.

The best way to reward others for communicating well with us is to attend to and respond to their messages. We **respond** by letting them know we have listened and received their message, and by acting appropriately in response to their message. That is, if we are asked a question, we should promptly provide a relevant answer. If we receive information, we should acknowledge its receipt, act on the information when appropriate, and let the speaker know that we have acted. Of course, if we want others to *stop* communicating with us, we can discourage communication by not responding.

Interpersonal communication scholars have identified *reciprocity* as an important communication variable (Fisher and Adams, 1994). They have observed that people tend to continue giving information to others only when others **reciprocate,** giving appropriate information in return. We have all experienced this principle in situations where we were giving information to someone who was withholding information from us. When this situation occurs, we tend to feel uncomfortable about giving information and to stop offering it freely. Conversely, when information giving is reciprocated, we tend to communicate more fully and freely. Therefore, to ensure that others will continue to speak to us candidly, it is essential to reciprocate by talking to them with appropriate openness and honesty. Give useful information in return for useful information.

This final key to effective listening brings the listening process full circle. Responding and reciprocating when others communicate with us contributes to a conducive communication environment. In chapter 1 we observed that communication is an interactive, ongoing process, with no clear beginning or end. We can say the same thing about listening. Listening is an essential part of the communication process that is itself interactive and ongoing, with no clear beginning or end.

Conclusion

Listening is but one of the many communicative roles we play in our social interaction at the workplace. Sometimes our role is to listen passively, nonjudgmentally, and empathically, while at other times this role calls for an active, critical, comprehensive, and evaluative listening strategy. As you build a repertoire of listening knowledge and skills, you are likely to become more adaptive, flexible, and practical in selecting an effective listening strategy to achieve your goals.

By approaching listening as a communication skill that improves with practice, you will learn much about yourself, about the speaker, and about the issue at hand. You will also become more effective at listening and responding to messages. The more you know about listening, the more you will appreciate how vital a communication skill it is in the organization. Ability to listen effectively at work will not only facilitate a more free flow of information; it will communicate to others that you value them as individuals. In these ways, listening becomes a path to your own and to others' empowerment.

Summary

Our aim in this chapter was to help you become a better listener by explaining the advantages of listening well and by describing ways to improve your listening. Effective listening is important because listening brings us information that enables us to function appropriately and make intelligent decisions. Information is a potent source of power in organizations, and listening is therefore an avenue to power. Conversely, poor listening is a cause of misunderstandings, conflicts, and functional failure. Listening is an interactive process that begins before speaking. Organization members listen for three basic reasons: to learn, to evaluate, and to help. One's reason for listening influences the way one listens. With these reasons for listening in mind, we described key ways to improve listening: establish a conducive environment for speaking; assume equal responsibility with the speaker for communication; focus your attention *fully* on the task of listening; seek to comprehend what the *speaker* means; use verbal listening skills to check and clarify meanings; use nonverbal listening skills to read nonverbal cues and to provide feedback; take notes; increase intercultural communication competence; and respond and reciprocate, giving back appropriately in return for the messages you receive.

References

Adler, R. B., & Elmhorst, J. M. (1996). *Communicating at work: Principles and practices for business and the professions.* New York: McGraw-Hill.

Arnold, V. D. (June, 1992). The communication competencies listed in job descriptions. *The Bulletin of the Association of Business Communication, 15.*

Barker, L., Edwards, R., Gaines, C., Gladney, K., & Holley, F. (1981). An investigation of proportional times spent in various communication activities by college students. *Journal of Applied Communication Research, 8,* 101–109.

Berko, R. M., Rosenfeld, L. B., & Samovar, L. A. (1997). *Connecting: A culture-sensitive approach to interpersonal communication competency.* Fort Worth, TX: Harcourt Brace College.

Borisoff, D., & Purdy, M. (1991). *Listening in everyday life: A personal and professional approach.* Lanham, MD: University Press of America.

Brownell, J. (1990). Perceptions of effective listeners: A management study. *Journal of Business Communication, 27,* 401–415.

Canary, D. J., & Cody, M. J. (1994). *Interpersonal communication: A goals-based approach.* New York: St. Martin's Press.

Cupach, W. R., & Spitzberg, B. H. (1994). *The dark side of interpersonal communication.* Hillsdale, NJ: Erlbaum.

DeFleur, M. L., Kearney, P., & Plax, T. G. (1998). *Fundamentals of human communication.* Mountain View, CA: Mayfield.

Devito, J. A. (1995). The interpersonal communication book. New York: Harper Collins College.

Fisher, B. A. & Adams, K. L. (1994). *Interpersonal communication: Pragmatics of human relationships.* New York: McGraw-Hill.

Guffey, M. E. (1997). *Business communication: Process and product.* Cincinnati, OH: South-Western College.

Kaufmann, P. J. (1993). *Sensible listening: The key to responsive interaction*. Dubuque, IA: Kendall/Hunt.

Nichols, R. G. (September, 1987). Listening is a 10-part skill. *Nation's Business, 75*, 40.

Sypher, B. D., Bostrom, R. N., & Siebert, J. H. (1989). Listening, communication abilities, and success at work. *Journal of Business Communication, 26*, 293–303.

Verderber, K. S., & Verderber, R. F. (2001). *Inter-Act: Interpersonal communication concepts, skills and contexts* (9th ed.) Belmont, CA: Wadsworth/Thomson Learning.

Weaver, J. B., & Kirtley, M. B. (1995). Listening styles and empathy. *The Southern Communication Journal, 60*, 131–140.

Wolvin, A. D. & Coakley, C. G. (1996). *Listening* (5th ed.). Dubuque, IA: Brown & Benchmark

Presenting oneself is an every-day task in organizational life. In Chapter 4, Pamela Koch draws on Goffman's classic work, The Presentation of Self in Everyday Life, and on a broad range of communication research to explain and offer suggestions on effective self presentation in an organizational context.

Ms. Koch is a Ph.D. candidate in Communication at the University of Arizona. She has considerable intercultural experience, including teaching and studying in China, and is an experienced teacher of organizational communication at the University of Arizona. She is currently at the City University of Hong Kong working on dissertation research in cross-cultural organizational communication that is supported by funding from Rotary International.

CHAPTER 4

Managing Impressions: Presenting Yourself Effectively

Pamela Tremain Koch
University of Arizona

Key Terms

impression management	audience	assertive behavior
impression formation	script	defensive behavior
actor	performance	tactical impression management
role	reviews	strategic impression management
stage	goals	first impression
backstage	nonverbal cues	
frontstage	verbal cues	

Objectives

This chapter discusses the importance of impression management in the organization and presents principles of good performances in the workplace. It also illustrates the usefulness of understanding how we form and manage impressions. By the end of this chapter you should understand:

1. What impression management is and how it is used within an organization.
2. What impression formation is.
3. Goffman's (1959) dramaturgical model of impression management.
4. General principles of how to competently manage impressions.

5. The meaning and classification of assertive, defensive, tactical, and strategic impression management behaviors.
6. How impression management strategies may be used in contexts such as interviews, performance reviews, and communicating with superiors and subordinates.
7. How gender, ethnicity, age, and other physical attributes of a person may influence impression management strategies and bias our interpretations of these strategies.

On the morning of your interview, you carefully choose an outfit to wear, check, then double-check your appearance in the mirror, and prudently schedule your travel to arrive at the interview site 15 minutes before the scheduled time. During the interview you seek to control any nervous behavior. You work to appear as knowledgeable, self-confident, and professional as possible in your appearance, behavior and speech. After successfully interviewing for the job, you continue working to maintain a good image. Your speech, appearance, gestures, use of space, time, touch, and a multitude of other behaviors all work together to ensure that you present the image of a competent, trustworthy, and personable employee. Success in this presentation will assist you to advance in the organization, while failure will hinder potential promotions, raises, and success in getting your work done.

Why do we concern ourselves about these details of our appearance, behavior, and speech? Like most people, we believe the impressions others build about us are important and we know that we can choose to emphasize certain aspects of our selves and to downplay others to influence this impression creation process. We want our prospective employers to see us as reliable, competent, and motivated; our romantic partners to see us as attractive and interesting; and our friends to see us as fun and empathetic.

Impression management is exercising control over communicative behaviors in order to make a desired impression (Gardner, 1992; Morrison & Bies, 1991; Rosenfeld, Giacalone, & Riordan, 1994; Schlenker, 1980; Schneider, 1983; Villanova & Bernadin, 1989). Because the impressions we make influence how others perceive, treat, and evaluate us, we often behave in ways that will create certain desired impressions in others' eyes (Leary & Kowalski, 1990). Although at times we are barely conscious of the impact our actions may have on others, we become more conscious when we are potentially subject to evaluation by other people. For example, we might work at a desk in the office without consciously thinking about the image we are projecting until we notice our supervisor walking down the corridor. At that time our attention to our work and the image we are projecting may become extremely important.

Within the organization, as in other areas of our lives, we seek to influence the impressions others develop about us. The success of our individual efforts, as well as the success of the organization, depends upon the skill with which impressions are managed (Baumeister, 1989; Gardner, 1992). Impression management is related to success within the organization (Gardner & Martinko, 1988) as well as in job interviews (Baron, 1986), and are an important influence mechanism (Pfeffer, 1981). Importantly, while many of our behaviors generally run on autopilot, we can learn to consciously control them for a more successful presentation.

Knowing how to manage the impressions others form of us is important. Equally important is knowing how we form impressions of others. **Impression formation** is the process of making judgements about others based on situational cues, appearance, and behaviors. Unfortunately, research shows that the impression formation process occurs both swiftly and in a biased manner. We are quick to judge others when their behavior deviates from expected norms or when it confirms negative preconceptions we might have. In order to better evaluate others' abilities and potential, we need to be aware of how this process works.

Organizational Impression Management

In much the same way that an actor on a stage seeks to induce the audience to believe in the character being portrayed, members of organizations seek to act out particular roles. This analogy drawn between impression management and acting underlies much of the foundational thought in this area. As Shakespeare eloquently wrote several hundred years ago:

> *All the world's a stage*
> *And all the men and women merely players;*
> *They have their exits and their entrances,*
> *And one man in his time plays many parts.*

Shakespeare wrote that we are actors, assuming and shedding roles as we move from one stage to another. While we should not completely accept this metaphor (Wilshire, 1982), there are certain aspects of playacting in our daily lives. In fact, one of the foundational thinkers in impression management used the acting metaphor to understand how these processes work.

Goffman's Dramaturgical Analysis

In *The Presentation of Self in Everyday Life* (1959), Erving Goffman wrote that our self-presentation helps define our place in the social order and sets the tone and direction of the interaction. Goffman argued that self-presentation is a constant, never-ending process similar to that of putting on a play for an audience. People actively develop consensus about the requirements for social situations and our behaviors are guided by these expectations and norms. Thus, any situation, or **stage,** will have attendant **scripts** that the social **actors** are expected to follow. **Roles** are the combination of social scripts that the person is supposed to follow in that situation. Goffman also describes the conflict between appearance and reality as the **frontstage** and the **backstage.** For example, a service employee is supposed to don a happy smile and cheerfully greet his customers even if he just experienced an emotional breakup with his girlfriend.

The organization provides one such stage whereupon we can act out organizational roles such as manager and employee, board member and stockholder, salesperson and client. Just as a successful actor knows how to 'put on' his part, an organizational role player knows how to present herself to properly act out her role in the organization. The appearance of the role player, the manner in which she communicates, and the setting in which the interaction takes place all serve to present the 'correct' image within the organization.

Thus, according to Goffman's portrayal of human interaction, our behavior in organizations can be understood using this metaphor. Other researchers have followed in his footsteps. Following is Gardner's (1992) elaboration of this metaphor.

The Actor is the key player in the drama, seeking to lay claim to a role. The success of that identity construction is dependent in part upon physical attributes such as gender, race, age, height, weight, attractiveness, and body shape, as well as the actor's particular skills, attitudes, values, beliefs, and personality. Even the actor's belief in her ability to achieve the impression management goal will influence the effort and type of strategies used. For example, if an actor believes that competition is too stiff, or that her abilities are not sufficient, then the amount of effort put into managing the impression often decreases (Palmer, Welker & Giacalone, 1993).

The Audience is the recipient of the role-playing drama. Key characteristics of the audience, such as power, attractiveness, and familiarity may influence the way an actor presents herself. The way we interact with our superiors is different from the ways we interact with our peers or subordinates. The higher the status of the audience, for example, the more the actor will work hard to ensure the performance is done well (Palmer, Welker & Giacolone, 1993).

The Stage is the context in which the drama is acted out. The particular stage, such as the office, break room, hall, company picnic, or parking lot has great influence upon the drama enacted. Behavior expectations as well as interpretation varies according to the stage on which it is performed. We expect more formal behavior during a performance evaluation, for example, for example, while interactions in the lunch room between the same two people would not be accompanied by such expectations. As a result, the same behaviors will have different interpretations in different contexts.

The Script is the expected sequence of events which unfolds upon the stage. Certain stages provide more rules governing the possible actions and interpretations of those actions, while others are more loosely scripted and thus allow for impromptu action. A board meeting generally follows certain prescribed rules of interaction, while more casual interaction in the halls of the organization leaves greater freedom for more varied presentations and interpretations. Yet other situations may be so ingrained that we merely follow the script mindlessly, going through the appropriate steps without thought to their meaning and interpretation.

The Performance is the total combination of verbal and nonverbal cues enacted by the actor. The words we say have great influence on the impressions others develop of us. At the same time, the way we say those words, as well as our dress, posture, gestures, and other nonverbal cues will also add meaning to our interactions. Good impression management and accurate impression formation demands attention to these multiple aspects of communication.

Reviews provide feedback to the actor from the audience about the success of the drama, as well as other audience reactions. A good actor is in tune with the audience's reviews, and adapts her or his performance to elicit positive audience feedback. A good manager provides timely and adequate reviews so that employees are aware of the impressions being formed of them and have the opportunity to ensure the creation of positive impressions and correct negative ones.

The Goals of the impression management attempt are the desired outcome of the event and also influence impression management strategies (Palmer, Welker, & Giacalone, 1993). The more desirable the outcome, the more effort is generally put into managing an impression. Interviews, performance appraisals, and interactions in which a goal is very important will elicit more conscious effort in impression management than those in which the goals are less salient or important.

Performance Principles

Based on this **dramaturgical** analysis, Goffman established principles for successful impression management performances. Below is a summary of five such principles (Burgoon, Buller, and Goodall, 1994):

1. **Segregate your audiences.** Different audiences and stages exert differing performance demands—thus the criteria for a successful performance may differ. For example, the organizational stage and the 'out with the pals' stage should not overlap to a great degree as it would be difficult to successfully maintain these roles at the same time. In the same manner, the methods that you use to successfully interact with your superiors may undermine the role requirements of successful management of your subordinates. Therefore, it is best to avoid situations where different roles compete with each other.

2. **Know and follow the rules for performing particular social acts.** Your audience has certain expectations about proper behavior based on the context of the situation and the role you are playing. If you are an employee speaking to your supervisor, the general expectation is that you will be deferential and attentive. If you are interviewing for a position in a company, you are generally expected to be interested in the job and to have adequate expertise. If you are a manager communicating with underlings at the office, you are expected to be organized and authoritative. If you are enacting the same roles at a company social event, yet different behaviors would be expected.

   Some research, however, points out that violation of expectations, and refusing to adhere to proper rules, may actually work to your benefit in certain cases (e.g., Burgoon, 1979). For example, wearing something other than the standard suit to an interview might make you be noticed more than the 101 other perspective employees who all dressed alike. Before breaking any role expectations, however, careful considerations of your audience's potential reaction should be taken.

3. **Your verbal and nonverbal cues should complement each other.** Conflicting cues will confuse your audience and might make your performance unbelievable. Burgoon, Buller, & Woodall (1994) point out that when spoken words conflict with actions accompanying them, adults usually give more weight to the actions. When you are managing your impression, how you say words and what you do as you say them is important.

4. **Give a sincere performance.** Fake-seeming performances will almost always result in negative impressions. Actors are more favorably evaluated when they are sincere—or at least perceived to be sincere. In many cases, the easiest way to achieve this goal is to actually *be* sincere, as only an extremely good actor can manage to convincingly carry off an unfamiliar role for more than a short period of time. At times, however, the issues of sincerity presents a conundrum, as the behaviors required to appear sincere might not be the ones you would enact in the absence of such social rules. At a minimum, however, being perceived as authentic can be helped by strategic effort (Grayson & Shulman, 2000) so actors should pay attention to audience perceptions and feedback about their performance.

5. **Express satisfaction with the role.** If an actor appears to dislike the role he is playing, then the performance may not be accepted by the audience. For example, if you dislike your job and are open in voicing this dislike, your co-workers and supervisor may judge your performance as unsatisfactory whether or not the physical evidence backs ups such an evaluation.

In organizations, Goffman would argue, the members fill 'roles' which have scripts we act out. Each position has attendant actions, words, and behaviors which are appropriate to it. Successful performances involve knowing the expectations for certain situations and audiences. In addition, Goffman also identified three typical factors that lead to unsuccessful performances. First, an actor may momentarily lose muscular control and accidentally convey incapacity, impropriety, or disrespect. Stuttering, sneezing, and other difficult to control behaviors may cause an audience to doubt an actor's performance and ability. Second, extremes of involvement or lack of involvement may cause an audience to question the actor's motivation. Baron (1986) found that either perfume or nonverbal behaviors by themselves enhanced their ratings by interviewers, but both together resulted in negative ratings by male interviewers. In short, there can be either too little or too much of a good thing. Third, if an actor is unfamiliar with the setting, available props and equipment, or is unfamiliar with the proper appearance or performance for a role, his performance may fail. For example, arriving at the organization's end-of-the-year party dressed in an evening gown while all other members are casually dressed indicates inadequate familiarity with the role, its setting, and attendant props (Burgoon, Buller, & Woodall, 1994).

Types of Impression Management

Impression management behaviors are very relevant to life in organizations. They can affect workers' morale and productivity, interviewing and selection of personnel, performance evaluation and upward mobility in the organization. Impression management behaviors can be divided into four categories according to whether the behaviors serve assertive or defensive functions and tactical or strategic goals (Tedeschi and Melburg,1984).

Assertive behavior is actor-initiated in order to establish a particular identity for an audience. It is proactive as it anticipates the demands of a particular situation. A person seeking to be a group leader, for example, may initiate more ideas, give more suggestions, and in other ways seek to be more visible. **Defensive behaviors,** on the other hand, are reactive and occur when an actor is faced with a predicament. For example, when undesirable qualities are attributed to an actor, the actor may react defensively to salvage his or her positive identity and reputation.

Tactical impression management is directed toward clear, short-term goals, such as dressing well for an interview, or appearing industrious and productive during a visit by the CEO. **Strategic impression management,** on the other hand, seeks to build reputational characteristics that serve long-term interests. Employees with aspirations to move up in the hierarchy and improve their positions are concerned with building a competent and responsible image.

Examples of assertive-tactical behaviors include ingratiation, intimidation, self-promotion and exemplification. Examples of defensive-tactical behaviors are excuses, justifications, apologies, and self-handicapping. Assertive-strategic behaviors build positive impressions like attraction, esteem, prestige, credibility; while defensive-strategic behaviors indicate problems such as alcohol or drug abuse, mental illness or phobias.

In a performance appraisal, subordinates may use assertive behaviors to create a positive image of themselves, such as ingratiating themselves by acting humble, asking for advice, or doing favors for the boss (Kozlowski, Chao, & Morrison, 1998). These behaviors may serve both tactical (short-term) and strategic (longer term) interests.

In general, focusing on assertive-strategic behaviors will have the greatest payoffs in long-term relationships within an organization. Burgoon, Buller, and Woodall (1994) note that nonverbal behaviors are particularly associated with this category of impression management. Dress, vocalics, eye gaze, posture, and a range of other nonverbal behaviors can greatly assist managing impressions of prestige, status, credibility, and trustworthiness.

In a job interview, however, assertive-tactical behavior would be also appropriate. Telling about your accomplishments, showing interest in the interviewer and organization, and showing how you are good enough to be an example for others will all assist the development of a good impression in the mind of the interviewer. Exemplification and ingratiation tend to enhance perceptions of leader effectiveness and follower satisfaction, while self-promotion and intimidation appear to have a negative effect (Gardner & Cleavenger, 1998).

Defensive-tactical behaviors can be used to excuse, justify, or apologize for behaviors which made you appear in an undesirable light. Making restitution or ensuring that others see you engaged in positive behaviors may help ensure that negative impressions are overridden and changed. While temporary defensive behaviors may serve a good purpose, apologies and excuses generally have a negative influence on evaluations (Gundersen & Tinsley, 1996). Proactive impression management strategies generally work better in both the short and long-terms.

Impression Management—Situational Contexts

Interviewing

During an employment interview the following sequence of events usually occurs: interviewers form an initial impression of an applicant based on paper credentials, ask questions in order to gather additional information, evaluate the applicant with respect to the job, and then make a decision to hire, reject, or seek more information (Macan & Dipboye, 1988). Impression management is particularly important during the interview process as interviewers form impressions, then confirm or reform these impressions. The interview situation is one such time when good impression management is very critical.

According to Bovee and Thill (1983), the top six reasons interviewers gave for rejecting candidates for a job were:

1. Poor personal appearance.
2. Appearing overbearing, aggressive, conceited, "know it all."
3. Unable to express oneself clearly.
4. Lack of career planning.
5. Lack of interest and enthusiasm.
6. Lack of confidence and poise.

Clearly, all six of these reasons imply poor impression management on the part of the job applicant. They are all areas that an astute student of impression management should be able to control for a more successful outcome.

First impressions develop quickly during an interaction, perhaps in as little as 20 seconds (Burgoon, Buller, & Woodall, 1994). Therefore, managing your image to achieve the goal of a good first impression is very important. In the interview situation this is particularly important. When interviewers have favorable first impressions of job applicants, they tend to interact in a more favorable way with these applicants than with those who have made negative first impressions. For example, interviews provide more job information to candidates creating a good first impression, gather less information from these candidates, and use a more positive interviewing style. As a result, positive job applicants respond with more confident and effective behavior, and show more rapport with the interviewers. Interviewers who have positive first impressions of job applicants also show much more positive regard for these job applicants later (Dougherty, Turban & Callender,1994).

Snyder and Swann (1978) found that the first impressions interviewers develop about job applicants influence the questions they later ask. For example, if interviewers believe that the applicant is an introvert, they tend to ask questions that solicit responses from interviewees confirming this initial diagnosis. Interviewers' initial evaluation of an applicant's job suitability also biases the kinds of questions asked (Macon and Dipboye, 1988). Interviewers given weak resumes ask fewer questions about positive characteristics, are less favorable toward these applicants, and tend to ask the more poorly qualified applicants more difficult questions. Thus, both interviewer and job applicant engage in a process of self-fulfilling prophecy during the interview process.

Because initial impressions are so important in the interview process, researchers have investigated the most successful ways for applicants to conduct themselves. The primary goal of the applicant is to convince the interviewer that she or he is the best applicant for the position. Both the applicant and the interviewer try to appear to fit the needs of the other (Godfrey, Jones, & Lord, 1986). Applicants engage in tactical-assertive tactics (Tedeschi & Melburg, 1984), which may be either self-focused or other-focused. **Self-focused tactics** maintain attention on the candidate and allow her to focus the direction of the conversation in areas which allow her to excel. Exemplification (convincing the interviewer that her behavior is good enough to be a model for others), entitlements (taking major responsibility for positive events in one's background), enhancements (attempting to increase the value of an event to make it look even more positive) and self-promotion (describing positive qualities she possesses) are examples of self-focused tactics.

Overall, self-focused tactics were more successful in creating positive impressions and obtaining more job offers. **Other-focused tactics,** however, can also be used to exert more subtle influence mechanisms. For example, other-enhancement (flattering the interviewer or organization), opinion conformity (agreeing with comments made by the interviewer), and favor doing (offering to do something for the interviewer) are other-focused and may successfully be used in certain situations.

Performance Evaluations

The manner in which we present ourselves to others can also have great influence on our performance evaluations. Impression management affects the degree to which a manager likes and perceives similarities with a subordinate. This in turn influences perceptions of the subordinate's performance (Wayne & Liden, 1995). One of the most common and easiest means of presenting ourselves to others is through verbal accounts of our accomplishments (Giacalone & Riordan, 1990). Giacalone & Riordan found that the manner in which information was disclosed affected the credit given to a presenter, perceived difficulty of the accomplishment, and the suggested recognition given to the presenter. Information that disclosed obstacles involved in completing a project increased the amount of credit given to a manager in comparison to a presentation in which the manager discounted the difficulty of the accomplishment and his or her contribution to it. Information that downgrades the effort involved in a project often reflects negatively on the presenter. Group members offering justifications or disclaimers about the quality of their work are more likely to be seen as loafers who don't pull their own weight (Mulvey, 1998).

Nevertheless, there are important differences depending on whether the person being evaluated is a male or female. In one study, if a male manager disclosed obstacles, he was seen as more deserving of recognition, while if a female manager disclosed obstacles, she was seen as less deserving of recognition. In other words, perceptions of the degree of effort expended worked favorably for the men, but unfavorably for the women. The outcome of impression management tactics also has been shown to differ according to sex (Kipnis & Schmidt, 1988). Men were more favorably evaluated when they used reasoning tactics, such as providing explanations for requests, whereas women were more favorably evaluated when they use ingratiation tactics, such as making the supervisor feel important.

Impression management tactics should be used carefully in these situations. If such tactics differ markedly from an employee's usual behavior, they can be interpreted with a negative bias since they contrast with that person's normal behavior. One manager even commented that an individual's tactics had "the effect of detracting from, rather then enhancing my impression" (Wayne & Liden 1998, p. 193), as they were seen as abnormal behavior.

Nonverbal Presentations

Nonverbal communication is particularly important in the formation of initial impressions and successful impression management (Burgoon, Buller, & Woodall, 1994). The success of our performances depends upon how well our nonverbal messages are coordinated with each other and with our verbal messages. **Nonverbal cues** such as physical appearance and vocalics are particularly important in initial interactions such as interviews as people develop initial impressions of our competence, personalities, and abilities. Dress, for example, is significantly related to perception of status (Gorden, Tengler, & Infante, 1982) and to perceptions of personality.

Think of some of the behaviors that are related to good listening skills—these behaviors not only help you to listen better, they also enable you to convey the impression that you are being attentive. Both aspects are important. Open body posture, forward lean, attentive eye gaze, touch, increased use of gestures, and close proximity often convey impressions of attentiveness, liking, and acceptance. Other nonverbal behaviors can be manipulated to increase perceptions of attractiveness, competence, credibility, and persuasiveness.

An understanding of how we nonverbally control our impressions extends beyond what we do with our bodies. Your use of your private space also contributes to the impressions others form of you. The objects you place on your walls and your desk will be interpreted as speaking of your personality and status, as will the arrangement of your office furniture. One need only reflect on the months spent towards the end of the Korean war over disagreement regarding the shape, size, and seating arrangements to be used during the peace negotiation process to realize both the symbolic importance and the meanings attached to these factors. In general, office arrangements that create more barriers between yourself and others lead to impressions of status and powers. On the other hand, more open office arrangements lend themselves to impressions of openness and equality. You must decide what kind of impression you desire to convey.

Vocal cues are also important in creating impressions of credibility, which is conveyed by moderately fast speaking rates, fewer fillers (such as 'um,' 'er,' etc.), vocal variety, and moderately high intensity (Buller & Aune, 1988). Tag questions, overuse of polite forms, hesitations, fillers, rising intonation and the use of hedge words, on the other hand, convey what is called **powerless** speech. Think of the difference between a sentence such as "Yes sir, the presentation .;tn.;tn. went kinda .;tn.;tn. not too bad, didn't it?" and a clear, concise and certain statement. Research consistently shows that listeners will judge speakers of the former sentence as less credible, less attractive and not able to do a good job (Conley & O'Barr, 1990).

Unfortunately, personal features that are more difficult or impossible to control—such as age, sex, height, skin color, and attractiveness—also contribute to the impressions others form. This warning leads us to reflection on how we form impressions of others.

Impression Formation—the Other Side of the Coin

Knowledge about impression management can help us create the impressions we want. Knowledge about impression formation can assist us in making informed judgments about other's impression management performances. Burgoon, Buller, and Woodall (1994) comment that impression formation is based upon several underlying principles:

People develop evaluations of others from limited external information. The amount of information we know about someone in initial meetings is quite limited. Nevertheless, we form impressions of others quickly based on this limited information. These impressions provide some level of necessary predictability (Berger & Calabrese, 1975), and help us judge how the interaction with the person might precede.

Impressions are partly based on stereotypes the perceiver holds. We rely on previous general knowledge to help make judgments about other people due to the fact that the amount of initial information we derive during an initial encounter is quite limited. For example, not only do we often rely on racial or gender stereotypes, but height (tall men are aggressive), hair color (redheads are hot-tempered), dialects (people who drawl are laid-back), and other cues also influence stereotypic judgments we might make about other people.

First impressions are often initially based on outward appearance cues. People rely heavily on physical cues when first meeting another person. Physical appearance is often the most readily available information in initial encounters. Physically attractive individuals are usually seen as more "responsive, sensitive, kind, sexy, modest, poised, sociable, extroverted, intelligent, well-adjusted, and interesting than unattractive individuals" (Burgoon, et. al., 1994, p. 223). They continue that these initial impressions form a baseline for subsequent impressions and judgments.

Thus in predicting and evaluating people's behavior we often rely on stereotypes based on the sex, race, age, or other background of the other. We also rely on expectations—we expect people to behave in particular ways in given situations (remember Goffman) and these expectations form baselines with which to compare the actual behaviors.

These feed into the impression formation process in ways that lead to both **self-fulfilling prophecies** and **self-perpetuating biases.** For example, in the interview situation, the pre-formed biases of the interviewer will greatly influence her behavior. An interviewer will make it easier for the person expected to perform well to actually do so. And, unfortunately, vice-versa. Thus, our expectations of other people influence our treatment of them—which in turn influences their behavior. In short, we contribute to making the other person fulfill our prophecies about his expected behavior. In the end, our biases are then confirmed and perpetuated into succeeding interactions—both with that particular person, or with other members of their group.

Cultural Impression Management and Formation

While impression management research and theory are helpful in understanding the behavior of people in general, there are differences in behavior and interpretation across sex, culture, and ethnic lines. The way in which men, women, and people from different cultural backgrounds enact impression management behaviors differs. Lack of eye contact by a Puerto Rican listener may only indicate deference and respect to the person who is speaking, while lack of eye contact by a Anglo-American listener is more likely to indicate lack of respect or uneasiness. Our interpretation of behaviors also differs according to sex, culture and ethnicity. Ingratiation behaviors, for example, are generally more accepted from a woman, while enhancement behaviors are rated more highly when coming from a man. Thus, familiarity with expected differences as well as our own preformed biases should help us be better judges and interpreters of behavior.

Cultural Issues

The cultural environment surrounding us has a significant influence on our values, choices, and interactions and plays an important role in shaping our work and social institutions. Even if we hold similar values, the degree of importance placed on these values may differ from one society to another. In Goffman's terms, the expectations for any actor or stage may be different. The same script may get you very dissimilar reactions. For example, there are differences in how people offer compliments and respond to compliments (Spencer-Oatey, Ng & Dong, 2000), as well as in how to properly express disagreement (Bond, Zegarac, & Oatey, 2000), among others. Apart from differences in expectations regarding appropriate language use, studies also find significant cultural variation in the use and interpretation of the nonverbal behaviors which play a part in impression management (Burgoon, Buller, & Woodall, 1994).

For example, U.S. based research found that group members offering justifications or disclaimers about the quality of their work are more likely to be evaluated negatively. (Mulvey, 1998). In Asian countries, however, this type of discounting language is more common. In fact, if you call attention to your work and praise yourself, you may be considered self-centered and rude. Thus, members of these disparate cultures may misinterpret each others' behavior negatively because it does not conform to appropriate social rules. Even in presumably similar cultures such as those of post-reunion West and East Germany, organizational members encounter problems in enacting appropriate behaviors and correctly interpreting behaviors from those in the other group (Birkner & Kern, 2000).

Thus, in cross-cultural situations, you should be sensitive to differences in behavioral norms. When interacting with members of different cultural groups, take the time to become familiar with common differences in communication styles and attempt to both adapt your own behavior as well as withhold interpretations of other's behavior until more information is gathered.

Sex and Ethnic Issues

Impression formation also is influenced by the sex of the actor. Men are generally viewed as more task-oriented, aggressive, and ambitious, while women are seen as relational, nurturing, and emotionally expressive. These sex-role stereotypes create perceptual sets through which we filter information. We attend to events that confirm our expectations and interpret actions in ways that typically confirm our biases.

In general assertive behavior is evaluated positively in the workplace. Since this conforms to expectation of male behavior, when a man is assertive it is viewed as part of his personality, whereas when a woman is assertive, it is seen as "out of character" and an isolated unique event. There is often a threshold of acceptable assertive behavior that, if exceeded, may result in negative evaluations. Because men are expected to be assertive, they have more leeway than women in this area. Thus, the same behavior may be evaluated differently.

Men's use of nonverbal behaviors that show connectedness and liking generally increases favorable nonverbal impressions in other areas. When the same behaviors are used by women, however, they may increase perceptions of similarity and liking, but damage impressions of status and power. There is also a strong association of touch with increased perceptions of power and liking. When women interact with men, however, the commonality of sexual interpretations associated with touch moderate these power and liking perceptions (Burgoon, Buller, and Woodall, 1994). The research suggests that men and women interpret impressions differently. For example, Baron (1986), showed that women and men make different attributions based on the same impression management strategies. While male interviewers reacted negatively to a combination of nonverbal cues and perfume, female interviewers did not did not exhibit this negative reaction.

Women may face a double-bind in their attempts to successfully manage impressions in the organization. They are often strongly encouraged to set aside their feminine behaviors in favor of more masculine ones (Riordan, Gross, & Maloney, 1994) that presumably contribute to greater organizational success. Enactment of these masculine behaviors, however, may not lead to the same success that men might achieve. If they do not enact such behaviors, they may not be able to create impressions of power and status needed for success. Enactment of masculine behaviors by a female, however, may violate the audience's customary preferences, and these violations of expected behavior often result in negative evaluations (Goffman, 1959). In addition, due to their lack of familiarity with proper performance of 'masculine' roles, women may not be able to successfully enact the part, thereby violating one of Goffman's principles of good performances.

Just as women encounter difficulties managing their impressions within the organization, members of ethnic minorities face similar problems. Kanter (1977) wrote that "tokens" are more likely to be stereotyped by others in addition to having the differences between them and the dominant group exaggerated. Because women and minorities in token positions are more likely to be stereotyped; their most visible group categorization, that of their sex or ethnicity, thus plays a major role in interpretations of their behaviors. As a result of these stereotypes and difference exaggerations, identical behaviors may have widely varying interpretations.

Conclusion

Impression management is a powerful tool we all use to project the image we desire within the context of a given situation and audience. Knowledge of how actions and speech influence the development of impressions, and cultivation of our ability to consciously control our actions and speech to achieve a desired impression will greatly aid us in the organization and in other contexts of life. Through impression management, we can highlight our strengths while hiding or avoiding our weaknesses (Giacalone & Beard, 1994).

Gardner (1992) makes some invaluable suggestions to assist **constructive impression management:**

1. **Be aware of your impression management behavior and the image you project.** Often impression management strategies are unconscious reactions to certain situations and interactions. Awareness of how we present ourselves, however, will help us avoid creating unwanted impressions.
2. **Size up your audience and the situation.** Know your audience and be aware of how its characteristics and the situational context influence your behavior. Also, effective impression management techniques are tailored to the particular audience and context.
3. **Carefully choose a desired image and present yourself accordingly.** People are often conditioned to project images counter-productive to success. Know what kind of image you wish to portray, learn how verbal and nonverbal cues contribute to the development of this image, and present yourself accordingly.

4. **Recognize the dangers of the strategy you have chosen.** All impression management techniques have their drawbacks. Knowledge of these dangers will help you minimize the probability they will occur.

5. **Perform.** Impression management cannot substitute for actual performance. In fact, one of the best ways to manage a positive impression to be a high performer.

6. **Be yourself.** Deceptive impression management strategies often backfire and only work in the short term. Make every effort to put your best foot forward, but make sure that this is a real representation of yourself and your abilities. High personal integrity is another excellent way to create a good impression in the minds of your audience.

In addition, here are some guidelines offered for those in the process of *forming impressions of others:*

1. **Be aware of your personal characteristics and the situational features that make certain types of impression management strategies more likely.** Since the salient characteristics of the audience and the context exert influence on the impression management strategies used by an actor, be aware of how your position, gender, age, and other characteristics, as well as the interaction context might bias the actor's presentation. For example, recruiters should be careful to separate pure self-promotion from legitimate applicant qualification.

2. **Minimize personal, situational, and organizational features that foster undesirable performances.** Ambiguous situations tend to foster ingratiative and manipulative impression management strategies, while clear goals and appraisal criteria foster more honest presentations. Careful attention to these type of features which lead to undesired techniques can minimize their use and aid more open communication.

3. **Look for ulterior motives and avoid being overly influenced by dramaturgical behavior.** Impression management strategies are inevitable. They also may be either honest representations of a person or manipulative and deceptive. A competent organizational member should be able to distinguish between the these types of impression management in order to make good decisions.

I would also add a forth important guideline to these three:

4. **Be aware of your predisposition to form stereotypical impressions of others based solely upon race, age, dress, or any singular characteristic and behavior.** Our own cultural background, prior experiences, and personal characteristics will bias the impressions we form of others. Awareness of how we are influenced by these biasing factors will help us guard against unwarranted bias and make fairer decisions.

References

Baron, R. A. (1986). Self-presentation in job interviews: When there can be "too much of a good thing." *Journal of Applied Social Psychology, 16,* 16–28.

Baumeister, R. F. (1989). Motives and costs of self-presentation in organizations. In R. A. Giacalone & P. Rosenfeld (Eds.), *Impression management in the organization*, (pp. 57–71). Hillsdale, NJ: Erlbaum.

Becker, T. E. & Martin, S. L. (1995). Trying to look bad at work: methods and motives for managing poor impressions in organizations. *Academy of Management Journal, 38,* 174–199.

Berger, C., & Calabrese, R. (1975). Some explorations in initial interactions and beyond: Toward a developmental theory of interpersonal communication. *Human Communication Research, 1,* 99–112.

Birkner, Karin & Kern, Friederike. (2000). Impression management in East and West German job interviews. In Helen Spencer-Oatey (Ed). *Culturally Speaking: Managing Rapport Through Talk Across Cultures*, pp. 255–271. Continuum: New York.

Bond, Michael Harris, Zegarac, Vladimir, & Spencer-Oatey, Helen. (2000). Cultural as an explanatory variable: Problems and possibilities. In Helen Spencer-Oatey (Ed). *Culturally Speaking: Managing Rapport Through Talk Across Cultures*, pp. 47–71. Continuum: New York.

Buller, D., & Aune, R. K. (1988). The effects of vocalics and nonverbal sensitivity on compliance: A speech accommodation theory explanation. *Human Communication Research, 14,* 301–322.

Burgoon, J. K. (1979). A communicative model of personal space violations: Explication and initial test. *Human Communication Research, 4,* 129–142.

Burgoon, J. K., Buller, D. B., & Woodall, W. G. (1994). *Nonverbal communication: The unspoken dialogue.* Columbus, OH: Greyden Press.

Dougherty, T. W., Turban, D. B., & Callender, J. C. (1994). Confirming first impressions in the employment interview: A field study of interviewer behavior. *Journal of Applied Psychology, 79,* 659–665.

Drummond, H. (1993). The power of impression management. *Management Decision, 31,* 16–20.

Gardner, W. L. III. (1992). Lessons in organizational dramaturgy: The art of impression management. *Organizational Dynamics, 21,* 33–35.

Gardner, W. L. & Martinko, M. J. (1988). Impression management in organization. *Journal of Management, 14,* 321–338.

Giacalone, R. A., & Beard, J. (1994). Impression management, diversity, and international management *American Behavioral Scientist, 37,* 625.

Giacalone, R. A., & Riordan, C. A. (1990). Effect of self-presentation on perceptions and recognition in an organization. *The Journal of Psychology, 124,* 25–38.

Godfrey, D. K, Jones, E. E., & Lord, C. E. (1986). Self-promotion is not ingratiating. *Journal of Personality and Social Psychology, 50,* 106–115.

Goffman, E. (1959). *The presentation of self in everyday life.* Garden City, NY: Anchor/Doubleday.

Gorden, W. I., Tengler, C. D., & Infante, D. A. (1982). Women's clothing predispositions as predictors of dress at work, job satisfaction, and career advancement. *Southern Speech Communication Journal, 47,* 422–434.

Grayson, Kent & Shulman, David. (2000). Impression management in services marketing. In Teresa A. Swartz & Dawn Iacobucci (Eds). *Handbook of Services Marketing and Management,* pp. 51–67. Thousand Oaks:Sage Publication, Inc.

Gundersen, David E., & Tinsley, Dillard B. (1996). Empirical assessment of impression management biases: The potential for performance appraisal error. *Journal of Social Behavior and Personality, 11,* 57–76.

Kacmar, K. M., & Carlson, D. S. (1994). Using impression management in women's job search processes. *American Behavioral Scientist, 37,* 682–696.

Kacmar, M. K., Delery, J. E., & Ferris, G. \R. (1992). Differential effectiveness of applicant impression management tactics on Employment interview decisions. *Journal of Applied Social Psychology, 22,* 1250–1272.

Kanter, R. M. (1977). *Men and women of the corporation.* New York: Basic Books.

Kipnis, D., & Schmidt, S. M. (1988). Upward-influence styles: Relationship with performance evaluations, salary and stress. *Administrative Science Quarterly, 33,* 528–542.

Kozlowski, Steve W. J., Chao, Georgia T., & Morrison, Robert F. (1998). Games raters play: Politics, strategies, and impression management in performance appraisal. In James W. Smither (Ed). *Performance Appraisal: State of the Art in Practice,* pp. 163–208. San Francisco: Jossey-Bass Publishers.

Leary, M., & Kowalski, R. (1990). Impression management: a literature review and two-component model. *Psychological Bulletin, 107,* 34–44.

Macan, T. H., & Dipboye, R. L. (1988). The effects of interviewers' initial impressions on information gathering. *Organizational Behavior and Human Decision Processes, 42,* 364–387.

Morrison, E. W., & Bies, R. J. (1991). Impression management in the feedback-seeking process: A literature review and research agenda. *Academy of Management Review, 16,* 522–541.

Mulvey, Paul W. (1998). The effects of perceived loafing and defensive impression management on group effectiveness. *Small Group Research, 29,* 394–416

Palmer, R. J., Welker, R. B., & Giacolone, R. (1993). The context of anticipated performance evaluation, self-presentational motivation, and performance effort. *The Journal of Psychology, 127,* 179–193.

Pfeffer, J. (1981). Management as symbolic action: The creation roader conception. In J. T. Tedeschi (Ed.), *Impression management theory and social psychological research* (pp. 23–40).New York: Academic Press.

Snyder, M., & Swann, W. B., Jr. (1978). Behavioral confirmation in social interaction: From social perception to social reality. *Journal of Personality and Social Psychology, 35,* 656–666

Spencer-Oatey, Helen, Ng, Patrick, & Dong, Li. (2000). Responding to compliments: British and Chinese evaluative judgements. In Helen Spencer-Oatey (Ed). *Culturally Speaking: Managing Rapport Through Talk Across Cultures*, pp. 98–120. Continuum: New York.

Tedeschi, J. T., Ed. (1981). *Impression management theory and social psychological research.* New York: Academic Press.

Tedeschi, J. & Melburg, V. (1984). Impression management and influence in the organization. In S. Bacharach & E. J. Lawler (Eds.), *Research in the Sociology of Organizations.* (Vol. 3, pp. 31–58). Greenwich, CT: JAI Press.

Villanova, P., & Bernadin, H. J. (1989). Impression management in the context of performance appraisal. In R. A. Giacalone & P. Rosenfeld (Eds.), *Impression management in the organization*, (pp. 299–313). Hillsdale, NJ: Erlbaum.

Wayne, S. J., & Liden, R. C. (1995). Effects of impression management on performance ratings: A longitudinal study. *Academy of Management Journal, 38,* 232–260.

Wilshire, Bruce. (1982). The dramaturgical metaphor of behavior: Its strengths and weaknesses. *Symbolic Interaction, 5,* 287–297.

Sooner or later, almost every member of an organization will be required to deliver an oral presentation. Effective oral presentations are important to individual in terms of their careers and to organizations in terms of their survival and their success.

In Chapter 5, Michael Dues draws on his many years of experience teaching public speaking, and more than twenty years' experience giving oral presentations as an organizational consultant to provide a helpful, basic step-by-step guide to creating and delivering oral presentations.

Effective Presentations

Michael Dues
with Gates Matthew Stoner
University of Arizona

Key Terms

oral presentations
audience
objective
interaction
signpost
redundancy
introduction
body
conclusion

ethos
pathos
logos
target audience
main points
supporting points
chronological order
spatial order
causal order

problem-solution order
topical order
visual aids
stage fright
extemporaneous delivery
four dimensions of meaning
presentation software

Objectives

In this chapter, we offer a basic, practical guide to preparing and delivering oral presentations at work. Specifically, our objectives are to:

1. explain six key principles that govern oral presentations,
2. provide a step by step guide to preparing and delivering presentations,
3. offer helpful suggestions regarding potentially troublesome aspects of oral presentations, and
4. provide helpful guidelines for using presentation software to enhance presentation effectiveness.

This guide should help you achieve a minimum level of presentation competence. We strongly suggest that you continue developing your skills in this area, and, at the end of the chapter, we list several sources of more detailed advice.

A sales manager reports to the Board of Directors on sales trends and projections for the coming year. An architect describes to a group of investors the design of for a new building to be built with their invested funds. A supervisor instructs her crew of delivery drivers how to fill out the new forms for reporting lost merchandise. A police lieutenant briefs his squad on tactics for an important surveillance operation. A manager presents the case reorganization of the administrative services unit. These are common examples of oral presentations in organizations. Presentations are a regular aspect of organizational life. They are used when: (1) there is reason to inform a group about a subject, and one individual possesses the necessary information, and (2) one organization member seeks to secure the support of other members for a policy, action, or position.

Almost every member of an organization who functions at a professional, supervisory, or managerial level is required on some occasions to deliver oral presentations. Ability to develop and deliver competent presentations is essential to adequate performance in many job roles. Ability to develop and deliver exceptionally effective **presentations** is a significant asset for career advancement.

Fundamental Principles for Presentations

Six key principles are useful to keep in mind when preparing and/or delivering an oral presentation. These are:

1. It's about the audience; it is not about the presenter.
2. It's an interaction; it is not a solo performance.
3. Audience attention and effort are voluntary and temporary.
4. Every presentation needs an introduction, body, and conclusion.
5. People are complex: they respond to the speaker's personal appeals (Ethos), emotional appeals (Pathos), and logical appeals (Logos).
6. Every communication is complex: each includes four messages which must work together for a presentation to be effective.

Following, we explain each principle.

1. It's about the Audience; It Is Not about the Presenter

The purpose of any presentation is to bring about a change in the audience. As a presenter, your purpose is to have members of the audience know something they didn't know before, have an opinion they didn't have before, or do something they wouldn't have done before your presentation.

This focus on change means the presentation is about the **audience;** it is not about you, the speaker. You will be much more effective if you clearly establish in your own mind not only the topic of your presentation, but also your exact objective. Your **objective** is what (exactly) you want to be different in the audience as a result of your presentation. Your objective is what you want them to know, or believe, or do when you have finished speaking that they would not have known, believed, or done if you had not spoken to them. You may have a single objective, or several.

To set an objective and design your presentation effectively, you will have to know something about the audience. What information is important that may influence their reception of your message? Who are they? What do they know already? What do they believe now? What do they do now? Age mix? Gender mix? Ethic, religious, cultural mix? Levels of education? Professions? Jobs? Job roles in an organization? Related specialized training? Relationship to one another? Relationship to you? Previous history relative to your topic? You need answers to many of these questions to intelligently set your purpose and design your presentation.

In most instances your audience will be a relatively small number of persons (5 to about 30) who are your professional colleagues. Therefore, you will already know much of what you need to know about them, and you can readily get answers to your additional questions. When an audience is unknown to you, *ask about them; your interest will be appreciated.*

2. It's An Interaction; It Is Not a Solo Performance.

In Chapter 4 we explained how presenting one's self is always in some way a "performance." The performance principles discussed in Chapter 4 apply during any oral presentation. It is equally important, however, to remember that your performance in an oral presentation is not a *solo* act. In Chapter 1 we explained that communication is an ongoing interactive process. Like any other face to face encounter, a presentation is an **interaction.**

For you to succeed, the audience must play an active role and work with you. They must listen to, evaluate, store, and provide feedback about whatever you say. And you must read their feedback and adjust what you are saying as you speak. So you must make eye contact, watch their faces and bodily movements, and listen to the sounds coming from the audience. You may even have to ask them questions and get verbal responses to guide yourself as you go along.

You cannot interact adequately with your audience if you try to read your presentation to them, or to recite it from memory, or if you have such detailed notes that you must refer to the notes more than to the audience. You will need to know well what you plan to say, and how you plan to say it, but you will also need to be flexible. A really good presentation never goes exactly as planned. That is because you cannot fully plan the audience responses.

3. Audience Attention and Effort Are Voluntary and Temporary.

It takes effort to sit and pay attention to a speaker. The longer and more complicated the message, the more effort it takes to listen well, and to really try to understand, and to evaluate what is being said. Human attention spans are extremely short; audience members actually stop paying attention several times each minute, and then come back to attending and try to catch up. If what you are saying is dull or too difficult, they stop trying.

Consider all that is involved in good listening, which we discussed in Chapter 3. Good presenters honor the fact that their audiences are voluntarily working with them to make the presentation successful. Good presenters show appreciation for an audience's effort, and work to make their presentations as easy and as interesting for the audience as possible. The principle is to give the audience maximum message and interest for minimum audience effort.

To achieving maximum impact for minimum audience effort:

- Make everything as clear, and easy to understand as possible.
- Think and present in outline form. Outlining helps keep clear the relationships between your main points and sub-points.
- Use between 2 and 4 main points in the outline (do not exceed 5).
- Follow the "Tell em" Rule. That is: "tell them what you are going to tell em, tell em, then tell em what you told em."
- Always "**signpost.**" That is, use transitions that clearly let the audience know what is coming next, where you are in the overall presentation, and what they are supposed to be doing with what you are saying.
- Keep it simple.

- Use **redundancy.** That is, use multiple media—especially visual aids—to reinforce your message. "Show and tell" is more interesting, and is easier to comprehend and remember than just "tell." Research has shown that people are more likely to pay attention, more likely to comprehend, more likely to remember, and more likely to be persuaded by messages when they receive the information through two or more of their senses at the same time. It is especially important to use visual aids when the information is difficult to understand (Lucas, 1995). Today, presentation software is widely available, providing easy ways to generate multi-media presentations. Detailed advice for using presentation software is provided later in this chapter.
- Do not run long. Audiences seldom mind if you end early, but they get bored and angry when presentations take longer than the time allotted.

4. Every Presentation Needs an Introduction, a Body, and a Conclusion.

There are three separate parts to each presentation, and each part has it's own purposes. The **introduction** prepares the audience to listen effectively.

The introduction should:
1. Get the audience's attention and focus that attention on your topic and on you,
2. Set an appropriate tone for the presentation,
3. Preview the main ideas and organizational structure of the presentation, and
4. Guide the audience as to what will be expected of them during the presentation.
5. Establish your credibility with your audience.

The **body** provides the actual content needed to accomplish your presentation objectives.

The body of the presentation should:
1. present the ideas and/or information you wish the audience to receive,
2. provide any explanation and/or support necessary for the ideas to be understood and/or convincing,
3. offer any illustrations or demonstrations that may be helpful.

Finally, the **conclusion** summarizes the content and purpose of the presentation in a memorable way.

The conclusion should:
1. Summarize the body of the presentation,
2. Tell the audience what you wish them to do with the ideas presented in the body,
3. Clearly tie the main points in your presentation to your over all thesis,
4. When appropriate, stimulate or inspire action, and
5. Clearly punctuate the ending of the presentation.

---

5. People are Complex; They Respond to the Speaker's Personal Appeal (Ethos), Emotional Appeal (Pathos), and Logical Appeal (Logos).

In ancient Athens, Aristotle taught effective speakers one appeal to the audience in three ways. The Greek terms for these three kinds of appeal are *ethos*, *pathos* and *logos*. Twentieth century communication research has repeatedly demonstrated that Aristotle was correct on this point.

"**Ethos,**" or *personal appeal*, refers to how a speaker is perceived and regarded by an audience. Speakers can be effective only if their audiences perceive them to be trustworthy in general, knowledgeable about the topic of their presentation, and free of excessive bias on the topic. It also helps for the speaker to be someone an audience feels it can "relate to," as "one of us."

Good speakers give their audiences information that establishes their expertise, their general good character, and their ability to look objectively at the topic. They also consciously build a relationship with each audience. This can be done by sharing information with the audience about yourself, using personal examples, letting the audience know that you share some experiences or perspectives with them, or by letting the audience know you empathize with in some way.

"**Pathos,**" or *appeal to emotions*, refers to the fact that an audience is more likely to listen and understand or be persuaded if a message is presented in a way that induces caring about what is being said. Good speakers are careful to include stories, examples, and information that touch the feelings of audience members. Emotional appeal does not have to be heavy, and should not be over done; but it must always be present.

"**Logos,**" or *appeal to logic*, refers to the fact that an audience will listen to, and accept what you say only to the extent that it appears to them to make clear, rational sense. Audience members will evaluate what is being said, usually by applying what we commonly call "common sense" as a test. Good speakers present what they have to say in a clear, rational sequence, and provide appropriate support where it is needed.

6. Every Communication is Complex; Each Includes Four Messages, which Must Work Together for Your Presentation to Suceed.

In Chapter 1 we explained that four dimensions of meaning are present in every message: **Sense, Feeling, Tone,** and **Intention**. **Sense** is the verbal message given to receivers that carries the surface meaning. **Feeling** is the message given to receivers expressing how the speaker feels about what is being conveyed in the sense message. **Tone** is a statement about the relationship between the speaker and the audience. **Intention** is the message given to receivers about the speaker's purpose in communicating.

The value for presenters in recognizing the presence of all four messages is that one can work to ensure that all four messages are consistent with one another and with audience perceptions and values. Giving presentations with compatible messages greatly increases the likelihood of successful presentations. If the dimensions of a presentation's message are not consistent with one another, or if some dimensions are objectionable to the audience, the presentation will at best be confusing, and at worst be rejected altogether.

Basic Steps in Preparing a Presentation

With these basic principles in mind, we suggest that you employ the following step-by-step approach to prepare your presentation.

1. Select Your Topic.

Choose the topic, or subject matter, you will discuss in the presentation. Often the subject matter is assigned to you. Generally, the topic should be sufficiently familiar and interesting to you that it stimulates enthusiasm and good ideas about what to present.

2. Analyze the Audience.

Find out where your audience stands concerning your topic and you. What do they know about it already? What interests do they have that might relate to the topic? Consider such factors as gender, age, ethnicity, profession, economic status, status in the organization, educational background. Ask about the audience if necessary to gather this information. Your purpose in learning about and analyzing the audience is to help identify your objectives in discussing your topic with the audience, and to help your choose strategies for speaking, and relevant examples.

Often, there is a broad range of opinion, experience, and knowledge represented in the group that will be your audience. When this occurs, it helps to identify those members of your audience with whom you believe you can succeed in the presentation, and for whom you message is important. This is your "**target audience**," and you can focus primary attention on this group. It is also helpful to decide how you will handle the non target members of your audience; find a way to include them while recognizing that they are not your primary targets.

Step 3. Narrow Your Topic and Establish Your Specific Objective(s).

Keeping in mind what you know about your audience decide exactly what you want to accomplish with your audience in the presentation. If your basic purpose is to inform, answer the question *What do you want them to know when your have finished that they do not already know?* If your purpose is to persuade, answer the question *What do you want them to believe that they do not already believe?* Or, *Precisely, what do you want them to do in response to your presentation?*

Be realistic in setting objectives. Do not try to accomplish more than is possible in one presentation. You can inform people about a few main ideas. You can present a simple, clear argument that can be persuasive. If you focus your objectives on what realistically can be accomplished, you will be more likely to succeed. If you attempt to accomplish more than is realistically possible, you may fail to accomplish anything, and damage your personal credibility with your audience.

Aim your objectives at your target audience. You may also wish to set secondary objectives for non-target members of your audience. Examples of secondary objectives are:

For audience members who already agree with what you are advocating:

"To reinforce their support of your view, and to provide them with additional information about it."

For audience members who are so committed to an opposing view that they cannot be persuaded to your point of view:

"To get them to recognize that intelligent, ethical people can disagree on this issue."

4. Investigate, Gather Information and Materials, Create Ideas, Develop Your Approach.

Gather all the information you can that may be helpful in building your presentation. Be careful and critical in your information gathering. Assess the credibility of your information sources, and select only material for which you can verify accuracy. Then creatively generate ideas. It helps to start with more information than you can use, and to generate more ideas than you can use. Then decide what ideas are most valuable, and what information is most useful regarding those ideas.

5. Develop the Body of Your Presentation. Do This By Outlining the Main Points and Supporting Points of Your Presentation.

Individuals differ greatly in their creative styles and processes. No one can tell you exactly how to create the content of your presentation. We do suggest, however, that you create the outline first. We also suggest that you limit yourself to between 2 and 4 main points, and that you generate a mixture of kinds of material, including some concrete description, examples, narratives, as well as some hard data.

It is important to build the body of your presentation using a clear, easy to follow, organizational pattern. Arrange your **main points** in a recognizable pattern if possible. Obvious patterns include:

Chronological order, with points arranged according the time,
Spatial order, with points arranged according to place,
Causal order, with points arranged in sequence of cause and effect,
Problem-solution order, with points arranged in sequence of problem, then solution.
Topical order, with topics arranged according to a list of sub topics into which you have divided your main subject.

Make sure the **supporting points** for each of your main points actually support the main point. Audiences will find it difficult to follow your presentation if it does not follow a clear, obvious organizational pattern.

If your speaking objective is to persuade your audience, consult Chapter 7 for guidance in developing the arguments that will constitute the body of your presentation.

6. Construct Visual or Other Presentation Aids.

We communicate more effectively with people when we deliver our message through two or more of their senses at the same time. Roughly translated, this means think in terms of "show and tell." **Visual aids** include charts, graphs, pictures, artifacts, live examples, demonstrations, slides, overheads, hand outs, films, videos, scents, sounds, power point projections, audience activities, and more. A few simple and clear visual aids are generally more effective than too many, or very complex visual aids, so plan carefully. Make sure you can use visual aids in a way that allows all members of the audience to see them clearly (including reading all the numbers and print). Plan how you will physically display the visual aids so that they will be shown at a time that matches the content. Plan carefully how you will physically handle and manipulate your visual aids, so that this can be done smoothly, and with a minimum of distraction.

Below are 10 general tips for gaining the benefits of visual aids while avoiding the pitfalls. As you make decisions about design and consider how you will use visual aids, keep these tips in mind.

1. Aids should be attractive, interesting, but also clear and simple. Avoid too much complexity.
2. A few good visual aids go a long way. Don't try to use so many that you clutter up the presentation.
3. Visual aids should be shown to the audience at the same time you are speaking about their content; not before and not after. Bad timing in the display of visual aids can be distracting, especially if they are interesting.
4. Hand outs are often the best form of visual aids, but never pass them out while you are speaking. Do it before or after you speak. The process of distributing hand outs always constitutes a distraction from what you are saying to your audience.
5. Think carefully through the logistics of all you will need and how you will use each aid. Will you need a plug? Lights turned on or off? Can all in the audience see? How much attention will you have to give to the aid? Where will you be relative to the visual, and relative to the audience? How will the aid be placed before the audience? How will you remove the aid from audience view when you are ready for them to attend to something else? How will you transport the aid to and from the presentation? How will you accomplish transitions to remove one visual from audience view and display another?

6. Make sure all print and numbers are big enough and clear enough for all to see.
7. Color contrast between text or images and background should be high. Use dark colored images on light backgrounds, or very light colored images on dark background. Low color contrast makes visual aids difficult for audiences to see and read.
8. Audiences will cooperate. Ask them to move to better positions, or to participate when appropriate.
9. Do not be timid about aids. Boldness is more interesting.
10. All aids should be in good taste, of course. Offending an audience will usually prevent your accomplishing your objective.

Using Presentation Software Presentation software, such as Microsoft Powerpoint, is a potent tool for creating and displaying visual images that can greatly enhance your presentation. Misuse or overuse of presentation software, however, can seriously damage the effectiveness of your effort. Given the great potential of software to help or hurt your presentation, we offer more detailed suggestions for its use in the box at the end of this section.

7. Develop the Conclusion to Your Presentation.

Keeping in mind the five functions of conclusions we listed above, develop the conclusion of your presentation. Invest some genuine creative effort in your conclusion. The final impression you make tends to stick with your audience.

8. Develop the Introduction to Your Presentation.

Keeping in mind the five functions of introductions we listed above, develop your introduction. Even more than conclusions, good introductions require creative effort. Your introduction will not only get the attention of the audience, announce your subject, and preview your main ideas; it will also establish your relationship with the audience for the presentation.

9. Create the Set of Notes You Will Use During the Presentation.

The ideal set of notes for most speakers is in outline form, large print, and on large enough paper so that turning pages in unnecessary. Ideally, everything in your notes can be readily seen at a glance. Key words and phrases should serve as cues for complete ideas which you present without additional reference to your notes. The time and energy you spend creating a really good set of speaking notes is almost always a good investment.

10.　Practice Presenting Your Presentation. (But Avoid Memorizing It.)

Business presentations are delivered exptemporaneously; that is, they are carefully pre-pared and rehearsed, but they are flexible, and include spontaneous adaptations in re-sponse to audience feedback during the presentation. To accomplish this requires prac-tice. The best way to practice is to pretend—fantasize—doing the presentation several times. Always follow your outline, but do it a little differently each time. You will want to be familiar enough with what you are going to say that you won't have to depend too heavily on your notes. On the other hand, avoid memorizing your material; memorizing will interfere with your ability to observe and adapt to audience feedback during your presentation.

Guidelines for Using Presentation Software

Ask yourself and carefully answer these four questions whenever you consider using presentation software. Going through this process will help you apply communication principles to generate and display effective visuals aids.

a. *Should I use presentation software in this presentation?*　The first consideration con-cerning use of presentation software is whether to use it at all in any given presenta-tion. In making this decision, think about your purpose in using visual aids? Consider whether software created slides will genuinely enhance your impact. Software slides can effectively retain the interest of your audience for a longer and complex presen-tation, but they might be overkill for a short presentation. The effort might not be worth the trouble and you may create distractions that impair the effectiveness of your message.

b. *How much should I rely on the slides to convey my message? How much is too much?*　A second key consideration is how much to rely on software in your presentation. To what extent should you employ the color, sound, and animation capabilities provided in Powerpoint and other similar programs? A recent article in the *Wall Street Journal* reported that Gen. Hugh Shelton at the Pentagon issued an order to "skip the bells and whistles in Powerpoint" and just "get to the point." Overuse of presentation software's "bells and whistles" damages presentations. An audience absorbed in reading the material on slides is not listening to the speaker. If what you display on the screen competes with you for audience attention, it functions as a distraction that interferes with your effort to communicate. For this reason, experts, including the makers of Powerpoint, caution against overuse. In terms of visual aids, the best presentations are usually simple ones.

Overuse can take the form of too many bells and whistles, too many slides, or too much information per slide. In general, it is best to avoid using sound effects or animation altogether. If you use these at all use them very rarely, and then only for some very special effect.

The most common mistakes regarding the number of slides are creating a slide for every point, and delivering more than one slide per minute. To avoid these mistakes, pace the presentation to have no more than one slide per minute. Avoid the temptation to have a slide for every point.

A third common error is inclusion of too much information per slide, often repeating every word spoken by the presenter. Remember that slides should serve as signposts for your audience and highlight your main points. Do not rely on your slides to speak for you. A golden rule regarding the number of words on software slides is "the fewer the better."

c. ***What kinds of information should I present on the slides?*** Slides and visuals aids are especially useful for presenting numbers and relationships among numbers with charts. Budgets, cash flow projections, and survey data can be difficult to convey orally to an audience. Charts and images can provide pictorial representations of abstract concepts to show trends and relationships that might not be evident if delivered orally. In a marketing presentation, for example, a chart can serve to show expected sales of a new car, and a digitally projected drawing can show what the car will look like. Two important roles of charts and images in a presentation, are to convey what words cannot, and reinforce abstract concepts while aiding retention.

d. ***How can I best format my slides?*** Slides should be formatted so that they are simple, clear, and easily read from the back of the room. Use bold lettering, at least 20-point font the text, and high color contrast to ensure readability. Avoid complexity; slides should have no more than three or four sub-points. Limit each slide to 25 words or less. Avoid use of italics in computer-projected visuals; they are difficult for audiences to read. It is best to stick with standard fonts, such as Times and Arial.

Some Suggestions for Delivering Presentations:

There are five potential problem areas where presenters can encounter problems even when they have carefully prepared their presentations. These are: (1) handling stage fright, (2) using notes, (3) delivering the presentation, (4) facility and equipment arrangements, and (5) controlling the audience and the situation. Below are some suggestions to help with each of these areas.

1. Handling Stage Fright:

Fear of speaking before an audience is the most common fear in the United States. Most people experience some level of anxiety about making presentations; many people experience an extreme amount of anxiety about speaking before an audience. The truly bad news is that nobody has yet discovered a solution to the problem. The good news is that almost everyone can do a good presentation even with extreme anxiety, and most audiences don't know how badly a speaker's knees are shaking.

Actually "stage fright" is the wrong name for fear of speaking. "Communication apprehension" is a more accurate term. And it helps to remember that you are not "on stage;" rather, you are working together with your audience to help them understand something.

Here are some tips that help fear of speaking, though they do not solve the problem:

- Be well prepared. Know your topic, and your planned presentation well.
- When you practice, do it a little differently each time, and imagine different audience responses. This builds experience with the presentation, if only in your fantasy life.
- Take several full, deep breaths before beginning to speak. Then keep breathing as you speak.
- If you're afraid your nervousness is showing, or that you will get confused or stuck, tell the audience you are nervous. This breaks your tension. Most audiences are on your side, and can well empathize with the spot you are in. (NOTE: Be careful, and very limited in using this one, though. It can damage your credibility with an audience.)
- Most importantly, *go ahead and make eye contact with members of your audience!* Pick a few friendly looking faces; make contact with those people, looking

them in the eyes to see if they are getting your point. Notice their feedback. This will help to put you at ease more than anything else you can do. DO NOT AVOID EYE CONTACT WITH YOUR AUDIENCE. That will increase your fear.

2. Using Notes Effectively:

There is no single "right" way to use notes in a presentation. It's a matter of what works best for you. You need notes enough to keep yourself on track - - to prompt you about what you're supposed to say, when. On the other hand, if you have too much detail in your notes, you will be referring to them too much, and this will interfere with your ability to stay in contact with your audience.

Here are some useful tips on notes and their use:

- Most speakers find that notes work best if they are in outline form. Do not write out notes in paragraph form; if you do, you will be tempted to read them.
- Notes are easiest to use if they are printed in large, bold letters; if they are on one or two sheets of paper large enough so that you won't have to turn pages to find what you're looking for, and if they are placed near your line of vision with the audience.
- Audiences expect you to use notes; they even appreciate your using notes to stay on track. It is absolutely silly to try to hide notes from an audience.
- Most importantly, DO NOT LET NOTES DRAW TOO MUCH OF YOUR ATTENTION AWAY FROM THE AUDIENCE.

3. Delivering Your Presentation:

How you deliver your message is extremely important. Here are some suggestions to help assure effective delivery.

1. Delivery style should be extemporaneous. "Extemporaneous" means that you know what you're going to say, but much of the wording is decided as you are speaking. Do not memorize or read it.
2. Stay in contact with your audience. Pay attention to them as you speak, and adapt your presentation based on their feedback as you proceed.

3. Speak clearly; make sure people in the back row can hear you.
4. Use language that is familiar to and appropriate to your audience. Speak at an educational and professional level suitable to your audience. Also use appropriate technical terms, but be sure to explain meanings when necessary.
5. If you are using visual aids in your presentation, avoid obstructing audience members' view of your visuals. Speak to the audience, not to the screen.
6. It helps to be animated. Do not lock you hands in your pockets, or behind your back, or onto the podium; let hands be free to move, and make whatever gestures are natural to you. Also, it helps to move around some (but not constantly) as you speak.

4. Facility and Equipment Arrangements:

Check on the facility and equipment, including the room, the seating, PA system, audio visual equipment, etc. Make sure that what you need is provided. It's a good idea to go to the room before speaking, and walk through the logistics of the presentation; then make any changes that appear useful. If possible, test all the equipment you will use before the audience enters the room.

Consider the configuration of the room. What is the working mood you wish to create? Does the arrangement of the room suit that mood? What is the relationship you wish to have with the audience? Does the arrangement of the room facilitate that relationship? Physical structuring of the communication context has a significant impact on communication. If, for example, you want to promote some interaction, and to address your audience as a professional equal, it would be a mistake to have the room arranged in theater style, and you standing behind a podium. The podium constitutes a barrier, and the seating arrangement would discourage interaction.

5. Taking Charge:

Finally, it is important to remember that when your are speaking to a group of people you must take charge. Many presenters feel constrained to simply accept and work with unfavorable speaking conditions. They find themselves confined behind podiums that keep them from using their visual aids well, or speaking from too far away from the audience, or speaking to too many people without a microphone, etc. Speak up for what you need to do the presentation well; take charge of the room and of your presentation.

Arrange the room and the people to best facilitate your presentation. Ask for the co-operation you need, and expect to receive it. The speaker's role is a leadership role; step up and lead.

Summary

In this chapter, we provided a practical guide to preparing and delivering oral presentations at work. First, we discussed six key principles which are important to understand, and which should guide you in preparing and delivering presentations. Second, we provided a ten step guide to preparing presentations. Finally, we offered suggestions for handling common problem areas that tend to arise in delivering presentations.

Remember that this is a beginner's guide. It is designed to help you achieve a basic level of presentation competence at work. For more detailed instruction in preparing and delivering oral presentations consult the references below.

For More Detailed Instruction:

Ronald Adler and Jeanne M. Elmhorst, *Communicating at Work*. New York: 1996.

Lani Arrendando, *How to Present Like a Pro: Getting People to see things Your Way. New York: McGraw-Hill, 1991.*

References

Hamilton, C., with C. Parker. (1997). *Communicating for results: A Guide for business and the professions* (5th ed.). Belmont, CA: Wadsworth Publishing Co.

Lucas, Stephen E. (2001). *The art of public speaking* (7th ed.). New York: McGraw-Hill

Brydon, S. R., & Scott, M. D. (2000). *Between one and many* (3rd ed.). Mountain-View, CA: Mayfield Publishing.

Organizations rely on written messages both to communicate and to provide records of activity. Ability to write well in an organizational context is an important and often essential skill in almost any organization role.

Mary Brown is a doctoral candidate in Communication at the University of Arizona. She is an accomplished business writer, editor and teacher of business communication. In Chapter 6, she draws on her 12 years of professional experience in public service as an analyst, information officer, research coordinator and manager, as well as on several years of teaching and studying business communication, to provide a clear guide to effective writing in organizations.

Connecting with Others in Writing

Mary Brown
University of Arizona

Key Terms

rhetorical goals
communication functions
personal benefits
paralanguage
static
audience-centered
purpose statement

primary source
secondary source
clarity
coherence
interest
economy
accuracy

format
style and tone
memorandum
report
issue memo
proposal
new media

Objectives

This chapter presents basic principles and recommendations for effective writing at work. It will help you understand and produce competent business writing from a communication perspective. Its objectives are to:

1. Describe the functions of business writing;
2. Distinguish how written communication differs from oral communication;
3. Explain the principles of good business writing;
4. Describe in detail the eight major steps in the writing process;
5. Outline the characteristics of style and tone in a quality written message; and
6. Provide models for four common documents used in organizations.

In the world of work today information is expanding and communication forms are evolving at unprecedented speed. Thousands of messages, in multiple forms, are generated and received every day. If we think of communication as the "life blood" of the organization, messages can be considered the blood cells in the circulatory system. Through messages, organizational members give direction, clarify roles, enact power, maintain social relationships and coordinate activities (Stohl, 1995). In short, messages enable us to accomplish the work of the organization. If messages are not clear, or if blockages prevent them from reaching their destination, vital parts of the body will fail to function. So all across organizational levels, members are challenged to make informed choices about what kinds and forms of messages will be appropriate and effective in different situations. These choices must be made in an environment characterized by ever-increasing information quantity, complexity and ambiguity.

In this message-saturated environment, successful writers need to be strategic and mindful of their audience's point of view, as well as their own goals. So in this chapter we will discuss writing in organizations from a perspective that rests on two foundations: rhetoric and relationship. First, writing in the workplace is rhetorical: it involves designing messages that are intended to achieve multiple **rhetorical goals.** In any writing assignment, the author aims, at a minimum, to inform, persuade or request (*content goal*); to project a positive self-image (*identity goal*); and to manage a relationship with the reader (*relational goal*). So several layers of meaning are embedded in organizational messages. Whether we realize it or not, we use rhetorical principles to create and to interpret messages. A rhetorical approach assumes that messages are instrumental, and that their effects depend on properties of the communicator, the message itself, the audience, and the context in which the message is received. Organizational messages are always situated in evolving personal, relational, social, technological, and cultural contexts. Understanding some basic rhetorical aspects of messages, and using a rhetorical approach to designing messages, can help writers make informed decisions that generate successful written products.

Second, when we write, we form a connection with our readers. Among other goals, we write to maintain organizational relationships. Our messages "make sense" in the context of our relationships (Stohl, 1995). Anderson, Benjamin and Paredes-Holt (1998) suggest that a good connection requires two working elements: a relationship between the parties, and a physical or technological medium through which they communicate. As you read this chapter, think of writing at work as a process of making meaningful connections with others who are in relationship with you. You make these connections through written words and symbols via a communication medium which may be either print or electronic.

Writing well is no small task. Despite our best efforts, written messages rarely achieve all their goals with all readers. Based on years of studying and teaching, Osmo Wiio developed four "laws" of communication in the workplace that have enduring value when it comes to thinking about writing at work (Goldhaber, 1979; Wiio, 1978). Although they are tongue-in-cheek, Wiio's laws convey truths about written messages that are worth stating as a prelude to this chapter:

1. **Communication usually fails, except by chance.** This law suggests that if we are careless, indifferent, lazy or unskilled communicators, we will usually fail in our communication.
2. **If a message can be understood in different ways, it will be understood in just that way which does the most harm.** This law warns that despite our most careful intentions, misunderstandings will most likely occur in ways that do maximum damage.
3. **There is always somebody who knows better than you what you meant by your message.** In other words, after a message is sent someone will always appear to advise us after-the-fact, or second-guess what we really intended to say (and how we should have said it!).
4. **The more communication there is, the more difficult it is for communication to succeed.** This law reminds us that because human beings have limited capacity to process information, the more messages ours is competing with, the less likely ours is to accomplish its goals.

With these cautions in mind, let's begin.

The Importance of Writing

Writing is one of the most common and important communication tasks we face at work, yet few professionals feel confident about their writing skills. Most people can communicate fairly well on short, routine assignments such as simple memos and letters, but when given the task of drafting a report or proposal, they struggle. Sometimes they even succeed in passing off a complex assignment to a better writer on staff, claiming that management will get a quicker, better product that way. But "passing the buck" is a shortsighted solution. Because of the pervasive need for accurate and efficient written communication, professionals and managers alike should know how to write effectively. Effective business writing sustains and does not obstruct the work process by making its point with brevity and clarity. As both producers and consumers of growing amounts of written messages, members of organizations benefit from effective writing.

Each of us starts with a different native ability to write, and clearly some are better writers than others. Fortunately, by applying and practicing some basic methods for effective writing, everyone in the organization can learn to write well. This chapter guides students through the writing process, and provides criteria for judging message quality from a communication perspective. The approach is practical and skill-based, with lesser emphasis on theoretical concerns. We will discuss how to approach and successfully execute a writing assignment, and how to identify the characteristics of a quality finished product.

Before we begin, though, it's important to understand the vital role writing plays in your career. Many business students in specialized areas don't see the need for writing skills. After all, why would an accountant, a sales representative, or a computer programmer need to write well? Can't others in the organization do the writing? Yes, and no. Others can write for you, but they may or may not convey your message accurately and in the way you intended. Time and effort must be devoted to instructing the writer, reviewing and editing the work. Even then the message will not be the same as if you wrote it. And if you have a good idea or recommendation, it is important that you write it. Only you can communicate the idea as you see it, and as its author you should receive credit for your idea. Furthermore, well executed writing assignments are persuasive evidence for promotional considerations.

On the other hand, some future-oriented business students think that with advancing technology, writing will become obsolete. Oral messages and voice recording will be the predominant mode of communicating in business, since speaking is quicker, conveys additional information through nonverbal channels, and requires less effort than does writing. Sophisticated computer software programs will translate voice messages into writing if necessary, generating perfectly phrased and formatted documents ready for signature. Think again. Will a computer-generated written version of your spoken words suffice as a proposal for a new project, or even for a quarterly activity report? Writing accomplishes different purposes than does speaking, and there will always be a need for good writing in the workplace.

Functions of Business Writing

Good writing matters . . . to everyone in the organization. It serves three critical **communication functions.** First, writing *informs.* Routinely at work, we need to clearly communicate in writing to coworkers, supervisors, managers, and subordinates. A team member needs a summary of last week's meeting; our boss wants a report on this month's project activities; we need to formally notify staff of changes in attendance policy. In delivering information, we are primarily interested in accuracy and efficiency.

Writing also *explains.* Internal documents often serve to explain procedures, policies, or positions to staff. For example, an explanatory memo is sent to staff who are confused about new performance standards; new employees are given written procedures for completing attendance forms and travel claims; and a statement is distributed to staff explaining an executive decision to relocate a certain division. In explaining actions, positions or procedures, accuracy, logic, clarity and efficiency are paramount.

Third, writing *influences thoughts, decisions and actions.* Because people are rational beings, members of organizations need good reasons, or rationale, to change their position or take action on an issue. Writing for business often involves providing those good reasons in a formal fashion. In other words, we document the facts, data and premises for organizational decisions or actions. Such documentation may be used immediately or stored and reproduced for future use. In this way we not only provide a written foundation for decision-making, but we avoid having to reinvent the rationale for action when the need for understanding or communicating why we did what we did occurs in the future. Persuasive writing emphasizes the combining of facts, evidence, and reasoning into compelling arguments.

Beyond these communication functions, writing also has two important **personal benefits** for the writer which also enhance the quality of the final written product. First, writing *clarifies our thoughts.* Good writing obligates us to think clearly. Putting ideas on paper requires us to explain and justify them for our readers. It thereby helps us judge the merit of our ideas, evaluate the ways we have expressed them, identify weaknesses, and rectify them. Done well, business writing is a powerful analytic exercise which involves dissecting ideas, assessing their quality, revising them if needed, and finally organizing and explaining them in a way that can be most easily understood by their audience. In this way, writers hone their critical thinking skills.

Finally, writing *permits self-expression*. When we write, we not only convey information, but we add our own unique perspective, knowledge and style to the message. Even composing routine, fact-based, messages involves using our own creative expression, within approved constraints. In other words, writing provides a disciplined way to apply your personal creative ideas to the task or issue at hand; it serves as a vehicle for self-expression. Self expression is challenging and satisfying.

Purposes of Written Documents

Written business messages, be they memos, letters, reports or proposals, have different purposes than oral messages. If a message is put in writing, its originator probably intended it to serve one or more of the following purposes of written documents:

1. To provide an accurate permanent account or written record of an issue;
2. To provide identical versions of a message for discussion or concurrent review by multiple staff;
3. To place information in a form which can be easily retrieved for future reference or reproduction; and
4. To efficiently, consistently and directly convey reasons for holding a position or pursuing a course of action.

Characteristics of Written Communication

Both speaking and writing are forms of communication with strategic goals of bringing about some change in the audience's knowledge, attitudes or behavior. However, written communication differs from oral communication in two important ways.

1. **Written messages have only one communication channel.** Words are the only means of written expression, while oral messages have multiple channels for conveying meaning. There are no nonverbal cues to supplement the meaning of the words. Unlike listeners, readers cannot infer additional meaning through visual cues or **paralanguage** (variations in vocal tone, rate, rhythm, loudness, and emotional quality). Information and meaning are confined to a singular, linear channel. In contrast, listening audiences receive and make sense of information in nonlinear fashion, at many levels simultaneously. Thus, oral presenters have more routes by which to send information than do writers.

2. **Written messages are static.** Documents are composed by the author at an earlier time, in a different place, than when and where they are read. This tempo-
   ral and spatial separation from the message receiver means that writers do not
   have the benefit of immediate feedback from their audience, as speakers do.
   Writers cannot make spontaneous adjustments or clarify meaning when the
   reader becomes confused, since the author and receiver of the message are not
   in each other's physical presence. Without opportunity to adjust the message as
   one delivers it orally, writers must complete all refinements and clarifications
   "up front." Once the written message is sent, it is static and unchangeable.

These characteristics place both constraints and freedoms on business writers. On
one hand, writers must rely solely on words to convey all the information in a message,
and must plan ahead so that their reading audience receives the right message in timely
fashion. On the other hand, writers are free to maximize the meaning and impact of a
written message through careful composition, formatting and timing of delivery.

Principles of Good Writing

The principles of good business writing are similar to those for oral presentations presented in Chapter 5. Since both written and oral business messages aim to efficiently and
effectively bring about some change in message recipients, these two message forms share
several common elements. Good business writing reflects these seven principles:

Good Writing:

Is audience-centered	Is economical
Adds value	Is interesting
Is easy to understand	Is accurate.

---

1. Good writing is *audience-centered.* The reader's needs and concerns are foremost. Remember you have a relationship with the reader to maintain. Write
   for your reader, not for yourself.

2. Good writing has something **valuable** to say. The message content is worthy of the reader's time and attention. The document adds valued information to the reader's base of knowledge.

3. Good writing is **easy to understand.** The meaning is clear and concrete. Words and thoughts flow coherently and logically. The document says all it is intended to say simply, without ambiguity.

4. Good writing is **economical.** The message properly fits the purpose and the situation. The document conveys all it needs to say in as few words as possible. Unnecessary verbiage which contributes nothing to the meaning of the message is eliminated.

5. Good writing is **interesting.** It is the writer's responsibility to engage and maintain the reader's interest in the message content. Boring writing is an almost-sure recipe for message failure.

6. Good writing is **accurate.** It accurately represents ideas and factual data, and gives appropriate attribution to original sources of ideas. Bias is minimized. The document itself is a reliable and credible source of information.

The principles outlined above serve as guides for the writing process. The steps presented next are appropriate for more complex documents such as reports, proposals and position papers; however in abbreviated form they are also applicable to shorter documents such as memos and letters.

Two cautionary notes are important to consider here. First, the writing process may not be linear or chronological, even though it is presented that way. Many studies show that good writers are involved in several stages of the process simultaneously, moving back and forth among the steps as they rework their information and refine their ideas (Berman, 1995). If you find a different sequence fits better for you, use it.

Second, excellent writing takes discipline, even for the gifted. Writing experience and skill can vary from person to person and from assignment to assignment. You might be an excellent writer of memos or letters, but have considerable difficulty with reports. On the other hand, your strength may lie in more in-depth proposals, while memos baffle and frustrate you. Just because writing requires practice and effort doesn't mean you can't be a good writer or that you can't enjoy the process. If you follow the basic steps outlined in this section, you're likely to end up with a well thought-through, efficiently written message.

Steps in the Writing Process

1. *Identify your purpose and situation.*
2. *Start the process right away.*
3. *Get in the right frame of mind.*
4. *Plan your schedule.*
5. *Analyze your audience.*
6. *Research and reflect.*
7. *Organize.*
8. *Write.*

1. Ask Yourself the Question: What Is My Purpose and What Is the Situation?

Are you writing to inform or to persuade? What goals do you want to achieve with this written message? What is it that you want the reader to know or agree to after reading your message? How do you want the reader to feel about you, about her/himself, and about the subject after reading this document? What are the circumstances surrounding this document? How might they affect the written product? In one simple sentence, write a **purpose statement,** or thesis statement, which specifically defines why and for whom you are writing this document. Put the statement in a place where you can easily refer to it. It will serve as a compass to guide and direct your writing. Examples of purpose statements are:

To inform Accounting Division staff of the new fiscal year closing procedures so that staff have adequate lead time to plan their schedules.

To persuade the two supervisors in the Planning Division that we need additional staff to manage the workload with the new projects that have been assigned to the Division.

2. Start the Process Right Away; Don't Wait Till the Last Minute.

Good writing takes time. Give yourself enough lead time to ensure you can produce a quality product. A one-page memo may take as little as 15 minutes to compose, and an annual report may require 20 or more person-days with multiple authors collaborating.

Additional time must be scheduled for circulation, comment and approval by reviewers. Negotiate these time frames with the person who assigns you the document.

Business writers seldom have the luxury of taking all the time they need for an assignment. Often, perhaps even usually, you will receive writing assignments in the workplace under less than optimal conditions. These vagaries may include: lack of clear direction; unrealistic time constraints, rigid style requirements and contradictory edits from different reviewers. As the author, it is up to you to develop a quality product in spite of these difficulties.

Get used to the fact that good writing isn't necessarily easy or orderly. Sometimes words flow smoothly onto the page in perfect form. More often, though, writing is an effortful and messy process. Winkler and McCuen (1995, p. 9) tell us:

> Remember that the best writing occurs by accretion—the same process used by the oyster to make a pearl. It is a laborious search . . . for the right theme, note, idea, or word. The process consists of repeated tinkering, revision, and rethinking of the subject.

3. Get in the Right Frame of Mind.

Prepare mentally for the task of writing. Just as in giving an oral presentation, many people are anxious about important writing assignments. After all, written messages test one's ideas and verbal skills against the scrutiny of the reader. Good writing therefore takes courage and conviction as well as skill. As the author of a document, begin with the confidence that (a) what I have to say makes sense and has value; and (b) I can write the message effectively. Armed with this conviction, proceed to write. Don't allow doubt to sabotage or delay your progress. You can always enlist the help of others to improve your drafts. Make a strategic choice to believe in yourself as a good writer.

4. Plan your Schedule.

Allow adequate time for writing assignments—preferably blocks of time without interruptions. Writing quality suffers and writing time drags on if you try to fit writing in between phone calls, meetings, or other activities. For larger assignments like reports, break the writing process into manageable steps or components and estimate the amount of time necessary to complete each step. Adjust the amount of work for each step to the available time for the assignment, so that you will meet your completion deadline. (This planning approach works for college writing assignments as well as those at work.) For ex-

Report Writing Schedule

Task	Est. time needed
1. Outline the report and get approval to proceed.	4 hrs.
2. Collect and organize all data for the report period, including weekly reports, monthly reports, project summaries, etc.	16 hrs.
3. Complete the body of the report.	32 hrs.
4. Complete all figures, tables, appendices and the reference list	16 hrs.
5. Complete introduction, conclusion and executive summary	16 hrs.
6. Complete first draft of report; circulate for comments	12 hrs.
7. Receive comments from reviewers	16 hrs.
8. Incorporate comments into final draft; submit to management	8 hrs.
TOTAL:	**120 hrs.**
	(15 days)

ample, suppose your manager has given you three weeks (15 working days) to complete a bi-annual report on your division's activities. You might subdivide the report into eight steps and estimate the time needed to complete each step, as shown in the following schedule:

Some of the time estimates may seem long to you, but they are actually prudent estimates with built-in time for interruptions and delays. With a realistic schedule like this you can monitor your progress, track where you are versus where you need to be in your writing process, and make necessary adjustments along the way. You can also avoid last-minute overtime or, worse yet, missing your deadline. It's a handy planning tool.

5. Analyze Your Audience.

Identify who will be primary and secondary consumers of the document. Based on knowledge of your readers, analyze what their needs, interests and concerns are. Take a moment to figuratively "walk in their shoes." What are their circumstances? How much time do they have to read the document? How interested are they in it? How much specificity do they need? What is their attitude toward the subject? The answers to all these questions will influence the choices you make in composing the document. Remember, it's up to you to see that the reader understands your message. As Strunk and White admonish in their famous writer's guide, *The Elements of Style* (1972), "Most readers are in trouble about half the time."

6. *Research and Reflect.*

With your purpose and situation in mind, gather and read all relevant background materials pertaining to the subject you are writing about. Research is necessary so you can write from a knowledgeable, credible position. If your purpose is to inform, you are interested in finding answers to the questions, "what, where, why, when, how, and who." If your purpose is to influence decisions, you will need to answer all these questions, with special emphasis on the "why."

The internet has become the major resource for researchers, and today you can conduct much of your research online. Using the internet has many benefits. Information searches using electronic indexes and internet search engines are quick and easy, saving valuable time. An enormous variety of source materials greatly expands your information base to include published and unpublished material which may be very current. Some web sites are updated daily or weekly; whereas information in print journals and books may be many months and even years old by the time it is published. Information is available immediately, eliminating or greatly reducing the need to travel to libraries or other institutions. Since much information is digitized, it can be downloaded and printed on site wherever you are working. You can save and store information on your hard drive or zip drive as long as you like, and you can copy and paste quotable material directly into your documents, ensuring accuracy.

It is necessary to identify and give proper credit to your sources. As a rule of thumb, any idea that you use in a document that is not your own and not generally known by the public needs to be cited. Distinguish between *primary and secondary sources.* A **primary source** is the original author of an idea or collector of data. Primary sources include authors of journal articles, reports, and books with original ideas. A **secondary source** conveys information about the original idea of another. Textbooks, newspaper articles, popular literature, and many web pages are considered secondary sources, since they are "one generation removed" from the original source. Be cautious about secondary sources; they may or may not interpret original ideas and information accurately. Worse yet, they may make unsupported assertions. These assertions often sound reliable and factual, but they lack supporting evidence and should be suspect. They may be based on hearsay, anecdotal evidence or simply on the author's own opinion; all of which are flawed bases for accepting the truth of the assertion. It is prudent to evaluate secondary source information by assessing the credibility of the author and checking the content of primary sources listed as references. This approach is particularly important with internet sources. Other than the relying on the authority and integrity of the author or institution, there is no assurance that information posted on web pages is accurate or unbiased, so be a critical consumer.

It's a good idea to create a central file with all notes on sources plus full citations. The citation includes all the information necessary for the reader to locate the reference, including, at a minimum, author, publication date, full title, name and volume number of publication, and publisher. Citations should be included in all larger documents to enable the reader to further investigate facts and other evidence. Smaller documents may not include reference lists, but you should always be able to find the answer to the question, "where did you get that information?" in your records. Your integrity and credibility, as well as the organization's reputation, may depend on being able to back up the information in your document.

Think. Good writing requires clear thinking, and poor thinking leads to poor writing. Reflect on what you know and what you've read. Think about how the material you've collected is applicable to your purpose. Jot down your thoughts. What are your reactions? Are there gaps? Unanswered questions? Complex assignments call for synthesis, not merely summarization. Synthesizing involves combining and applying existing information together with your ideas in new ways. Use only the relevant and useful information for your synthesis. Not all published information is correct, or useful. Are the facts substantiated? Are the inferences reasonable? Evaluate the quality of the information, and use only information which is well supported by evidence. Responsible authorship recognizes the importance of conveying reliable, accurate information. As a communicator, you have an ethical responsibility to the reader to ensure that the information you use in your writing is accurate, unbiased and traceable to its original author.

7. Organize.

There are many good ways to organize information and ideas. The goal of all of them is to present ideas in a logical, easy-to-follow fashion for the reader. Examples of organizational patterns are presented in Chapter 5. These patterns may be used for written as well as for oral messages.

Here are some useful ideas to help you organize. First, refer often to your purpose statement. It should state your overall purpose and specifically describe what you intend to accomplish in the document. The purpose statement guides the structure and content of your document. It is the standard against which you measure all information in the paper.

Second, identify all main ideas related to the thesis. One useful method for doing so is brainstorming. To **brainstorm** related ideas, list as many topics as you can think of in a given time period, such as ten minutes. As you generate this list, resist the temptation to evaluate the idea or information. Simply list. Once you have developed a complete list of ideas, then go back and identify the most appropriate ones to include in the document. This selection process may take some time, and you may need to shift choices as you consider your purpose, your audience, and your situation.

Once you have selected your main ideas, **outline** your document. Use an organizational structure which most logically and effectively sequences your information and achieves your purpose. Fit your main and supporting ideas into the organizational structure. Include an introduction, body and conclusion, just as recommended for oral presentations in Chapter 5.

Your outline will help you decide on the best **format** to accomplish your writing purpose. Format refers to the visual arrangement or spatial layout of the message on the page. The format should be congruent with the message content, the purpose and the situation. Sometimes formats are predefined; on other occasions you, as author, have the liberty to choose the most effective format. Clarify your format options with the person who gave you the writing assignment. Different formats are used for memos, reports, proposals, and newsletters. Any of these documents may include a variety of ways to visually display information, such as itemized lists; charts or graphs; tables, columns, pictures, boxes, borders, or font variations. Your guiding question should be: what is the most efficient and effective way to visually present the different parts of my message to this audience?

8. Write.

Good writers in organizations are sensitive to the four dimensions of meaning inherent in all communication mentioned in Chapters 1 and 5. These dimensions are *sense,* or the substance or content of the message; *feeling,* or how the writer feels about the content of the message; *tone,* or the relationship between the writer and her/his audience; and *intention,* or the writer's purpose for the message. Before you write, clarify your goals for the sense, feeling, tone and intention of your document. (I will say more about *tone* later.) Think about not only *what* you need to write, but *how* it should come across to the reader. As you write, remain aware of these important aspects of your message, and realize that much of the meaning in your writing is contained "between the lines." Before you transmit your message, check to ensure that it meets your "meaning" goals. Remember that your documents do not merely convey information; they also reflect your purpose for writing, how you feel about the information, and how you relate to your readers.

Effective writing also necessarily involves a process of drafting, revising and editing. Only through a careful rewriting process will you produce an optimal finished document. Plan on at least three drafts, or successive versions of the document (Winkler and McCuen, 1995). There may, however, be multiple iterations and refinements of the document, depending on available time and reviewers, the sensitivity and importance of the document.

A. First, create a ***rough draft.*** In writing this draft, be concerned more with content than with style or mechanics (Ober, 1995). This first attempt may be awkward and ragged, but the important thing is to get down on paper a complete set of all your ideas, plus an introduction and conclusion. Then let the draft alone for at least 24 hours. Give yourself time away from the work so you can come back to it with "new eyes"—with a fresh perspective, not locked into yesterday's thinking and writing patterns.

B. ***Edit and revise.*** After 24 hours, it's time for your first rewrite. At this stage, you are "cleaning up" the roughness and awkwardness of your first draft. Your aim is to focus on both content and style to make the document say clearly what you want it to say. Edit your draft for **clarity, economy, coherence, interest** (Barzun and Graff, 1970) and **accuracy.** Each of these qualities is explained in the chart on the following page. It is best to edit for one or two purposes at a time, rather than to try to attend to several at one time. No particular order is needed in applying these edits. Here you also have an opportunity to modify earlier formating choices to best meet your rhetorical goals. Beyond the content of your document, optimal appearance and placement of text and graphics can mean the difference between success and failure. After editing, your second draft should be significantly more effective than the first.

C. *Final rewrite:* During this final stage of revision, you act as a finish carpenter, polishing the document so that it "shines." Now is the time to replace those last few awkward phrases, to take care of technical details: to make the format uniform; to correct grammatical and spelling errors, to ensure that sources are properly cited. A final overall edit for clarity, coherence, economy, interest and accuracy is wise. To catch problems you may have missed, get a coworker, friend or advisor who is a good writer to do a final proofread.

EDIT DRAFTS FOR:

1. *Clarity:* clarity requires that every word, sentence and the document as a whole say all they are intended to say and nothing else. Possibilities for misreading are minimized. To edit for clarity, get skeptical: read everything literally; misread wherever possible. Look for words or phrases that have multiple meanings, terms that lack specificity, needless abstractions, and unquantified quantities. Clearly define terms.
2. *Coherence:* a coherent message flows easily from sentence to sentence and from paragraph to paragraph. There is a logical and orderly relationship of all the parts. The reader immediately recognizes why one line follows its predecessor. The message holds together to form a comprehensible whole. To edit for coherence, look for places where the writing appears choppy, or appears to jump from one subject to another. Notice whether the order in which ideas are presented appears sensible and easy to follow.
3. *Interest:* interesting writing captures and holds the reader's attention. To edit for interest, replace passive verbs with active verbs, replace abstract terms with concrete terms, and adjust sentence structure and length to provide variety.
4. *Economy:* An economical message is one that says everything it should say in as few words as possible. To edit for economy, take out words that contribute nothing to the meaning of the sentence. Aim to reduce verbiage by one-third without cutting any content from the message.
5. *Accuracy:* An accurate message correctly represents the facts and information it contains. To edit for accuracy, again read with the eyes of a skeptic, looking for any possible misrepresentation of ideas or data. Correct any errors or omissions left from the first draft, such as citations, statistics, and other supporting evidence.

Generating a Quality Product

Quality business writing is characterized by the **substance,** or content of the message, as well as by its **style** and **tone.** Ober (1995) presents a helpful analysis of style and tone which guides the following discussion.

Writing **style** refers to the ways in which ideas are expressed. Good writing style creates a message that is *clear, accurate, complete, and appropriate for the audience and the occasion*. Words are specific, concrete, short and simple, leaving little room for confusion. Cliches and buzz words are avoided. Active voice emphasizes the doer of the action, while wordiness and redundancy are averted. A mixture of simple, compound and complex sentences provides variety and increases interest. Paragraphs are coherent, and paragraph length is generally limited to a topic sentence and three to five supporting sentences. These style characteristics minimize the effort a reader must devote to understanding the message, while maximizing message comprehension.

The **tone** of a message reflects the writer's attitude toward the reader and toward the subject of the message (note that this use of the word combines the meaning dimensions of feeling and tone mentioned earlier). The overall tone of business writing should be *direct, positive, confident, courteous and sincere*. Directness is strongly preferred for most written messages in today's busy workplace. Except in sensitive matters, people don't want to waste time getting to the point. Positive language is more likely to be accepted by the reader than is negative language. Language that stresses what is true and what can be done is stronger than a negative approach. Try to avoid negative words like cannot, will not, should not, failure, refuse and mistake. A confident tone is persuasive. Confident writers show conviction, but do not appear arrogant, condescending or pushy. Courtesy and sincerity build goodwill and increase the likelihood that the reader will read and accept your message. Flattery, ingratiation and overstatement can offend the reader. Together, the characteristics of tone should maintain a favorable relationship between the writer and reader.

Basic Organizational Documents

I. Memos: the "Notes" of the Organization.

The word **memorandum** is derived from the Latin *memorandus,* meaning *to be remembered*. Today, the abbreviated form, memo, refers generally to a written internal message. Memos may range from one-sentence notes dashed off on E-mail to several hard-copy pages painstakingly composed for official reasons. Routine memos are used as requests for permission to take some action, advisories of scheduled meetings, reminders that a report is due, questions about a team member's responsibilities, transmittal and explanation of an attached document, even suggestions for the annual picnic. Despite differences in content, length and medium, most memos have two common features: (a) they are in-house messages; that is, they are sent to and from staff within the organization; and (b) they are designed to be simple and direct, dispensing with formal salutations and closings present in letters. Many organizations use basic memo formats or templates with the following headings:

MEMORANDUM

To:
From:
Date:
Subject:
Message:

In drafting a memo for routine internal communication, get to the point right away, preferably in the first one or two sentences. Don't make the reader search for your purpose. Avoid using stilted language like, "the purpose of this memo is . . ." As Paxson (1981) suggests, "Lead off with a simple and specific statement that plunges the reader into the subject." Since most routine memos are brief messages between coworkers that know one another, the language used in memos is typically less formal, more direct, and more like speaking, than in letters or reports. Examples of leading statements for memos might be:

"As you requested, I have called ABC Company to confirm our meeting next week."

"Last week we agreed that I would get three bids on a new fax machine. Here they are:. . . ."

Finish the memo by clearly asking for action. Don't leave the reader wondering, what should I do with this information? In short, a memo should be concise and direct.

E-Mail Messages

In and between most larger organizations, people write messages primarily via e-mail. E-mail messages have some special characteristics. First, e-mail is marvelously efficient, saving time and paper. E-mail messages are composed, sent, read and stored electronically. They may never be printed on hard-copy. They may be deleted immediately or saved in an electronic file for future reference. They may be distributed simultaneously to one person, to a designated group, or to all employees in the organization. They may also be forwarded electronically to other interested parties. Since e-mail delivery is almost effortless and virtually immediate, it is often the quickest and easiest way to connect with others. Some people overuse this communication medium, and many members of organizations must contend with dozens, or even hundreds of messages each day, many of which are irrelevant to their work. Given the growing prevalence of e-mail overload, it is important to use subject headings which are short, relevant and easily understood, so that users can sort and prioritize their reading. Also, respect your readers' time and storage capacity by keeping your message concise and appending only necessary parts of prior messages (Anderson, et al., 1998). Resist the temptation to pass on every good joke or juicy tidbit to your mailing list members.

Second, because of the quickness and informality of the electronic medium, e-mailed messages may be less formal, or less carefully composed than hard-copy memos. A busy staffer may dash off a message without capitalizing, punctuating or correcting misspelled words. This lack of formality may send unintended, ambiguous nonverbal messages which may be interpreted by receivers in positive or negative ways, such as "this person can't spell," or "she must not care enough about me to use complete sentences," or "this casual style is a way of telling me we have a close relationship." Because these unintended messages are prone to misinterpretation, it is wise to watch your writing style, grammar, spelling, punctuation and tone when composing e-mail messages. Also, because of e-mail's informality it is easy to write things in ways that can offend readers. Make a habit of proofreading the message before you send it, placing yourself in your reader's shoes. Especially when you're in a hurry or if you have strong feelings about the issue, editing the message with your reader in mind is well worth the trouble to avoid unintentionally damaging work relationships.

The informal, personal nature of e-mail also invites users to "chat." Check with your superior for the organization's policy on personal use of e-mail. Chances are it is discouraged. Resist the temptation to misuse the system for idle chat, gossip, or non-business related (personal) concerns. If you have internet access, limit your online use to official business. Internet browsing costs the organization, and sites you have visited, as well as time charges are trackable to your work station. A recent survey of 1,627 organizations by the American Management Association showed that 63 percent monitor internet access, and almost 50 percent store and review e-mail. In short, don't abuse the privilege of having access to new technology. Your internet activities could be limited, and your relationship with your employer jeopardized.

Third, e-mail is not confidential and message integrity is not assured. Messages may be easily copied and distributed to unintended receivers. E-mail messages can be altered, and senders' addresses can be concealed or misrepresented by unscrupulous persons. Remember that incoming and outgoing messages may be scrutinized. Even with casual messages, always be professional and observe rules of politeness and good taste. It is unwise to send confidential or privileged information via e-mail. Never send an e-mail message that you wouldn't want to be seen, or questioned about later, by a third party. If your message is private and confidential, either put it on paper and ensure it is read only by its intended recipient, or perhaps a better solution is to talk to the person face-to-face, in private.

II. Internal Reports: Keeping Management Informed

Business and professional writers generate a variety of internal **reports.** Monthly activity reports, annual reports, management reports and technical reports are just a few examples. Different reports have certain principal parts in common. If one becomes familiar with these core parts, it becomes relatively easy to organize and write a report tailored to specific needs. Reports generally contain the following principle parts, or a variation of these parts (Ober, 1995; Paxson, 1981).

Parts of a Report

I. **Prefatory Matter**
   A. *Cover & Title Page;* Acknowledgements (if desired).
   B. *Preface* (introductory statement by the author of the report); or *Forward* (initial statement made by someone other than the author).
   C. *Authority: statement of the agency, statute, or official authorizing the report.*
   D. Table of Contents, including lists of tables and figures.
   E. *Executive Summary:* Summarizes topics covered, including specific information from within the report, such as the issue, report highlights, conclusions, recommendations. May range from 1 to 5 pages. Or:
   F. *Abstract:* Indicates the topics covered in the report but gives few details. Maximum length is approximately 150 words.

II. **Body of Report**
   A. *Background:* orients the reader to the subject of the report and explains why the question or issue is being investigated.
   B. *Statement of the Problem:* defines and thoroughly describes the question or issue to be answered in the report.
   C. *Method:* describes precisely and comprehensively how the question or issue was investigated.
   D. *Results:* systematically reports the data or findings of the investigation. The findings are not discussed; only presented in this section.
   E. *Discussion or Conclusions:* presents the author's reasoned interpretation of the findings. The conclusions answer the question, what inferences does the evidence in the report logically lead to?
   F. *Recommendations* (if appropriate): If the issue addressed by the report is a question of policy (see Chapter 7), this section presents the author's suggested courses of action to follow based on the conclusions.
   G. *Comments* (if appropriate): presents noteworthy insights gained by the author as a result of having completed the research, including cautions, additional questions, and areas for further research.

III. **Supporting material**
   A. *Reference List* or *Bibliography:* a comprehensive list of references used.
   B. *Appendix:* supplementary material provided to explain methods or findings.

III. Issue Memoranda: Arguing For or Against an Idea or Course of Action.

An **issue memo** is a formal, brief internal document which provides executives with concise, yet sufficient information to make policy decisions. To accomplish its purpose, an issue memo must have a narrow, clear focus. It should briefly describe the issue, present alternative courses of action, and recommend the best course of action. The format of an issue memo may differ from one organization to another, but there are five basic parts to an issue memo, which are well described by Paxson (1981). These parts may appear in slightly different order, depending on executives' preference. A sample issue memo format is shown next, followed by an explanation of its five parts.

XYZ Organization

Issue Memo   # 97-17

Subject_____

Author_____   Division Chief_____

Issue:

Recommendation:

Discussion:

Fiscal Impact:

Suggested Action Steps:

---

1. The **Issue** section clearly and briefly states the issue to be decided. A simple, declarative sentence is common; however the issue may also be phrased as a question.
2. The **Recommendation** section follows the statement of the issue . It briefly relates the writer's recommended action. In this way the solution is offered immediately after the problem is stated.
3. The **Discussion** section briefly summarizes the background on the issue, the alternatives and their advantages ("Pros") and disadvantages ("Cons"). It may also contain brief historical information, but this should be kept short, since most readers are familiar with the history of the problem.
4. The **Fiscal Impact** section includes a concise analysis of potential costs and savings, and and the work involved in implementing the recommendation. Any unresolved fiscal or workload questions should be mentioned here.
5. The issue memo ends with the **Suggested Action Steps** section, which outlines immediate action steps necessary to implement the recommendation.

This issue memo follows a "thesis first" format, the standard, deductive form of argument (Fulwiler, 1995). The advantage of this direct approach are that your audience knows where you stand right away, and your position occupies the two strongest places in the memo—first and last. Most issue memos follow this standard form of argument.

IV. Proposals: Vehicles for Ideas

A **proposal** not only defines and describes a problem; it also considers alternative solutions and recommends a best solution. A proposal may be brief, such as a suggestion for improving internal distribution of mail; or it may be comprehensive, as in the case of government budget change proposals. Whether brief or comprehensive, proposals generally follow this basic problem-solution format derived from the John Dewey's (1910) rational problem solution method:

Format for a Proposal

I. **Analysis of the problem**
   A. Definition of the problem
      1. How does the status quo differ from organizational goals? What is wrong? What are the symptoms? What evidence points to the problem?
      2. What is the meaning of the problem? Define or clarify terms.
   B. Scope of problem: How big is it? Is it increasing? Whom is it affecting? In what ways? Under what conditions? At what times, in what places?
   C. History of the problem: What conditions led to the problem?
   D. Causes of the problem: What are the main and contributing causes of the problem?
   E. Present efforts: what is being done to meet the problem? In what ways are these efforts ineffective?
   F. Implications: what results can we expect if the problem is not solved? What are the short-term and long-term consequences of the problem?

II. **Identification of alternative solutions**
   A. What are the criteria for a satisfactory solution? An effective solution must make an effective attack on the operating causes of the problem.
   B. What boundaries must an effective solution observe? An effective solution must preserve to the greatest possible extent other values, operations, laws, policies in the situation.
   C. What are the possible solutions, given criteria and boundaries? Exactly what does each possible solution involve? Describe the solution specifically.

III. **Evaluation of alternative solutions** What are the advantages and disadvantages of each solution?
   A. Suitability: To what extent would each solution attack the causes of the problem?
   B. Acceptability: To what extent would each solution preserve other values and requirements in the situation?
   C. Feasibility: To what extent is each solution doable? Affordable?

IV. **Selection of Best Solution**
   A. Which solution should be adopted as the best potential remedy for the problem?
   B. Do more than one solution form a "solution package?"

V. **Implementation of Solution**
   A. What steps must be taken to fully execute the solution?
   B. When shall the solution be implemented? What time lines must be met?
   C. Who will implement the solution? What division of authority or labor is appropriate to implement the solution?

The above four models represent a cross-section of document types used to inform and influence decisions in organizations. Memos, reports, issue memoranda, and proposals are the among the most common written forms of routine internal messages. Because of limited space, we have not discussed messages external to the organization. However, one area deserves brief consideration.

New Media: Communicating via Web Pages

Increasingly, organizations are recruiting good writers and training them to serve as web masters who are responsible for designing and managing their web sites. Web page development is a new form of written communication for use internally (intranet), and externally (internet). It requires a specialized combination of knowledge of design and page layout principles, an understanding of how users navigate through web sites, and technical knowledge of HTML (Hypertext Markup Language), file management, multimedia elements, and hyperlink strategies. Building web pages is also a highly creative endeavor. Many of the basic principles of good writing still apply, but because the environment is web-based, multi-media and interactive, additional knowledge and skills are needed. If you are interested in web page development, take some courses that specialize in this new technology. You can also visit web resources listed at the end of the chapter.

With a basic understanding of the functions, characteristics, methods and common forms of business writing, you are now better prepared to write well and to recognize good writing at work. Before we part, let me leave you with one last set of lists.

Common Writing Mistakes to Avoid

Here are some common mistakes made by student writers in organizational communication courses and by young professionals in organizations. These mistakes detract from the quality of the finished document, making it appear weak and unprofessional, even if the ideas are outstanding. The result for a student may be a lower grade; the result for a professional may be a career setback. It's a good idea to use these checklists to help spot problems prior to submitting a written assignment. If you tend to make such mistakes, get help from an experienced writer or writing advisor BEFORE you submit your work for a grade. More comprehensive assistance is available by taking a college composition course. Although such a course is designed for college writing, the information you will gain from it will be extremely valuable and transferrable to the workplace.

Punctuation, Grammar and Spelling Error Checklist

_____ Inappropriate use of commas; using commas instead of semicolons, colons.

_____ Misuse of possessive forms, e.g., *there* for their; *their* for singular possessive (his or her), such as: a person showed *their* intent to communicate by. . . .

_____ Misplaced apostrophes, confusing contractions for possessive forms, e.g., *it's* for its; *childrens'* for children's.

_____ Misspelled words. (Use Spell Check! There's no excuse for incorrect spelling).

_____ Poor sentences: run-ons, lack of verbs.

Style Error Checklist

_____ Lack of a purpose statement or thesis.

_____ Lack of a clear introduction, body or conclusion.

_____ Beginning sentences with pronouns having vague or unknown referents, e.g., *This* means we should proceed . . .

_____ Inappropriate use of paragraphs, including several unconnected ideas in one paragraph or failure to break paragraphs when a new idea is introduced.

_____ Incomplete, inconsistent and improper citations, e.g., reference list doesn't match citations; uncited ideas that are not the author's (this is plagiarism).

_____ Unnecessary repetition and excessive verbiage.

_____ Unsupported fact claims and assertions.

_____ Lack of concrete examples or illustrations to explain an idea.

_____ Excessive loaded language and overstatement.
_____ Improper use of quotations: too many and/or too lengthy.
_____ Poor transitions between main points; lack of logical flow.
_____ Vagueness; lack of clarity; muddy writing.

Summary

Writing at work is rhetorical and relationship-based. Good writing matters to the organization and to its members. We use writing to inform, explain or influence organizational decisions. Written messages are more constrained than spoken messages in that writing has only one channel to convey the message: words; and writing is static, with no opportunity for feedback. Good business writing is marked by its focus on the reader, its utility, its clarity, interest, accuracy and efficient use of words. The writing process involves eight major steps. Generating a quality document requires careful attention to the message substance, style and tone. Models were presented for four common internal documents: memos, reports, issue memoranda and proposals. New media, including e-mail, intranet and internet web sites, pose special challenges to writers. Business students should avoid common writing pitfalls. Being a good business writer takes knowledge of the right tools to use, and practice.

References

Anderson, D., Benjamin, B., & Paredes-Holt, B. (1998). *Connections: A guide to on-line writing.* Boston, MA: Allyn & Bacon.

Barzun, J. and Graff, H. F. (1970). *The modern researcher* (2nd ed.). New York: Harcourt Brace & World Inc.

Berman, Elena. (1995). *A short guide to improving student speaking and writing.* Unpublished manuscript, University Composition Board, University of Arizona at Tucson.

Dewey, John. (1910). *How we think.* Boston: D. C. Heath.

Flesch, Rudolph. (1962). *The art of readable writing.* New York: Collier MacMillan Publishers.

Fulwiler, Toby. (1995). *The working writer.* Englewood Cliffs, NJ: Prentice Hall.

Goldhaber, G. M. (1979). *Organizational communication* (2nd ed.). Dubuque, IA: Wm. C. Brown Co.

Ober, Scott (1995). *Contemporary business communication* (2nd ed.). Boston, MA: Houghton Mifflin Company.

Paxson, W. C. (1981). *The business writing handbook.* New York, NY: Bantam Books.

Stohl, C. (1995). *Organizational communication: Connectedness in action.* Thousand Oaks, CA: Sage.

Strunk, William Jr., and White, E. B. (1972). *The elements of style* (2nd ed.). New York, NY: Macmillan.

Wiio, O. (1978). *Wiio's laws and some others.* Espoo, Finland: Welin-Göös.

Winkler, A. C. & McCuen, J. (1995). *Pocket guide for writers.* Englewood Cliffs, NJ: Prentice Hall.

Web Resources

Anderson, D., Benjamin, B., & Paredes-Holt, B. (1998). *Connections: A guide to on-line writing.* Boston, MA: Allyn & Bacon.

Nielsen, Jakob. (2000). *Designing web usability: The practice of simplicity.* Indianapolis, IN: New Riders Publishing.

Writing for the Web: Online sources

http://www.useit.com/papers/webwriting

http://www..useit.com/papers/webwriting/rewriting.html

http://webreview.com/97/10/10/imho/index.html

Persuasive efforts are integral to organizational decision-making processes. To engage effectively in decision-making, members must be skilled at both constructing and evaluating persuasive arguments.

In Chapter 7, Michael Dues explains persuasion processes and provides a guide to presenting and evaluating persuasive arguments. In writing this chapter, Dr. Dues draws on his experience directing a nationally ranked debate team, his considerable study of argumentation theory, and 25 years of experience as an organizational consultant.

Sound Arguments and Persuasive Messages

Michael Dues
University of Arizona

Key Terms

argument	policy claim	informal fallacies
Toulmin's Model	presumption	one-sided and
claim	burden of persuasion	two-sided messages
warrant	status quo	ethos
data	problem-solution model	logos
expert testimony	comparative advantage	pathos
inference	model	Monroe's Motivated
fact claim	Stock Issues	Sequence
value claim		

Objectives

1. Use Toulmin's Model to describe the basic components of an argument, and explain how these components are joined to produce a persuasive message.
2. Describe three kinds of claims made in persuasive messages (claims of fact, value, and policy), and explain ways to provide rational support for each.
3. Explain the fundamental principles which guide classical theory of argument, and describe how these principles are applied in the Problem-Solution and Comparative Advantage models of policy argument.

4. Describe 13 common reasoning fallacies which should be avoided in building arguments.
5. Identify key strategic choices which must be made in developing persuasive messages.
6. Describe Monroe's Motivated Sequence for constructing and presenting persuasive messages.

Persuasion is an integral part of organizational life. Coordinated effort, a defining factor in organizations, requires getting people to agree about what will be done, and how it will be done. Bringing members of an organization to recognize *and to do* what should be done requires persuasion. Thus, every member of an organization regularly confronts two persuasion tasks: (1) construction and presentation of persuasive messages, and (2) evaluation of others' persuasive messages. This chapter provides information that is helpful with both tasks.

In organizations a conscious effort is usually made to make *rational* decisions. Moreover, organizational decision-makers are held accountable, and accounting for decisions is a matter of providing sound reasons for decisions that are made. Thus, when competent organization members attempt to persuade one another regarding a decision, they emphasize the rational aspects of their messages. The rational element of a persuasive message is called the **argument.** There is more to persuasion, of course, than argument. However, due to its organizational emphasis, this chapter focuses primarily on building and evaluating persuasive arguments. It contains an explanation of the fundamental structure of argument, models for constructing rational arguments, common fallacies to avoid in developing arguments, and a model that uses rational and emotional appeals to motivate audience change.

A word of caution to the reader who is new to argumentation theory: As a guide to rational argument, this chapter necessarily contains extended discussions of abstract concepts. It is not an easy read. Take it slowly. Read parts more than once and let the ideas sink in. Treat it like a condensed instruction manual or a complex recipe book and it will serve you well.

Toulmin's Model of Argument

In attempting to understand how to construct or evaluate an argument, it helps to have a model in mind that identifies the fundamental parts of an argument and describes how those parts come together to support a conclusion. Stephen Toulmin (1959) created a model of argument that has proved broadly useful in analyzing persuasive discourse. He observes that arguments grow out of information (data) on a particular issue that leads to an inference or conclusion (claim). There is also a bridging statement, which he calls a **warrant,** that allows the data to be linked to the claim. Every persuasive message presents an idea or course of action that the communicator advocates; it then suggests reasons why listeners should agree. Thus, most persuasive arguments include the three basic components in the **Toulmin Model:** *claim, warrant,* and *data* (Toulmin, 1959). These elements workData and warrant combine to support the claim.

Basic Diagram of Toulmin's Model:

Claim

A **claim** is any statement, implied or explicit, with which a communicator wants the audience to agree. A particular claim can serve as the major point of several related arguments, or it may be used in one part of an argument to support an assertion (claim) made in another part.

There are three kinds of claims that can be used in a message: *policy claims, fact claims,* and *value claims.* In a *policy claim,* the speaker calls for a specific course of action. The statement "Abortion should be available to women on demand," is an example of a policy claim. In a ***fact claim*** the speaker asserts that a condition does or does not exist.

For example, the speaker might claim: "In Sweden, abortion is available to women on demand." A **value claim** asserts an evaluation of some kind. For example, "The Swedish system that allows for abortions on demand is superior to the abortion policies in the United States." Regardless of the kind of claim used, the claim alone does not in itself provide a reason for audience acceptance.

Warrant

To persuade, the communicator must support each claim with two other message parts: a *warrant* and *data*. A **warrant** is a general belief or principle that supports a claim. Warrants may be explicitly stated, or (more commonly) they may be unstated. Unstated warrants are silently supplied by receivers who share the belief or opinion. To be effective, a warrant must be accepted (or supplied) by the audience; otherwise, it remains just another claim. For example, a communicator who says, "Our organization should be environmentally conscious" is making a claim. He may then support the claim with the general statement "Environmental concerns are important in today's society." Such a statement would be a warrant. Members of Green Peace might accept this warrant and so accept the claim. Indeed, members of Green Peace could be counted upon to silently supply this warrant without the speaker explicitly stating it. But disposers of toxic waste or activists from other groups might not believe the warrant and so would reject the claim as unwarranted. To address an audience whose members did not already believe environmental concerns are important, the warrant itself would have to be treated as a claim, and would have to be supported with data and a new warrant.

Data

Data are specific sets of information, opinions, or beliefs stated in support of a claim. Like warrants, data must be accepted by the audience to be persuasive. Data to support claims can take several different forms:

Forms of Data

1. **Specific beliefs or information shared by the communicator and his or her audience.** It may be claimed, for example, that all cigarette advertising should be banned. Such a claim might be warranted by the generally accepted belief that cigarette smoking causes lung cancer. The communicator might then of-

fer as data the information that cigarette advertising encourages smoking. The success or failure of this argument depends upon whether or not the audience already shares the belief that advertising encourages smoking. If not, the data itself must be treated as a claim which the communicator will have to support by further argument.

2. **Beliefs or information held by the communicator, but not necessarily known or shared by his or her audience.** This type of data asks the audience to accept something just because the speaker says it is so. It is effective to the extent that the speaker is viewed as a credible source. For example, a speaker might assert that consistently poor nutrition retards the mental development of children. If his or her credibility on this issue is high enough—let us say that the audience knows him or her to be an established and respected member of the medical profession—the assertion itself becomes sufficient data.

3. **Citing the testimony of an expert.** When the communicator is not recognized by the audience as an expert on the subject being discussed, he or she can present *expert testimony* from a third party who is credible to the audience concerning the subject. Consider an example:

Data:	**In her book *The Change Masters,* R. B. Kanter, Ph.D.** tells us that employees are far more likely to accept major change, if they are given a genuine opportunity to "buy in" to the change before it is made.
Warrant:	R. B. Kanter is a credible source on this issue.
	[Therefore, we can conclude]
Claim:	Affected employees should be consulted before a decision involving a major change in company strategy is made.

For this type of data to be persuasive, the audience must trust that Kanter is a credible authority concerning the issue being discussed. In evaluating the credibility of expert testimony, professionals may consider three key issues, *expertise, bias, and method.* Consider each of these tests briefly.

Expertise: The expertise issue addresses the question "How do we know this person is an expert?" In the case of Kanter, her Ph.D. is some evidence that she is an expert, but a speaker might want to further "qualify" her in the eyes of the audience by pointing out that she is an internationally recognized authority on organizational management.

Bias: Most experts have a certain amount of bias about issue they address. Bias is not a moral issue (we are not discussing prejudice here). Bias arises from the perspective from which one approaches a subject, or from taking a point of view publicly. If bias may be significantly influencing what an expert says about an issue, credibility is reduced.

Method: Perhaps the best test of the credibility of expert testimony is to evaluate the *method* by which the expert reached the conclusion that is being reported. This is why all scholarly articles, and most professional reports clearly describe the methods used in the research being reported. A brief description of method can be provided to an audience to support the credibility of expert testimony. EXAMPLE: "Kanter found in a two year study of organizations that had successfully implemented major change that. . . ."

When the expert cited is known to the audience, it is generally not necessary to provide "qualifying" information to establish the expert's credibility. However, when the expert is unknown to the audience, some qualifying information is usually required. In constructing persuasive messages, it is important to identify when qualifying information is useful, and to provide it. In evaluating persuasive messages, it is important to consider whether the "experts" cited have actually been "qualified" as experts by the speaker.

Toulmin's Model shows us the common elements of rational arguments. The rest of this chapter contains suggestions for combining these elements to construct rationally sound arguments.

Constructing Persuasive Arguments

Many logical and organizational patterns are available for structuring persuasive arguments. As you grow in your professional career you will want to develop a broad repertoire of persuasive message patterns. In the rest of this chapter we provide a beginner's book of recipes for building sound arguments and persuasive messages. Below, we describe four ways to build arguments supporting claims of fact, three ways to build arguments supporting claims of value, and two models for building arguments supporting claims of policy, the **Problem-Solution Model,** and the **Comparative Advantage Model.** At the end of this chapter we will describe Alan Monroe's (1962) formula for constructing rationally sound messages that are emotionally appealing to the audience. Additional patterns for constructing strong persuasive messages are discussed in Chapters 5 and 6.

Supporting Claims of Fact

We indicated above that a *fact claim* is one in which the speaker asserts that a condition does or does not exist, without attaching any assertion about whether that condition is good or bad. Arguments supporting claims of fact may be simple or complex. Simple support for fact claims can be created by citing the three kinds of data we discussed above. One can cite:

(1) information that is known to both the speaker and the audience,
(2) information that is directly known to the speaker, allowing the audience to supply the warrant that they trust the speaker to report truthfully, or
(3) a credible third party as an expert source, allowing the audience to supply the warrant that they trust the credibility of the source.

Often, supporting a claim of fact requires guiding the audience through a chain of reasoning. As we described above, a chain of reasoning involves a series of inferences, each of which represents a claim, supported by data and a warrant.

Common Reasoning Patterns

Many reasoning patterns can be used to support claims of fact. Six of the most common are listed below:

Reasoning by example involves using one or a few examples to illustrate, and thus support an claim. EXAMPLE: "Printers tend to be creative people. Bob, for example, is also a song writer and an excellent musician." (Notice that the support here is in the form of an illustration of the point. If we really try to conclude that all printers are creative based on this one example, we engage in the informal fallacy of *hasty generalization*, which is discussed later in this chapter.)

Reasoning by analogy involves making a comparison between two similar cases, and inferring that what is true in one case must be true in the other. EXAMPLE: "College is more like a marathon than a series of sprints. If you really want to succeed at college, therefore, you must maintain a good, steady pace, and keep going." (The analogy in this pattern serves as the *warrant* in the argument. The argument works only if the audience accepts the analogy.)

Reasoning from cause to effect: When we know that one factor usually causes a certain kind of result, we can infer that the result is present, based on citing the presence of the cause. EXAMPLE: "Television advertising usually increases the sales of the advertised product. Widgets have recently been advertised on television in Tucson, so we can expect sales of widgets to increase."

Reasoning from effect to cause: When we know that one factor usually causes a particular result, and we know that result is occurring, we can infer that the cause is also present. EXAMPLE: "In weather, we know that low pressure systems cause rain. When it is raining, we can infer that a low pressure system is present."

Sign reasoning is based on knowing that two factors tend to vary together (not necessarily that one causes the other). With this knowledge, when we see one variable, we can infer the presence of the other. EXAMPLE: "A frown on the boss' face is usually a sign that she is displeased with someone's work. The boss is frowning, so she must be displeased with someone's work."

Process of elimination (method of residues): This method of reasoning lists possible alternatives, identifies reasons why all alternatives except one must be eliminated, then concludes that the remaining alternative must be correct. EXAMPLE: "We know it had to be one of the four of us. Harry couldn't have done it because he was in Louisville at the time. Jane couldn't have done it because she doesn't have the pass word. I know I didn't do it. So, it must have been you who erased the accounts data."

Supporting Claims of Value

Claims of value are more complex than claims of fact. A claim of value begins as a claim of fact, and becomes complex by attaching a value to the fact. EXAMPLE: "The MIS Program at University of Arizona is one of the best in the world." (Embedded in the value claim is the *fact claim* that "there is an MIS program at University of Arizona." The value claim is created by attaching a value to that fact, i.e. "one of the best in the world.") The *fact* element of the value claim can be supported using any of the methods described above for supporting fact claims. But what about the *value* element? Values are subjective; at their core they represent personal needs, wants, beliefs, or ethical standards. Many people mistakenly believe that because values are subjective they cannot be the subjects of rational argument. As a consequence, they may limit themselves to expressive strategies in discussing value issues. It is certainly true that some of our core values are learned before we are five years old, and are so deeply ingrained in us that they are very unlikely to change. But many of our evaluations—beliefs about values—are more tentatively held, and are quite amenable to reconsideration. Despite their subjective nature, value claims can be supported by rational arguments in three ways: *appeal to authority, appeal for consistency, and citing new, valued information.* Each of these is explained below.

Appeal to authority: Every culture has certain people who are considered wise and good. The opinions of such people on issues of value carry weight. To appeal to authority is to cite the opinion of such a person on an issue of value, using that person's statements as third order data to support the claim. EXAMPLES: "Thomas Jefferson believed that every citizen has a right to a basic education." or "The Bible says Thou shalt not kill."

Appeal for consistency: People hold many values, some of which are related to one another. And people prefer to be consistent with themselves. Consistency appeals in support of value claims ask the listener or reader to agree on the value in question on the ground that it is consistent with other values he/she holds, and on the ground that it would be inconsistent with other values he/she holds to not do so. EXAMPLE: "If you agree that a woman has a right to control the uses and functions of her own body, then you must agree that she has a right to choose when she becomes pregnant whether to carry the fetus and give birth or to terminate the pregnancy."

Citing new, valued information: People can be induced to reconsider values by introducing new information which involves values upon which all agree. The new information is presented as a claim of fact, and can be supported in any of the ways we described above for supporting fact claims. EXAMPLES: "A motorcycle rider who is not wearing a helmet when an accident occurs is fourteen times more likely to be killed than a rider who is wearing a helmet." or "The State of California spends more than $4 million per year of tax payers' money to cover medical costs of motorcycle riders' head injuries, which could have been prevented by wearing a helmet."

Notice that each of these methods of supporting value claims asks receivers to be consistent with themselves in the values they hold—consistent with an authority whose wisdom they respect, consistent with other values they hold, consistent with the values attached to the new information cited. Thus, rational argument about values honors the personal subjectivity of values while offering the audience logical reasons to change.

Supporting Claims of Policy (Proposals)

Policy claims propose action of some kind. Arguments supporting policy claims always involve complex chains of reasoning, which include several fact claims and at least one value claim. Two well established prescriptive models are particularly useful. These models, derived from classical argumentation theory, provide useful patterns for building persuasive cases, and can serve as checklists for evaluating cases others present.

Prescriptive models state how people *should construct and evaluate arguments. The "shoulds" in the models below are derived from the concepts and principles of classical argumentation theory, which are derived from the writings of nineteenth century theorist Richard Whately (1872), who based his work on the* Rhetoric of Aristotle. Those principles and concepts are described below, followed by the two models.

Classical Principles of Argumentation

Whately articulated three principles on which models of policy argument rest, and gave us several argumentation terms denoting those principles. I have exercised considerable liberty in translating Whately's work into contemporary terms. His fundamental principles of argumentation, interpreted in today's terms, are these:

1. We value rational behavior, which means that we think action should be based on reasons. Conversely stated, this principle says we shouldn't do anything for which we don't have at least one good reason.
2. We think that in the absence of a reason to change, people will and should go on behaving as they are. (Behaving as they are equals the **status quo.** In classical argument theory this principle is called a **presumption** *in favor of the status quo.* In argument theory, the **burden of persuasion** is on a person who proposes change. Burden of persuasion simply means a requirement to offer at least one complete reason to do what is proposed.)
3. Argument models for supporting policy claims rest on the above principles. They are models that constitute recipes of constructing one complete reason. They also serve as useful tests of policy reasoning. A **stock issue** is an issue that arises as a necessary part an argument model. If any necessary part is missing from reasoning following a particular model, the reason is not complete. In that case we say the **burden of persuasion** has not been met, and *presumption* says people will and should go on with the **status quo.**

Basic Policy Argument Models and Their Stock Issues

Based on these principles, there are two models for supporting policy claims: the **Problem-Solution Model,** and the **Comparative Advantage Model.** In each model there are four issues that are *stock issues*, which means that they are always present. Each stock issue is logically necessary for the argument using the model to add up to one complete reason. If the argument fails on any one stock issue, the argument fails, period.

Problem-Solution Model

In problem-solution reasoning, the argument is that the reason to do a proposed action (policy) is because it solves a problem. The four stock issues in this model are:

Problem-Solution Model
Stock Issues

1. Existence
2. Harm
3. Inherency
4. Solvency

The requirements for meeting each of these stock issues are explained below.

1. **Existence:** To establish this issue we need a supported claim of fact, showing that a condition actually exists which we are going to identify as a problem.
2. **Harm:** To establish this issue we need a supported claim of value showing that the condition we have identified is harmful (or at least less than optimal).

   NOTE: A harmful condition is a "problem." If we cannot show that the condition in fact exists, we cannot claim there is a problem. And, if we cannot show that the existing condition is harmful, there is no problem. If there is no problem, there is no need to do anything. In many argumentation texts, these two "problem" stock issues are lumped together, and called "need."
3. **Inherency:** We need to show that the problem is a function of whatever it is that we are proposing to change. Otherwise, changing something else might

solve the problem as well or better than what we propose. And if changing something less could solve the problem, we do not have a reason to make the particular change that is proposed. To demonstrate inherency we need a supported fact claim that says "We can't solve this without doing what is proposed."

4. **Solvency:** To establish solvency we need a supported fact claim that shows it is reasonable to predict that if we do what is proposed, we will solve the problem. One common and effective way to argue solvency is to detail how the proposal could be implemented, and then use the details to illustrate how the proposal would solve the problem. This is called presenting a plan. It is logically necessary to address the solvency issue because unless we can credibly predict that the proposed action will solve the identified problem, we have not supplied a complete reason in problem-solution terms.

In summary, the four stock issues of the problem-solution model say:

1. This condition is occurring,
2. and it is a problem,
3. which cannot be solved unless we do what I propose, but
4. it will be solved if we do what I propose. Therefore, we should do what I propose.

EXAMPLE: Problem-Solution Model Stock Issues

Existence: Our delivery van breaks down at least twice each month.

Harm: This costs us an average of $280 per month in repairs, and makes our customers angry when deliveries are late—which costs us business.

Inherency: This problem inheres in the fact that the van is six years old and has over 300,000 miles on it. It's just old and worn out, so it will keep breaking down and needing repairs.

Solvency: A new van would not break down often, and would allow us to make deliveries reliably on time.

Conclusion/policy claim: Therefore, we should buy a new delivery van.

Comparative Advantage Model

In this model, the argument claims that adopting the proposal will yield a result that is in some way better than the results of continuing the *status quo*. Typically, the maker of the argument selects one or more criteria on which to compare results of the proposal against results of continuing the *status quo*. Examples of criteria for comparison might be: cost, number of people served, attractiveness of the product, or time required.

For each of the points of comparison with this model there are four stock issues:

Comparative Advantage Model
Stock Issues

1. Importance
2. Accrual
3. Significance
4. Uniqueness

---

1. **Importance:** To establish importance we need a supported value claim which shows that this point of comparison matters.
2. **Accrual:** To establish accrual we need a supported claim of future fact which indicates that the claimed better results will actually accrue from adopting the proposal being advocated.
3. **Significance:** To establish significance we need a supported claim of fact which indicates that the *extent* to which the better results will be achieved is sufficient to make the change worth the effort. It is necessary to address this issue of degree because this model deals in degrees of difference.
4. **Uniqueness:** To establish uniqueness we need a claim of fact indicating that the claimed comparative advantage cannot be acquired without doing what is proposed. (This is exactly the same as the inherency issue in the problem-solution model.)

In summary, in the Comparative Advantage Model, the reason to do what is proposed is that:

1. Regarding something that really matters,
2. we gain an advantage by doing what is proposed, that is
3. great enough to make it worth our effort to change, and this advantage
4. cannot be gained in any way short of doing what is proposed.

NOTE: If any of the four issues is not adequately addressed, the advantage claim in question is not supported by a complete reason.

EXAMPLE: Comparative Advantage Model Stock Issues

Importance: Money is important to all of us.

Accrual: Riding a bicycle to school saves money because it avoids the costs of gasoline and parking.

Significance: The savings adds up to at least $60 per month, which is well worth the effort to anyone on a limited income.

Uniqueness: Since walking is too slow, and busses to slow, unreliable, unsafe, and almost as costly as driving, riding one's bicycle is the only realistic way to save this $60 per month.

Conclusion/policy claim: Therefore, we should all ride our bicycles to school.

Which Is More Effective, Problem-Solution or Comparative Advantage?

Research indicates that the problem-solution pattern is generally more effective in changing attitudes, both immediately following the message and over a period of time (Cohen, 1957). The problem-to-solution message sequence is more interesting, and the solution is more understandable when presented as the answer to a specific problem or need. In our Western Culture, the notion of solving a problem is somewhat more compelling than is gaining some relative advantage. Problem-solution reasoning deals in absolutes; there either is, or is not a problem, and the proposed action either will, or will not solve it.

Often, however, the data available to construct arguments is quantitative. Quantitative data is always relative. It is well suited for supporting claims about "more" or "less," or "to what degree." It is generally not well suited to supporting absolute claims about "is" or "is not." When the data available to support an argument are quantitative, it is often best to employ the Comparative Advantage Model, which deals in relative terms. Which is more effective, then, Problem-Solution or Comparative Advantage? The answer is "it depends." It depends on which model is best suited to the reasons you are citing to support your claim, and on the nature of the available support data. We suggest that when a Problem-Solution Model accurately reflects your thoughts, and when you have data that clearly support all four problem-solution stock issues, you build a problem-solution argument. When you are working primarily with quantitative data, and/or when your reasons themselves deal with relative claims (more and less, instead of yes and no), the Comparative Advantage Model may serve best.

Errors in Reasoning: Informal Fallacies

The suggestions and recipes above will help greatly in constructing arguments, but they will not ensure that your argument will be rationally sound. An argument can fail to persuade because it is rationally flawed. A fallacy is a rational flaw in an argument that eliminates or reduces its effectiveness. A "fallacious" argument may appear to lead to a conclusion, but that appearance is false. Fallacies are to be avoided in making arguments. When evaluating the arguments of others, it helps to be able to recognize **informal fallacies** when they are present. Below are **thirteen common fallacies** which should be avoided in constructing arguments.

- **Unsupported Assertion:** An assertion which is not supported, but is nevertheless used as part of an argument. EXAMPLE: "Domestic violence usually increases on Superbowl Sunday." (This unsupported assertion was widely broadcast several years ago. No evidence was offered to support the claim; it turned out that *was no evidence*. The claim was fraudulent.)
- **Equivocation:** Using terms that may have two or more meanings, or that have broad, vague meanings. Conclusions may depend on wrong interpretations of the meanings of such terms. EXAMPLE: "We need a team approach on this, because evidence shows that a team approach works best over time. So I'm going to appoint a task force, and I'll expect the people I appoint to

meet regularly, and do everything by consensus." (Notice that "team approach" dopes not necessarily mean "do everything by consensus.")

- **Loaded Language:** Using words that attach overly strong emotions to what is being discussed, then relying on those emotions instead of the facts to secure agreement. (EXAMPLE: "We simply can't trust a government that uses Gestapo tactics the way the FBI did against the Branch Davidians at Waco." (The FBI may or may not have botched its role in the Waco tragedy, but the FBI is hardly the Gestapo.)

- **Hasty Generalization:** Generalizing from a small number of specific cases to a general rule. EXAMPLE: "The last time we hired a college student for that position she quit in less than two months. Now this college student is quitting in less than three months. If we want somebody in the position who will stay there awhile, we'd better not hire a college student." (It is irrational to generalize to all students, based on two examples.)

- **False Analogy:** Using an inaccurate comparison to reason from analogy. EXAMPLE: "Lovers are like trolley cars. There will be another one along in twenty minutes. So your departure is of little concern to me." (People are not like trolley cars; they cannot be boarded at will, and relationships with lovers are not accomplished for a dollar.)
NOTE: **False Sign** works the same way.

- **False Cause (*post hoc, ergo propter hoc*):** Claiming a causal relationship exists where we have no good reason to believe a causal relationship exists. One very common way this happens (post hoc fallacy) is to claim that because one event followed another in sequence, we can infer that the former event caused the latter event. EXAMPLE: "Most users of hard drugs, smoked marijuana before they tried harder drugs. Therefore, we can conclude that smoking marijuana leads to using harder drugs." (Sequence does not necessarily indicate a causal relationship. Most smokers of marijuana drank milk before they began smoking, but no one would suggest a causal relationship between those two behaviors.)

- **Slippery Slope:** Basing an argument on the unsupported assumption that one step in a given direction will lead to more steps in that direction, and, eventually, to going to extremes in that direction. The name of this one is based on the analogy of stepping onto a "slippery slope;" with that one step you begin a slide which you cannot stop until you reach the bottom. EXAMPLE: "I know our people worked very hard and did a spectacular job this year, and that as a result we made huge profits. But we should not give them bonuses this year, because if we do it will set a precedent, and they'll think they have a bonus coming every time we make a profit." (There is no reason to believe bonuses will be expected in years when large profits are not made.)

- **Attacking the Person Instead of the Issue (*ad hominem*):** Diverting attention from the actual issue in question by personally attacking a participant in the discussion. EXAMPLE: "John says they're having a problem with the new software, and are unable to capture the data we need, but he's always whining about something." (Notice that in focusing on John, the real issue of whether there is a problem with the software is avoided.)

- **Circular Reasoning:** Using unsupported premises to support each other. EXAMPLE: "The Clintons hid this box of records for over a year before they turned it over to the committee. Therefore, there must be evidence in these records which ties them to the Whitewater scandal. The Clintons say this box was missing and that they just found it, so they're turning it over to the committee now. But we know there is evidence in the box tying them to the Whitewater scandal. Therefore, they must have been hiding the box, and withholding evidence from the committee." (Notice that this is a closed loop. The premises are used to support one another.)

- **Begging the Question:** Assuming the conclusion, and using it as a premise in the argument. This is logically the same as circular argument. EXAMPLE: "Gun control is unAmerican. Therefore no patriotic American can support it." (Notice that the "Americanness" of supporting gun control is the claim that is in question, and that the "unAmericanness" of gun control is assumed as data to support it. Begging the question is also circular reasoning.)

- **Popular Appeal:** Using majority opinions about an issue as evidence about the issue itself. EXAMPLE: "Most Americans believe O. J. Simpson committed the murders. Therefore, he probably did." (The truth is whatever it is, no matter how many people do or do not believe it. Popular opinion, therefore, cannot serve as rational support for the actual truth of a claim.)

- **Attacking a Straw Man:** This fallacy occurs when someone sets up an issue that is not really an issue, then knocks it down. This is referred to as "setting up a straw man," which is easy to knock down instead of taking on a real man. Focusing on the "straw man" diverts attention from the real issue. EXAMPLE: "Including these proposed restrictions on old growth logging in the bill won't help to balance the budget." (Restrictions on old growth logging are designed to save forests; they are not intended to help balance the budget. The real issue is whether they will help save old growth forests. That issue is avoided by focusing on the "straw man" concerning the budget.)

- **Non Sequitur:** (Latin words meaning "does not follow") An argument in which the conclusion simply does not follow from the premises. EXAMPLE: "Most Americans are now convinced that our bureaucracy is wasteful and inefficient. Therefore, we need to fundamental change our system of public service, and literally reinvent government. (Even if it were true that American public service is wasteful and inefficient—a claim widely made, but not well supported by the evidence—that would simply not lead to the conclusion that radically restructuring our public service system is warranted.)

Deciding Whether to Present One or Both Sides of an Argument

Most claims represent only one side of an argument. In constructing persuasive messages, one is often confronted with the question of whether or not to cite opposing arguments. In a **one-sided message,** a claim is made, and the communicator attempts to support it (as we have described above in this chapter). In a **two-sided message,** the same claim can be made but there is acknowledgment of opposing arguments, with some attempt to demonstrate why the claim being advocated is superior to those in opposition. The decision to present a one-sided or two-sided message depends on several factors residing with one's audience. The issue memo format described in Chapter 6, which is a standard decision-making tool used in many organizations, simply dictates using a two-sided message. In most situations, you must consider the circumstances in order to decide. There are three conditions in which **one-sided messages** are usually the better choice. When an audience already agrees with the claims of a speaker, a one-sided argument will increase or confirm that support (Hovland, Lumsdaine & Sheffield, 1949). If the audience is unaware of counter arguments, the speaker will probably do best simply to avoid mentioning them. By mentioning them, one risks persuading listeners against one's claim by providing reasons not to support it. Finally, if you are playing the role of advocate for one side of an issue, then other individuals are expected to offer counter arguments. When you are expected to adopt the one-sided stance of an advocate, it's best to stay with what is expected and present a one-sided message.

On the other hand, if an audience is hostile, if its sympathies are unknown, or if there is any possibility that an audience is aware of opposing arguments, a speaker is best advised to present a **two-sided message.** Even when people are in agreement with the speaker, the more educated they are (a strong likelihood in the corporate setting), the more likely such an audience will be persuaded by a two-sided argument (Hovland, et al., 1949). Educated people are usually capable of thinking of at least a few opposing arguments for themselves and, therefore, might be suspicious of the motives or intelligence of a speaker who does not consider these same arguments. Most experienced executives prefer to be presented both sides on an issue before making a decision.

Building Persuasive Messages

In this chapter I have concentrated on recipes for building sound rational arguments because rational decision-making is valued in organizations and sound arguments provide accountability for decisions. However human beings are influenced both by rational and emotional considerations. In the workplace it's best to build your persuasive messages primarily as logical appeals and to make sure you are personally credible to your audience, then to take steps to add emotional appeal to your rational foundation.

About 2500 years ago, Aristotle identified three basic kinds of persuasive appeals: (1) appeal to reason (**logos**), (2) appeal to emotional (**pathos**), and (3) the personal credibility of the persuader (**ethos**). He observed that effective persuasion usually required the combination of all three kinds of appeals. Twentieth century research on persuasion has generally supported Aristotle's observation.

Although it is clear that certain messages are more logical or more emotional than others, it is probably not very useful to view logical and emotional appeals as completely separate and distinct. Persuasive messages typically contain both emotional and logical appeals in addition to the personal credibility of the persuader, which is inherently part of any persuasive message.

One especially useful formula for building emotionally appealing cases on a sound logical framework was proposed many years ago by Alan Monroe (1962), of Purdue University. He offered a five-step sequence of steps to motivate an audience to action using the framework of a problem-solution argument model. Known as **Monroe's Motivated**

Sequence, this formula continues to serve business professionals, government leaders, and academicians well after almost four decades of widespread use. It is described below. Notice that Monroe adds steps to involve the audience personally and emotionally so that they are emotionally as well as rationally engaged in a decision-making process, and motivated to take action.

Monroe's Motivated Sequence

Step 1: Attention. As indicated in Chapter 5, it is important at the beginning of any presentation to gain the audience's attention. Do this in a way that focuses attention and audience interest on your topic, in a manner that supports your own credibility as a speaker (or writer).

Step 2: Need. This step addresses the first two stock issues in the problem-solution model—existence and harm. Monroe suggests including four elements in demonstrating a need for your proposal.

1. State the nature of the problem.
2. Illustrate the problem with one or more detailed examples.
3. Show the extent and ramifications of the problem using statistics and/or expert testimony.
4. Point to the relationship between the audience and the problem. Indicate the personal implications for each listener (or reader).

Step 3: Solution. Propose a solution and show that it will satisfy the need you have demonstrated. This step addresses the last stock issue in the problem-solution model—solvency. Depending on the complexity of the problem and on your proposed solution, this step may have as many as five elements.

1. State the attitude, belief, or action you want the audience to adopt.
2. Explain your proposal clearly enough so that the audience well understand it.
3. Show the logical connection between your proposal and the need you have demonstrated.
4. Show that your proposal is practical and feasible, given the available resources and the conditions under which the group is functioning.
5. Overcome any objections members of the audience may have.

Step 4: Visualization. Ask the audience to visualize what will occur if your proposal is adopted, and if your proposal is not adopted. Vividly describe the positive conditions that will result from adopting your proposal and the negative conditions that will result from failure to adopt your proposal.

Step 5: Action. Ask your listeners to take specific, overt action to begin enacting your proposal. If appropriate, state your personal intention to take specific action. Then close in a way that has emotional impact.

A Concluding Comment

In this chapter, we have discussed several issues that are important to the communicator who wishes to structure effective persuasive messages. Let us end with a few words of caution. Even the best persuasive efforts, built upon perfectly sound arguments, can fail. Other variables are always present. Persuasion is not the same as controlling others. Others have free wills; they have a part to play in whether or not our persuasive efforts succeed. The mark of any successful communicator is adaptation. Following the general suggestions offered here, however, will increase the probability that your persuasive efforts will succeed, and, even when unsuccessful, will help you contribute to sound decision-making processes in your organization.

Summary

This chapter is meant to serve as a beginner's guide for constructing persuasive messages built on sound rational arguments. The main points are:

1. Although persuasive messages always involve a combination of logical, emotional, and personal appeals, organization members are expected to emphasize logical appeals in constructing persuasive messages.
2. The Toulmin Model of argument describes the three basic components of a persuasive argument, shows how these components are put together to constitute a persuasive message.
3. There are three kinds of claims: claims of fact, claims of value, and claims of policy.
4. There are several ways to provide logical support for claims of fact, and three ways to provide logical support for claims of value.

5. The fundamental principles of classical argumentation theory are explained.

6. The Problem-Solution and Comparative Advantage Models of argument, which are derived from classical argumentation theory, can be applied to construct logical support for a claim of policy.

7. It is important to avoid thirteen common informal fallacies in developing arguments.

8. Monroe's Motivated Sequence is a useful model for building rationally sound and emotional appealing persuasive messages.

For further information on how to construct and present effective arguments, see:

Ronald Adler, (1996). *Communicating at Work: Principles and Practice for Business and the Professions.* New York: McGraw-Hill. Chapter 15.

Austin J. Freeley, (1986). *Argumentation and Debate: Critical Thinking for Reasoned Decision-Making*, 6th ed. Belmont, CA. Wadsworth Publishing Company.

Stephen Lucas, *(1995)*. The Art of Public Speaking, 5th ed. New York: MaGraw-Hill. Chapters 15 & 16.

References

Cohen, A. R. (1957). Need for cognition and order of communication as determinants of opinion change. In *The order of presentation in persuasion* (pp. 102–120). In C. I. Hovland (Ed.), New Haven, CT: Yale University Press.

Hovland, C. A., Lumsdaine, A. A., & Sheffield, F. D. (1949). *Studies in social psychology in World War II*, vol. 3. Princeton, NJ: Princeton University Press.

Monroe, A. H., (1962). *Principles and types of speech*, 5th Ed. Chicago: Scott, Foresman, & Co.

Toulmin, S. (1959). *The uses of argument.* Cambridge, England: Cambridge University Press.

Whately, R. (1872). *Elements of Rhetoric.* New York: Sheldon & Co.

Meetings are a primary mechanism of organizational communication. It is in meetings that members communicate with one another to make decisions, plan and coordinate activity, and share sensitive information.

Len Silvey is an experienced executive who has managed both public service organizations and his own highly successful consulting firm. In his many years as an organizational consultant, he acquired a reputation as an exceptionally able facilitator of successful meetings. In Chapter 8, Mr. Silvey draws on his experience as well as his considerable study of the subject to explain how to ensure successful meetings.

Leading Useful Meetings

Len Silvey
State of California

Key Terms

meeting	strategic planning	consensus
agenda	group leader	RISE
meeting content	group facilitator	silent writing
meeting process	group recorder	open interaction
problem-solving	group memory	human factors
decision-making	group member	warm openings
action planning		

Objectives

This chapter presents fundamental concepts and principles necessary to understand how to effectively lead work group meetings. The chapter objectives are:

1. to describe principles that make meetings work,
2. to point out significant contributions to meeting technology, and
3. to provide a basic guide to help meeting facilitators ensure productive meetings.

Meetings are a primary means of communication in organizations. A **meeting** is a "get together with a purpose", and it is important to ensure that meetings produce what we intend them to produce. Meetings are the means by which some of the essential tasks of an organization are accomplished, including decision-making, coordination of work activities, and consensus building. Meetings also consume time, energy, employee attention, space, and other resources. From the standpoint of the organization, ensuring useful and efficient meetings affects the bottom line issue of productivity. The "technology" of meetings is a body of knowledge, based on research, providing sound guiding principles to help ensure that meetings are efficient and useful.

Principles for Guiding the Conduct of Meetings

In my judgment there are ten principles that should guide the conduct of meetings:

1. Useful meetings require agendas; useful agendas must fit the purpose of the meeting, the culture of the organization, and personalities of the meeting participants.
2. Every agenda item should have an identifiable purpose.
3. Process is different from content, and every bit as important.
4. There are four distinct roles in the conduct of any meeting: leader, facilitator, recorder, and member. Meetings work best if these roles are recognized, legitimized, assigned, and honored.
5. Consensus is a reasonable goal of any meeting.
6. In any meeting, whether it be face to face, teleconference, or computer mediated, "human factors" abound; humans misbehave.
7. People develop the best ideas in a meeting when they write their ideas silently in the presence of one another, prior to expressing their ideas.
8. People do the best job of ranking or selecting the best ideas, and are more likely to arrive at consensus when discussion is open and interactive.
9. Voting can either interfere with consensus or help identify consensus, depending on how it is done.
10. Warm openings contribute to productive closings.

Below are explanations of these ten principles.

1. Useful meetings require agendas.

An **agenda** for a meeting is like a road map with the destination marked for a trip; it identifies where you wish to go, and how you intend to get there. The absolute minimum agenda required for a meeting is a clear statement of its purpose(s); an agenda is more useful if it also lists, subjects to be discussed, processes to be employed, and time frames for specific agenda items. Agendas provide focus, and focus matters.

Variables to Consider in Building Agendas

In my role as professional facilitator, I am often called upon to assist group leaders in developing agendas for meetings. Here are seven categories of variables with which we typically struggle in deciding what an agenda should include:

A. *Professional Protocols and Styles*

Each profession has its own professional culture, and that culture influences the protocols and styles with which members interact in meetings. When medical doctors meet, for example, a "high tell" approach is evident in their agenda, and much of what they do is like having a select few, who have the latest or best information in some specialized area, deliver formal "papers" to the rest of those present. Lawyers, on the other hand, have a "high debate" style, and their meetings are characterized by polemics, frequently summarized near the conclusion by someone who can fairly represent the opposing points of view. Sales people tend toward a style of interaction characterized by high enthusiasm and voiced mutual support. When members of the cloth of the same religion meet, benediction, blessing, and prayer are important parts of the interaction. Educators, scientists, police, termite inspectors, legislators, finance directors, business managers, and trainers all have histories about how they work together; all have styles and protocols that govern their meetings. These represent a kind of cultural baseline for a meeting. One can judiciously choose to attempt to change such protocols, but they cannot be ignored.

B. *Mandates and Statutes*

Both private and public service organizations are governed by mandates and statutes which regulate organizational processes. Legislatures, boards of supervisors, city councils, and regulatory boards build agendas according to legal mandates and procedural rules. Organizational boards of directors, professional associations, ad hoc task forces, and quality circles build their agendas according objectives and procedures mandated by organizational by laws or by management. When a meeting occurs in the context of an organization, both its outcomes and its processes must conform to the legal and organizational mandates and statutes which govern the organization.

Many of the rules and procedures governing meetings, especially in public service organizations, were established before the development of contemporary collaborative meeting processes. Among the most complex challenges I have faced over the years has been to build agendas for efficient, productive meetings in organizations encumbered by rules requiring inefficient, unproductive meeting processes. For example, I have struggled with clients to devise ways to bring wholesome collaborative processes to meetings whose legislated protocols are ANTI-collaborative, and sought ways to allow open, free flowing discussion in meetings where there were strict confidentiality requirements.

However cumbersome they may be, mandates governing an organization's meeting processes must be honored in developing agendas. Whether it be Robert's Rules of Order for a home owners association, the docketing procedure for a County Board of Supervisors, Murphy's Manual for the California Legislature, the Articles of Incorporation of a company, or Lincoln's Log for the United States Congress, procedural mandates will affect an agenda. In developing an agenda for a meeting it is important to become familiar with, and to conform to any mandates that apply.

C. *Organizational Culture*

Organizations, like societies, build identities over time that come to characterize the way people treat each other, the way people react to certain stimuli, and the face that people present to one another and to the outside world (Deal and Kennedy, 1982). As we pointed out in Chapter 2, each organization develops its own unique culture. An organization's culture includes all the informal rules and patterns for how things are done, and it definitely affects what is appropriate in building agendas for meetings. Culture affects what can be discussed in a meeting, who may speak about what, who may disagree with whom, even whether or not meetings start on time. In planning the agenda of a meeting, it is important to know and honor the organization's culture.

In some organizations the culture about meetings has been to conduct meetings with aimless agendas or no agendas at all. In such organizations members often bemoan the many hours spent and wasted in meetings. When this is the case, the best way to honor the organization's culture concerning meetings is to acknowledge it, and thoughtfully change it. It is actually a joy to work with these organizations, showing them how thoughtful agenda building can save time and frustration while producing useful, efficient meetings.

D. Available Time and Resources

Every meeting requires time, space (computer mediated meetings require cyber space), and people. All three of these are finite resources; all are limited, and all are used at some cost to the organization. In building the agenda for a meeting it is critical to know, and to work within the available resource limits. Agendas set expectations for a meeting, and it is a mistake to set unrealistic expectations. If an agenda calls for a meeting to accomplish more than is possible, or includes too many items, the meeting will probably fail, participants will be frustrated, and cohesiveness and motivation will be damaged.

E. Personal Styles of the Leader and Members

In addition to the organizational and group cultures that affect meetings, individuals have personal styles of thinking and interacting. These, too, should be taken into account in developing agendas. One of the great contributions of organizational scholars has been the development of instruments (paper and pencil questionnaires) which, when filled out, create insight into a person's approach to the world, and, thereby, to the organization (Parker, 1990). These can be very helpful in identifying the wide variety of styles and approaches individuals will bring to a meeting. Some instruments, for example, help in distinguishing between people who tend to be dominant and controlling of others, and people who are more reserved and analytical, or between people who are more autocratic and those who are more collaborative. Today, we know that collaborative styles are more useful in most situations, but the personal styles of individuals must nevertheless be recognized and honored for meetings to be successful.

F. Ownership of the Agenda

An agenda that takes into account all of the above variables is crucial to ensuring a useful meeting. A final variable concerning agenda building concerns the agenda building process itself. This is the variable of agenda ownership. The participants in the meeting must feel that they "own" the meeting and its agenda. Therefore, whatever the style, protocol, tradition, culture, or resource limits, a goal I bring to the agenda building process is to engage people enough in the process so that they will in fact own the agenda; it will clearly reflect their ideas and intentions. The task of building such an agenda must be accomplished, for the most part, before the meeting begins, and access before the meeting to some of the participants may be limited. Therefore, the agenda itself should be the first item of discussion at any meeting, and the agenda should be agreed upon before proceeding to other items.

G. *The Long Term Impact of Agendas*

It may sometimes seem that an unwarranted amount of time and effort go into building an agenda for a single meeting, and that the meeting might run as well, or almost as well, without that effort. I have noticed over the years, however, that agenda decisions about a single meeting often carry over to many future meetings, and can even affect the organizational culture as a whole. Frequently, when we are considering what should be included in an agenda, we are building an agenda format that will be at the core of how we do business for months, years, even decades to come. The fact that agenda decisions for specific meetings can have long term, unanticipated affects makes it all the more important that they be as right as they can be.

Check List for Agendas

Distributed agendas should clearly indicate:

- Who called the meeting
- Name of the meeting group
- Title of the meeting
- Who is invited/expected to participate
- Date, starting time, and ending time
- Intended outcomes (purposes, objectives)
- Methods or processes to be used
- Background materials, preparation required, and/or items to bring
- List of specific agenda items in their anticipated order
- Any special notes about the meeting that may be useful

Sometimes it is also advisable to specify the following:

- Purposes of specific agenda items
- Decision-making method to be used (See chapter 9)
- Final decision-maker of items involving decisions, if other than the group itself
- Individual person responsible for discussion concerning specific agenda items
- Specific processes to be used regarding specific agenda items
- Time allocated to discuss specific agenda items

Distributing the Agenda in Advance

For any important meeting a tentative agenda should be distributed in advance of the meeting to all potential participants. Distribution may be in hard copy or via E-mail.

Seldom have I seen all the items on the above checklist on a single agenda, and never have I seen two agendas, in two different organizational settings using exactly the same format. The important thing is that an agenda must serve to focus and structure the meeting, and that participants agree on it.

2. Agenda Items Have One of Six Purposes

When organization members get together in a meeting, they generally do so for one of six purposes (Doyle and Straus, 1976):

A. **Problem-solving:** developing, evaluating alternatives to dispose of a problem.
B. **Decision-making:** choosing from among proposed alternatives the one believed to be best suited for solving a problem or gaining an advantage.
C. **Action Planning:** laying out the action steps, and identifying the resources required to carry out a decision, or to accomplish an objective)
D. **Strategic Planning:** identifying the mission or purpose of an organization or work unit; establishing a vision of success; setting goals and objectives; and agreeing on ethical values which will guide the conduct of business.
E. **Reacting and Evaluating:** assessing newly emerging conditions and issues, evaluating progress in carrying out previously selected courses of action, and identifying existing problems or opportunities.
F. **Reporting and Presenting:** sharing information.

Reporting and presenting consumes a significant portion of most meetings, and is the sole purpose of some meetings. That so much meeting time is consumed in reporting and presenting reflects considerable bad judgment on the parts of people setting agendas. Reporting and presenting is the *least* valid purpose for incurring the expense of bringing people together to spend time with one another; there are other, less expensive ways to inform one another. Meetings should be called only when we value the intellectual capacity of participants to make contributions. Besides, it has been my experience that reporting and presenting, after the first twenty minutes, doesn't accomplish much informing; people are much better "informed" by having them participate in the other five purposes, when they are actually expected to grapple with, and respond to what is being said.

3. Process is different from content, and every bit as important.

Much of the work on effective meetings in the last three decades has been on the distinction between the **content** of a meeting (the topics discussed, ideas expressed, decisions made, and plans developed) and the **process** by which a meeting is conducted. Irving Janis attracted interest to the issue of group meeting processes with his ground breaking study of how groups of intelligent people can get together in a meeting and make a truly foolish decision (Janis, 1967). Extensive research on group dynamics, which identified important elements of group communication processes was done in the 1960's (Pavitt and Curtis, 1994). But organizational and professional cultures tend to resist change. In some organizations and professions, the traditional emphasis on content is so firmly in place that it is difficult for members to understand what process is, or even that process exists.

To ensure useful meetings participants must be able to clearly distinguish meeting content and meeting processes. A colleague of mine who is a professional facilitator describes the difference between content and process as the distinction between the "what" and the "how" of meetings (McCarthy, personal communication, 1994). He has so attuned himself to the process, or "how they are operating with one another," that he does not even hear the content, or "what issues are being addressed" in a meeting. His professional task is about process, and, to better focus on his task, he literally tunes content out.

In my own work, I find it necessary to attend to both process and content. Meeting content is made up of the substantive issues, problems, conditions, and activities that are placed on the agenda and discussed. Meeting processes are the methods employed by group members to address the content. Processes must be selected and adapted to fit appropriately with the content. Appropriate processes are as essential to successful meetings as appropriate content.

Today there is, in my opinion, a markedly enhanced sophistication among people in key roles in organizations about process skills, where to get them and how to use them. The last thirty years have seen us move from having to explain what process skills are to having entire graduate programs in universities devoted to building organizationally useful process skills. Facilitating is now a profession in its own right, and there is a considerable variety of meeting processes available so that processes can be matched to a variety of content issues, organizational cultures, time frames, and resource limits.

More will be covered on process in each of the remaining segments of this chapter.

4. There are four roles present in every meeting.

Perhaps the most enduring element of the work done by Doyle and Straus on "making meetings work" (1976) is their clear identification of the four roles present in any meeting. Whether these roles are played by the same person or by different people, they are either all present at the meeting, or the meeting fails to achieve its full potential. In my experience, the more roles can be distributed to different people, the better an individual can do with the role she/he is assigned. The Doyle and Straus framework for identifying roles has served well in the hundreds of meetings I have conducted or facilitated over the last fifteen years. The four group roles are the leader, facilitator, recorder, and member.

A. Group Leader

The group leader is the "boss", the project leader, the person who is authorized to make decisions about the issue at hand or to designate who will have authority. In a meeting the group leader has responsibility for sponsoring and legitimizing people who are to play the other three roles.

   The group leader (though not necessarily building the agenda) ensures that an appropriate agenda is developed and distributed to participants. She/he ensures that the meeting is directed and that participation is structured, but generally does not take on the role of directing the meeting or structuring participation. Group leaders lend support to decisions about what processes will be used in meetings and what agenda items will be discussed. Finally, the leader is responsible for bringing appropriate closure to agenda items (and to the meeting), and for ensuring that accountability for further work on agenda items is clear.

B. The Group Facilitator

While the group leader's responsibilities tend toward matters of content, the responsibilities of the **group facilitator** are normally limited to matters of process. To "facilitate" means to "make easier." The role of the facilitator is to make it easier for the group to efficiently accomplish the purposes of their meeting—to help the group get what it wants from the meeting.

Responsibilities of the Facilitator

- Ensure the meeting has a clear agenda, and that members own the agenda.
- Ensure that appropriate facilities and equipment are provided and in place for the meeting.

- Help the group focus on a common problem and a common process.
- Ensure the use of processes that are appropriate to the organizational and professional culture, meeting content, and time and resource conditions, and participant styles.
- Guide and manage the meeting process and movement through the agenda.
- Induce everyone to participate, and protect group members from personal attacks.
- Remain neutral and build trust.

Facilitators do not contribute their own ideas or evaluate the content of the ideas expressed by group members. The facilitator's job is to keep the process on track and moving, and to keep the meeting content in the hands of the group members. This often requires that the facilitator sublimate his/her own ego. It is difficult to keep quite about one's own ideas while others are speaking freely about theirs. The facilitator must be driven by a genuine desire to serve the **process** needs of the group, and must be flexible enough to adapt to the changing conditions and to changes in the group's needs. A good facilitator avoids defensiveness, and adjusts as required.

Facilitator Tasks

Some of the common tasks facilitators perform during meetings are:

1. Manage the pace of the meeting, picking up the pace or slowing it down as needed.
2. Regulate communication traffic, managing who speaks, when, and for how long.
3. When the group gets stuck, help it to move on by framing issues, and/or offering alternative approaches.
4. Deal with problem participants, controlling interrupters and monopolizers, busting late comers, stopping rude behaviors.
5. Handle silences by acknowledging low energy levels, offering breaks, or asking needed questions about process.
6. Ensure participation, drawing timid or reluctant participants into discussion.
7. Punctuate filibusters, cutting off those who attempt to monopolize discussion.
8. Keep quiet when appropriate, blending into the woodwork when things are going well.
9. Admit mistakes. "Owning" occasional bad calls when they occur.

10. Carefully observe all that goes on in the meeting, verbally and nonverbally.
11. Minimize repetition, calling attention to frequent revisits to prior issues.
12. Suggest methods and approaches for addressing content issues.

C. Group Recorder

The role of the **group recorder** is to create an immediately visible record of ideas considered, commitments, and conclusions. Visibly recording agreements helps make members accountable to one another for action on the agreements; it helps assure that things get done, and that commitments made in meetings will be kept.

Whether this record be produced on chart pads mounted on easels in the front of the meeting room, or on a lap top computer, and projected on a screen, it is important that the recording be done in "real time," as ideas are presented and decisions made, and that the record be immediately visible to all participants, so that edits and corrections can be made immediately. The more traditional method of having someone "take minutes," then reviewing and attempting to "correct" them weeks later at a subsequent meeting was never adequate. Hardly anyone remembers perfectly from one meeting to the next exactly what occurred. Doyle and Straus call the process of creating a simultaneous record of the meeting, maintaining the "**group memory**" (1976).

In addition to generating the "group memory" of the meeting, recording properly also helps focus attention on the content of ideas being discussed. The record as it is created serves as the physical point of attention for participants. It keeps participants informed on what has been decided. It frees group members from taking notes, and it assures individual participants that their ideas have been heard and duly noted.

Especially when a meeting moves quickly, with many ideas expressed, the recorder's role can be difficult and exhausting. A good recorder must be able to: (1) listen well (See Chapter 3), and be able to capture the meanings participants intend, (2) write or type the record quickly and clearly, and (3) gracefully ask for clarification when needed without unnecessarily interrupting the flow of ideas. Recorders benefit from being familiar with the content of ideas being discussed, and with professional jargon (even alphabet soup acronyms) used by the group they are serving. The recorder must depend on the meeting facilitator for sponsorship and support in carrying our her/his role. The facilitator must monitor the recorder's efforts, and break in as needed to check the spelling of a name or term, to clarify the meaning of an idea so that it can be accurately recorded, or to slow down discussion so that the recorder can catch up. Finally, it should be noted that contemporary electronic meeting technologies have contributed much to making recording easier and more accurate. Computers speed up the recording process, provide clearly readable recording, permit immediate correction and editing, and make it possible for participants to leave meetings with complete print outs of the meeting record in hand.

D. The Group Member

The role of the **group member** is often overlooked in discussing meetings and roles. It is the group members, however, who do the *primary* work of the meeting. Most of what the leader, facilitator, and recorder do is done to help the group members do the work of the meeting. Group members are the primary resources in a meeting; they are the sources of vision about the future, awareness of problems and issues, determination about goals, opinions about objectives and how to meet them, ideas about alternatives and solutions, and about refinements of ideas under discussion. Their job is to bring their wealth of information, creativity, and critical analysis to the tasks of the meeting for the benefit of one another and the organization.

Freed to do their work by the efforts of facilitators, recorders, and group leaders, group members can initiate ideas, listen to one another, elaborate on ideas, present information, and evaluate ideas. Members can also take time to pause from time to time to summarize, seek information and opinions of others, offer clarifications, or move toward compromise. To further nurture a wholesome meeting, members can share in providing gate keeping, harmonizing, testing for ground rules and group norms, and encouraging one another. If we genuinely value the intellectual capacity of group members to participate in a meeting, these are the things members do.

Now that we have described what group members can contribute to a meeting, it may be useful to recall what we said above about the purposes of meetings. Recall that we said "reporting and presenting information" is the least valid reason to conduct a meeting. When meetings are conducted primarily for this purpose, members are limited to listening and absorbing, or, as a colleague of mine once put it, "receiving a brain dump from the boss." Given that group members are a vital organizational resource with information, ideas, and evaluation of their own to contribute, such a limitation constitutes a serious waste of resources. And, given that information can usually be conveyed in other ways that consume less time, long periods of reporting in meetings generally constitute a serious waste of time.

5. Consensus is a Reasonable Goal of Any Meeting

"**Consensus**" is difficult to define, and more difficult to achieve. Consensus does not mean that a decision is unanimous. It means there is broad, general agreement among group members on a course of action, and strong support for that course of action. The problem of definition here is in the question: How much agreement is enough to constitute a consensus? The answer to the question is "It depends." It depends on the importance of the issue to the participants; it depends on how much the players are willing to invest in time, energy, and creativity; it depends on the urgency of the issue at hand; it depends on the stakes. I have seen meetings close with members satisfied that 80% in favor of a decision was as close to full agreement as they could get, and that, given what they had to invest, 80% was good enough to call it consensus. I have seen other groups stay with an issue relentlessly for hours because they felt that "on this important issue" nothing less than 100% would do.

Pursuit of consensus is relevant only when there are differences among the group members concerning issues on which agreement is desirable, i.e. when there is conflict. Thomas and Kilmann (1975 identified five basic approaches, or "styles" for managing conflict: *Avoidance, Accommodation, Competition, Compromise, and Collaboration*. Four of these five styles (80%) assume that a conflict is a kind of competition in which, for one party to win, the other must lose. Avoidance and accommodation allow the other party to win. Competition is an effort to win at the other party's expense. Compromise is a way of having neither party lose and neither party win by splitting the difference. Only collaboration represents a win-win strategy. Interestingly, Morton Deutsch, who coined the term "win-win," found in his research that 80% of conflicts can be resolved with win-win solutions.

Why are we so focused on competing to win at one another's expense when there is disagreement? Historically, the human race has been scripted by the battle field and the playing field to adopt strategies that involve strong positioning and combative methods based on the belief that for me to win, you must lose. This point will be discussed further in Chapter 11. My purpose here is to point out how this preconditioning prevents pursuit of consensus. When my winning requires your losing, consensus is not a possibility. For pursuit of consensus to become a general pattern, humans will have to do a lot of unlearning. The metaphors of combat and competition are firmly established in ways of doing business.

In my view, consensus is about arriving at win-win, collaborative resolutions to differences. And, we are babes in the woods when it comes to practicing collaborative processes in meetings. The reasons are twofold: (1) To the extent that we have been scripted by centuries of practice to enter the problem solving arena with opinion, points of view, and commitment to a position, we are scripted to not find consensus. (2) We are only beginning to find the tools for participating in a win-win collaborative process, and we have a lot more to find. Morris Massey, Ph.D. (*What You Are is Where You See*) makes a strong case for the importance of people setting aside their preconditioning on an issue long enough to define the needs of the various parties in an issue. He argues that we must learn to check preconditioning, points of view, positions, and above all, posturing at the door at least long enough to learn about the needs of others in the process. Massey then gives a formula for reaching win-win consensus conclusions. "RISE," he says. Get high enough above the issue to see all the alternatives from your viewing point. He then turns **RISE** into an acronym:

> **Relax.** Let go of the tension that goes with positioning.
> **Insulate** against preconceptions and points of view.
> **Sense** the mood of the environment and the others around you.
> **Empathize** with the needs (not the positions) that others have about the issue.

These admonitions make sense, but Massey offers little guidance on exactly how to accomplish them. I believe some of the important work of the twenty-first century will be to develop methods for accomplishing these four steps, and to strengthen our permission to use them. Our combat scripts are deeply rooted, and they are antithetical to building consensus. Consensus tools rub against the grain of the very principles on which many of our institutions are founded.

How stuck in traditional combative approaches are we? Consider an example. A colleague and I were contracted to facilitate a series of meetings with a group of well intentioned public service executives who held sharply differing points of view on a complex web of key issues. All of the members of the group had been appointed to their positions by the state governor. They had set this series of meetings and hired professional facilitators because they sincerely wanted to find consensus on their major points of difference. The first meeting was characterized by tight jaws, clinched fists, rattling vocal cords, and posturing. At the beginning of the second meeting, everyone in the room joined the consensus on one point: "We all have to agree that nobody can walk away from here at the end of this process feeling like they got everything they wanted." If consensus means win-win, as I believe it does, they had achieved consensus on only one point - - that consensus is not possible. Stuck in their traditions of combat and compromise, they had defeated themselves before they began.

Is consensus a reasonable goal in any meeting? Certainly. And if participants are able to set aside their preconditioning, and pursue consensus, it can be achieved more often than not.

6. In any meeting, human factors abound; humans misbehave.

Even in meetings among highly educated professionals, humans continue to be human; and humans tend to misbehave. They engage in disruptive behaviors; they arrive late, leave early, gossip, whisper, attack, interrupt, drop out. The typical meeting will include its quota of doubting Thomas's, head shakers, loud mouths, interpreters, know-it-alls, back seat drivers, and teacher's pets. With computer mediated meetings come the additional misbehaviors of flaming, hacking, and eaves dropping.

To ensure useful meetings, it is necessary to deal effectively with such all too human misbehaviors. A framework that has served me well over the years is to assume that most disruptive behavior in meetings has one of three causes: (a) the disrupter didn't know the rules; (b) the disrupter feels powerless as a group member, or (c) the disrupter feels s/he has no defined role in the meeting. The solutions for these are straightforward:

Cause of Disruptive Behavior	Solution
a. Doesn't know the rules	Give him/her the rules
b. Feels powerless	Empower her/him
c. Has no role	Assign him/her a role

This framework has helped me deal effectively with most of the disruptive behavior that occurs in meetings. Occasionally, disruptive behavior results from some other underlying condition, such as fear of making a mistake, fear of losing power, or fear of not being noticed. There are no complete or perfect solutions to the problem of human disruptive behavior.

A challenge directly ahead will be learning how to deal with the extra layer of detachment that occurs among group members in computer mediated meetings. Computer mediated communication provides a kind of anonymity that does not occur in face to face settings. Anonymity, combined with unworthy intentions, or with any of the causes of misbehavior mentioned above, can be a dangerous mix. It will take more than facilitation to address the potential manipulation of cyber meetings. (See Chapter 17 for further discussion of this issue.)

7. Silent writing produces the best ideas.

Some of the most useful research done to build a technology on the conduct of meetings is the work of Andre Delbecq. His experimentation with a wide range of groups produced three primary findings, and a list of secondary findings illuminating group process, and identifying ways to make meetings work best (Delbecq, Ven de Ven, and Gustaphson, 1986). I want to focus here on the first of the three primary findings, a finding that has served particularly well in groups with which I have worked over the years. It is a finding that provokes doubt and skepticism when it is described, but which quickly converts skeptics when experienced. Experimenting with a variety of ways in which people can work together to generate ideas, Delbecq found that open, interactive "brainstorming" by a group is only second best. More and better ideas are produced by a group of people who sit together in the same room and write ideas silently.

Delbecq's demonstration of the value of silent writing surprises professionals like me who have long been convinced of the value of open, interactive group process tools. Delbecq was careful to note that this finding is a very narrow one, applying only to the process of generating ideas to consider. No one has fully explained why silent writing works better for generating ideas, but some reasons are evident. **Silent writing** allows people to express themselves without being influenced by formal or informal power dynamics in their group, thus avoiding the group and self censorship symptoms of groupthink (Janis, 1967). It also appears that in silent writing, individuals who think and speak more slowly than others have more opportunity to express their ideas than they would have in interactive brainstorming. Also, in interactive brainstorming, when a particularly attractive idea is expressed, there is a tendency for other group members to similar suggest ideas; silent writing prevents this pattern, promoting a broader variety of ideas.

Silent writing of ideas is the first step in a six step group problem-solving process called Nominal Group Technique (NGT) developed by Delbecq and Andrew Van de Ven (1975). Nominal Group Technique is described more fully in Chapter 9. Modifications to NGT include the Crawford Slip technique which assures confidentiality in the reporting of ideas to the group. At the University of Arizona, where extensive research on the technology of cyber meetings is underway, NGT has been computerized so that silent writing can be accomplished, and ideas then anonymously reported to the group using interactive computers (Vogel, personal communication, 1996). Contexts, specific techniques, and media will change over time, but the underlying principle that silent writing of ideas works best will remain useful in meetings.

8. Open interaction produces the best conclusions.

Once ideas are generated and reported to the group as a whole, interactive discussion is the best means for people to examine, explore, learn from one another, and select the best ideas. This was the second of Delbecq's primary findings. Open interaction allows ideas to be clarified, narrowed, and finally ranked, so that decisions can be made. Open discussion is also the method of evaluating ideas that is most likely to lead to consensus.

9. Voting can either interfere with consensus, or help identify consensus, depending on how it is done.

Delbecq's third primary finding was that in any democratic decision making process where decisions are made by voting, a single round of voting tends to produce nonconsensus decisions which tend later to be viewed as mistakes. When he experimented with adding a second round of voting, with an open discussion period in between, he found that in the second round, members benefitted immensely from examining and discussing the outcome of the first round of voting.

The traditional voting process in which votes are cast for or against a proposed idea is based on the metaphor of competition we discussed above. "For/against" voting always leads to a majority of "winners" and a minority of "losers," a divisive condition which prevents consensus. Delbecq found that by employing a numerical voting process in which members "vote" by awarding points to proposed ideas to indicate their relative merit, the divisiveness of "for/against" voting could be avoided. I have been continually amazed over the years at how often consensus is clearly identified in a group by a second round of voting, using a numerical voting process. Typically, there is nearly 100% consensus on the merit of the two or three ideas receiving the highest voting point totals. Done manually, casting and tabulating numerical votes can be tedious and time consuming; done using interactive computers, however, it is almost instantaneous.

10. Warm openings contribute to productive closings.

One of Delbecq's secondary findings that I have found particularly helpful is this: the level of productivity of a group is measurably higher when, at the beginning of their process, they are greeted with warmth. The principle is straight forward. It seems obvious to some, but it is often not practiced. When a group plunges into the work of a meeting without first warmly greeting one another, it is at increased risk of failing the reach necessary decisions, and of failing to achieve consensus. I have noticed that in teleconferences or computer assisted meetings there appears to be an increased tendency to skip the kinds of warm greetings that occur in face to face meetings. So, I suggest that greater attention be given to **warm openings** in non face-to-face meetings.

A Checklist of Things to Consider in Facilitating a Meeting

1. **Agenda:** Is there a process for building one? What will ensure the agenda meets all its purposes? Will the group members own it? Can I attribute one of the five purposes for a meeting to each item on the agenda?
2. **Process:** Does the agenda identify processes for handling items?
3. **Facilities & Equipment:** Has a suitable meeting room been reserved? What equipment is needed? Has needed equipment been acquired for the meeting?
4. **Roles:** Are the roles (leader, facilitator, recorder, member) clearly assigned and properly distributed?
5. **Consensus:** What does consensus really mean for this group in this meeting? Has the meeting sponsor (leader) committed to the time, energy, and creativity required to achieve genuine consensus? Do we have the tools to achieve consensus in this meeting?
6. **Human Factors:** Do I have the tools to address behavior problems when they occur? Has the meeting sponsor (leader) legitimized my use of interventions to address behavior problems?
7. **Silent Writing:** Have we designed the meeting process to take advantage of the value of silent writing to generate ideas?
8. **Open Interaction:** Have we provided for open discussion at the right times? Does our process ensure that the ideas people want to express will be heard?
9. **A Vote for Consensus:** Have we provided for two rounds of voting on issues, with open discussion in between? Have we provided for numerical voting so that consensus can be identified, and divisiveness avoided?
10. **Warmth:** No matter how "urgent" your feel at the opening, put task aside long enough to lay the foundation for people being warmly welcomed first.

Summary

In this chapter we have discussed ten principles which should govern the conduct of meetings, and described how they can be applied to ensure that they are efficient and productive. We have pointed out the important contributions to the technology of meetings provided by Doyle and Straus, Morris Massey, and Andre Delbecq which relate to these principles. The checklist below should serve as a reminder concerning the keys points in these principles and their application.

For more about how to conduct useful meetings, see:

Clyde Burleson, *Effective Meetings* (1990). New York: John Wiley & Sons.

Doyle and Straus, *Making Meetings Work* (1976). New York: Playboy Books.

Gerald Wilson, *Groups in Context, 4th ed.* (1996). New York: McGraw-Hill, Inc.

References

Deal, Terrence, and Kennedy, Allen, *Corporate Cultures: the Rites and Rituals of Corporate Life* (1982). Reading, Mass: Addison-Wesley.

Delbecq, Andre, and Ven de Ven, Andrew, and Gustaphson, David H., Group Techniques for Program Planning: A Guide to Nominal *Group Techniques and Delphi Process, 2nd ed.* (1986). Glenview, Illinois: Scott, Foresman.

Doyle, Michael and Straus, Robert, *Making Meetings Work* (1976). New York: Playboy Book Publishers.

Janis, Irving, *Victims of Groupthink* (1972). Boston: Houghton-Mifflin.

Kilmann, R., and Thomas, K., "Interpersonal conflict handling behavior as reflections of Jungian personality dimensions," *Psychological Reports 37,* (1975), 971-980.

Massey, Morris. *What You Are is Where You See.* [CBS Fox (TM) Video].

Parker, Glenn M., *Team Players and Teamwork: The New Competitive Business Strategy* (1990). San Francisco: Josey-Bass Publishers.

Pavitt, charles, and Curtis, Ellen, *Small Group Discussion: A Theoretical Approach (2nd ed.)* (1994). Scottsdale, AZ: Gorsuch Scarisbrick, Publishers, 134-175.

A central communication function that occurs in meetings is cooperative decision-making. Understanding the processes by which small groups of organization members make decisions is essential for members who wish to exercise influence in organizations.

Virginia Kidd (Ph.D., Speech Communication, University of Minnesota) has taught small group decision-making for twenty twenty-five years and has served as consultant to a variety of public and private organizations. She is the author of *Coptalk: Essential Communication Skills for Community Policing.* In Chapter 9, she explains the processes of small group interaction and principles of group decision-making.

Making Group Decisions

Virginia V. Kidd
California State University, Sacramento

Key Terms

group communication
decision-making groups
task dimension
social dimension
cohesiveness
norms
ad hoc groups
groupthink
primary tension
fantasy themes
roles

orientation
forming
conflict
storming
emergence
norming
reinforcement
performing
reflective thinking
brainstorming
teleconference

Nominal Group Technique
nominal question
buzz group
consensus
majority vote
negotiation
decision emergence
asynchronous meetings
synchronous meetings
audio conference
video conference

Objectives

This chapter provides students with knowledge of the basic skills needed to make decisions effectively in organizational work groups. After reading this chapter, students should be able to:

1. Identify the elements of small group communication.
2. Describe the four phases of group development and deliberation.
3. Explain Dewey's Reflective Thinking process for group decision-making.
4. Describe Brainstorming and Nominal Group Technique.
5. Identify four procedures to reaching group decisions: voting, negotiation, consensus, and decision emergence.
6. Point out eight ways to improve one's skills in group communication.

What's the difference between, on the one hand, eggs, sugar, flour and butter, and on the other hand, a cake? The answer is, what they can do together. It's a nice metaphor for working in groups. A cake is a lot more appetizing than a raw egg.

Unfortunately, when someone says "group work," most of us don't immediately think "a piece of cake." This may be because we have an idyllic view of what group decision making ought to be, and grow frustrated when reality does not match it. Like the ingredients in a cake, a group does not proceed directly from butter and cream to dessert. It has to go through the mixing and baking steps. And it helps to have the right ingredients.

Task-Oriented Small Groups

The term "group" is used informally to mean anything from three people discussing issues over coffee to representatives from various agencies getting together in conglomerations of thirty or thirty-five. In organizations, however, **group communication** means *structured groups of people who have a decision to make together, a task to accomplish together, or a problem to solve*. Group members are *interdependent*; they must work together in order to make sound decisions.

In today's environment, it is impossible to escape group work. Whether you participate in a standing committee, a staff meeting, an ad hoc group, a Total Quality Management team, a board of directors or a jury, you will be doing group work. One current estimate holds that "if you work in a corporate setting, you may spend over three hours a week in formally scheduled meetings and another nine and a half hours in informal meetings. The numbers go up as you assume more organizational responsibility" (Ross 1). And the trend is that the hours will increase: "The emphasis on teams and teamwork is increasing rapidly in the United States. It's a sort of teamwork revolution . . ." (Lumsden and Lumsden 11). One 1993 survey found that "Federal Express has over 4,000 employee teams; Motorola has over 2,200 problem-solving teams, Cadillac has over 60 percent of its work force working in teams; and Xerox has over 75 percent of its work force working in teams" (Blackburn & Rosen, qtd. in Tubbs 10). Knowing how to work efficiently in such groups is essential.

Elements of Small Group Communication

Purpose

Groups meet for various reasons. Most research on groups by communication scholars has focused on task-oriented, decision-making groups. Groups that do not make decisions also exist, however, and research scholars are beginning to give them more attention. Very likely you are in such groups. They might be informal gatherings such as study groups or social alliances; interest groups like clubs or computer-user networks; active groups like sports teams, bands, theater casts, video production crews, hospice volunteers; support groups such as Alcoholic Anonymous or Al-Anon or weight control groups; psychological encounter groups; religious groups; even families. All of these involve dimensions of the group process. However, they differ from **decision-making groups** in that generally individuals do not have to reason together to reach a common conclusion.

Size

Research has shown that the optimum number for task-oriented decision-making groups is five to seven people (Bormann, *Small Group* 2). This provides a group with enough people to do the work and to offer a variety of perspectives, but at the same time is small enough for everyone to voice an opinion or share an idea. If the group gets much bigger than this, cliques start to form, and when the number reaches thirteen, five to seven people really discuss the issues and the rest become quiet (Bormann, *Small Group* 2). Sometimes when people say they don't like working in groups, their experience has been with groups that are too large.

Dimensions of Communication

Every group meeting operates at two levels simultaneously. One is obvious: the **task dimension.** This loosely translates into what business items are on the agenda, what the group needs to get done. To many people, the task dimension is all the group is about, and they grow impatient with the inability of a group to "stick to business." They want a group meeting to proceed in a linear fashion: to address the issues before it, make decisions, plan actions, and then, adjourn.

What task-oriented people ignore is that every meeting also has a **social dimension.** Scholars also call this the *relational dimension* (Wilson and Hanna 21), the *climate* (Beebe, Barge and McCormick 10), or *group maintenance* (Wheelen 32). The social dimension refers to the interaction between group members, their perceptions of one another, how well they like or dislike one another, how much they enjoy their time together, how attracted they are to one another, how much—or how little—status they feel they have, whether they look forward to group meetings or dread them, how they feel they are treated in the meetings, and so on. This is the dimension in which a person's value as an individual is acknowledged. Ernest Bormann used a computer metaphor to explain it:

Five carefully programmed computers, their memory storage filled with information, can be connected with one another so that information is fed back and forth among them. This information can be processed and its output transferred to another machine. . . . The computers in this small group can be programmed so they are completely task oriented. Such a group has no social dimension. One of the computers will not short circuit communication because he feels a loss of status within the group, nor will one computer resist instructions transferred from another because it dislikes the attitude of that computer. (Bormann *Discussion* 138)

Human beings, however, will. How individuals treat one another very much affects how willingly they communicate and by what process they do so. Clearly this subsequently makes a difference in the quality of the decisions the group makes and the actions it takes. The social dimension, consequently, is vitally important. A group in a class I taught, for example, discovered in casual interchange that they had much in common: Jose went to high school in the town where Laurie's grandparents lived; Cassie's cousin was good friends with Bill's brother; Willie used to go to summer basketball camp at Laurie's high school. None of these was earth-shaking, nor did any reflect on the group's work topic. However, the commonalities created a warmth between group members that made conversation easy. They became one of the most successful groups in class. Unfortunately, too often the social dimension is neglected or even deliberately repressed. People fear it will detract from the group's work.

Acknowledging the social dimension does not mean people can vary from the agenda at will, or expose the entire group to all the photos of the family in grass skirts at the luau on the Hawaiian beach. It means valuing the casual chit-chat before and after meetings, appreciating the value in occasional quips or stories that release tension in the group, and noticing the particular ways in which ideas are voiced when people discuss issues. Careful wording, attentive listening, and thoughtful consideration of other group members' ideas make considerable difference in the social dimension.

Norms

Every group operates according to certain shared expectations about what is appropriate—or NORMAL—to do in a group meeting. These expectations reflect standards for both task accomplishment and social interaction. In time group members expect these behaviors, and that expectation becomes part of the group dynamics.

If you think back over groups you have been in, you can probably recognize some group norms. If you arrived late, did people frown or did they pull up a chair and welcome you? If you interrupted someone, were you chided or did the speaker stop talking? Did people frequently talk over one another? Did you eat at your meetings? Could you use expletives or tell knock-knock jokes? If you showed up unprepared or missed a meeting or failed to return a phone call, what happened? If you think about what you consider appropriate behavior in a church setting versus appropriate behavior at a basketball game, you are identifying norms.

Groups that will meet only once or twice such as **ad hoc** groups-groups established to accomplish one task and then disband after one or two meetings-frequently follow the standard norms of social etiquette of the larger society rather than working out their own norms. In groups that will meet for longer time periods, however, such as standing committees or even class project groups, each group develops its own individual patterns. These norms are often implicit-not stated directly; nonetheless, they govern group action.

Norms are informally negotiated within a group and reflect the values of those in the group. In my own department of Communication Studies, for example, many professors were formerly college debaters. We have faith in the value of open expression of ideas, in the power of reasoned discussion to lead a group to strong decisions. Our meetings, therefore, are regularly marked by vigorous argument, often culminating in unanimous decisions. When outsiders remark on the conflict that goes on in our meetings, we have been known to respond with surprise. "What conflict?" we will say, not regarding our arguments as any kind of negative conflict. They are simply our normal way of proceeding effectively.

Norms begin being set from the moment a group first gets together. First meetings are particularly important in the process since what seems to work at that meeting is often followed in subsequent meetings. A wise teacher, for example, who wants class participation will spend time the first day asking students questions as he or she calls roll. This sets a norm that students may speak in class. In class project groups, if no one expresses disappointment the first time someone fails to carry through on an assignment, it is likely that others will subsequently fail to do their work. A norm has been set that it is okay to slack off on work.

Often group norms reflect the larger organization in which the group operates. To illustrate, university class groups are generally influenced by the length of class periods, the general rules for appropriate classroom conduct, the common pressures of time, and the standard ability level that group members bring to the class. As well, norms reflect the cultures of individuals in the group. For example, a norm of politeness turns on what a person considers polite. Is it polite to be casual and friendly or formal and respectful? In an increasingly multi-cultural world, basic standards are increasingly difficult to determine.

When someone does not conform to established group **norms,** group members react, tending to evaluate the violator negatively and possibly to engage in some kind enforcement behavior to encourage conformity to norms. Enforcement can range from mild teasing to direct confrontation, depending on the strength of the norms and severity of the violation.

One easy way to identify a norm is to note the reaction when it is broken. In one class I taught, at one point the class engaged in a general discussion. One young woman voiced an opinion. Another said to her, "Oh, you aren't going to talk about that dumb idea, are you?" The class was suddenly very quiet. Students calling one another's ideas dumb was not a class norm they appreciated. The young woman instantly realized her mistake and explained: "It's all right. She's my sister." The class laughed and relaxed. Apparently students in the class felt comfortable speaking much more directly to siblings, or at least understood that they were observing a family norm, not a group norm.

Roles

As people interact in groups, they generally repeat certain communication behaviors, establishing patterns. After a few meetings, other group members expect these behaviors of them. For example, at the first meeting group members feel shy. People don't know each other. Takasha is very outgoing and makes a joke that gets people laughing. At the next meeting, discussion gets a little tense. Takasha makes an off-hand remark that starts the group smiling. The next time the group has a problem, people will expect similar from Takasha. Such behaviors are called **roles.**

In 1948, Benne and Sheats compiled the findings of over 50 studies about roles people contributed in groups. Their seminal report still stands as the description of group roles. Understanding that such roles exist in groups is useful because the center of much unspoken conflict in groups comes from competition for high status roles. Benne and Sheats divided roles into three patterns: task-related roles, group-maintenance roles, and self-centered (negative) roles. Among the functions that people contribute in the task area are such behaviors as initiating discussion, orienting and energizing the group, seeking information or opinions, supplying information or opinions, elaborating, clarifying, evaluating, summarizing, coordinating ideas, testing for procedure, coordinating procedure, and keeping records. In the maintenance area, people manage the conversational flow, encourage members, harmonize when differences exist, relieve tension by joking or telling stories, express solidarity, and set standards for the group process. Often such roles are combined, resulting in roles such as leader.

The self-centered roles are ones you have undoubtedly encountered before: dominators, who talk much too much; blockers, who are negative about every idea; recognition seekers, who tie every discussion to themselves; withdrawers, who won't participate if they don't get their way or who simply vanish from the group; special interest pleaders, who are interested primarily in their own cause.

Cohesiveness

Cohesiveness refers to the *esprit de corps* of the group. Wilson and Hanna define it as "the degree to which the members of a group are attracted to one another and to the group" (204). Ellis and Fisher say it is "the ability of group members to get along, the feeling of loyalty, pride, and commitment of members toward the group. It would not be inaccurate to say that cohesiveness is more than anything else, the degree of liking that members have for one another" (23). An early definition offered by Cartwright and Zander was simple and to the point: "Group cohesiveness refers to the degree to which the members of a group desire to remain in the group" (91). It generally encompasses group loyalty, the feeling of belonging to the group and the willingness to work for its good.

Groups can potentially succeed without a cohesive bond. However, one reason to work in groups is for the pleasure of group interaction. Such pleasure is vastly enhanced in cohesive groups. In addition, Ellis and Fisher point out that the more a group "raises its level of cohesiveness, the more likely it is to raise its level of productivity. Conversely, the more productive the group the greater the likelihood that it will be more cohesive" (24). They warn, however, that this relationship "breaks down toward the upper end of the two continuums" (24), possibly because a cohesive, productive group may have been together so long it has lost sight of its original goal.

What makes groups cohesive? According to Renz and Greg, groups are more likely to be cohesive if members joined voluntarily, communicate freely, receive equal treatment, participate in decision making, have established clear roles, have a clear goal and achieve an early success. Baird and Weinberg say that groups with long common histories, whose members participate and enjoy activities together, and who have democratic leadership tend to become more cohesive. They point out that large groups have difficulty bonding. And they add that groups held in high esteem by society are groups which members want to be part of (Baird and Weinberg 190-191).

Groupthink

Cohesiveness can strengthen a group. However, blind cohesiveness to the point of conformity to the wrong norms can silence needed difference of opinion. Irving Janis terms this "**groupthink.**" In this condition, needed critical thinking is stifled, often leading a group to make decisions which turn out to be poor. Voicing opinions contrary to the majority view is seen as a violation of norms. Johnson and Hackman sum up the problems: "Groups that suffer from this syndrome fail to: consider all the alternatives, weigh the risks of their choices, work out contingency plans or discuss important ethical issues. In sum, these groups are ineffective creative problem solving teams" (143).

Janis described several symptoms of groupthink. First, group members overestimate the quality of the group; they believe they can do no wrong, operating out of their own illusion that they are invulnerable. Second, if group members do encounter any information contrary to their position or any indications that their decisions may be inadequate, they construct rationalizations to dismiss the feedback. Third, either the group pressures all members to conform, or group members who have reservations simply do not express them. Fourth, group members stereotype those who oppose them as weak, evil or stupid, thus once again justifying the dismissal of contradictory evidence.

Conditions that can lead to groupthink include moderate to strong cohesiveness, having no contradictory opinions or information, lack of impartial leadership, and lack of norms or rules about procedures for making fact-based decisions.

Fantasy Themes

Group discussions often get off task. The group is trying to plan an advertising campaign for glow-in-the-dark cat litter, and Andrea starts talking about when she was a girl and her parents took the family on a road trip to Yellowstone Park. It was a long trip, but they had a lot of laughs. This sparks Shane's hilarious tale of running out of gas twenty miles outside of Tonopah, Nevada, at midnight. Then the group recalls car games. Is this bad group work? Not necessarily.

Fantasy themes are stories, or references to stories, told in groups. Sometimes listeners respond eagerly; sometimes they return quickly to the task. Such stories serve many functions. First, they help people get to know one another in the social arena. Second, when a group laughs together or finds common ground, they are more likely to be cohesive. Third, such stories are often "breaks" in word form, letting tempers cool down or ideas flourish or simply letting minds rest. Fourth, sometimes fantasy themes have hidden meanings, not realized at the time even by those telling them. They convey values. Later, individuals look back and see implications in what was said. For example, this group could indirectly be saying they want to have fun on the long trip to solving their problem. Typically, the more involved group members get in a story, the more it reflects group values. Finally, sometimes group tensions are resolved indirectly through what is said in stories.

Phases of Group Deliberation

Primary Tension

When you meet with a group of people for the first time, you experience something Ernest Bormann labeled **primary tension** (*Small Group* 132-135). You don't know one another, don't know what's okay to do and what isn't, do not yet understand the group norms, are uncertain whether, if you crack a joke, the group will laugh or look at one another and roll their eyes. Will you be seen as a comic or as an irritant? In the uncertainty, most people opt for politeness. They are quiet, shy, careful. They sit up straight, wait their turn to speak, stop immediately if someone else starts. On video tapes of primary tension, with the sound off, members look very apathetic. Viewers might think they are bored. They are not. They are very aware of what's going on and are cautiously feeling out the group trying to determine its norms.

Orientation

Primary tension expands into the first phase of group development. Different researchers give this phase different names, but their descriptions of what happens here are relatively similar. B. Aubrey Fisher calls the first phase **orientation** (Ellis and Fisher 157). He describes it as a process of internally forming opinions about group goals and members. Bruce Tuckman calls this first phase **forming** (396). Tuckman's seminal work examines 50 articles which described different stages in groups. He compresses these to produce a common frame. He says that during forming the group clarifies its task, attempts to determine what behaviors are approved of or frowned upon, and through nonverbal communication explores how each member will fit into the group.

Fisher speaks particularly about the kind of communication that goes on in this phase. Participants are uncertain about the norms, and so comments are offered tentatively and statements are ambiguous. Because issues are so vague, people find it easy to agree with one another, and thus conflict is avoided. This is not because conflict does not exist. It is because the group is very inhibited. Everyone is nice and careful. After a while, however, the honeymoon is over.

Conflict

The second phase is one of the reasons people don't like working in groups. You have come up with a great idea, a perfect solution, and when you present it to the group, people have the effrontery to disagree.

In this phase, people are getting down to work. They are clear now on what the task is, what the general operating rules of the group will be, and what the issues are. More confident of themselves, they take positions on the issues that have been identified. Disagreement follows. The ambiguity is gone and firm comments replace them. People have grown fed up the "over niceness" of orientation, and they blast their way out of it into what Fisher calls **conflict** (Ellis and Fisher 158).

Tuckman calls this **storming** (396). He sees struggle occurring on two levels. At the task level, group members become aware of inconsistencies between the group goals and their personal motives. On the social level, they reassert the individuality they abandoned by their overly-polite behavior. They may rebel against group norms and group structure.

The good news is that this is just a normal phase of decision-making. Nothing is wrong with the group. In fact, disagreement leads to stronger decisions, to well-thought-out conclusions, and it prevents the blind conformity known as groupthink. Productive conflict is characterized by critical evaluation of ideas—not evaluation of people. Members understand their common group goals, their different points of view, and tend to remain flexible. This can generate new ideas and lead to better decisions.

Problems occur when conflict becomes dysfunctional. This happens when group members begin to evaluate one another; display very rigid attitudes; and show concern only for themselves, not for the group. They feel hurt when their ideas are rejected, as if they themselves have been put down. Interestingly, the group can also experience dysfunctional conflict when group members pretend nothing is wrong and suppress their own opinions in the name of group "cohesion." But the group is not cohesive at all. In cohesive groups, members feel free to express differences; here group members are hiding their true ideas and values. Without open discussion of ideas and problems, no truly examined solution can emerge.

In this phase of group development, many students deeply regret ever having taken a class involving group work, and people working in groups within organizations or in the community gnash their teeth and wonder what imbecile appointed the lunatics on their committee. Everyone despairs of ever achieving success.

Emergence

And then, the miracle occurs: the group hits upon a solution. Fisher calls this emergence (Ellis and Fisher 158-160) and notes that in this phase, dissent lessens and ambiguity reappears, allowing people in conflict to change their positions without losing face in order to unite. Tuckman calls this **norming** (396). He says that groups sometimes develop standards by which they will reach their decisions as a precursor to this phase. They may develop a new set of norms. Within the social dimension, harmony blossoms again. Frequently groups feel closer than they ever have, displaying the strength of those who have listened to one another's differing opinions, survived conflict, and are still willing to work together.

Reinforcement

The final phase of the decision making process is reinforcement (Ellis and Fisher 160-161). Decisions which emerged ambiguously in phase three are now stated clearly, and members spend their time providing reasons for accepting the decisions. Dissent disappears, agreement abounds, and unity develops as members become committed to their decision. Maintaining his rhyming scheme as well as he can, Tuckman calls this phase **performing** (396). At the task level a specific decision or solution emerges and at the social level, members become comfortable with the contributions they are making.

Agendas for Decision Making

A number of techniques help group members move through various stages of the group process. Each achieves a different purpose. The most widely accepted have been around for many years and have survived the test of time.

Reflective Thinking

Still recognized as one of the best agenda formats for problem solving or logical decision making is **reflective thinking,** advanced by John Dewey in 1910 in his book *How We Think.* Dewey says reasoning about an issue should proceed through systematic steps. Before choosing a solution, the group makes sure it is thoroughly clear about the issue before it. The problem under consideration is defined thoroughly, and factual data about issues relevant to the problem are gathered and brought before the group. Only when the problem is thoroughly understood are possible solutions considered. The strengths and weaknesses of potential solutions are then weighed against one another. Out of this careful procedure, the best solution is selected. Steps to putting the solution in place are designated by the group and follow-up plans laid out.

Reflective thinking is a very logical procedure for ensuring open, fair, logical decision making. To engage in reflective thinking follow these procedures:

REFLECTIVE THINKING

1. Analyze the problem (including definition of terms and establishing group goals)
2. List possible solutions
3. Weigh alternative solutions
4. Select the best solution
5. Take steps to implement the solution.

Reflective thinking is essentially a guide for discussing an issue. It requires little more than sticking to the agenda and proceeding systematically. That, however, is easier said than done. Creativity does not always flow in prescribed patterns and group members often discover ideas out of sequence. The best adaptation to make in such conditions is to record the ideas as they emerge, proceeding logically to discuss them as the group gets to them on the agenda.

Brainstorming

Brainstorming is a technique developed by advertising executive Alex Osborn and explained in his book *Applied Imagination*. Since its description in 1953 it has been so widely accepted that today **"brainstorming,"** used informally, just means thinking up ideas. Its formal procedure, however, follows basic rules that enhance its application.

The person using brainstorming forms a "brainstorming pool" for the issue under consideration. Osborn says the optimal size is about a dozen people of approximately the same rank. One of these facilitates to keep the group focused on the process and one records ideas. Of the others, five are directly involved in the problem and five are "guests," people who are aware of the kind of problem facing the group but who are not directly involved in it. Too many of the same people meeting over and over fall into predictable patterns; new people add variety, which spurs ideas.

Osborn suggests that about two days before the meeting, the facilitator provide group members with a one-page background memo about the problem to start them thinking. At the meeting, the facilitator presents the problem as simply as possible but in very specific terms. The facilitator then explains the procedures shown in the following boxes.

BRAINSTORMING GUIDELINES

1. Absolutely no criticism
2. The wilder the idea, the better
3. Build on others' ideas
4. Aim for quantity, not quality

BRAINSTORMING

1. Set a time aside and clearly designate it for brainstorming.
2. Designate a person to keep a list of the brainstormed ideas.
3. Explain the issue to be brainstormed.
4. All members of the group should call out ideas as they get them, operating in random order. No one should hesitate because an idea seems impractical or repetitious or obvious or outright stupid. The more, the merrier!
5. All group members must withhold judgment of ideas until another time. The purpose is to generate ideas, no matter how impractical they may later seem.
6. One person's ridiculous suggestion is another person's inspiration. Use every idea to help you generate more ideas. Combine ideas, modify ones already suggested, turn them around, add to them.
7. Quantity breeds quality. The more ideas you generate, the greater your chances of having generated the one you need!

Fundamental to these procedures is the absolute acceptance of any idea, the wilder the better. No evaluation is allowed at any time. This is generally the most difficult of all of Osborn's precepts to actually be true to. Evaluation is inherent in our society and we tend to immediately leap to "But we don't have the money" or "They'll never approve that." Such remarks absolutely must be prohibited. Negative feedback causes creativity to wither. Bizarre ideas generate other ideas, and among them may be the solution you seek.

Nominal Group Technique

NGT was developed in 1968 by Andre L. Delbecq and Andrew H. Van de Ven as a technique to blend the benefits of brainstorming with the advantages of quick decision making (Delbecq and Van de Ven). In this system a group of informed people are brought together to give their views on an issue. **Nominal Group Technique** is a tightly structured, facilitated process which produces a ranked list of ideas. The entire process can be completed in less than two hours, and the results usually reflect group consensus on the highest-ranked ideas.

In NGT group participants are seated around three sides of a table. The facilitator stands at the open side. Also at the open end is a chart pad for recording ideas. The participants are presented a single question (called the "nominal question"), then guided by the facilitator through six structured, time-limited steps.

In **Step 1,** participants brainstorm responses to the question silently, writing down responses as they think of them. Eight minutes are allowed for this step.

In **Step 2,** participants take turns reporting ideas to the group, one idea at a time, going around the table in "round robin" fashion. Each idea is recorded on chart paper as it is reported, and given an identifying number. The entire charted record of ideas is kept visible to all participants. Twenty minutes are allowed for this step.

In **Step 3,** the meaning of each idea is checked to ensure that there is no confusion or misunderstanding. Only *meaning* is discussed in this step; discussion of the *merits* of the ideas occurs later. Often ideas are combined when it is discovered that their meanings are closely similar. Twenty minutes are allowed for this step.

Step 4 establishes the level of group support for each idea prior to group discussion. In this step, a preliminary "vote" is taken, using a numerical point system (5 points for the best idea, 4 points for second best, etc.). Preliminary votes are tabulated, and scores are recorded on the chart paper, so that preliminary levels of support are visible to all (see Chapter 8 for an explanation of the advantages of preliminary voting). This step may take approximately ten minutes.

In **Step 5** participants explain their views and discuss the merits of the ideas. Sometimes additional combining of ideas occurs at this step. Discussion is limited to twenty minutes because Delbecq found that longer discussion produces very little additional change of views.

Finally in **Step 6,** a final "vote" is taken, following the same numerical voting procedure as Step 4. Votes are tabulated and recorded on chart paper. Results of the final vote often differ significantly from those of the preliminary vote, reflecting the impact of the discussion. Typically on the final vote, there is strong consensus support for the top-ranked two or three ideas. The final vote may take approximately ten minutes.

The NGT process is outlined below.

NOMINAL GROUP TECHNIQUE

1. Silent generation of ideas in writing   (8 minutes)
2. Round-robin recording of ideas   (20 minutes)
3. Serial discussion for clarification   (20 minutes)
4. Preliminary vote on item importance   ($\approx$10 minutes)
5. Discussion of the preliminary vote   (20 minutes)
6 .Final vote   ($\approx$10 minutes)

(Delbecq, Van de Ven, & Gustafson, 1975)

The creators of NGT acknowledge that the "mechanics of NGT become burdensome with a larger group. Satisfaction drops off as members have less opportunity to participate" (Delbecq, Van de Ven, Gustafson 69-70). They designate the ideal NGT group size as "from five to nine members. . . . A group made up of less than five members lacks resources in terms of the number of critical judgments available to analyze the problem and arrive at a decision. On the other hand, adding beyond ten members often does not increase group accuracy . . ." (Delbecq, Van de Ven, Gustafson 70).

NGT is used widely in business and public service agencies, in part because it "provides equality of participation among group members. In a less structured group, personality or status differences often sway the direction of group discussion" (Van Gundy 345). As well, research has shown that the NGT technique generates more ideas and ideas that are generally regarded as better than other techniques generate (Van Gundy 345). It has the disadvantage, however, of limiting genuine discussion of ideas and the potential of new solutions that come from a blending of divergent positions.

Buzz Groups

The **buzz group** technique encourages input rather than leading to decision making. It is often used in conjunction with a conference or a public speech. After hearing information on an issue, a large group is broken up into smaller groups where discussion can take place. These groups may brainstorm, use NGT, engage in reflective thinking or just ramble. By whatever process they use, however, they come to some conclusions. Each group then shares their conclusions with the large group. A variation of this is to put six people in each group and allow them six minutes to discuss. Named for the originator of the idea, Donald Phillips, it is called Phillips 66 (a pun on the Phillips 66 Petroleum Company well known in some parts of the country).

Procedures for Reaching Decisions

Once groups have gathered all their data, and they fully understand problems, they must reach some decision. This is accomplished in a variety of ways.

Consensus

Reaching consensus is often seen as ideal decision-making. As Wood and Phillips explain, "Consensus decisions reflect the views of all members and ideally have unanimous acquiescence and support" (52). At the very least, a consensus implies the decision is at least minimally acceptable to all group members. Such common agreement encourages group unity and creates a common front. It is especially valuable for standing groups that will go on meeting together over time. In order to reach consensus through discussion, group members tend to be cooperative and supportive. Confrontation is avoided. The assumptions that underlie consensus are that the good of the group is more important than individual goals and that everyone's ideas are equally valuable.

As affirming as that sounds, consensus has some disadvantages. In the interest of creating a climate in which consensus can be reached, people are careful about what they say. Talk is constrained. Individuals may tend to avoid even legitimate disagreements. This can lead to watered-down decisions or even groupthink. Almost always, decisions tend to be moderate.

Voting

An alternate to consensus is the majority vote. It is fast, the decision is clear, and the result is not necessarily moderate. Votes are frequently preceded by persuasive efforts and debate, often with some formal means of control such as parliamentary procedure so issues may have a fair hearing.

The problem with "yes/no" voting is obvious: it is divisive. Compromise is not part of the process. Voting produces losers who have no reason to be committed to the decision. As well, minority views can be ignored. Majority voting is useful when it is more important to reach a decision than to achieve harmony. With a large group, this is often almost the only way to reach a decision.

A variation on standard voting which **can** produce consensus is the procedure used in the Nominal Group Technique process. As mentioned above, each participant is asked to rank a limited number of items under consideration, usually five, in order of highest priority. Point counts are then assigned to rankings, so that a first-ranked vote may get five points; a second-ranked, four; a third-ranked, three and so on. As Oliver Cummings says, "Ranking ideas in this nonthreatening, private way makes possible the generation of a group judgment from each individual's judgments. This protects the anonymity of each individual of the group" (8). Individuals may see one of their more highly valued positions adopted, even if it is not their first choice. The divisiveness of standard yes-no voting is minimized through this process. As well, the NGT procedure itself restricts divisive discussion.

Negotiation

A third alternative that combines the best elements of consensus and voting is negotiating, in which group members strike a bargain rather than reaching a broad agreement that everyone endorses. This is an effort to achieve what is sometimes called a "win-win" decision in which a new solution allows competing goals to be achieved. Obviously negotiation involves much bargaining, many persuasive efforts, and some acceptance and adjustment to others' points of view.

Decision Emergence

Ernest Bormann studied groups without firm decision making processes to see what actually happened as they made decisions. He found what he labeled "decision emergence" (*Small Group* 245-251). Groups discussed alternatives, gradually eliminating the least favorable, providing reasons to choose one over another, until only one option remained. Often the choice made by the group was suggested as early as the first meeting. However, it could not be the group's choice until alternatives were considered and eliminated. One student in one of my classes described the process this way:

> When an idea or decision seemed right, we all became excited and it was adopted merely by expressions of excitement. Rarely was it specifically verbalized that we had made a decision. It was amazing how little conflict, or even need for compromise, resulted from our group decision-making processes.

This process works better for smaller groups than for larger ones. In this type of decision making, group members must present strong information and factual analysis during the process of discussion in order to reach solid conclusions.

Electronic Meetings

Various kinds of electronic meetings are increasingly available to groups. In **"asynchronous meetings"** group members are not all present at the same time. Typically, this means *bulletin boards* on the web. Group members post messages for one another related to specific issues. These are organized in "discussion threads." Such postings are useful for keeping group members updated on meetings, for discussing on-going issues and presenting various points of view, and for keeping a history of how ideas progress that new members can access. The weakness of such a system is the lack of direct interaction and the extremely linear nature of the process.

In **synchronous meetings,** group members are all present online together. A common version of synchronous meetings is the *chatroom.* All participants type their comments, which are viewed by all group members present. The group chat is very valuable for stying in touch when people are at a distance and for making simple decisions. However, complex issues are hard to discuss in a chat format. Using a chat room for a group meeting can be frustrating and limiting. People who cannot type fast are at a disadvantage. By the time you are ready to post your response to Marilyn, Robert has put up a message. Your message seems unrelated, as it is; it was intended to respond to the previous message. When participating in synchronous meetings, keep this advice in mind:

- Chat rooms are most useful when you have an agenda already set up and a limited, somewhat simple issue. Complex discussions are better in person or on electronic bulletin boards.
- Address your comments to people by name. Otherwise, the group can be confused about what your message is addressing.
- Avoid clever comments and jokes. They can be misinterpreted online when the nonverbal cues are missing.

Teleconferences include both video and audio (telephone). **Video conferences** allow group members to see one another while they are physically separated. Such conferencing is increasingly available, but it still involves enough production cost that such meetings should be judiciously considered and carefully designed. Members meeting via video—even when one group meets with another group-should remember that they are ALWAYS on camera. Never say or do anything you don't want heard or seen. Such meetings work best if they are prepared well in advance, with supporting material sent to all who will participate before the meeting time.

Audio conferences link group members by telephone. Such meetings via "conference calls" are very common, relatively inexpensive and efficient. However, unless participants know one another very well or their voices are very different, participants can become confused about who is speaking. Any audio conference should begin with a "hello" warm-up of pleasant discussion about some unrelated event such as the weather to allow participants to come to recognize one another's voice. Then, each person should state his or her name before speaking.

Improving Your Skills in Group Communication

Because group work inherently involves other people, you cannot improve your group skills as easily as you can improve your tennis swing. You can't go out and practice by yourself. What you can do, however, is rely on the principles of good communication whenever you are in a group situation and remember the group communication process.

1. Whenever possible, try to arrange for groups to be small, ideally five to seven. A large group is much more difficult to work in. Suggest sub-groups, small task groups, arrange for five to seven people to participate in projects.

2. Pay attention to the social dimension of the group process. Appreciate those who release tension, help others get along, and show an interest in other group members.

3. Help establish functional norms. Do your work thoroughly and on time, show appreciation to others who do the same, and treat people courteously.

4. Help other group members feel valued. Often this just means listening to everyone and making sure all points of view are heard.

5. Raise issues if you notice that everyone is agreeing. Don't let your group fall into groupthink.

6. Remember that some conflict is normal. Don't worry about your group if disagreement occurs. Express your own ideas directly and without rancor. In the conflict phase, remember to frame your arguments against ideas, not against people.

7. Suggest alternative agendas to achieve various goals. Brainstorming, NGT and buzz groups produce ideas; the reflective thinking pattern is a natural for solving problems.

8. Finally, use your best communication skills. Listen carefully, speak clearly, and remain flexible.

THE COMPETENT GROUP COMMUNICATOR

Group Task Competencies

1. *Define the problem:* Appropriately defines the problem that confronts the group.
2. *Analyze the problem:* Appropriately analyzes the problem that confronts the group.
3. *Identify criteria:* Appropriately participates in the establishment of the group goal and identifies criteria for assessing the quality of the group outcome.
4. *Generate solutions:* Appropriately identifies solutions or alternatives to solve the problem that the group is seeking to solve.
5. *Evaluate solutions:* Appropriately evaluates the solutions or alternatives identified by group members.
6. *Maintain task focus:* Appropriately helps the group stay on the group task, issue or agenda item the group is discussing.

Group Relational Competencies

7. *Manage conflict:* Appropriately manages disagreements and conflict.
8. *Maintain climate:* Appropriately provides supportive comments to other group members.
9. *Manage interaction:* Appropriately manages interactions and invites others to participate.

General Problem-Solving Competence

10. *Problem-solving skill:* Uses appropriate and effective group communication problem solving skills.

(Beebe, Barge and McCormick 10)

For Further Reading

Cathcart, Robert S. and Larry A Samovar, eds. *Small Group Communication: A Reader.* 7th ed. Dubuque, Iowa: Wm. C. Brown, 1996. This edited text includes articles by different authors on a variety of group areas. It is very practically based, with many articles coming from business sources. Of particular interest are two articles on intercultural communication in groups, explaining how different ethnic groups follow different norms.

Ellis, Donald G. and B. Aubrey Fisher. *Small Group Decision Making.* 4th ed. New York: McGraw-Hill, 1994. A strong text on small group communication principles, this book clearly explains Fisher's theories about phases of group development and as well explains how roles develop, theories of leadership in groups, and issues around conflict.

Johnson, Craig E. and Michael Z. Hackman. *Creative Communication: Principles and Applications.* Prospect Heights, Ill.: Waveland, 1995. This book covers creativity, including a useful chapter on group techniques that can be used to enhance a group's creative output.

Klubnik, Joan P. and Penny F. Greenwood. *The Team-Based Problem Solver.* New York: Irwin, 1994. The material focuses on specific techniques for addressing problems. It comes with a P.C. disk that includes various written forms groups can use to coordinate their activity.

Larson, Carl E. and Frank M. J. LaFasto. *Team Work: What Must Go Right/What Can Go Wrong.* Newbury Park, CA: Sage, 1989. In this short book, the authors report the results of their interviews with some of the most successful teams in the U.S. and pull out ten elements that they say make teams successful.

Parker, Glenn M. *Team Players and Teamwork.* San Francisco, Jossey-Bass, 1990. This book focuses heavily on the skills team members bring to a team and the roles that evolve from their skills. The author urges a balance of skills for effective teams.

Ross, Raymond S. *Small Groups in Organizational Settings.* Prentice Hall: Englewood Cliffs, NJ, 1989. Ross' text focuses, as its title implies, very specifically on small groups as they operate within larger organizations. Chapters focus on relational effectiveness, conflict, leadership, boards, and how to observe groups.

Tropman, John E. Making meetings work: Achieving High Quality Group Decisions. Thousand Oaks, CA: Sage, 1996. Tropman offers the results of his interviews with what he calls "master meeting managers." He provides a system drawn from their insights for how to plan and carry out effective meetings. Of particular interest is what he calls the "bell-shaped agenda," in which controversial items fall in the middle of the meetings and items that are only for discussion are scheduled at the meeting's conclusion so that the group leaves on a pleasant note.

References

Baird, J. E. Jr. and S. B. Weinberg. *Group Communication: The Essence of Synergy.* 2nd ed. Dubuque, Iowa: Wm. C. Brown, 1981.

Benne, Kenneth D., and Paul Sheats. "Functional Roles of Group Members." *Journal of Social Issues,* 4 (1948): 41–49.

Blackburn, Richard, and Benson Rosen. "Total Quality and Human Resource Management: Lessons Learned from Baldridge Award-Winning Companies." *Academy of Management Executive* 7 (1993): 49–66.

Bormann, E. G. *Discussion and Group Methods.* New York: Harper & Row, 1969.

_____ *Small Group Communication: Theory and Practice.* 3rd ed. New York: Harper & Row, 1990.

Beebe, S. A., J. K. Barge, and C. McCormick. "The Competent Group Communicator: Assessing Essential Competencies of Small Group Problem Solving." *Speech Communication Asso. Convention.* San Antonio, Nov. 1995.

Cartwright, D. and A. Zander. *Group Dynamics.* 3rd ed. New York: Harper & Row, 1968.

Cummings, Oliver W. "A Quick Look at the Nominal Group Technique." St. Charles, Ill: Arthur Andersen & Co. Center for Professional Education, 1987. ERIC ED 290788.

Delbecq, Andre L. and Andrew H. Van de Ven. "A Group Process Model for Problem Identification and Program Planning." *Journal of Applied Behavioral Science* 7 (1971): 466–492.

Delbecq, A. L., A. H. Van de Ven, and D. H. Gustafson. *Group Techniques for Program Planning: A Guide to Nominal Group and Delphi Processes*. Glenview, Ill.: Scott, Foresman, 1975.

Dewey, J. *How We Think*. Boston: D.C. Heath, 1910.

Ellis, D. G. and B A. Fisher. *Small Group Decision Making*. 4th ed. New York: McGraw-Hill, 1994.

Janis, I. L. *Victims of Groupthink*. Boston: Houghton Mifflin, 1982.

Johnson, C. E. and M. Z. Hackman. *Creative Communication: Principles and Applications*. Prospect Heights, Ill.: Waveland, 1995.

Lumsden, G. and D. Lumsden. *Communicating in Groups and Teams*. Belmont, Ca.:Wadsworth, 1993.

Osborn, A. *Applied Imagination*. New York: Charles Scribner's Sons, 1953.

Phillips, D. J. "Report on Discussion 66." *Adult Education Journal* 7 (1948): 181–182.

Renz, Mary Ann and John B. Greg. *Effective Small Group Communication in Theory and Practice*. Boston: Allyn and Bacon, 2000.

Ross, R. S. *Small Groups in Organizational Settings*. Prentice Hall: Englewood Cliffs, NJ, 1989.

Tubbs, Stewart L. *A Systems Approach to Small Group Interaction* 7th ed. Boston: McGraw-Hill, 2001.

Tuckman, B. W. "Developmental Sequence in Small Groups." *Psychological Bulletin* 63 (1965): 384–399.

Van Gundy, A. B. *Techniques of Structured Problem Solving*. 2nd ed. New York: Van Nostrand Reinhold, 1988.

Wilson, G. L. and M. S. Hanna. *Groups in Context*. 3rd ed. New York: McGraw-Hill, 1993.

Wheelen, S. A. *Group Process: A Developmental Perspective*. Boston: Allyn and Bacon, 1994.

Wood, J. T. and G. M. Phillips. "Teaching Groups Alternative Patterns of Decision Making." *Teaching How to Work in Groups*. Ed. Gerald M. Phillips. Norwood, N.J.: Ablex Publishing, 1990.

As organizational theory developed during the twentieth century, the importance of building and maintaining healthy, productive human relationships in organizational environments became clear.

Lawrence Chase (Ph.D., Communication, Bowling Green University) brings his experience researching and teaching interpersonal communication, as well as his experience as an organizational consultant and team developer to this subject. In Chapter 10, he outlines the primary factors affecting development and maintenance of productive relationships, organizational communication networks, and organizational team building.

Building Productive Relationships, Networks and Teams

Lawrence J. Chase
California State University, Sacramento

Key Terms

relationships
communication climate
supportive climate
interpersonal confirmation
collaboration
defensive climate
confirming responses
disconfirming responses
stages of relational growth
 and decay
contacting
independent flow

coordinating
collaborating
contrasting
circumscribing
constricting
recommended roles
 for supervisors
traditional roles for
 for supervisors
networks
information flow
life cycle of a team

sequential flow
reciprocal flow
team flow
opinion leader
liaison
isolate
gatekeeper
team building
Total Quality
 Management
self-directed teams

Objectives

This chapter describes how, through communication, productive relationships among coworkers working on teams are developed and maintained. In this chapter we:

1. Describe the communication characteristics of a productive organizational relationship.

2. Identify the stages of growth and decay in organizational relationships.
3. Explain and provide examples of confirming and disconfirming messages.
4. Describe communication networks, and discuss their impact on work relationships.
5. Discuss the importance of four types of communication flows within an organization.
6. Discuss four individual network communication roles, and describe the five phases of the team life cycle.
7. Describe two approaches to forming an effective work team.
8. Identify obstacles and key factors involved in successful team building.

Much of the daily work of managers and supervisors involves the development and maintenance of productive relationships among workers. This work is focused on building strong, efficient teams, and it is accomplished through communication.

In their *Harvard Business Review* article titled "Report cards on the MBA," Jenkins, Reizenstein and Rodgers (1984), asked Fortune 500 presidents about the business school graduates who had just joined their companies. Specifically, these researchers requested that the executives identify the areas in which their newly hired MBAs could improve. Of fourteen key attributes, the CEOs were *least* satisfied with the interpersonal skills of their new employees. Ranked second and third in need of attention were administrative and leadership skills, respectively. A more recent study echoes their findings. In a 2001 survey of 482 employers nationwide, the National Association of Colleges and Employers found that the "ideal job candidate knows how to communicate, interact, and work with others effectively" (Luckenbaugh, 2001).

How individuals develop productive working relationships, networks, and teams is the focus of this chapter. We begin by looking at communication in human relationships. We also discuss those factors which typically enhance interpersonal exchanges, such as communication climate and message structure. Next, we examine groups as communication networks. Specifically, we are interested in the effects of different networks upon leadership, problem solving, and group member satisfaction. Individual communication roles in networks are examined as well.

Finally, we look at the organizational unit as a team, and address some general strategies and specific tactics one can use to begin the process of team building, and discuss various obstacles to team building and other employee involvement efforts.

Relationships

A relationship is an ongoing interaction between two or more people in which each person has some stake in maintaining the association. We have relationships with persons in an organization whom we see and work with regularly. For these associations to thrive, attention must be paid to our interpersonal communication with colleagues.

Productive relationships in an organization are generally characterized by three communication factors: A supportive climate, interpersonal confirmation, and a high degree of collaboration. The communication climate sets the stage for effective relationship building. Confirmation deals with the interpersonal costs and rewards involved in interaction, and collaboration concerns the degree to which individuals are able to work together.

Climate

The communication climate, according to Gibb (1961), may be supportive, defensive, or both. A supportive communication climate encourages individuals to communicate in an open—or more open—manner, while a defensive climate tends to create barriers between people.

To establish a supportive climate, parties should focus on an accessible rather than closed-minded approach to problems. By describing rather than immediately evaluating a situation the possibilities for creative problem-solving are expanded. Both people should attempt to empathize, or see the problem from the other's perspective, before rendering a judgment. Finally, as Quincy Jones put it during the making of the "We are the World" video, the two should, "check their egos at the door." That is, the two should cultivate a creative, spontaneous exchange of ideas instead of trying to control the conversation. The characteristics of supportive and defensive climates are presented below.

Supportive and Defensive Climate Characteristics

Defensive Climate	Supportive Climate
evaluation	problem description
control	problem orientation
strategy	spontaneity
neutrality	empathy
superiority	equality
certainty	provisionalism

Awareness of how we interact with one another is the first step toward developing a more benign communication climate. Perhaps the most important realization is that organizational groups that foster open and honest communication will outperform those that are mired in interpersonal games. A more productive climate both increases and is increased by the degree of confirmation and collaboration present in a relationship.

Confirmation

When two people interact, they can come away from the event with one of three feelings: One-up, one-down, or equal. These are the relational consequences addressed by those who view communication from the interactional or pragmatic view (Watzlawick, Beavin and Jackson, 1967). Communication theorists who subscribe to the interactional view begin by looking closely at how messages are constructed. Messages contain two components: The *content component* concerns the specific denotation or dictionary meanings of the words used. The *relationship component* results in some attribution by the receiver of the esteem that the sender holds for him or her. Ruesch and Bateson (1951) would term these the report and command functions, respectively. According to Watzlawick, Beavin, and Jackson (1967, p. 52), "The command aspect . . . refers to what sort of a message it is to be taken as, and, therefore, ultimately to the relationship between the communicants."

When individuals perceive themselves to be one-down, they believe that they have been diminished in some manner by the other person. Often, this was not the intent of their partner, but meaning, of course, is in the mind of the receiver. Care must be taken, therefore, to monitor our messages to ensure that we have not inadvertently caused someone to feel one-down.

Another way of saying that a person has been one-upped is to say that he/she has been *disconfirmed*. A person who has been disconfirmed feels as if what s/he says or does isn't important to other members of the group. Any message or behavior that communicates to a person that he/she is not important can be disconfirming. In a relationship where one has a real stake in what others think of them, disconfirming communication can be devastating. Disconfirmation may even exceed rejection as the most destructive force in human relationships. Conversely, being confirmed by a valued other constitutes a real reward in a relationship, and can motivate an individual to seek out the other person more frequently. There are several ways to communicate confirmation and disconfirmation. Some of these are (Beebe, Beebe, and Redmond, 1996, p. 192–194):

Confirming Responses

Direct Acknowledgment:
Example: Joan: "It certainly is a nice day for a canoe trip."
Mariko: "Yes, Joan, it's a great day outside."

Agreement about Judgments:
Example: Nancy: "I think the steel guitar player's riff was fantastic."
Victor: "Yes, I thought it was the best part of the performance."

Supportive Response:
Example: Lionel: "I'm disappointed that I only scored 60 on my economics test."
Sarah: "I'm sorry to see you so sad, Lionel. I know that test was important to you."

Clarifying Response:
Example: Larry: "I'm not feeling very good about my family situation these days."
Tyrone: "It is tough with you and Margo working different shifts."

Expression of Positive Response:
Example: Lorraine: "I'm so excited. I've just been promoted to associate analyst."
Dorette: "Congratulations! I'm so proud of you! Heaven knows you deserve it!"

Disconfirming Responses:

Impervious Response:
Example: Rosa: "I loved your speech, Harvey."
Harvey: (No response. Verbal or non verbal.)

Interrupting Response:
Example: Anna: "I just heard the news on that. . ."
Sharon: "Oh yes. The stock market just went down 100 points."

Irrelevant Response:
Example: Arnold: "First we're flying down to Rio, and then to Quito. I can hardly wait to . . ."
Peter: "They're predicting a hard freeze tonight."

Tangential Response:
>   Example: Richard: "This new program will help us stay within our budget."
>   Samantha: "Yeah, I think I'll save some bucks and send this letter by regular mail."

Impersonal Response:
>   Example: Diana: "Hey, Bill. I'd like to talk with you for a minute about getting your permission to take my vacation in July."
>   Bill: (ignores Diana; continues working)

Incoherent Response:
>   Example: Paula: "George, here's my suggestion for the merger deal with Antrax. Let's offer them forty-eight dollars a share and see how they respond."
>   George: "Huh? Well . . . So . . . I'm not sure."

Incongruous Response:
>   Example: Sue: "Honey, do you want me to go grocery shopping with you?"
>   Steve: (Shouting) "OF COURSE I DO! WHY ARE YOU ASKING?"

Collaboration

To collaborate is to work together toward a common goal. Collaboration requires co-operation, which requires communication. Collaboration has been a central theme in Chapters 7, 8, and 9. The co-active approach to persuasion is essentially collaborative; conducting useful meetings is a matter of efficiently achieving collaboration; and group decisions should be made collaboratively whenever possible. In Chapter 11, we will suggest that the best approaches to managing conflict are collaborative. In Chapter 2 we traced the history of organizational theory, and noted the development of collaboration as a central theme. In the context of discussing the building and sustaining of productive relationships, the point we need to make about collaborative communication is that every genuine effort to collaborate at work tends to help build productive working relationships. When we communicate in efforts to agree on goals and processes, and to coordinate our actions for mutual gain, the relational components of our messages tend to be supportive and confirming. Collaboration builds both rapport and trust.

Stages of Relational Growth and Decay

In considering the building and maintenance of relationships it is important to recognize that relationships do not develop instantly. Developing relationships requires that we invest time and energy. In successful organizational relationships, individuals develop the ability to collaborate with each other on a variety of projects. It is also important to accept the fact that most relationships are temporary. Knapp (1978) noted that relationships evolve through several stages of growth and decay. Knapp focused on intense personal relationships, but by adapting his model to contemporary organizational relationships, we can characterize where an organizational relationship stands at any given point in time. The growth stages begin with the first hello and culminate in a strong bond. The decay stages are characterized by emphasizing differences, avoiding direct dialogue about problems, and eventually, disengagement. Knapp (1978) also describes several dimensions of communication which may be used to assess where a relationship stands.

Contacting, coordinating, and collaborating are the three stages of relational growth among co-workers. During the contacting stage, communication is primarily limited to ritualistic greeting behavior. At best, our two employees are merely acquaintances. Coordinating—comparing background and attitudes to determine if they have some common experiences or interests—can lead the way to a closer, more interdependent association. Organizational friends can become allies should their interaction style and professional objectives permit. If this occurs, we might classify them as members of the same team, or partners. It is at this stage that the two are able to genuinely collaborate on projects and problem solving.

Citing areas where two co-workers differ is the hallmark of the contrasting stage. Should this become a pattern, the two could fall into a more stagnant form of interaction. Usually because of a series of incidents in which the two find themselves on opposite sides of an issue, the interactants may arrive at the circumscribing stage. Here, care is taken to avoid topics which may cause friction. Because the two have found that working together is at best problematic, the relationship generally devolves into the constricting stage. Here, the two avoid contact, and if they must interact, those episodes are usually very narrowly focused and kept brief. Should the two reach this degree of disengagement, they occupy the constricting stage.

Our adapted stages of growth and decay are presented below. Also provided are examples of messages that might typify that particular stage.

Relational Development Stages among Organizational Employees

Growth Stages

Contacting   "Hi, have a good one!"
Coordinating "How's your project coming? Let me know if I can help, OK?"
Collaborating "We really need to keep on top of this personnel issue. What's your take on this?"

Decay Stages

Contrasting   "I can't believe that you approved that resolution."
Circumscribing "I think we should avoid discussing this issue."
Constricting   "Yes I received that memo. Thank you.""

Of course, a sentence or two out of context is insufficient to portray an entire relationship stage. It is worthwhile to note, however, that the degree of engagement or responsiveness is often related to increased interpersonal solidarity. It is also noteworthy that, even in the decaying stages, co-workers will often attempt to maintain a positive exterior with each other. Efforts to maintain the appearance of solidarity can make accurate assessments of relational stages more difficult.

In addition to the message examples provided above, there are dimensions of communication that can illustrate further whether a relationship tends to be growing or stagnating. By assessing the nature of the dialogue between two people, we can better identify the direction in which a relationship is heading.

Seven semantic differential-type scales are used by Knapp to discuss the kind of communication that occurs during either the growth or decay of a relationship. These dimensions are: Public-personal, narrow-broad, awkward-smooth, hesitant-spontaneous, stylized-unique, difficult-efficient, and judgement suspended-judgement given. Let's look closer at each of these important aspects of communication.

Public _____**Personal**

This dimension concerns the depth of interaction between two parties. If topics are discussed on a superficial level, we classify their interaction as public. If topics are delved into on a more substantial basis, the interaction is characterized as personal.

Narrow _____**Broad**

This dimension refers to the breadth of interaction. The more topics two people discuss, the broader their communication.

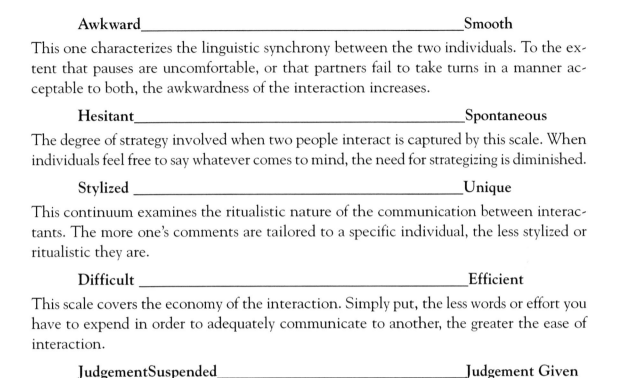

Awkward_____Smooth

This one characterizes the linguistic synchrony between the two individuals. To the extent that pauses are uncomfortable, or that partners fail to take turns in a manner acceptable to both, the awkwardness of the interaction increases.

Hesitant_____Spontaneous

The degree of strategy involved when two people interact is captured by this scale. When individuals feel free to say whatever comes to mind, the need for strategizing is diminished.

Stylized _____Unique

This continuum examines the ritualistic nature of the communication between interactants. The more one's comments are tailored to a specific individual, the less stylized or ritualistic they are.

Difficult _____Efficient

This scale covers the economy of the interaction. Simply put, the less words or effort you have to expend in order to adequately communicate to another, the greater the ease of interaction.

JudgementSuspended_____Judgement Given

This scale concerns the degree of candor present in a relationship. With most people, we tend to withhold interpersonal evaluations. However, with those we truly care about, we are more likely to level.

To understand how these scales can be used to assess the extent to which a relationship is growing or decaying, consider two examples from your own life. Focus on two relationships that you have had. One should be a growing, intimate relationship. The other should be one which was at one time very strong, but has now become virtually nonexistent. According to Knapp and Vangelisti (1994), in growing the relationships, communication should fall along the right hand side of the scales. In a decaying one, the left hand side of the scales should predominate.

Special Organizational Relationships

A unique relationship exists between a manager and the person s/he supervises. While this is not a chapter on leadership per se, it may be profitable nonetheless to look at the interpersonal dimensions of this relationship. According to Tom Peters, co-author of *In Search of Excellence*, the role of the manager is changing dramatically. Peters and Austin (1985) see the manager as a coach, sponsor, and counselor, as opposed to the more traditional images of the supervisor as a nay-sayer, cop, or devil's advocate. Peters (1985) contrasts the new recommended roles for supervisors with traditional supervisor roles as follows:

Recommended Roles	Traditional Roles
Cheerleader	Cop
Enthusiast	Referee
Nurturer	Devil's Advocate
Coach	Nay-sayer
Facilitator	Pronouncer

Thus far in this chapter we have described how the probability of developing successful organizational relationships is enhanced when the climate is supportive rather than defensive. The extent to which individuals recognize and exchange confirming as opposed to disconfirming messages can also contribute to a positive relational outcome. Apart from specific message strategies, a collaborative orientation toward work-related tasks and interpersonal association is necessary to optimize organizational relationships.

Understanding the essentials of relational communication is a necessary yet insufficient step toward building productive organizational teams. How people interact on the job is substantially affected by the way in which personnel are organized. Such factors as proximity (where employees work vis-a-vis one another), chain of command (who is responsible to whom), and frequency of interaction will also influence organizational relationships and the overall effectiveness of organizational communication. To appreciate the impact of these factors, an introduction to organizational communication networks is required. Once we have considered the basics of communication networks, we can then move on to discuss team building.

Networks

Farace, Monge and Russell (1977, p. 180) define communication networks as "repetitive patterns of interaction among the members" of groups. The way in which a network is configured will impact subsequent leadership emergence, the effectiveness of group problem-solving efforts, and the morale of group members. The way information flows in an organization provides a good starting point for analyzing communication networks.

Information Flow

As information passes through an organizational unit, members of the organization will perform some function in relation to the message. The way in which the tasks and individuals are configured—the way the shop floor and work stations are laid out—will have an impact upon the accomplishment of tasks as well as on the relationships among organizational members. There are four types of work/information flow. In *independent flow*, work and information enter the work unit through the supervisor, who distributes assignments and information to individual workers. In a *sequential flow*, work and information flow from member to member through the work unit, but mostly in one direction, beginning with the supervisor. In a *reciprocal flow*, information flows back and forth between the supervisor and individual members, but not between individual members. In a *team work flow*, work comes into the unit through the supervisor, but information enters through all members; members meet regularly to coordinate work, diagnose and solve problems, and share information; information flows in all directions and among all members. Below we briefly discuss each flow pattern and note its impact on relational development.

Independent Message Flow

In this case, a message is passed into the unit and then leaves the unit after only one contact with the group. None of the other group members are involved, so no coordination is required. The relationships between group members are almost irrelevant in this type of situation. Independent information flow inhibits development of strong working relationships.

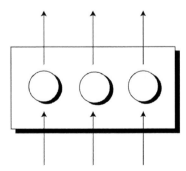

Sequential Message Flow

Here, a message enters the unit and is passed along from one individual to another before it leaves the group. Message flow is one way only, and each member's performance is directly dependent upon the accuracy and completeness of the message as it is received from the preceding member in the flow sequence. The opportunity for message distortion is a function of the number of individuals who must monitor and then disseminate the message.

You have no doubt played the telephone or rumor game, where one person whispers a story into someone else's ear, who in turn tells another, and another, and so on. After the story has passed through several individuals, the final version appears very different from the original. This is the information accuracy problem associated with sequential message flow. In addition to the problem of message distortion, this flow pattern has the disadvantage of providing only very limited opportunity for the kind of interaction that promotes development of productive relationships.

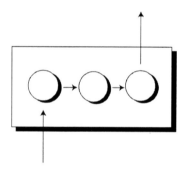

Reciprocal Flow

In reciprocal message flow, messages may travel back and forth between any pair of individuals, but no others are involved. Here, a preliminary check on message accuracy is provided as it returns through the links in the chain to the originator. However, communication is still severely restricted, and message accuracy will often be sacrificed. Also sacrificed is opportunity to develop productive relationships among individual members of the work group.

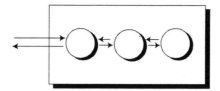

Team Flow

In team message flow, the opportunity to check and double-check the message is abundant. No member of the group can be held totally responsible, as is the case in sequential message flow, and the output of the group is likely to be improved with free-flowing communication. The cost of team flow, of course, is time. This is often a small price to pay when accuracy or effectiveness is the desired goal. Team work flow is a staple building block of employee involvement programs. Team flow is the most collaborative pattern, and maximizes opportunity to build productive work relationships among all team members.

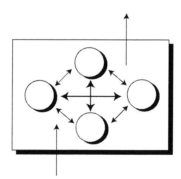

Communication Roles

Another approach to understanding communication flow in a given organization involves determining the various roles the members play. There are four key communication roles individuals may occupy: *Opinion leader, liaison, isolate, and gatekeeper*. Knowing who is performing each role is especially useful when attempting to convey information to the entire group. Recognizing the roles individuals occupy is also helpful in understanding the nature of members' relationships with one another.

The *opinion leader*, who may be particularly knowledgeable on any given topic, becomes the target of interaction when that topic is under consideration. During a re-engineering effort, for example, an employee who is up to speed on organizational change may be the center of attention when such a program is being discussed. A *liaison* connects two groups, but is not a member of either group. A *bridge* is a member of one group that has regular interaction with one or more members of another group. These individuals are, according to Farace, Monge and Russell (1977), generally considered to be more influential and more competent communicators. A *gatekeeper* controls message flow between one person, typically a high status individual, and the rest of the organization. Administrative assistants, for example, are often gatekeepers. A person who monitors information from the outside environment and then must decide whether or not to share that information with the group also functions as a gatekeeper. Individuals who keep contradictory or undesirable information from reaching the group, are sometimes termed "mindguards" (Janis, 1972). An isolate is a group member who does not communicate on a regular basis with most group members. Generally, this individual is dependent upon one group member for his or her information on what others are saying or doing.

Understanding and appreciating organizational communication networks and network roles is especially useful when attempting to introduce a team approach in modern organizations. As we will see in the following section, creating an awareness of the value of a pending organizational change, such as increased employee involvement, can aid in the acceptance of that program by organizational members. Knowledge of the interaction between task and interpersonal factors can enhance the selection of team members and facilitate the dissemination of information to affected employees.

Teams

Team Building

When we think of teams, athletic groups such as the Green Bay Packers, the Los Angeles Dodgers, and, more recently, the New York Liberty come to mind. Yet, many modern organizations also rely upon effective work teams to function optimally. In fact, Peter Drucker contends that "the modern organization cannot be an organization of boss and subordinate. It must be organized as a team." (1992, p. 101). Teams are a central part of most employee involvement efforts, such as Total Quality Management (TQM). While not all organizations will use a high involvement approach, it is probable that the use of teams will continue to grow. According to the Center for Effective Leadership, one of the ten fatal flaws that derail modern executives is over-managing, that is "failing to delegate or build a team." (McCall and Lombardo, 1983).

Orsburn, Moran, Musselwhite and Zenger, in *Self Directed Work Teams: The New American Challenge*, define a self-directed work team as "a highly trained group of employees, from 6 to 18 on average, fully responsible for turning out a well-defined segment of finished work.(1990, p. 8)." Peters (1987, p. 299) describes a business team as "a highly autonomous group responsible for scheduling, training, problem solving and many other activities." Team building is the process by which work groups are transformed into teams.

According to Orsburn, et al. (1990), the life cycle of a team typically progresses through five stages: (1) start-up, (2) state of confusion, (3) leader-centered teams, (4) tightly formed teams, and finally (5) self-directed work teams. Each point in the process requires specific communication skills to maximize the likelihood of program success.

The *start-up* phase is perhaps the most important. After an initial expression of high expectations, the reality of putting the program into practice must be tackled. During this phase, team members typically "learn the ABCs of communication and group dynamics, begin using administrative procedures, and expand their repertoire of technical skills. . . . Supervisors . . . if they've been carefully selected, generally do their best to facilitate, rather than control, the operational and decision making efforts of the teams." (Orsburn et al., 1990, p. 20).

The **state of confusion** stage occurs in part because of the absence of a central authority figure. Without clear directions, teams can work very hard and make some decisions, but not be sure whether they are doing the right thing. There is often second-guessing at this stage, and some employees express doubt as to whether a team approach is feasible. Clearly, a leader is needed at this point.

Assuming that the organization continues to support the team concept through the confusion stage, **leader-centered teams** appear in stage three of the process. One member of the group emerges as the leader, and helps to clarify work assignments and settle internal disputes. This person also represents the team in their dealings with the organization. During this stage, there is a chance that the group can become too dependent upon the leader. To avoid this problem, team members take turns at leading the group.

The next stage in the process involves **tightly formed teams.** The group is functioning well and accomplishing its major objectives, but problems may lie just beneath the surface. For example, a poorly performing team member may be protected by the group, or the team may find it difficult to accept a new member. In addition, there is often an intense rivalry between different teams, and care must be taken to ensure that what was once a healthy rivalry does not become destructive to the overall organization. Groups made up of members of different teams can then be used to review situations and keep the teams on track.

The fifth and final stage features **self-directed teams.** "Mature teams develop a powerful commitment to achieving corporate and team goals" (Orsburn, et al., 1990, p. 22). All of the team members display initiative, constantly attempting to improve their level of performance and service. Even at this stage, however, the organization must provide continual training in order to keep the teams working at an optimal level.

Obstacles to Team Building

While team building is a popular approach, there are several obstacles that must be overcome when attempting such a program. First and foremost, there must be support for the effort from the top down. As Tom Peters (1985) has observed, it doesn't matter what innovative programs are introduced if top management is not a hundred percent behind the campaign; lukewarm, or questionable backing from top management is actually an obstacle to success. Management must make a clear, sincere, and persistent commitment to the program if it is to have any chance of success.

Moreover, in the specific case of employee involvement and team building, workers must feel free to express themselves honestly, without fear of recrimination. The founder of TQM, W. Edwards Deming, lists "driving out fear" as one of his 14 Key Points for Management (1982). According to Ryan and Oestreich (1991), "fear of speaking up is a basic human barrier to improving an organization," and can lead to six negative consequences: (1) Lack of extra effort; (2) making and hiding mistakes; (3) failure to meet deadlines; (4) ineffective problem solving; (5) wasting time on low priority projects; and (6) lack of creativity, innovation, and risk taking. For a team-building effort to succeed, employees must be able to contribute, and management must create an appropriate climate to encourage this form of participation.

Unwilling supervisors represent yet another barrier to effective implementation of employee involvement programs. Klein (1984) identifies several sources of resistance frequently exhibited by middle managers, including job security, uncertainty about their responsibility and workload, philosophical problems with employee involvement, and perceived loss of power and status. For example, a group of resistant supervisors Klein calls "status seekers" are most concerned about losing prestige and control. Another category of supervisors, termed "deal makers," believe that the adoption of a quality circle or work team approach will interfere with their ability to reward employees on a one-to-one basis.

A Collaborative Approach to Team Building

A collaborative approach to team building begins with a clear indication of managerial support. Peters (1985) suggests that managers use MBWA (Managing by Wandering Around) to listen to employees. While this approach keeps managers both informed and visible, and provides symbolic evidence of managerial commitment, organizations must also follow through by responding to what employees tell them. E.g., it is common for organizational management to feign collaboration, soliciting employee input— which is then ignored. When management is perceived as giving only lip service to an employee involvement program, the effort is doomed. Trust is broken between management and employees; and once broken, trust is the most difficult component of a productive relationship to rebuild.

In addition, to accomplish collaborative team building, management must create and maintain a supportive communication climate within the organization. Employees need to know that they can speak their minds without fear of repercussions. This process takes time, and requires a substantial investment of energy by those in charge. For a collaborative model to work well, employees must feel empowered to go ahead and speak and act; they cannot be constantly afraid that management may change the rules of the game midstream. In *The Change Masters*, Kanter provides an insightful observation concerning successful teams:

> Note that it is not just *any* team that aids innovation but one with a tradition of drawing members from a diversity of sources, a variety of areas. Innovating companies seem to deliberately create a "marketplace of ideas," recognizing that a multiplicity of points of view need to be brought to bear on the problem. It is not the "caution of committees" that is sought—reducing risk by spreading responsibility—but the better idea that comes from a clash and an integration of perspectives (1984, p. 167).

To deal with potentially resistant supervisors, Klein suggests that the transition to the team format should include a "coordinated strategy to make supervisors an integral part of the change process" (1984, p. 94). Collaboration between organizational decision-makers and those responsible for accomplishing organizational objectives will facilitate the transition to a team-based structure. Supervisors should be involved in both the design and implementation of the program, and peer networking among supervisors should be encouraged.

Key Success Factors in Team Building

Peters (1987, pp. 215–17), based upon his analysis of employee involvement efforts at Hewlett Packard, Ford Motor Company, and DuPont, cites six success factors involved in team building. The first is *multi-functional involvement*. That is, the team should consist of individuals with different backgrounds and skills, thus maximizing the diversity of approaches to a particular organizational problem. He further recommends that, especially during the early phases, key team members work *full time* on the project. He also argues that team members should be located in close *proximity* to one another. This serves to increase the communication between the workers. Peters characterizes *communication* itself as a key success factor, and claims "it is essential that regular decision making sessions be held, with all functions represented" (1987, p. 216). Peters (1987, p. 217) warns against underfunding new teams, citing the *shared resource trap*. "The sharing of resources between new product/service teams and main-line activities . . . is a leading cause of sandbagged product development and introduction efforts." Peters concludes by encouraging *outside involvement* in team projects. This would allow customers and suppliers to act as consultants for new products and services, and stimulate the development of cooperative, as opposed to adversarial, relationships between the organization and its constituents.

Effective Team Building: Two Approaches

According to Lumsden and Lumsden (1993, p. 79), "a team starts developing in the context of an organizational culture. . . . It begins creating its own team attributes as it goes through phases of development, and it guides and nurtures its own development by using feedback." They offer nine guidelines for developing a strong team: (1) Members must get to know one another. (2) Members must connect with one another through shared experience, mutual supporting, and enjoyable interaction. (3) Team members must develop and share a vision of the team's mission and goals which reflects that of the parent organization. (4) The group must develop its own team culture. (5) It must be safe for individual members to fully participate; diversity must be valued; conflict must be constructively managed. (6) Members must recognize and discuss phases of team development as they go through them. (7) Communication must be open, clear, and supportive, and include sound analytic processes. (8) Team self assessment and improvement must be ongoing. (9) The team must recognize and celebrate its successes as they occur.

Paralleling the Lumsden guidelines, Orsburn et al. (1990) provide a seven-step procedure for effective team building: (1) Conduct awareness training, (2) select initial work team members, (3) specify team boundaries, (4) revise the preliminary plan, (5) begin training for team members, (6) prepare the managers, and (7) encourage responsible participation. This sequence, if applied properly, can go a long way toward avoiding the problems that Klein (1984) discusses.

Awareness training enables individuals to comprehend the value of teamwork and anticipate how the team-building effort will work. This sort of informational campaign can serve to allay employee fears as well as to involve them in the transition from square one. Specifying the team's boundaries enables team members to clarify their charge and avoid encroaching upon the territory of other organizational entities.

The revision stage involves both the newly formed team and those who designed it. The idea here is to involve the young team in charting its own course in collaboration with the individuals who are conducting the team-building effort. This serves to increase the team's ownership of the process.

Based upon the new plan, team members can now begin their training in earnest. Technical, interpersonal, and administrative skill development are the staples at this stage. The final two steps, preparing the managers and encouraging responsible participation, function to fine-tune the team-building effort. Managers require training in order to develop meaningful performance objectives and to establish a plan for shifting responsibility from the manager to the team.

Responsible participation in the program is essential for team building to succeed. In this follow-through phase, managers and other upper level personnel need to demonstrate their support for the team-building effort. This may necessitate the expansion of the team's role in planning, and/or doing away with special perks formerly available to those in authority. Whatever mechanism is used, the team members need to be assured that the organization is behind the effort.

Summary and Conclusion

In this chapter we have given a basic introduction to key communication concepts associated with relationships, networks and teams. We identified three key characteristics of effective organizational relationships, namely, climate, confirmation, and collaboration, and gave examples of each factor. We also looked at special types of relationships within modern organizations, touching on leadership, gender, and cultural considerations.

Our examination of networks focused on fundamental information flow models, and typical small group communication network configurations. We linked both topics to leadership emergence, group problem solving, and the morale of group members. In the teams section, we discussed the typical phases that teams go through, and provided two approaches to developing effective teams. We identified a number of obstacles to introducing a team-based approach in organizations, and discussed key success factors associated with team building.

For Further Reading:

Bass, B. M. (1990, Winter). From transactional to transformational leadership: Learning to share the vision. *Organizational Dynamics*, pp. 19–31.

Bolman, L. G., and Deal. T. E. (1992). What makes a team work? *Organizational Dynamics*, autumn, 34–44.

DeVito, J. A. (1996). *Messages: Building interpersonal communication skills*, 3rd. ed. New York: Harper Collins.

Kinlaw, D. C. (1991). *Developing superior work teams: Building quality and the competitive edge*. Lexington, Massachusetts: Lexington Books. *Concerning relationships:*

Knapp, M. L., and Vangelisti, A. L. (1994). *Interpersonal communication and human relationships*, 2nd ed. Boston: Allyn and Bacon.

References

Beebe, S. A., Beebe, S. J., and Redmond, M. V. (1996). *Interpersonal communication: Relating to others*. Boston: Allyn and Bacon.

Deming, W. E. (1982). *Quality, productivity, and competitive position*. Cambridge, MA: MIT Center for Advanced Engineering Study.

Drucker, P. (1992, Sept.–Oct.). The new society of organizations. *Harvard Business Review*, 95–105.

Farace, R. V., Monge, P. R., and Russell, H. M. (1977). *Communicating and organizing*. Reading, Massachusetts: Addison Wesley.

Gibb, J. (1961). Defensive communication. *Journal of Communication*, 11, 141–148.

Gudykunst, W., Ting-Toomey, S., Sudweeks, S., and Stewart, L. P. (1994). *Building bridges: Interpersonal skills for a changing world*. Boston: Houghton Mifflin.

Janis, I. L. (1972). *Victims of groupthink*. Boston: Houghton Mifflin.

Jenkins, Roger L., Reizenstein, Richard C., and Rodgers, E. G. (1984). Report cards on the MBA. *Harvard Business Review*, September–October, pp. 20–30.

Kanter, R. M. (1984). *The change masters: Innovation and entrepreneurship in the American Corporation*. New York: Touchstone.

Klein, J. A. (1984). Why supervisors resist employee involvement. *Harvard Business Review*, September–October, 87–95.

Knapp, M. L. (1978). *Social intercourse: From greeting to goodbye*. Boston: Allyn and Bacon.

Leavitt, H. J. (1951). Some effects of certain communication patterns on group performance. *Journal of abnormal and social psychology*, 46, 38–50.

Luckenbaugh, C. (2001, Mar. 30). New college grads with communication, interpersonal, teamwork skills have the edge say employers. *National Association of Colleges and Employers Press Room*. http://www.naceweb.org/press.

Lumsden, G., and Lumsden, D. (1993). Communicating in groups and teams: Sharing leadership. Belmont, California: Wadsworth.

McCall, M. W., Lombardo, M. M., and Morrison, A. M. (1983). *The lessons of experience: How successful executives develop on the job*. Lexington, MA: Lexington Books.

Orsburn, J. D., Moran, L. Musselwhite, E., and Zenger, J. H. (1990). *Self directed work teams: The new American challenge*. New York: Irwin.

Peters, T. (1985) *A passion for excellence: An evening with Tom Peters*. Washington, D.C.: Public Broadcasting System.

Peters, T. (1987). *Thriving on chaos: Handbook for a management revolution*. New York: Knopf.

Peters, T., and Austin, N. (1985). *A passion for excellence: The leadership difference*. New York: Random House.

Ruesch, J., and Bateson, G. (1951). *Communication: The social matrix of psychiatry*. New York: W. W. Norton Company.

Ryan, K. D., and Oestreich, D. K. (1991). *Driving fear out of the workplace: How to overcome the invisible barriers to quality, productivity, and innovation*. San Francisco: Jossey-Bass.

Shaw, M. E. (1954). Some effects of problem complexity upon problem solution efficiency in different communication nets. *Journal of experimental psychology*, vol. 48, pp. 211–217.

Shaw, M. E. (1971). *Group dynamics: The psychology of small group behavior*. New York: McGraw-Hill.

Tannen, D. (1990). *You just don't understand*. New York: William Morrow and Company.

Tubbs, S. L., and Moss, S. (1977). *Human Communication*, 2nd ed. New York: Random House.

Van de Ven, A. H., and Ferry, D. L. (1980). *Measuring and Assessing Organizations*. New York: John Wiley.

Watzlawick, P., Beavin, J., and Jackson, D. (1967). *Pragmatics of human communication*. New York: W. W. Norton.

Critical to maintaining productive relationships, to coordinating work, and to sustaining individual motivation are the communication skills of constructive conflict management.

In Chapter 11, Michael Dues explains the importance and principles of constructive conflict management, and provides a step-by-step guide to effective conflict resolution. His Six Step Process has been widely adopted in public service organizations as the recommended method for informally resolving conflicts among organization members and work units.

CHAPTER 11

Managing Conflict

Michael T. Dues
University of Arizona

Key Terms

conflict
interdependence
opposition
expression
micro conflict management
macro conflict management
win-win resolution
competetive conflicts

dysfunctional strategies
avoidance
reduced communication
imposition
triangulation
payback
bargaining and compromise
constructive conflict management

negotiation
interests vs. positions
mutual gain
objective criteria
Six Step Process
conflict issue
mediation process

Objectives

This chapter describes the communication skills required to deal constructively with conflict at work. Chapter objectives are to:

1. Define conflict, and identify its essential characteristics.
2. Distinguish between individual efforts to resolve conflicts and organizational level efforts to prevent destructive conflict, and to promote constructive conflict management.
3. Identify erroneous ideas about conflict which interfere with effective conflict management.
4. Identify five dysfunctional conflict management strategies, and explain how these strategies are harmful.

5. Describe seven principles of constructive conflict management.
6. Explain Fisher and Ury's four principles for principled negotiation.
7. Describe the Six Step Process for resolving conflicts by mutual agreement.
8. Explain conflict mediation, describing how third parties can act as facilitators to help resolve conflicts.
9. Describe steps managers can take to reduce incidence of unnecessary conflict, promote constructive resolution of conflict, and mitigate the harmful effects of conflict aftermath.

Conflict is an absolutely natural aspect of human social life. It occurs wherever humans interact. Organizations where people work together are natural locations for conflict, and the manner in which conflicts are managed significantly affects the functioning of organizations. Other than force, communication is the primary means for managing conflict.

What is Conflict?

Experts offer a variety of definitions of conflict, but they generally agree that certain components are present whenever conflict occurs. Wilmot and Hocker (2001) define **"conflict"** as: *"an expressed struggle between at least two interdependent parties who perceive incompatible goals, scarce resources, and interference from others in achieving their goals."* Jordan (1990) says that *"conflict arises when a difference between two (or more) people necessitates change in at least one person in order for their engagement to continue and develop."* In my consulting practice, I have used a somewhat simpler definition, describing "conflict" as *"a discomforting difference between two or more people"* (Dues, 1990).

While these definitions employ different wording, each includes, either explicitly or implicitly, recognition of three fundamental elements of a conflict. These elements are: *interdependence, opposition,* and *expression.* Consider how each of these elements is an essential part of the conflict.

Interdependence. Conflict only occurs between persons who are in positions to affect one another's lives. If the condition of interdependence is not present, a difference between people will be only a difference; it will not cause discomfort; no one will be required to change to preserve anything. Another way to describe this condition is to say that each party in the conflict must have some *power* relative to the other parties. Each party must control some consequences that affect the other parties.

Opposition.   When one party perceives that he/she is being harmed or prevented from achieving a goal by the behavior of another party, a perception of opposition exists. When two or more parties clash in pursuit of goals, resources, or outcomes which they perceive to be incompatible with one another, these parties are in opposition.

Expression.   Most experts agree that conflict begins to be present when one or more opposing parties *expresses* his/her opposition in some way. That is, until there is some behavioral manifestation, there is no visible conflict.

Combining these three essential elements, we can say that when two or more inter-dependent parties perceive themselves to be in opposition to one another, and act on their opposition, they are in conflict.

Conflict Management at the Micro and Macro Levels

The term **"conflict management,"** widely used in the literature on conflict, has two related, but different meanings. In the literature of social science, where conflict has been the subject of serious research for fifty years, "conflict management" generally refers to the behavior with which an individual or organization responds to, or attempts to handle an existing conflict. In the field of organizational management the term "conflict management" refers to the set of structures, policies, and procedures by which managers attempt to minimize the potential damage conflict may cause to an organization. We shall refer to the former definition as "micro conflict management," and the latter definition as "macro conflict management." Specifically, **Micro Conflict Management** includes the behaviors by which individuals, attempt to deal with an existing conflict. **Macro Conflict Management** includes the structures, policies, procedures, and behaviors by which organization managers attempt to minimize conflict damage, and promote efficient, constructive conflict resolution.

Wrong Ideas About Conflict

Given that conflict is a common aspect of organizational and individual life, and that conflict has the potential to do considerable harm, one might expect that people in general, and managers in particular would have evolved methods for handling conflict that are as effective and reliable as any other aspect of social or organizational life. In fact, however, most individuals and most organizations handle conflict poorly, and reap the painful consequences. Poor handling of conflict results, at least partly, from erroneous ideas about conflict. Some of these ideas are present in the metaphors we use to think about and describe conflicts. One extremely common metaphor for conflict is "war." We think of conflict in terms of battles, attacks, defense. We think and talk in terms of "winning" and "losing." Another common conflict metaphor is "explosion." We describe conflict situations in terms of "pressure building up;" we talk about parties having a "short fuse." We say one party "blew up" over some action;" we talk about "pushing people's buttons," and about "cleaning up the damage" afterwards.

These problematic metaphors for conflict are rooted in, and help perpetuate four fundamentally wrong ideas about conflict. These wrong ideas are that:

- Conflict should not occur; when conflict occurs it is a sign of flawed relationship, and someone is at fault.
- Conflict is competitive; for one party to win, another party must lose.
- Winning requires acquiring and exerting more power than the other party; and
- Exertion of power is always harmful, and has no legitimate place in the resolution of conflict.

Consider what is wrong about each of these ideas.

- ***Conflict should not occur; when conflict occurs it is a sign of flawed relationship, and someone is at fault.*** Conflict is always discomforting; often conflict is deeply painful. Conflict produces anger, and angry people sometimes do seriously harmful things. Given the human condition, and our experience of pain and harm in the context of conflict, it is understandable that we are afraid of conflict, and that we might conclude that conflict should be prevented. Acting on this view, individuals and organizations frequently see a conflict as an aggressive act, and attempt to identify who is to blame. Even when there is fault on the part of one or more parties, finding fault, and assigning blame contribute nothing toward resolving the conflict.

- ***Conflict is competitive; for one party to win, another party must lose.*** The issue of whether conflict is always competitive—whether one party must lose in order for another party to win—was a major concern to Morton Deutsch, whose research provided the basis for much our contemporary understanding of conflict and conflict resolution (Deutsch, 1973). Deutsch found that in about 80% of conflicts, it is possible to find a resolution with which all parties achieve their goals. He labeled this kind of resolution "win-win." He called conflicts in which **"win-win"** resolution is possible, "pure conflicts," which he distinguished from **"competitive conflicts."** In "competitive conflicts," the remaining 20%, alternatives for resolution included only "win-lose," and "no win-no lose." "Win-lose" obviously refers to having a winner and a loser; "no win-no lose" refers to a compromise in which neither party really wins, but neither party really loses. Deutsch explained that in wrongly believing that all conflicts are "competitive," we pursue "win-lose" resolutions which damage both the loser and the relationship; or, to preserve relationships, we pursue compromises in which all parties settle for less than optimal solutions.

- *Winning requires acquiring and exerting more power than the other party.* In battle, victory is accomplished by exercising power, "forcing" another party to change in order to achieve our goals. Force need not be physical; it is exercised in degrees by imposing consequences, or threatening to impose consequences. When opposing parties exert their power in an effort to force one another to comply, both sides suffer damaging consequences. This approach always harms (and may destroy) the relationship between the parties. Despite the obvious downside of resorting to power to resolve conflicts, organization members commonly attempt to increase their ability to handle conflict by increasing their power relative to other organization members. In hierarchical organizational structures, conflict is macro managed by having the person with higher authority and greater power unilaterally impose "resolutions" upon subordinates. Interestingly, research shows that the greater the difference in power between conflicting parties, the less likely they are to achieve satisfying and lasting resolutions of their conflicts (Lulofs, 2000). Power differences tend to force opposition underground; they do not eliminate it.

- *Exertion of power is always harmful, and has no legitimate place in the resolution of conflict.* Observing the harm done by misuse of power, some conclude that power itself is harmful. This conclusion is misguided. Power is the ability to influence or control outcomes. Power over another person is ability to influence or control outcomes which affect that person. Power itself is neither good nor bad, but can be used for good or bad; it is an essential fact of organizational life—it is the very interdependence that is an essential condition of conflict. And interdependence, power relative to one another, is what motivates people to attempt to resolve conflict. Interdependence needs only to be mutual to motivate resolution efforts. Constructive conflict resolution is most likely when no party has enough power to dominate others, and when all parties have enough power to induce cooperation from others.

Dysfunctional Conflict Management Strategies

Thinking in terms of problematic conflict metaphors, guided by wrong ideas, and influenced by anger and fear, organization members tend to engage in dysfunctional conflict management strategies at both the micro and macro levels. By "dysfunctional," we mean that whether or not the strategy yields the desired result, it produces a result that harms the parties, their relationship, or the organization.

Below are six common dysfunctional conflict management strategies:

```
Avoidance
Reduced Communication
Imposition
Triangulation
Payback
Bargaining and Compromise
```

Avoidance.   The most common strategy for managing conflict in organizations is to ignore it, or postpone addressing it in the hope that it will simply go away. Usually, of course, the conflict does not go away; generally, it festers, grows more severe, and/or spreads. Avoidance allows conflicts to worsen and grow. Moreover, it causes resentment and demotivation among workers affected by the conflict.

Reduced Communication.   Closely related to avoidance as a strategy are attempts to close off channels of communication to make conflict less visible or less felt. In this category are such tactics as physically separating conflicting parties, limiting who may communicate with whom, or requiring transactions to go through buffering or screening parties. At the individual level this tactic includes such behaviors as finding reasons to be away from the office, or simply closing off conversation. This approach fails to confront the actual issue in the conflict; it literally prevents the very communication needed to resolve it. Moreover, reducing communication always weakens an organization's ability to function.

Imposition. This strategy involves a direct resort to power in which one conflicting party, or a supervisor with authority to do so, imposes a specific solution without consulting, or securing genuine consent from one or more of the interested parties. Imposition of solutions always produces resentment, and demotivates the "loser." Moreover, imposed solutions are generally less effective, and less efficient over time than solutions generated by discussion and mutual agreement.

Triangulation. Triangulation occurs when one party appeals to a third party for support in a conflict *instead of* directly confronting the other conflicting party. This creates and "triangle," and places participants in the roles of "victim, villain," and "rescuer" (Lerner, 1985). These roles are harmful to all three parties. The "innocent victim" claim, with which one appeals to a third party, almost always distorts the truth. Viewing one's self as an "innocent victim" requires regarding one's self as unable, and as not responsible. Such psychological baggage tends to become a self fulfilling prophecy, and to undermine self respect. The "rescuer" role can feel powerful and righteous temporarily, but it embroils the third party in a conflict that is not her/his own. To rescue, however, a supervisor (or other helper) must accept (or appear to accept) the "innocent victim" claim, and the "villain" charge, both of which are probably false. This compounds the conflict, making an enemy of the alleged villain, who becomes resentful, and may retaliate. It tends to confirm the view that the "victim" is unable and unresponsible. At best, it produces solutions that require third party policing; at worst, it generates wider and more harmful conflict.

Pay Back. Revenge is a common conflict strategy in organizations. The cliche says "Don't get mad, get even." Among criminals who live outside the law (or in prison), exacting revenge for perceived wrongs is viewed as ethical and necessary to deter attacks. They call such revenge "pay back," and it does serve to prevent them from attacking one another by instilling fear in potential attackers. But the system has a costly downside which few organizations can afford. This approach never addresses the original conflict. It reduces communication and destroys the trust necessary to genuinely resolve a conflict. It tends to create an on going, escalating cycle of conflict which damages not only the conflicting parties, but bystanders, and the organization as well.

Bargaining and Compromise. Compromise is a useful, sometimes necessary strategy in the 20% of conflicts that are truly competitive. But compromises, frequently reached through a competitive bargaining process, are employed to settle many conflicts that are among the 80% that are not truly competitive. In compromising when they could have reached a "win-win" resolution, all parties settle for less than they could have achieved. Moreover, the competitive bargaining process leads conflicting parties to withhold information from one another, and to seek to gain at the other's expense; this damages trust and cohesion.

Each of the above strategies is dysfunctional in that it produces undesirable side effects. It is important to note, however, that each of the strategies can, at least sometimes, produce some desired effects. Occasionally, a dysfunctional strategy is the best available alternative. At times, for example, when the risks involved in confrontation are too great, avoidance is the best available response to a conflict. Compromise can be the best available strategy when the conflict is truly competitive in nature. When dealing with volatile personalities or a long standing pattern of conflict, reduced communication may be the best alternative. And sometimes people really do need to be rescued. The point is not that these strategies should never be used. Rather, the point is that they are used too often, and used when they are not the best available alternative. Thus, individuals and organizations unnecessarily reap the harmful side effects. Below, we discuss key principles that should guide both micro and macro conflict management, and describe methods for more constructively resolving conflicts.

Principles of Constructive Conflict Management

In place of the four wrong ideas discussed above, we suggest that managers and organization members be guided by ***seven principles of constructive conflict management.*** These are: (1) Conflict is natural in human interaction; conflict will occur. (2) Conflict management requires time and energy, and involves risk. (3) Unnecessary conflict wastes time and energy. (4) Poor conflict management damages individuals, relationships, and organizations. (5) Good micro conflict management involves direct communication and mutual agreement between conflicting parties. (6) Third parties help best to resolve conflicts when they serve as facilitators and teachers, not when they intervene as rescuers or arbitrators. (7) Good macro conflict management focuses on general patterns and long term relationships; its primary purpose is to promote and facilitate constructive micro conflict management. Consider each of these principles briefly.

Constructive Conflict Management Principles

1. **Conflict is natural in human interaction; conflict will occur.** That a conflict occurs does not mean something is wrong or that someone is a fault. Each human is unique; each has different perceptions, different needs, different ways of pursuing goals. When people work together there are bound to be occasions when differences will generate discomfort, and discomfort will be perceived as opposition, which will be expressed. Conflict is a natural event that will happen, not a bad event that should not happen.

2. **Conflict management requires time, energy, and risk.** Every conflict must be managed. That is, attention, energy and effort must be expended in responding to it. Even avoidance requires thought, effort, and stress. Since conflict occurs in every organization, and every conflict requires management, conflict management is part of every organizational job. The time and energy required are not taken from the job; they are part of the job. Conflict management always yields consequences, some of which are controlled by other parties, and some of which can be negative. Hence, conflict management always involves risk. Risk must be accepted as part of human interaction.

3. **Unnecessary conflicts waste time and energy.** In addition to the unavoidable conflict that naturally occurs, unnecessary conflicts occur, which could have been avoided. These arise through careless behaviors, failures to communicate, and avoidable role conflicts. Whether or not a conflict could have been avoided, when it occurs, it must be managed, which requires time, energy, and risk.

4. **Poor conflict management damages individuals, relationships, and organizations.** Everyone knows conflict can result in harm ranging from wounded feelings, to chilled or broken relationships, to missed promotions or lost jobs, to organizational failures, even to violence. When conflict occurs, individuals, relationships, and organizations can find themselves in harm's way. It is important to observe, however, that most of the damage is done, not by the initial conflict, but by dysfunctional conflict management strategies. An important corollary to this principle is that *constructive conflict management is part of every member's job.*

5. **Constructive micro conflict management requires direct communication and mutual agreement.** We know that avoidance, triangulation, and imposition produce harmful side effects. Research also shows that satisfactory conflict

resolutions are most likely to be generated when the conflicting parties communicate directly with one another in an effort to mutually agree on a resolution (Yarbrough and Wilmot, 1995), and that the best solutions are produced when there is a balance of power between the conflicting parties (Lulofs, 2000). The corollary to this principle is that *individuals can manage conflict most constructively by discussing conflicts directly with one another in a genuine effort to find a mutually agreeable solution.*

6. **Third parties help best in managing conflicts when they serve as facilitators and teachers.** Occasionally, when power imbalances are too great, a third party must rescue a conflicting party. And, occasionally, especially in a competitive conflict, a supervisor, manager, or outside party must arbitrate a conflict. But these occasions are exceptions. In most instances, when two conflicting parties are having difficulty resolving a conflict, a third party can help them best by serving as a facilitator and/or teacher, guiding the parties through a constructive conflict management process, but allowing them to reach their own solution.

7. **Good macro conflict management is focused on general patterns and long term relationships; its primary purpose is to promote and facilitate constructive micro conflict management.** Since the advent of the Human Relations Approach to management, experts have agreed that a major function of executive management is to design and maintain an organization's communication system. We know that an organization's communication system includes both formal and informal mechanisms. And we know that, other than using force, all strategies for handling conflict involve communication. Working through the formal communication system, managers can minimize unnecessary conflict by clearly defining tasks, procedures, roles, and lines of authority, and by establishing formal grievance and disciplinary procedures to handle conflicts when informal efforts fail. Working through the informal communication system, they can model and encourage constructive patterns of managing conflict. In addition, they can provide conflict management training for employees, and conduct periodic team building with the help of an outside consultant when needed.

Constructive Micro Management of Conflict

Principles for Effective Negotiation

As principle #5 states, good conflict management requires direct communication and mutual agreement. In a word, it requires *negotiation*. Roger Fisher and William Ury, co-founders of the Harvard Program on Negotiation, provide clear and succinct principles of effective "win-win" negotiating in *Getting to Yes* (1981), a book which has guided individual, corporate, and international negotiation efforts with evident success. Fisher and Ury discuss a process they refer to as *"Principled Negotiation,"* which focuses on finding the best solution for all parties, and avoids competitive bargaining and compromise. They suggest that negotiation be guided by four key principles: (1) *Separate people and roles from the problem.* (2) *Focus on interests not positions.* (3) *Generate options for mutual gain.* And, (4) *Use objective criteria to choose among options.* Each of these principles is explained below.

Principled Negotiation

1. **Separate people and roles from the problem.** Instead of viewing one another as opponents to be overcome, Fisher and Ury suggest viewing the issue in the conflict as a problem which can be solved to everyone's satisfaction by working together.
2. **Focus on interests, not positions.** There are two basic kinds of "positions" taken in conflicts, "bargaining positions," and "battle positions." A bargaining position is a stand one takes expecting to negotiate a compromise in which each party will give up something. A battle position is a point on which one attempts to "stand firm," refusing to compromise. Either way, taking a position assumes the conflict is competitive; it prevents pursuit of a win-win solution. To avoid this trap, Fisher and Ury suggest focusing on "interests." An interest is a need, a desire, or a goal. To focus on interests, each party must state her/his needs, desires, or goals. Identifying interests requires trust, because it often ex-

poses vulnerabilities. However, when all parties identify their interests which may be affected by the conflict, they can then work cooperatively to create ways to satisfy all the identified interests. Fisher and Ury's work supports Deutsch's earlier research in showing that in most conflicts mutually satisfying solutions can be found without compromising.

3. **Generate options for mutual gain.** Fisher and Ury suggest placing the list of identified interests clearly in front of the conflicting parties, then brainstorming to generate a list of suggestions for satisfying the interests. This involves working creatively and cooperatively to find a solution that will please all the parties. (See Chapter 8, "Making Group Decisions," for more detail on the brainstorming process.)

4. **Use objective criteria to choose among the options.** A criterion is a factor to be considered in evaluating options. A criterion is objective if it is (a) measurable, and (b) agreed to by all parties. Before making a decision on which options to choose, it helps to first identify and agree upon objective criteria to guide the choice.

Adhering to these four principles in working together to resolve conflicts greatly increases the likelihood of reaching a resolution that truly satisfies all parties. Perhaps more importantly it engages the parties in a cooperative, mutually supportive effort that builds trust and understanding. Another way of thinking of these principles, therefore, is to view them as honoring the kind of relationship we wish to maintain with our work colleagues (Fisher and Brown, 1988).

"Conflict to Contract:" The Six Step Process

The **Six Step Process** for resolving conflicts by mutual agreement (Dues, 1990) has been widely applied in pubic service and private organizations. The process incorporates Fisher and Ury's concepts, and a number of research findings into a step by step guide, and can be applied in any conflict in which two conditions are present. These conditions are: (1) It must be possible to define the conflict issue in terms of the voluntary behavior of one or more of the conflicting parties. (2) The parties to the conflict must be willing to discuss the issue with one another in an attempt to reach a solution. The first condition is essential because the process is one of negotiating to reach a contractual agreement. The only thing humans can truly negotiate about, and contract about, is voluntary behavior. The second condition is obviously required since negotiation will not occur unless the parties are willing to negotiate.

The six steps in the process are:

Six Steps for Resolving Conflicts Constructively

Step 1: Define the conflict issue.

Step 2: Decide promptly whether to seek to resolve the conflict by negotiation.

Step 3: Approach the other party and request assistance in resolving your conflict.

Step 4: Talk in an effort to understand and resolve the problem.

Step 5: Contract to resolve the conflict.

Step 6: Follow through on your contract.

M. Dues, 1990

Below, each step is briefly explained.

Step 1. Define the Conflict Issue.

The "issue" in a conflict is the point of difference or disagreement. Every conflict is complex, and each conflict issue can be described in various ways. The way we conceptualize and state the conflict issue significantly affects the likelihood of constructively discussing it and reaching a workable agreement. In general, it is important to state the issue simply, clearly, and concretely in terms of voluntary behavior.

Useful guidelines to follow in defining the issue are:

A. **Identify behaviors the parties can voluntarily control.** Notice that past behavior can no longer be controlled. Focus on present and future voluntary behavior.

B. **State the issue clearly and concretely.** Point out specific behaviors; avoid abstractions and generalizations.

C. **State the problem. Do not prescribe a specific solution.** Unilaterally prescribing solutions in advance of discussion with the other party precludes cooperative problem solving, and reduces the likelihood of finding a mutually satisfactory resolution.

D. **Do not object to the way a person feels.** Humans do not have direct voluntary control over feelings; feelings are not negotiable. It is not helpful, for example, to object to someone's being angry; anger is not negotiable.

E. **Do not label a person's character.** Character can be improved over time, but it is generally stable. People can't agree to change their character, then simply do so by an act of will. A "lazy" person, for example, can't simply decide to become energetic, and do so. Character is not negotiable.

A Simple formula for defining an issue constructively is:

Identify the behavior (or behavior pattern) and state
what is wrong with that behavior (or pattern).

> **EXAMPLE:** "Henry is giving assignments directly to some of my staff. Then, when I need them for a task, they are already occupied working for him, and I can't get my work done on time."

In some conflicts, it is difficult or impossible to identify objective harmful results of the other party's behavior. Sometimes, for example, their behavior just hurts our feelings, or makes us angry. Feelings are not negotiable, but they are real, and must be honored, even in work settings. In such conflicts, a formula widely applied in interpersonal conflicts is useful. This formula, often called the "tough love" statement, is as follows:

"When you/he/she (state the behavior), I feel
(state the feeling)."

> **EXAMPLES:** "When you let the others know what's going on and don't tell me, I feel angry." or "When you leave early and don't let me know, I feel very frustrated."

In stating an issue, it is not necessary to explain, or to justify a reported feeling. Feelings are important personal facts. They must be taken into account in discussing and resolving conflicts, but they are not negotiable.

If you are not able to define the issue in terms of voluntary behavior, following the above guidelines, or employing one of the above formulae, your issue is not negotiable, and you will be unable to apply the Six Step Process. The vast majority of conflict issues, however, can be defined in these ways. Once you have defined the issue in terms of voluntary behavior, proceed to Step 2.

Step 2. Decide Promptly Whether to Seek to Resolve the Conflict by Negotiation.

Once you have defined what is wrong, you can decide whether to try to resolve the conflict by negotiating with the other party. This choice may be difficult, but is *your* choice to make. There are risks involved in choosing to seek resolution. Confronting the conflict sometimes makes matters worse. There are also risks involved with choosing not to seek resolution. Unconfronted conflicts usually get worse.

Once the issue is defined you have only three options: (1) If you choose to do nothing (or to postpone taking action), you are choosing to *accept the situation as it is.* (2) If you choose neither to accept the situation as it is, nor to attempt to resolve it, you must *withdraw.* To remain in the situation would be choosing to accept it. (3) If you choose to attempt to resolve the problem, you must make an effort, and take a risk. You are choosing to *initiate a resolution effort and carry it through.*

Whatever you decide, *remember that you decided, and take full responsibility for your decision.* Also, whatever you decide, decide promptly. Remember that the most common dysfunctional strategy is to avoid dealing with the conflict, and the most common method of avoidance is procrastination.

Step 3: Approach the Other Party and Request Assistance in Resolving Your Conflict.

Having defined your issue and decided to attempt resolution, you are ready to act. You have an agenda. But the other party is **not** ready. To constructively negotiate a resolution requires the cooperative efforts of both parties. Therefore, before you can attempt to negotiate, it is necessary to secure the other party's agreement to cooperate in the negotiation effort. *Securing agreement to negotiate* is your central purpose in Step 3. Step 3 has three specific objectives:

1. to inform the other party of the issue,
2. to secure her/his agreement to meet with you at a mutually convenient time and place to discuss and resolve the conflict, and
3. to give her/him an opportunity to prepare for the resolution effort.

The outcome you seek in Step 3 is an agreement to meet at a specific time and place for the purpose of discussing and resolving your conflict. You also seek to enhance the probability of finding a mutually satisfactory resolution by arranging for the meeting to focus clearly on your issue, and by allowing the other party time to consider the conflict and prepare for the resolution effort.

Step 3 Guidelines for Approaching the Other Party:

A. If possible, approach privately. The presence of an audience can embarrass the other party, and provoke a defensive response.

B. Bear in mind that your purpose is to solve a problem, not to create one. Approach the other party with a request and a proposed task, not a complaint.

C. When you approach the other party, come quickly to your point. Do not visit about other matters before bringing up the issue. Conflict resolution is an unpleasant task required to manage relationships; treat it as a task.

D. State the issue *exactly* as you defined it in Step 1. Do not try to avoid the discomfort of confrontation by stating the conflict in vague or general terms. The other party will need to know the specific issue to prepare for discussion. And, it is important to establish a norm of openness and candor for negotiation.

E. If you have strong feelings about the matter, it is helpful to report those feelings to the other party. Emotions, such as anger or frustration, are internal facts that must be taken into account in a resolution effort. As with stating the issue, the other party will need to know about your feelings to prepare for discussion, and the norm should be openness and candor. Stating feelings does not include explaining or defending them. Feelings need no defense, and explanation can wait until the discussion.

F. Use the word "we," and avoid using "you" and "I." "We" promotes cooperation.

G. Make it clear that you are seeking a resolution that will *satisfy all parties*. You are not seeking to win at the expense of the other party.

H. Before approaching the other party, select an appropriate time frame for resolving your conflict. Decide, for example, whether it is important to resolve it today, or this week, or in a few days, or this month. This will allow you to set a time frame in requesting to meet and negotiate with the other party; the other party can then choose a time within that frame.

How to say it:

Keeping these guidelines in mind, when you approach the other party about the conflict:

- Tell him/her you have a problem you wish to discuss.
- State the issue exactly as you did in Step 1, indicating the behavior and the associated discomfort. Include stating your feelings about the matter as needed.
- State that you would like to resolve the problem in a way that satisfies both parties if possible.
- Make your request. Ask when (not whether), within your selected time frame, the other party can meet with you to discuss and try to resolve the problem.

> **Example:** "Ray, I've got a problem. Your department is taking two weeks to process purchase orders. My people are waiting for supplies, and that's slowing production. We're missing deadlines, and I'm pretty frustrated about it. I'd like to find a way to solve this problem in a way that works for both of us, and I think we can. When can we get together this week to talk about it and work something out."

However nicely you say it, in the Approach Step you are confronting the other party about a conflict. This is almost always uncomfortable for both of you. Typically, the other party will choose the most sensible, quickest way to relieve this discomfort, and respond by picking a specific time to meet. In doing so, she/he accepts everything in your question. That is, she/he agrees to (a) meet with you (b) at a specific time and place to (c) discuss your problem for the purpose of finding a mutually satisfactory resolution.

Most often, the other party will choose a time near the end of your stated time frame, thus securing time to prepare mentally and emotionally for the discussion. Some people prefer to discuss issues immediately once they are identified. It is advisable, therefore, to have time available for immediate discussion when you approach the other party. Occasionally, the other party begins discussion of the issue by asking questions, defending the problem behavior, or starting to explain. If this occurs, check to make sure he/she wishes to complete the discussion immediately before proceeding.

Often, the other party may claim to be too busy or otherwise attempt to evade the discussion. If this occurs, be persistent. Assure the other party that you seek a mutually satisfactory solution, and that you believe such a solution can be achieved. If you are unable to convince the other party to join you in the resolution effort, you must decide either to escalate your efforts, accept the problem and live with it, or withdraw from the relationship. In most conflicts, however, with some persistence, your approach will secure an agreement to meet and discuss the problem.

Step 4: Talk in an Effort to Understand and Resolve the Problem.

In meeting and talking with the other party you engage in a cooperative effort to:

- Discuss the issue to increase mutual understanding.
- Explore possible solutions, and find a resolution that will genuinely satisfy all parties.
- Make a clear, firm agreement regarding a resolution. That is, to make a contract on the resolution.

In Step 4 we focus on exploring the issue and generating a solution. Step 5 will focus on securing the contract. In Step 4 it is important to bear in mind that the meeting is yours. The conflict is your problem; you are the one who feels discomfort. In meeting with you, the other party is assisting you in solving your problem. Begin by thanking the other party for meeting with you. Take responsibility for guiding the meeting, keeping it focused to resolving your conflict. Below are some useful guidelines for the meeting.

Step 4 Guidelines:

A. Always model the behavior you wish to characterize the meeting.
B. Express yourself assertively. Clearly indicate your own thoughts, feelings, and needs. Be considerate of the other parties' thoughts, feelings, and needs.
C. Listen actively and empathetically. Listen in a genuine effort to understand the other party's position and feelings about the matter. (See Chapter 3, "Listening," for details on active listening.)
D. Show that you are listening, and that you expect the other party to listen. Make eye contact (unless direct eye contact is inappropriate in the other party's culture). Do not interrupt; do not allow the other party to interrupt you in the middle of expressing an idea. Acknowledge the other party.
E. As talk progresses, keep it focused on the issue and aimed at producing a resolution. This requires careful attention, assertiveness, and patience. Seek to understand one another, then to generate a solution to your problem. Do not deal with other issues until you have resolved the issue which precipitated the meeting.
F. Once some understanding has been achieved by discussion, offer suggestions for resolving the conflict. Ask for, and listen fully to suggestions from the other party. Consider combining suggestions.

G. Make every effort to find solutions that truly satisfy all parties before considering compromise solutions. Compromise only if you are unable to find a true "win-win" solution.

Following these guidelines, your meeting almost always increases understanding of one another's interests. Occasionally, understanding alone is sufficient to resolve the discomfort, and no further agreement is required. Usually, however, an agreement to change the behavior of one or more parties is needed to truly resolve the conflict. Persistence and patience in suggesting and considering potential ways to resolve the conflict can usually generate an agreement to resolve the conflict by changing specific behaviors. When this occurs, proceed to Step 5.

Step 5: Contract to Resolve the Conflict.

The purpose of Step 5 is to reach a clear and firm contract which, if carried out, will resolve the conflict. For a contract to be genuine, two conditions must be met: (A) All parties must clearly and overtly agree to (B) clearly specified, voluntary behaviors. Too often, negotiations which produce understanding and help the parties feel better end in a vague "agreement" that fails to meet one or both of these conditions. Then, when the vaguely described, but desired behavior changes do not occur, one or more parties feel betrayed, and the conflict is confounded rather than solved. Careful attention to Step 5 helps avoid this pitfall.

To accomplish Step 5, focus on the two conditions required for a contract:

A. **State what is being agreed to in concrete terms of voluntary behavior.** Clearly answer the question "What is each party agreeing to *do?*" Eliminate phrases like "try to" or "be sensitive to," or "make more of an effort." Such phrases are fine for other purposes, but they do not specifically identify voluntary behaviors. Voluntary behaviors are the only things humans can hold themselves and one another responsible for. So, only voluntary behaviors can be the subjects of your contract. Describing the agreement in terms of behavior may require creative effort, and even more negotiation. Persistence and patience may be required.

B. **After clearly stating the terms of the agreement, have each party explicitly state that he/she agrees to the terms.** As each party expresses agreement, listen and observe carefully. Mixed messages are common at this point. Observe nonverbal cues. If one's "agreement" appears less than genuine (Words saying "yes"; body language saying "maybe" or "no."), point out that the message appears mixed, and ask whether that party truly means to agree. Sometimes the party will clarify her/his message and agree. Sometimes more negotiation will be required to find terms that party can fully endorse.

It is not normally necessary the context of organizational work to put such contracts in writing. It is useful to build the kind of trust in which team members can count on one another's oral agreement. If the agreement is complex, however, or if there may later be doubts about its meaning, one party can agree to draft a memo of understanding on the point.

With completion of Step 5, the parties have a conflict resolving contract which, in most cases represents a "win-win" solution, satisfying both parties. A contract, however, is not a resolution unless it is carried out.

Step 6: Follow Through.

In Step 6, the focus is on carrying out the contract. Following through involves five behaviors:

1. **Act.** Do what you have agreed to do.
2. **Pay attention.** Notice whether the other parties do what they contracted to do. This does not mean that you constantly police the other parties' behavior; just that you generally pay attention.
3. When they do what they agreed to do, **show appreciation.** Give them positive feedback. Unless behavior changes are reinforced by positive feedback, humans almost always revert to the old, objectionable behaviors.
4. If other parties fail to do what they agreed to do, **point out the failure.** If they continue to fail, treat the problem as a conflict and renegotiate. Especially when conflicts involve habitual behavior patterns several renegotiations may be needed. Recognize that your best efforts may be insufficient to overcome the conflict. You cannot control another's behavior. If renegotiation fails, go back to Step 2; escalate, withdraw, or accept the situation as it is.
5. Consciously **accept responsibility** for your entire part in both the conflict and its resolution.

Neither this process, nor any other process, can guarantee satisfactory resolution of every conflict. In some conflicts, the issues are competitive, and defy resolution. Other parties' behavior, which we cannot control, always affects the outcome of a resolution effort. In most cases, however, applying the Six Step Process, or a similar direct, "win-win" negotiation approach, not only produces resolutions that minimize the damaging effects of conflict, but also promotes open, trusting relationships that enhance team effectiveness. If organization members can trust one another enough to express conflicts, feelings, and needs, and then make agreements that mutually honor one another's needs, they can sustain cohesive relationships, and optimize their communication climate.

Helping Others Resolve Conflicts

Usually, the best way to resolve a conflict is by direct discussion between the conflicting parties. And we noted above that triangulation is a common dysfunctional conflict strategy. It is also obviously true, however, that some people need help in resolving conflicts. Hence, the question arises for supervisors and work colleagues, as well as for professional consultants: How can we best help others resolve conflicts? Is there a constructive role for third parties that avoids the pitfalls of rescuing and imposition? The answer is "yes." And the correct term for that role is facilitator or "mediator".

The role of the conflict mediator is to assist the conflicting parties in their resolution effort by guiding them through a constructive resolution process. The purpose of mediation is to facilitate resolution, which means "to make resolution easier to accomplish." Yarbrough and Wilmot (1995) tell us that, done correctly, mediation helps in four ways: (1) It "reduces the costs of conflict to the organization." (2) It "increases everyone's satisfaction with the outcomes." (3) It "enhances relationships among people." And, (4) it "reduces the recurrence of conflict." (p. 3) They suggest the **mediation process** involves five stages:

1. Entry, which involves gaining mutual trust and establishing roles,
2. Diagnosis, which involves listening, analyzing, and suggesting a resolution process,
3. Negotiation, in which the parties negotiate with the mediator serving as teacher, and process regulator,
4. Agreement, in which the mediator helps synthesize and clarify agreements and responsibilities, and
5. Follow Up, in which the mediator serves as "cheerleader, monitor, and coach." (p. 11)

For mediation to be helpful, it is essential that the mediator (a) participate only with the full consent and trust of all parties to the conflict, (b) be genuinely neutral (on the sides of all parties, and on the side of the relationship between them), and (c) limit his/her role as much as possible to guiding the process, leaving the content of the solution to the conflicting parties.

Mediators can be co-workers, supervisors, or outside consultants. In most large communities there are certified professionals in mediation and conflict resolution who are skilled and experienced in mediating conflicts. Many organizational management consultants serve also in this capacity. When a conflict, or series of conflicts has reached a stage in which it is seriously crippling the ability of a group to work together, mediation can take the form of an off site meeting, which may last several days under the guidance of an outside facilitator. Such off site meetings are usually called "team building" meetings.

Macro Management of Conflicts: Attending to General Patterns

The role of upper management is to focus on general patterns of conflict management. In this role there are four general goals:

1. to minimize the occurrence of unnecessary conflict;
2. to promote constructive resolution of conflicts that occur;
3. to provide formal procedures, with enforcement mechanisms, to be employed when informal resolution efforts fail, and
4. to help mitigate the damaging effects of conflicts after they occur.

Let's briefly consider each of these goals.

1. Minimize the occurrence of unnecessary conflict. As we noted above, conflict is unavoidable. Unavoidable conflict occurs because people have different personalities, perceptions, and needs. Unavoidable conflict occurs because perfect communication is impossible; there will always be misunderstandings. Changes in conditions that bring roles into conflict also cause unavoidable conflicts. In most organizations, however, there are also many conflicts that could have and should have been avoided. Avoidable conflicts are caused by vague or overlapping role assignments, poor communication, withholding information, unrealistic expectations, win/loss decision-making processes, and by a generally negative social environment in which members feel unappreciated. To reduce occurrence of avoidable conflicts managers can:

- Clarify roles, authority, and lines of responsibility, and eliminate conflicting role assignments.
- Promote full, open communication, up, down, and across. Discourage withholding of information. Make information about organizational matters available to all members, except for personally confidential information.
- Implement participative decision-making, using consensus decision process whenever possible.
- Generate a positive work environment characterized by ample recognition and positive feedback.

2. *Promote constructive resolution of conflicts that occur.* To foster constructive micro conflict management in the organization managers can:

- Model constructive conflict management of their own conflicts with one another, with subordinates, and with customers and stakeholders. The behavior of upper managers profoundly affects the organizational culture.
- Develop employee conflict resolution skills by providing conflict resolution training. For supervisors, this training should include training in conflict mediation.
- Expect constructive efforts to resolve conflict. Deliver appropriate consequences (rewards and punishments) for employees' behavior in dealing with conflicts. Conflict management should be included as a significant factor in evaluating individual job performance.
- Make outside consultants available as needed for conflict mediation and team building.

3. *Provide formal procedures to be employed when informal resolution efforts fail.* Many organizations establish structured, formal processes, with written rules and procedures through which conflicts are presented to, and adjudicated by designated third parties. Designated third parties may be officials within the organization or outside arbitrators. Typically, there are formal procedures for implementing serious disciplinary action against an employee; grievance procedures which employees can apply to pursue complaints against superiors; and special procedures for handling certain difficult issues, such as sexual harassment or racial discrimination.

It is important that formal processes be used ***only when informal measures fail.*** Resorting to formal conflict resolution procedures usually damages relationships, and often damages individual careers.

4. Help mitigate the damaging effects of conflicts.   Even when conflicts are managed well there can be conflict aftermath. And, given that humans are imperfect, and that few people are really skilled in managing conflict, some conflicts will be handled badly, creating painful aftermath. Conflict aftermath in the forms of lingering anger, reduced motivation, or reduced sense of belonging and loyalty, is painful to individuals and costly to the organization. It can lead to further conflict. Aftermath cannot be wished, or ordered away. Managers, however, can help to mitigate and heal conflict aftermath in several ways. First, they can provide constructive outlets for members to talk about difficult feelings, and they can listen and acknowledge when people do speak about such feelings. Second, they can promote renewed communication among members whose relationships were strained by conflict; a new experience of working together and interacting constructively can help restore the relationship. Third, managers can sometimes take concrete action to compensate members for losses suffered in the conflict. Finally, managers can expect comfortable relationships to be restored over time, and clearly communicate that expectation.

Summary

This chapter has described constructive ways to manage conflict in organizations. Conflict was defined as a "discomforting difference" that includes three essential components: interdependence, opposition, and expression. Micro conflict management, which involves efforts to resolve conflicts that occur at an individual level, is distinguished from macro conflict management, which involves promoting constructive ways of handling conflicts, and minimizing the damage caused by conflict. Erroneous ideas about conflict are embedded in the metaphors commonly used to describe conflict, these ideas interfere with constructive conflict management. Five dysfunctional conflict management strategies block effective resolution: avoidance, reduced communication, triangulation, pay backs, and compromise. Seven principles underlie constructive conflict management. Fisher and Ury's four principles for effective negotiation of conflicts offer helpful guidelines for handling conflicts at work. Dues' Six Step Process for constructively resolving conflicts is a simple, behaviorally-based process that can be used to achieve mutual agreement. To assist parties in resolving their conflicts, principles and conditions for useful mediation were presented. In macro conflict management, there are several ways in which managers can minimize conflict damage by reducing occurrence of avoidable conflicts, promoting constructive resolution of conflicts that occur, providing procedures to formally resolve conflicts when necessary, and taking steps to mitigate conflict aftermath.

For more information:

Fisher and Ury, *Getting to Yes* fully explains the principles for effective negotiation, and offers a step by step guide as well as "trouble shooting" suggestions.

Fisher and Brown, *Getting Together,* is an excellent guide to building and maintaining a constructive conflict management climate.

Lerner, *The Dance of Anger,* offers useful advice for handling the anger associated with conflict, and for communicating effectively when angry.

Yarbrough and Wilmot, *Artful Mediation*, provides and explains clear directions for mediating conflicts.

References

Deutsch, Morton (1973). *The Resolution of Conflict.* New Haven, Connecticut: Yale University Press.

Fisher, Roger, and Brown, Scott (1988). *Getting Together: Building a Relationship that Gets to Yes.* Boston: Houghton Mifflin.

Fisher, Roger, Ury, William, and Patton, Bruce (1983). *Getting to Yes: Negotiating Agreement Without Giving In.* New York: Penguin Books.

Lerner, Harriet Goldhor (1985). *The Dance of Anger: A Woman's Guide to Changing the Patterns of Intimate Relationships.* New York: Harper and Row.

Lulofs, Roxane S. and Kahn, Dudley (2000). *Conflict: From Theory to Action* (2nd ed.). Boston: Allyn & Bacon.

Morrill, Calvin (1995). *The Executive Way: Conflict Management in Corporations.* Chicago: The University of Chicago Press.

Wilmot, William and Hocker, Joyce (2001). *Interpersonal Conflict* (6th ed). New York: McGraw-Hill.

Yarbrough, Elaine, & Wilmot, William (1995). *Artful Mediation: Constructive Conflict at Work.* Boulder, Colorado: Cairns Publishing.

Leadership is the central idea that guides positive personal and organizational change. This chapter describes how the theory and practice of leadership in today's organizations have been influenced both by changing conditions and evolving ideas about human behavior and motivation.

Kenci Lewis holds a Masters Degree in Organizational Communication from California State University, Sacramento and currently co-directs the organizational communication course at University of Arizona. Throughout her twenty year dual careers in post-secondary teaching and public affairs, she has studied and written about leadership, and conducted seminars in management and supervision skills to help raise the level of communication skills in organizations.

CHAPTER 12

Leadership in Contemporary Organizations

Kenci L. Lewis
University of Arizona

*"He who gains victory over other men is strong;
but he who gains a victory over himself is all powerful."*

Lau-Tzu

Key Terms

Leadership
Influence
direct message influence
indirect message influence
non-message influence
bases of power:
   reward, coercion, position,
   referent, expert, information
trait leadership

behavioral leadership
situational leadership
management
leader
knowledge management
modern organizations
post-modern organizations
emergent leadership models

Objectives:

This chapter will enable readers to

1. understand the elements of the leadership process
2. identify the finding of the three main categories of leadership theories
3. understand the differences between the purpose and function of management and leadership

4. recognize the differences between modern and post-modern organizations, the member perceptions, and the potentials for leadership in each
5. examine some methods of developing emergent leadership characteristics

In this chapter, we will describe the elements of leadership and the important findings of early theories, which will help us understand the leadership process in organizations. We will identify some important differences between leadership and management, terms that are often used synonymously in organizations. We will examine how the challenges facing modern and post-modern organizations have changed the expectation and occurrence of leadership behaviors. Finally, we will examine some of the current ideas promoted by organizational specialists and identify some ways to demonstrate leadership, regardless of position.

We begin with a definition: *leadership is influencing others through communication, resulting in a beneficial change in others and/or the situation for the greater good.* Let's examine the main elements of this definition.

Leadership Is . . .

When thinking about leadership, we can easily recall great men and women who have inspired others in times of trial, turmoil or threat. Presidents, civil rights champions, military or sports heroes, and others of great courage come to mind. We may also remember friends or relatives, business associates, or spiritual guides who have motivated or encouraged us with their words or actions. Yet if someone asked us to define leadership, we might have some difficulty. We may remember great speeches, super-human activities, courage in the face of oppression and other behaviors that influenced others to action. We also might remember specific crisis situations, such as a natural disaster, economic turmoil, or organizational disorder, and describe situational factors that allowed one person to rise above others and lead them to a more secure environment. Depending on the situation and the person relaying the story, leadership can be interpreted in many ways.

Most of us have a fairly good idea of what leadership is, but if we were asked to put those ideas down in words that all would agree with, we might answer, "Well, I don't know if I could define leadership, but I know it when I see it." We wouldn't be alone in our struggle to nail down this illusive idea. Through the years, authors, researchers, and philosophers have examined leadership, with each group claiming it as either art or science or both. And while it seems that leadership may mean courageous acts when we read about great leaders in literature, or behavior guided by known principles when we are being philosophical, there are common threads that run through all discussions. Leadership brings about a change in others or a situation, and leaders seem to have a great command of communication skills that influence others to work toward this change.

Some of us may wonder how that happened, or question what kind of magic occurred. Most of us, however, have more practical concerns. A manager in charge of a large production line, for example, wants to know, "How can I be more effective at leading my subordinates so we can be more successful?" College graduates taking entry-level positions in large organizations may think, "I know I have a lot of ideas to offer an organization" and then wonder, "How can I be effective in getting them across? Will my leadership skills ever be recognized?" Staff members in large organizations who select mentors and "learn the ropes" may ask themselves, "What is it about that person that I admire and want to emulate?"

Influencing Others through Communication . . .

To better understand leadership, let's first look at influence. *Influence is communication that is perceived to change another's beliefs, attitudes, values and/or behaviors*, and it can take many forms. As we learned in Chapter 1, communication can be intentional or unintentional on the part of the communicator. For example, when a CEO delivers a visionary presentation to the board of directors about a potential merger, the influence attempt is intentional. Influence can also be unintentional, when we see the new sales representative adopt a customer relations style similar to that of the sales manager, without the senior member being aware. The sales manager had no intention to influence others, but her success inspired others to pattern their behaviors after her. So whether an individual intends to influence others or simply acts in a way that others admire which in turn influences them to change their behaviors, the individual communicating this message can be perceived as having some impact on others.

Let's also look at how these messages can be communicated. Both direct and indirect communication can influence others. Even when communication does not occur, the implied message can have an impact. Even when we are not sending a message, there may be a perception on the part of the receiver that a message is being sent. Let's look at some examples of direct, indirect and non-messages and how they influence others.

In *direct messaging,* senders employ clear language, a logical sequence of information and supporting evidence to convey information, directions or advice as strategies to exercise influence. If a change on the part of the receiver occurs, some influence has taken place. For example, an engineering manager may write a memo to her staff detailing the need for speed and efficiency in finishing the XYZ project to meet the contract deadline. The team members recognize the urgency and the bottom line effects and are influenced to step up their activities to get the project finished on time and within budget.

Indirect messaging can be effective as well. In this form of influence, the sender does not overtly convey the entire message. Parts of the message are left unspoken and are silently supplied by the receiver. As you will remember in Chapter 7 about constructing effective arguments, warrants are premises that are typically not overtly presented, but are understood and filled in mentally by the audience. Allowing receivers to provide part of the argument can be especially effective in engaging the audience and convincing them to believe or behave a certain way. Let's look at an example in the organizational setting. The sales manager might suggest to the sales reps that bringing in new customers in outlying areas and expanding their sales territories might cause the CEO to consider building a new regional office. Without ever saying so directly, the sales manager is sending a message there would certainly be opportunities for advancement and growth, and that one or more of the sales staff could be promoted. The sales reps are supplying the missing information (increased opportunity) and may be influenced to increase their sales calls, introduce themselves to new customers, and overcome any satisfaction they have with the ways things are in the present. Influence has occurred.

We can probably relate to these examples of direct and indirect influence attempts, but what about the idea that, "**Non-messages** also send a message"? Think of a time when you have called a friend and he or she didn't return the call. You wonder if there is an unspoken message being sent: your friend doesn't have time for you; your friend didn't think your call was important; your friend didn't get the message. You may make any number of interpretations of this non-message from your friend, and it may or may not have influenced you in any number of ways, from rationalizing (she didn't get the call) to disengaging (she doesn't care enough about me to return my calls, so I won't bother to call her again).

In organizational settings non-messages also communicate. Consider what message is sent when a manager withholds both praise and criticism from her subordinates about their daily activities. In doing so, the manager may be intending to communicate her trust of her subordinates, sending the message, without ever saying so, "I know you will do your job to increase production figures to meet the estimates you gave me last month." The subordinates may or may not understand this message. If they understand the intent of their manager, they may feel empowered and trusted to do their jobs without being micro-managed. This non-message may influence them to be that much more productive, feeling they have some control over their own activities and enjoying the responsibility of making decisions and carrying out tasks in a way that will be most effective to get the job done without interference from the manager. As discussed in Chapter 1, the sense, tone, feeling and intention of a message, or in this case a non-message, depends on the sender understanding the receiver, the receiver understanding the sender, and both parties understanding the situation in which the communication takes place.

Influence can take many forms and can be communicated in different ways and still be effective. Let's look at some information that may help us understand what kinds of influence are used in organizations and some examples of the types of communication associated with each.

French and Raven (1959, 1965) identified six *bases of power* that people use to influence each other: *reward, coercion, position, referent, expert* and *information.*

- *Reward*—the perception that another can provide psychological and/or economic reward in exchange for compliance.

  Example: The CEO tells the engineering manager that if she takes a position at the company's new manufacturing plant in Cleveland, Ohio she will be promoted and given a salary increase. The CEO is using a "reward" as a way to influence the manager to agree to the relocation. The manager, also, perceives the CEO has the power to reward.

- *Coercion*—the perception that another can punish or withhold psychological and/or economic rewards for non-compliance

  Example: The CEO tells the engineering manager that if she doesn't accept the relocation offer to Cleveland, she may as well find employment elsewhere, because no more opportunities for advancement are available. The CEO is using "coercion," which in this case is withholding economic rewards, unless the manager agrees.

- *Position*—the perception that another has a legitimate right to influence others because of rank or role in an organization

  Example: A supervisor tells the line workers they need to attend a sexual harassment training class. The line workers attend the class, not because they will be rewarded in doing so, and not because their jobs are threatened, but because they recognize their supervisor has the authority over their activities and their time because of her position.

- *Referent or Charismatic*—the perception that another is attractive and similar and that his/her opinions, behaviors or attitudes are worthy of emulating

  Example: Remembering the sales manager in the previous example about unintentional influence, this manager conducted herself in such a manner, or was successful using certain sales strategies, that those around her wanted to perform in a similar way. Referent power can also be seen when someone is seen as charming or has a great number of friends who genuinely like that person because of her attitudes, opinions or behaviors. People like to be around those who have referent power.

- *Expert*—the perception of another being the most competent to perform tasks

  Example: In this technological age, we can readily think of examples of expert power. Ask anyone who has a computer whom they go to for advice about accessing a file on a bad disk, or getting a stubborn file opened. That person is perceived as having expert power. We are likely to take that expert's advice when we decide to buy a new pc or a laptop.

- *Information*—the perception of one person having information that is valuable to others

  Example: he financial manager of a company is often perceived as having a greater ability to influence the CEO in decisions than the managers who work directly with the product or the sales reps who work directly with the customers. All three aspects of the company are important, but the financial manager has information that is perceived to be the most valuable—the bottom line numbers on what it takes to keep the company's doors open.

While this is not an exhaustive list of power bases available to organization members, it does help us understand some of the perceptions people have of the means to influence others. We will look more closely at how these power bases are used in following discussions of different organizational structures, but first let's complete our definition of leadership.

When we recall instances in which someone influenced us, we may have felt it was for our own good, or we may have felt manipulated-that this person persuaded us for his or her own benefit. We may recognize that influence has taken place, but would we call this person a leader? Some other elements need to be added to our definition.

Resulting in a Beneficial Change in Others and/or the Situation . . .

Another key aspect of leadership is this: there is a beneficial change in people (followers) and a change in the situation. A change within people is often difficult to recognize: altered beliefs or values may or may not be observable. What we typically see as a result of personal change is a change in the person's behavior or attitudes and a resulting change in the situation or group outcome.

Imagine that a financial analyst in ABC Company proposes a change in the fiscal reporting procedures through a well-written and well-documented proposal to the CEO. The CEO is persuaded by the strong argument and approves the change. The CEO's beliefs in the merits of the previous system have been modified, although we may not see that change. What we do see is the change in the situation. The CEO communicates about this changed belief in the form of a decision to change the fiscal reporting procedures. She tells her managers and supervisors about this new procedure: why it is important, where to receive training in the new procedures, and how it will make the company more efficient. Decisions similar to this are made frequently in organizations, and in this case we see that some influence has taken place, both on the part of the financial analyst and the CEO. Those affected by the decision may see an improvement in this new procedure and a better annual financial report. The individuals and the situation have experienced a beneficial change, but has leadership occurred? Another factor must be examined.

For the Greater Good

A variety of persuasion methods can bring about change for someone's greater good, but these types of influence are not necessarily recognized as leadership. Inherent in the understanding of leadership is the notion that a greater good is attained for more than one or a few, or even a small group. Leadership is influencing others through communication, resulting in beneficial change in others and/or the situation for the greater good. Also implied in this understanding of "greater good" is that it will stand the test of time.

It is important to pause here to explain why the terms "beneficial change" and "greater good" are included in this definition of leadership. Leadership as influencing others to better themselves and to improve a situation includes a fundamental value judgment. If we take the scientific approach, we could operationalize the definition of leadership (strip it of value and make it measurable) as many have done and set up studies to examine influence, leader characteristics, follower characteristics and group outcomes from a clinical perspective. We would then need to include in our examination (in order to be objective) the behaviors and outcomes of those who direct or influence (manipulate) others for their own selfish intentions or for others' ill fortune. We could study the methods of Hitler and Capone, along with those of Martin Luther and Martin Luther King, Jr., and define either set of behaviors as leadership. That is not the purpose of this chapter.

Our purpose is to understand leadership in organizations, and to explore how one can demonstrate leadership behavior in different institutions. When we use the positive outcome criterion, we can identify whether we are being influenced by leaders or being manipulated by rulers or tyrants. When we are put in positions of authority where we have access to more power and ability to make decisions that affect or influence others, we might think we are demonstrating leadership, when in fact we are acting despotically. This definition, then, will serve as a way to examine our own behavior, examine other's behavior and learn how to demonstrate leadership. When we influence others to act on behalf of the greater good that stands the test of time, we are at the same time influencing ourselves to demonstrate higher principles. The effect is a change that influences the leader, the followers and the situation to a greater good. The effects of this form of leadership, then, are widespread and exponentially rewarding.

Learning from the Past

If we aspire to this level of influence, or if we simply want to understand more about how people may use influence in organizations, we can learn from many sources. Reading about courageous acts and the ways in which recognized leaders, such as Winston Churchill or Abraham Lincoln, have had positive impacts can help us form mental models of success. We can also learn from some of the research that has been done in organizations. These perspectives will help us see how leadership has been defined and taught to others, and how the understanding of leadership has grown through the years.

As early as Plato's definition of three types of leaders—the philosopher, the military commander, and the businessman—numerous philosophers, theorists and researchers have examined leaders and the leadership phenomenon. Decades of research and discussion about leadership can be sorted into three main approaches: *trait, behavior and situational.* The chapter also explores a fourth category—emergent. Each approach corresponds, for the most part, with the historical development of leadership research. Examining each approach will help clarify our understanding of leadership, and of leadership qualities that are needed in today's organizations.

Trait Theories

During the first half of the 20th century, theorists examined the traits of well-known leaders. **Trait**-focused theories of leadership are based on the premise that leaders have superior qualities or traits that enable them to influence others to accomplish a given task (Tead, 1929). Trait theories were the earliest attempt to formalize leadership research, and these models dominated the field from approximately 1904 to 1947. Stogdill's (1948) compilation of 50 years of trait research revealed leaders could be distinguished from nonleaders by the following characteristics:

1. capacity—intelligence, alertness, verbal facility, originality, judgement
2. achievement—scholarship, knowledge, athletic accomplishments
3. responsibility—dependability, initiative, persistence, aggressiveness, self-confidence, desire to excel
4. participation—activity, sociability, cooperation, adaptability, humor
5. status—socio-economic position and popularity

Certainly we can recall great men and women who fit these characteristics, from spiritual leaders to politicians. In the first half of the 20th century, executives, such as Henry Ford, were considered "leaders." These leaders of large organizations were revered, or feared for the power they held. The realities of harsh working conditions and the disparity between those who held power and those who did not was great. If we look back and examine the effects of the decisions and business practices of these "leaders," can we call their behavior "leadership"?

Some researchers continue to do both formal research and informal opinion studies on leader characteristics. While the trait model may help us develop a profile of characteristics that may be recognized in leaders, it does not take into account the communication used by leaders and how that communication influenced others to follow them and create a new reality.

Behavioral Theories

In the 1950s and 1960s, social science researchers expanded their thinking about leadership to include ideas about the role of the follower and the interaction among group members and the group leader. Gibb (1954) reasoned that without leadership, there was only headship or mere supervision, which is someone in a position of authority telling someone else what to do. After World War II, researchers studied the effects of managers' behaviors on the members of their work groups. We read about these studies in Chapter 2 discussions of the Human Resources approach to organizations. These studies culminated in **behavioral** models of leadership, also called leader-follower interaction theories. The main premise of this behavioral approach is that leadership is a result of effective group interactions, and that only those who influenced others toward a successful group outcome demonstrated leadership.

As a way of understanding what occurred when certain group members were seen as leaders, researchers began examining the kinds of communication that group members engaged in. After considerable research in organizational work groups, Blake and Mouton (1964, 1978) sorted managers' messages into two categories: communication about tasks and communication about relationships. Task messages are about the group goals, decisions to be made, or other concerns related to the work that must be done by the group. Relational messages are about the group members themselves, their personal interests or activities, and expressions of concern for or sensitivity to members' needs and feelings. For example, in a work group, members may talk about the project that must be completed, when it is due, to whom it will be sent and other types of discussion related to group success. This is task communication. In the same work group, members may discuss scores of their favorite ball team, what they are doing after work, feelings about each other or management, and other talk related to their satisfaction with being group members, which is considered relational communication. Behavioral studies examined how much of each type of communication (task and relational) a group leader would engage in and with what success.

Blake and Mouton (1964, 1978) charted and labeled these combinations of high or low task and high or low relational communication into leadership styles (see Figure 1). A

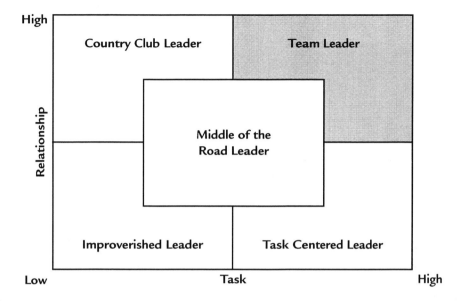

Figure 12.1 Blake and Mouton's Managerial Grid

group leader could demonstrate a leadership style known as *task centered* (high task, low relational), *country club* (high relational, low task), *impoverished* (low task, low relational), *middle of the road* (moderate task, moderate relational), or *team* (high task, high relational). The styles approach to leadership described this *team* leadership style as the most effective. Team leaders were thought to possess the greatest possibility to motivate others to accomplish group goals.

The shortcomings of Blake and Mouton's conclusion soon became apparent. Some scholars noted that certain managers were effective in accomplishing organizational objectives even though they exhibited very low concern for relational communication. Other managers were effective when they had low concern for task communication. In some cases, managers were effective when they had low concern for both people and production (Fiedler, 1967).

We will discuss the differences between management and leadership in more depth, but first let's examine the effects of the behavioral approach to "leadership". We read about the human relations and human resources approaches in Chapter 2 in which theorists recognized the importance of communication that flowed up, down and across the organization. Employees were given more of a voice and asked to participate in decision-making; in reality, managers retained the right to change those decisions if they felt differently and did so without consulting their employees. As a result, in many organizations, employees soon learned that providing input on how to improve operations made little impact on the day-to-day operations. Also, managers were being trained to show appreciation of their subordinates by using relational communication as well as task communication, but employees felt manipulated. At the management level, managers were not able to reap the expected benefits of participative management or to change their "leadership" styles at will. Other things were going on with regard to management/leadership that hadn't been accounted for by the behavioral model. Also, as we recall from Chapter 2, the organizational structure hadn't changed significantly in that period. Observing that the desired results were often not being achieved, researchers in the 1960s and 70s broadened their scope and definition of leadership, and began to look for other variables.

Situational Theories

Fiedler's research in the 1970's in church groups, student groups, sports teams as well as hierarchical organizations supported the new thinking that leadership was more than a mix of task or relational communication among leaders and group members and more than relative proportions of leader-follower participation in decision making. Fiedler and others recognized that depending on the situation and the communication style, the leader could have greater influence over group members. The key to leadership was this: **situational** variables, including the personal characteristics of group members, the amount of participation needed from group members, and the characteristics of the environment, should be considered when managers adopted a specific style. Furthermore, the leader must be able to change styles as needed. Fiedler (1973) maintained that a manager could adopt a particular leadership style that fit a given group, or the group could be engineered to fit the manager's leadership style.

Other theorists expanded this situational perspective, retaining the management styles idea and adding additional styles that could be used, depending on the needs of a given situation and the satisfaction felt by the followers. For example, Bass and Valenzi (1976) described directive, manipulative, consultative, participative and delegative styles. Studies revealed that the directive style might work in a crisis situation, while a delegative style would work in a less chaotic environment.

According to the situational theorists, this process of choosing and acting effectively demonstrates good management and thus, effective leadership. Many situational models, also called contingency models, use elaborate flow charts and decision-trees that help a manager choose among a variety of management styles, selecting the one that meets follower needs and situational factors.

At this point in our review of leadership studies, we might ask, "Have we lost the understanding of leadership while we were trying to be scientific? Of what use is a model that predicts which management style would be most effective in which circumstances, when the circumstances or situations aren't even clear?" Managers protested that it was enough to handle day-to-day interactions successfully with subordinates, and they had little time to study "what if's." An explanation of terms will help us understand where managerial studies have taken us.

Most leadership studies conducted from the behavioral and situational perspectives over the past 50 plus years used subjects who were in place in existing decision-making groups with positional leaders (managers) in existing hierarchical organizations. From this social science perspective, if the influence process was successful, and work groups were motivated by the manager's actions, such managers were thought to be leaders. Leadership, then, was considered to be effective management, which relied on positional authority, reward and coercion as the primary means of influence.

During the behavior and situational phases of leadership study, an interesting change occurred in the way leadership was discussed. The terms "management" and "leadership" began to be used interchangeably. Theorists described a set of "leadership styles" that managers could adopt to be effective in influencing or motivating their subordinates to accomplish work projects. Numerous books, training manuals, tapes, courses, and personal coaches promised any manager could learn to become a great leader given the training on what style to use. Also, by labeling all the management styles as leadership styles, the meaning of leader started to become lost in the language. Is an "impoverished leader" described in the list of leadership styles who fails to lead really a leader?

If we are to understand leadership, however, we must remember it is not just a style. It is an influence process that brings about a change in others and an *outcome regardless of position or role*, rather than an organizational process based on position or role. Let's examine the differences between management and leadership more closely.

Management versus Leadership

When we think about managers of organizations where we have worked , we don't usually think of them as leaders. After all, a manager's primary responsibility is to direct, facilitate, and coordinate the activities of people so the organization can be successful. **Management,** then, is the ability to motivate others to get their work done in a timely manner. **Leadership,** on the other hand, is an influence process resulting in a beneficial change in others and the situation. Managers are individuals in organizational positions for the purpose of completing work projects through others. **Leaders** are individuals in a variety of positions who influence others to change an outcome for the greater good. Managers bring about a change in a situation through controlling, directing, coordinating, and facilitating the work of others. They may use any means of influence, including coercion, to get the job done. Leadership is rarely associated with coercion, unless such coercion protects others from harming themselves. Leaders more often use passive resistance or persistent modeling of exemplary behavior if they intend to influence others to work toward a goal. Leaders effect change through a variety of means, most notably by richly communicating a vision that garners support from others. Effective managers may or may not demonstrate leadership. Leaders exhibit consistent, recognizable behavior that inspires others, and they can be found in any position within an organization.

As many theorists have noted, management is doing things right; leadership is doing the right things (Covey, 1991). Covey explains, "Management is efficiency in climbing the ladder of success; leadership determines whether the ladder is against the right wall." I would add that anyone may put the ladder against the right wall and not inspire others or influence them to the greater good. When executives and CEOs, who are in positions to make higher level decisions, make decisions for the greater good, they may be recognized as leaders.

Leadership Challenges in Today's Organizations

Today, those who study organizations and organizational leadership recognize change is the norm. Organizational contexts are changing and savvy organizations are restructuring to survive. For example, in an environment of stiff Asian competition, General Motors, a long-standing hierarchy in American auto manufacturing, created a team of employees to form the Saturn Corporation. Working with a blank slate, with no preconceived ideas of how a company should be structured or managed, the team researched manufacturing facilities and gathered ideas for creating a new and innovative production method. This empowered team, in turn, empowered employees by forming self-managed work teams. Saturn is recognized for producing high quality vehicles with few defects, and employees demonstrate ownership, offering to stay late to solve problems and exhibiting a relatively low absentee rate (2.5 percent compared with 10 to 14 percent in other GM plants) (Costley, Santana-Melgoza, & Todd, 1994).

Organizations that have not changed their hierarchical structures may be threatened in the face of changing economies and regulations. An organization's structure directly and indirectly affects the communication that takes place within it. Linked to this truth is the understanding that with the unpredictable nature of today's organizations, the predominant means of influence in organizations will change. Positional authority may give managers greater power to enact decisions, but the reality is it gives managers less power to influence others. What works in many organizations that are facing crisis is the ability of those in positional authority to communicate a clear vision of what can be accomplished to members who are then inspired to bring about the vision. Lee Iacocca, who led Chrysler Corporation out of near failure in the 1990s, communicated consistently and clearly to anyone who would listen, including the US Congress, his vision of the New Chrysler and the importance of the work of this company. Bill Gates of Microsoft, Inc. is known not for his charm, but for communicating his vision for the company's position in the global marketplace. Even in these chaotic times, the "I recognize it when I see it" idea of leadership is still dominant.

The Changing Environment

Today's business environment challenges organizations, from non-profits to multi-national corporations, to re-invent themselves in order to survive. From modifying the perception of the "average" customer to changing the foundation beliefs about the basic purpose of the company, organizations are making major changes.

Organizations are beginning to recognize a more culturally diverse marketplace. These consumers represent such a significant chunk of the buying power that companies are taking notice and changing their marketing strategies. Customer service departments are adding bilingual and multi-lingual representatives to meet the demands of this new market. Marketing professionals are designing strategies and promotional campaigns to capture a wider array of cultural norms and values.

And, the ways in which organizations respond to the market place requires different thinking about their management practices. Back in the late 1980s, organizational studies done at MIT predicted that information-centered enterprises would be smaller, more customized, and more work-team and project based, with an emphasis on open information systems and a need for adaptability to situational changes (Dertouzos, 1989). By the mid-90s, theorists were changing the management discussions to include knowledge and information as key organizational products. Lawler (1996) predicted managers need to think of their subordinates as information and knowledge processors rather than workers who crank out specific jobs. Organizations that do not recognize the change are becoming stuck. Gross (2000) reported in Business Week that of a survey of 200 executivess at 158 multi-national corporations, "80 percent said they had **knowledge management** projects in the works, and many had chief knowledge officers, or enlisted KM consultants." These knowledge management consultants help companies recognize that communication and information are the "most precious resources" in organizations, which are often buried in the rigid management practices of the hierarchy.

Other ways of thinking about the organization have changed also. In the past, organizations were created with the idea that growth and longevity meant expansion of the existing structure—this was success. AT&T is an example. Deregulation, which tore at AT&T's foundation belief of "we're the only game in town providing phone service," caused the organization's decision-makers to think outside of the box of land lines and fiber optics to satellite communication. This new kind of thinking is creating an entirely different perception of success. Some of today's entrepreneurs create an organization not for longevity, but for the expressed purpose of selling it in three to five years to competitors. These exit strategies are built into business propositions pitched to investors.

Change is the norm in today's organizations. Futurists predict that change will occur more rapidly and with greater intensity than it has in the past and that the way we think about organizations will continue to change. There is not one best way to organize—there are many ways. As potential organizational members, we will want to learn as much as we can about the organizations we join. One way we can re-conceptualize organizations to understand them better is to think of them in terms of being modern versus post-modern, depending on their structure and their approach to communication and information. We will examine these two types according to their structural characteristics, the members' characteristics, and the predominant use of influence. We will also look at some opportunities for leadership in each organization type.

Modern Organizations

The ideas of modernism center around reason, rationality, belief in science (we can discover the truth) and individual autonomy. Examples of modern organizations can be seen in the Chapter 2 discussion of classical, human relations and human resource approaches to organizations. We see the following characteristics in **modern organizations:**

- bureaucratic—isolated departments with separate functions
- hierarchical—multiple layers of authority
- chain of command—ideas and problems restricted to members in positions directly above and below
- communication—restrictive; formal upward communication, informal downward communication, grapevine or rumor mill lateral communication; restrictive external communication
- role dominant—individuals must perform within their specified roles
- logical—reliance on reason, rationality, accountability and accepted methods of justifying decisions
- sequential—small bits of information given only to those who have an immediate need to know.

Modern Organizational Members

Members of modern organizations typically exhibit the following characteristics:

- External locus of control—I do not have power or control over my destiny; others do. I expect the organization will take care of me. I am loyal to the organization. I will go where it wants me to go, even if that means relocating my family. In return, I can expect security: reasonable compensation, benefits and retirement.
- Expectation of consistency in policies, procedures, order, and status quo—I know the right thing to do because someone has told me what that is and how to do it. The "right way to do things" will not change and the organization will continue to grow. Change is disruptive.
- Work is seen as "work"—I expect a certain amount of slow, mundane work and should build a tolerance for repetitive or tedious activities.
- Technology is viewed as a challenge to order. Machines are costly, they change constantly, and, bottom line, machines will replace workers.

Use of Influence

When we look at the type of power or influence used most often in modern organizations, we can see a relationship between the organizational structure and the communication means available. The predominant uses of influence in these environments are *reward, coercion, and position* (Raven, 1965). Reward is communicated throughout the organization as job security, opportunities for advancement and guaranteed retirement in exchange for loyalty and hard work. Coercion may be used when necessary to assure compliance in unsatisfactory circumstances. "Either go along or get out," is the understood message. Position power is implied by the hierarchical structure of classic organizations. Even with the emphasis on employee needs in the human relations approach, and an increased emphasis on valuing humans in the human resources approach, the person sitting in the box higher in the organizational chart has more control and ability to influence than others sitting in boxes at lower levels. Communication in such organizations is generally formal, downward, and indirect, with information given in increments only to those who need to know. The bottom line message to organizational members who are not in positions of power is, "I don't trust you; I must control you."

Opportunities for Leadership

In modern organizations, leaders are typically recognized as benevolent executives who value others and who take the role of the loving parent. When people in positions of authority do not abuse their positional power, and when they bring about change for the better, we recognize their behavior as leadership. When individuals take personal responsibility for their actions and demonstrate high principles, such as honesty, dignity, and human respect, they typically have a positive impact on those around them. Often a modern organizational leader is perceived as having charisma (referent power) along with position. Leadership may also be found in management ranks as well as lower level positions. For example, a staff members might initiate a company recycling program, set up a charity golf match for employees, adopt a family for the holidays, or voluntarily train others in a skill or hobby. Creating strong, well-supported persuasive messages, delivering well-researched and well-organized presentations, and demonstrating effective conflict management skills are also ways to be influential.

Post-modern Organizations

The definition of post-modern is still being shaped in a variety of fields, including art, literature, architecture, and organizations. The ideas associated with post-modernism center around systems, environments, complexity, indeterminism (we cannot know the truth), pluralism (multiple truths), realism, and individual as well as organizational accountability. The term **"post-modern organization"** is associated with the changes occurring in organizational structures away from a classical and hierarchical to more flattened, technological and information based. In referring again to discussions in Chapter 2, post-modern organizations would be more closely aligned with the systems and cultures approaches. We see the following characteristics in post-modern organizations:

- Global: they are connected globally and are more global in understanding the entire economy, not just their niche
- Specialized: at the same time they understand globally, they fill specialized needs in the economy. For example, many companies outsource certain aspects of their organization, such as management information systems, creating a win-win situation for themselves and the vendor. The outside vendors enjoy economies of scale and can provide a necessary service and turn a profit. From the company perspective, vendors are held more highly accountable for accurate and reliable service than internal departments might have been. Outsourcing cuts overhead and releases upper level managers to spend their time on higher level decision-making.
- Tech'ed: technology is a requirement, not an option. Computers, networks, cell phones, cross-linked and multi-function communication systems help post-modern organizations survive. Many manufacturing organizations are turning production lines over to robotics, which are more reliable and safe.
- Environmental: organizations are understood as "systems," where everyone is connected to and part of the information base. The physical environment (work functions and work space) is a prime concern of employees; the natural environment is considered as well (use of natural resources and effects of usage)
- Information-knowledge based: The emphasis on information and knowledge (from compiled and processed internal data to global economic indicators) is a resource to be assimilated and used for profitability.

- Shape-shifted: organizational structure is flattened; middle managers are eliminated in many organizations and short or long term teams are assembled to complete a project and then re-assigned to other projects. Some organizations are temporary; they are created for the purpose of being sold or merged within three to five years. Organizations can be ethereal: members may interact without any face-to-face time. For example, some international companies have globally linked team members, telecommuting members who work from home or regional work centers who never see one another. Some on-line academic institutions report instances when their students who "walk" during graduation may be meeting their instructors or "classmates" for the first time. During their tenure as on-line students, they will have spent hundreds of instructional contact hours interacting with these individuals on course work and team projects and never met them face to face.

Post-modern Organizational Members

We have learned from human resources professionals, market researchers and sociologists that Generation X is making a greater impact than their predecessors, the Baby Boomers. This new generation is bringing a different set of skills and expectations to organizations.

- Internal locus of control: I have seen the results of my parents turning their lives over to the organization. The previous generation made the "company" their priority; and some were rewarded for their hard work and commitment. Some were downsized, laid off or otherwise disappointed. I will be the master of my own destiny, will follow my own path; I do not honor authority or position as powerful in and of themselves and will often rebel or shut down in response to direct orders. Do not expect me to uproot myself or my family for the convenience of the company. If it means I will lose my job, I'll find another one.
- Expect challenge and change: I am able to process a great deal of information rapidly, and I must see the importance and relevance of my work or I am not interested. I saw how my parent's generation brought about change through innovation and social movements. Change is positive and I expect it.
- Work must be challenging and fun: I am young and energetic. Do not put me in a mundane, boring job where I will lose my enthusiasm. I expect to be challenged, and I am adaptable and willing to learn. Also, I expect fun and excitement and that my work be an extension of my life, not compartmentalized and endured.

- Tech-tooled: I have grown up with technology. I can use the tools, and I expect to be equipped with the latest so I can perform at the highest level.
- Money, material and freedom focused: I have grown up in a materialistic society. I expect to have the money and materials to meet the norms of society. I also expect the freedom of choice and movement without constraints of tradition, custom or outside intervention.
- Relationships: I expect understanding and support from others, not rigidity. Relationships must be satisfying.

(Kelley (1985); Kay and Jordan-Evans (1999).

Use of Influence

We can immediately see that the predominant forms of influence and power in post-modern organizations rest on the bases of *expertise* and *information* (Raven, 1965). *Position power* is present as well, as is *referent power.* Expert power, or the perception of having more skill or knowledge in technology or complex task completion, is an understood form of influence in post-modern organizations. Along the same lines, information power (post-modern organizations are predominantly information and knowledge based) is clearly recognized as an influence base. Referent power is communicated among members who feel similar to, or attracted to, others for their admirable behavior, their friendliness, or their opinions that others determine were worth emulating.

When we remember that communication is the lifeblood in systems organizations, we can understand these bases of influence more readily. With the more informal, clear, direct and complete communication found across functions and departments within the organization, and with increased communication with stakeholders outside the organization, post-modern organizations send a message to their members, "I trust you and respect you. Do your job."

Opportunities for Leadership in the Post-modern Age

As we can imagine, opportunities for leadership in post-modern organizations will show up in unlikely places and are more than ever dependent on individuals who can demonstrate exemplary skills, desire for excellence and commitment to the greater good. A computer programmer who willingly takes on a challenging project, learns a new programming language, teaches the team and helps complete the project on time might be recognized as the key individual for an even bigger project. For going above and beyond what was required, she has positively affected others and the outcome.

As organizations are restructured, and as new organizations are formed, the opportunities for leadership during this chaotic time are phenomenal. Having a high level of technical skills and the ability to communicate a vision clearly and directly to others are essential. In a post-modern world, the situations themselves will provide opportunities for exceptional individuals with or without positional authority to influence others and achieve success. Current leadership theorists recognize the artfulness of leadership and offer a variety of perspectives or approaches to meet the needs of the future. I encourage you explore your own vision and see if you are up to the task.

Emergent leadership models

- New SuperLeadership—Manz and Sims (2001): A method of developing self-leadership: "behaviors, thoughts and feelings that we use to exert influence over ourselves" (p. 21). "A superleader is one who develops others to lead themselves" (p. 38).
- Wang and Chan (1995): Leadership surfaces when one can integrate complex variables (the individual is cognitively complex, can process complex information and can work in complex contexts.)
- Great Game of Business—Jack Stack (1994, 1992): Using the example of his own company, Stack describes an organization where every member is provided with all the information it takes to run the business. Essentially, each member takes ownership of the bottom line and works for growth. Stock ownership for all members is the rule.
- Principle-Centered Leadership—Covey (1990): "Principles are self-evident, self-validating natural laws . . . that apply at all time in all places. They surface in the form of values, ideas, norms, and teachings that uplift, ennoble, fulfill, empower and inspire people" (p. 19). "Principle centered leadership is based on the reality that we cannot violate these natural laws with impunity . . . individuals are more effective and organizations are more empowered when they are guided and governed by these proven principles."
- Warrior Image of Leadership (1985)—Leadership emerges when individuals of exceptional character strive to serve others in bringing about a better reality.

Leaders operate from a servant position, are cognitively complex, have a high tolerance for ambiguity, and use both intuition and logic. They are persistent and consistent in demonstrating principled behavior, meeting challenges, and communicating a vision of an attainable future for the greater good.

How to Emerge as a Leader

You can emerge as a leader, regardless of your role, position or level in an organization. However, if you hope to lead for the greater good, you must understand the complex environment in which you are functioning, interpret its opportunities for growth, and respond to challenges appropriately. As Castaneda (1973) pointed out, "Challenges are not a blessing or a curse. They are just challenges." Understanding environmental complexity will come through paying attention to news, information, and conversations. Reading, listening to and thinking about information are keys. Analyzing information and engaging in dialogue with others about situations, problems, and decisions are essential. Taking time to reflect is also important. Developing respectful, cooperative relationships in all areas of your life, and maintaining a high standard of ethical behavior are of prime importance. Also, developing character, incorporating principles such as honesty, integrity, fairness, dignity, respect, equality, is essential.

Develop Exemplary Communication Skills

To influence others in such complex environments, you must demonstrate exemplary communication skills. Essentially, communication is your primary source of power and influence in today's organizations. Whether these organizations use a modern or post-modern way of doing business, information and knowledge are the primary drivers. To gain information, you must be able to listen, and once you have information, you must be able to communicate it in an effective way so others can understand it. There may be great intrinsic reward in feeling as if you are an expert, but if you want to bring about change because of your expertise, you must be able to communicate your skills to others. Writing, speaking, listening, decision-making, working in groups, developing relationships, engaging stakeholders, and handling conflict are essential skills in any organization and are especially key in post-modern organizations. If you aspire to true leadership, you must develop these skills to the best of your ability and you must develop character to accompany these skills.

How to Develop Character and Leadership Capability

When your goal is service, when you honor others, and when are self-motivated, self-directed, and self-disciplined, you demonstrate character. You inspire others to the same attributes. When you have the necessary skills and information and can communicate a vision to others who are then inspired to work toward changing an outcome for the greater good, you will be recognized as a leader.

Things to do for yourself

- increase your knowledge of situations
- understand the groups and organizations you join
- define your ethical boundaries
- describe your personal vision and write your legacy
- set aside time to be
- practice communication behaviors that honor yourself and others in all situations

Ways to handle others

- Remember 80 to 90 percent of people are well intentioned and are doing the best job they can.
- Set standards for the 10-20 percent who are ill intentioned. You do them no favors by allowing them to manipulate you or use you or others in their race to do themselves in.
- Plant seeds for others' growth. Don't give advice—give them the information they need and let them decide.
- Give others all the information they need to do their jobs, manage their careers, and make decisions about the organization—teach them to work for the bottom line. The bottom line is about everyone's success.

"Be kind to each other. It is better to commit faults with gentleness
than to work miracles with unkindness."

Mother Theresa

References

Bass, B. M. & Valenzi, E. (1976) Contingent aspect of effective management styles. In J. G. Hunt & L. L. Larson (Eds.) *Contingency approaches to leadership*. Carbondale, IL: Southern Illinois University Press.

Blake, R. R. & Mouton, J. S. (1964). *The managerial grid*. Houston: Gulf Publishing Company.

Castaneda, C. (1973). *Tales of power*. New York: Simon and Schuster.

Costly, D. L., Santana-Melgoza, C. & Todd, R. (1994) *Human relations in organizations* (5th ed.). New York: West Publishing.

Covey, S. R. (1989). *The 7 habits of highly effective people*. New York: Simon & Schuster.

Covey, S. R. (1990). *Principle-centered leadership*. New York: Simon & Schuster.

DeRopp, R. S. (1979). *Warrior's way: The challenging life games*. New York: Delta Books.

Dertouzos, M., Lester, R., Solow, R. (1989). *Made in America: regaining the productive edge*. New York: Harper Collins.

Fiedler, F. E. (1967). *A theory of leadership effectiveness*. New York: McGraw-Hill.

Fiedler, F. E. (1973). Personality and situational determinants of leadership effectiveness. In E. A. Fleishman and J. G. Hunt (Eds.), *Current developments in the study of leadership*. Carbondale, IL: Southern Illinois University Press.

Feider, F. E. & Chemers, M. E. (1974). *Leadership and effective management*. Glenview, IL: Scott, Foresman.

French, J. R. P., Jr. & Raven, B. (1959) The bases of social power. In D. Cartwright (Ed.), *Studies in social power*. Ann Arbor, MI: Institute for Social Research.

Gibb, C. A. (1954) Leadership. In G. Lindzey (Ed.) *Handbook of social psychology*. Cambridge: Addison-Wesley.

Gross, Neil (2000). Mining a company's mother lode of talent. *Business Week* (3696) August 21–28 (135)

Kaye, B. and Jordan-Evans, S. (1999). *Love 'em or lose 'em. Getting good people to stay*. San Francisco. Berrett-Koehler Publishers, Inc.

Kelley, Robert. (1985) *The Gold collar worker*. Cambridge: Addison-Wesley

Lawler, E. E. (1996) *From the ground up: Six principles for creating the new logic corporation.* San Francisco: Jossey-Bass.

Manz, C. C. & Sims, H. P. (2001) *The new supeleadership. Leading others to lead themselves.* San Francisco: Berrett-Hoehler Publishers.

Raven, B. H. (1965). Social influence and power. In I. D. Steiner & M. Fishbein (Eds.) *Current studies in social psychology.* New York: Holt, Rinehart & Winston.

Schroeder, H. M., Driver, M. J., & Streufert, S. (1967). *Human information processing.* New York: Holt, Rinehart & Winston.

Stack, Jack (1992). *The great game of business.* New York. Doubleday.

Stogdill, R. M. (1948). Personal factors associated with leadership. *Journal of Psychology, 25*(1), 35–72.

Stogdill, R. M. (1974). *Handbook of leadership.* New York: Free Press.

Sun-Tzu (1963). *The art of war* (S. B. Griffith, Trans.). London: Oxford University Press.

Tead, O. (1935). *The art of leadership.* New York: McGraw-Hill.

Wang, P. & Chan, P. (1995). Top management perception of strategic information processing in a turbulent environment. *Leadership & Organizational Development Journal, 16*(7), 33–43.

Yager-Savasta, K. L. (1985). *A critical analysis of the applications of Castaneda's warrior imagine to the study of leadership.* Thesis: California State University, Sacramento.

PART III

Specialized Communication Functions

Training and Development are organizational communication processes that best serve their purposes when they are carried out by specialists. It is critically important, however, that every manager have a basic understanding of these processes.

In Chapter 13, Len Silvey draws upon twenty years' experience as a professional trainer, organizational developer, and training manager to explain the foundational principles and fundamental processes of his industry.

CHAPTER 13

Training and Organizational Development

Len Silvey
State of California

Key Terms

human resources	systems analysis model	outcomes and outputs
training	iterative	distance learning
organizational development	effectiveness	cost/return criteria
scarce resources	efficiency	action plans
needs assessment	performance analysis	implementation
training mandates	individual development plans	evaluation
transferability	goals and objectives	

Objectives

Our goal in this chapter is to give students a basic understanding of the nature, uses and limitations of the specialty of training and development from a communication perspective. In this chapter, we:

1. identify ten foundational principles which guide the training and development process,
2. briefly describe models and tools that can ensure effective use of the training and development resources.
3. establish that training and development are best viewed as communication processes.

297

Although training and organizational development are normally done by professional specialists, every manager and professional working in an organization should have a basic understanding of the nature, uses, and limitations of these processes. Training is a powerful communication tool used by organizations to guide employee behavior and achieve desired change. Almost all large organizations have some form of a training department, training and development unit, or human resources development program directed at the training and development of their **human resources.** An organization's people are often its most expensive resource, and training is a necessary investment to ensure that people are as productive as they can be. Some organizations attach training and development to their Human Resources or Personnel departments. Others attach it to the Chief Executive or Directorate offices. Others decentralize it to specialized parts of the enterprise. Many purchase training from outside providers. However it is organized and used, the training and development profession is rich with opportunity, and is a vital tool to assist in steering the organization.

Training and *organizational development* are usually carried out by specialists, including trainers, facilitators, diagnosticians, designers, organizational developers, technical writers, technologists, and evaluators. Organizations are wise to rely professional training specialists to do training and development. It is important, however, that every manager and every professional working with an organization have a basic understanding of the nature, functions, and limitations of these processes. To provide this understanding, we describe ten key principles that guide the work of training and development specialists, and briefly describe some widely used training and development processes and tools.

Definitions: By *training* we mean any event or process intended to inform employees, enhance employee understanding, or build employees' skills. By *organizational development* we mean any process intended to improve organizational processes or outcomes. The meanings and uses of these terms will become clearer as we discuss the important principles below.

Foundational Principles in Training and Development

Let's begin with a word about what training is *not*. It is common to find resources being used in organizations under the name of "training and development" for activities that clearly are *not* training and development. Misuse of resources occurs when policy makers and/or practitioners fail to recognize the nature, uses and limitations of training and development. Training is often wrongly viewed as the "feel good", the "fix all" or the "soft" side of an organization.

Some trainers contribute to such misguided views. In a recent conversation, for example, one professional trainer suggested: "The message I really want to get across to upper level management and executive people in organizations is that it is OK to use training as a way to get people away from stressful workloads and into a relaxed setting for a few days." He was seriously wrong. Use of training for rest and relaxation, or as a way to feel good, or as a general "fix all" solution does not reflect the principles at the foundation of the industry I embrace. Training and development are precise *and expensive* organizational tools, to be applied judiciously and accountably in pursuit of organizational goals. The ten principles discussed below provide a basis for understanding the nature and functions of training and development.

Principle #1

Training and development is a fast growing, multi billion dollar a year industry. And it will, and should, keep growing.

I remember reading in 1968, when I was an ambitious young organizational trainer, that the training and development industry had broken the billion dollar mark. I was impressed then by the size and apparent importance of my chosen field. Today, thirty years later, training is a fifty-five billion dollar a year industry that is still growing. This amount does not include the cost of higher education, where a great deal of professional development occurs. It includes only what organizations spend to train their employees and to improve teamwork or organizational processes.

What does training include? Here are just a few examples:

- orientations of new employees,
- core training of new recruits in technical job roles,
- sophisticated technical training, such as training of commercial air line pilots in the instrumentation of different kinds of air craft using electronic simulators,
- supervisory or management development training programs,
- customer relations programs,
- measurement of climate or attitudes in an organization,
- discovery of the different styles and approaches people bring to a team, disaster simulations.
- dissemination of information about innovations throughout the organization.

Where does training occur? It occurs in a variety of settings, from on the job processes, to rented meeting rooms, to teak paneled rooms with cushy chairs, to computer assisted, multimedia training rooms in an upscale training center, such as the FBI Academy in Quantico, Virginia, the Walt Disney University, Wells Fargo Bank's corporate training facility, or McDonald's Hamburger University.

This industry is likely to continue growing because it is not only an essential way to ensure that employees perform specified tasks correctly, but also an essential catalyst for organizational development. Training tells employees what to do, how to do it, and why. Beginning with Frederick Taylor (see chapter 2), organizational theorists and managers alike have recognized training as a necessary management tool.

Principle #2

The purpose of training and development is to improve individual, team, and organizational performance. Training and development create in individuals and teams the capacity to make reasoned changes that benefit the organization.

Approaches to training and development vary. Some professionals offer skill building opportunities that anybody in any industry must surely need to have (time management, stress reduction, sales skills, customer relations, etc.). Other professionals focus on directing training toward ensuring individual employees' ability to perform precisely defined tasks at measurably defined levels of expected performance. Still others apply training and development as vital tools for changing the direction of an organization, building harmony in a workforce, ensuring cohesion in management, supervisory or work teams, or engaging people in defining the direction of change.

All three of these approaches reflect the fundamental purpose of training. Useful training can take the form of (a) off-the-shelf training applications intended for wide application, (b) highly tailored training applications directed at mastery of specific and specialized tasks, or (c) organization development and team building. These approaches exist on a continuum from the strict behaviorist to the organizational change agent. Behaviorists argue that training has no place in affecting the attitudes, beliefs, or spirit of people in an organization. They insist training must focus on the behavior of people at work to assure they are performing defined tasks correctly. Organizational change agents (developers) argue that training is like the trim tab on the rudder of a ship at sea; a one degree twist in the trim tab can make a several thousand mile difference in the ultimate destination of the ship. They argue that shifting the direction of an entire enterprise has as much to do with capturing the imagination of the players, engaging them in the change and building supportive attitude and climate in the work force about the changes as it does with getting right performance.

Principle #3

Training is a scarce resource—it's use should not be squandered

Everybody wants to go to training. Most supervisors and managers want to provide training. It is possible for individuals or organizations to become training junkies, even when training does not produce change in performance. With organizations spending up to fifty-five billion dollars annually to provide it, training must be considered an expensive, as well as a limited resource. It is important that this resource not be squandered. The second part of this chapter introduces tools to aim the resource in directions yielding the greatest favorable outcomes.

Principle #4

Needs assessment *is an attempt to become informed about discrepancies between desired and actual levels of performance, and about where and what kinds of interventions can make the most difference.*

"Need" means any *condition (problem, issue, discrepancy or missed opportunity)* in the organization that, if addressed, could create a more productive or wholesome organization. Needs assessments seek information about conditions, forecast the continuation of conditions or trends, identify their potential ill-effects, and point out which conditions can be most usefully addressed. When people say, "We need sexual harassment training", the professional conducting needs assessment will ask, "Why? What are the conditions, (problems, or issues, or missed opportunities) in the organization's environment or in the environment of like organizations that lead you to this conclusion?" The professional will press for information on the scale and extent of the condition, where it is located and its particular characteristics. Needs assessment is a diagnostic process.

It is useful for managers and trainers to recognize that *there is no such thing as training needs assessment*. When we conduct a needs assessment, we cannot possibly know in advance if the findings will warrant a training solution or some other intervention to address the conditions revealed. Training is a solution, not a problem, condition, issue, discrepancy or missed opportunity (need). Robert Mager likens statements that "We have a training problem", to a situation where a person goes to his/her physician and says, "I have an aspirin problem." More likely the person will go to their doctor and say, "I have a headache," and the Doctor will say, "Try an aspirin" (Mager, 1974).

The parallel in training would be to say, "Other organizations in our industry are losing law suits and sizable sums of money to allegations of sexual harassment, and confidential interviews of members of our work force revealed that 42% of the respondents had either been the subject of or had observed others being the subject of unwanted sexual advances.", (findings of a needs assessment). The training professional would likely say, "Training in sexual harassment awareness may be a part of the comprehensive strategy for addressing these conditions."

When we conduct needs assessment in organizations, there are three possible outcomes related to training and development:

a. findings suggest that training is the right kind of intervention to resolve the conditions identified, or
b. findings suggest that training, only if it is accompanied by other types of strategies, can assist in resolving the conditions identified, or
c. findings suggest that restructuring, (or changes in policies and procedures, or personnel movements, or redirection to a different market, or a change in the mission or goals of the organization, etc.) is the appropriate intervention to resolve the conditions identified, and training is not part of the fix.

Principle #5

There are many methods by which we identify discrepancies and determine which discrepancies are fixable by training. Professional trainers and developers should have a broad variety of these methods in their repertoires.

Methods available for assessing needs and defining and diagnosing conditions that might be addressed with training include:

performance analysis	interviews
group approaches	individual development plans
debriefing of critical incidents	findings from inspections, etc.
examination of HR or other records	executive imperatives

The second part of this chapter briefly discusses each method. Varying conditions and organizational situations require various methods of data gathering. Moreover, best results are usually achieved through a mixture of methods. Hence, we expect that professionals in this field will be capable of employing a variety of assessment methods.

Principle #6

It is a responsibility of training professionals to question mandates to train people (if for no other reason than to discover the assessment of information underlying the mandate); training professionals should cause a dialogue with those issuing the mandate.

Executives often order that certain kinds of training be provided to employees. Such orders are **training mandates.** When training is delivered as a direct response to such a mandate it often misses the mark because it is *designed to meet the mandate* rather than to *address conditions that gave rise to the mandate.* Mandates usually come from higher authority, and higher authority can intimidate. Further, mandates often give a training course title (sometimes lacking precision of definition), which strata or type of personnel will be trained, how many of them, for how many hours and by when. The provision of a law or the directive of a CEO may state, "All first line supervisors in this organization will be trained in Interpersonal Communication by the end of the year." The job of the training professional is to ask with all due respect, "Why? What led to this conclusion?", and "May I conduct some fact finding (needs assessment) that will allow me to ensure that the training conducted is aimed at the right conditions?" The reason for raising questions about mandates is not that there is a belief that the mandate is wrong; rather such questioning is motivated by a desire to ensure that training addresses the conditions rather than simply meeting the mandate.

Principle #7

Organizations are legally responsible for training employees to perform tasks properly. If adequate training is not provided, and harm results from an employee's failure to perform properly, the organization is legally liable.

In many job roles, errors can cause serious harm to individuals and/or organizations. Mishandling of food in a food service operation, improper application of constraints to a hostile person arrested for violation of the law, improper posting of money amounts in a banking operation, failure to raise the wing flaps on an airplane after take off, failure to remove a surgical instrument prior to suturing a patient, inattention to spilled fluids on a supermarket tile floor,—all are errors that can yield major harm.

Organizations are morally and legally responsible to provide adequate training to ensure safety whenever serious harm can result from improper performance of an assigned task. Setting aside moral responsibility (which should in itself motivate managers to provide training), organizations often respond to the problem of **legal liability** and its potential cost. When harmed, people sue. Addressing the issue of liability, accused workers commonly seek to defend themselves by assigning responsibility to their employer. The employer is liable when the worker can show that he/she was either (a) not trained in the proper procedure for performing the task in question, or (b) was trained in the proper procedure, but that the training was inadequate.

Enormous sums are spent by organizations as a result of lawsuits involving claims of failure to train or failure to train properly each year. An adverse liability judgment can bankrupt an otherwise healthy organization. To minimize this risk, organizations invest large sums to provide appropriate training. The major **social benefit** is that training prevents countless incidents in which people might have been harmed by improper task performance.

Principle #8

Ensuring that training will produce actual improvement in work performance should be a central concern in training design.

The purpose of training is to improve work performance. Thus, it is important to ensure that skills learned in training are *transferred to actual work* performance. Unfortunately, this concern is often overlooked, and training is often designed and evaluated with more attention to its entertainment value.

When concern for **transferability** drives us, we design training to allow for practice of skill in task performance under conditions replicating those actually encountered on the job. We treat the safe environment of the training room as a place where trainees can make errors as a natural part of skill building. We sometimes have trainees accompanied to the work site by mentors who guide them in applying their newly acquired skill. Trainers lecture less, and participants practice more.

Principle #9

*It is important to recognize the common **misuses of training,** and to avoid them.*

Training is frequently seen as the fix-all for anything that goes wrong in the performance of tasks, and is, therefore, often wasted on problems that training cannot solve. Human beings, because we are human beings, sometimes have a hard time confronting performance problems with individuals at work. A supervisor who is reluctant to confront performance discrepancies of a performer can off-load the issue onto training and development professionals by framing the performance discrepancy as a training problem, even when the performance discrepancy may not warrant a training intervention. Mager

(1974) suggests examination of several causes of performance discrepancies prior to concluding that lack of training is the cause. Among others, he suggests (a) physical obstacles in the work environment, (b) non-performance is somehow rewarded, (c) acceptable performance is punished, (d) performance doesn't matter, or (e) work is structured improperly.

Principle #10

Sometimes training can be perceived as punishment. Training should never be required as punishment for poor performance, and it is important to avoid this perception.

A friend of mine spent the better part of an hour one evening explaining how she felt when her boss sent her an e-mail assigning her to go to a training course in "Interpersonal Communication" 500 miles from her work site, for five full days. There was no explanation of why the boss had made this assignment. My friend had sleepless nights for weeks wondering what awful transgressions she must have committed, or what others must have alleged to her boss, that he would conclude she needed a big dose of this kind of training. She felt she was being punished by being sent to training.

As a training professional, I have had frequent occasion to pause and remember my friend's agony about being assigned to training. Her anxiety about why she was being sent to training eliminated much of the value she might otherwise have derived from it. Today I take great care in thinking through how to approach a potential trainee or group of trainees about a training prescription. Training can and should be challenging, but it should never be punishing. Trainees who believe they are being punished with training are unlikely to learn very much.

Tools for Ensuring Effective Use of Training and Development

For planning and implementing sound training, I use and recommend a **systems model** that has nine steps. One key characteristic of this model is that it is **iterative.** Iterative means that it is a fluid process of non-sequential interacting steps. Steps in this model may not occur in order (i.e. first you do step one, and then you do step two, and then you do step three, etc.). Though I will discuss the nine steps though they do occur in order, realize that work on any one step is likely to affect prior work on one or all of the other eight steps, therefore requiring frequent revisits to steps already "completed." I call this the principle of *"The More You Know, The More You Know."*

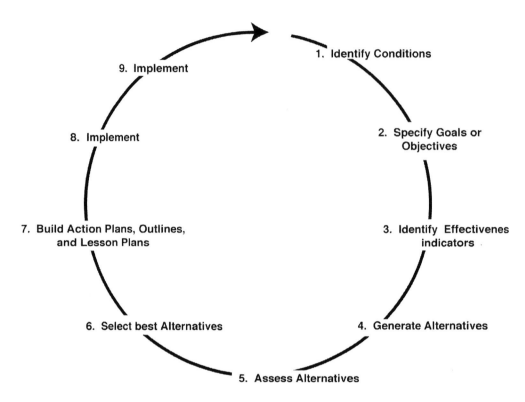

Figure 13.1 Systems Thinking and Behaving

The **systems model** is used as a way of sorting out the various steps, skills and roles in undertaking training and development planning and decision making. It divides into two main categories: *CONCEPT* and *ACTION* (see figure one).

Steps 1 through 6 attempt to determine what conditions are we trying to address with training, for whom, and why. Steps 1 through 6 also attempt to enlighten us about what we seek to accomplish with the training, the value of those accomplishments to the organization, and other ways we might favorably impact the conditions we want to address.

Steps 7 through 9 attempt to bring precision to action in the actual delivery of training. Concept has to do with considering what are we trying to accomplish for who, why and for what value. Action has more to do with how will we do it. Concept has to do with ensuring the ***effectiveness*** of our use of training resources (the degree to which we achieve the right goals). Action has more to do with ensuring the ***efficiency*** of our use of training resources. Below is a brief description of each of the nine steps.

Bringing Precision to Concept: Steps 1 through 6

Step 1: Identify the Condition to Be Addressed

This step involves conducting **needs assessment.** We begin by attempting to identify and describe condition(s) (i.e. problem, issue, performance discrepancy or missed opportunity) attempt to name conditions that exist in the organization. Statements about conditions may contain the following five kinds of information:

(a) **Facts:** Factual statements of condition(s) tell with data whom we are attempting to serve, how many, where, what characterizes them as a group, and what conditions they currently face.

(b) **Values:** Statements about factual conditions typically do not provide sufficient information to support judgments about how to respond. Thus, it is also important to respond to the question, "So what?", or "What are the probable *ill-effects* of the conditions identified. Statements identifying the positive or negative value of a condition are **value statements.** (Remember the distinction between fact and value issues discussed in Chapter 7. And remember that identifying a *problem* requires citing both the *fact* of a condition, and the negative value of a condition.)

(c) **Assumptions and Inferences:** Often, facts are not observable for every facet of a condition we are attempting to analyze. In the absence of directly observable facts, or to enrich our insights about the facts, we often operate on the basis of assumptions, or upon inferences we make, based upon facts we know. It helps to be explicit and clear whenever we make assumptions or inferences. Assumptions and inferences (1) express beliefs, and/or (2) identify relationships among conditions in the organizational environment we are characterizing.

(d) **Forecasts:** Conditions are usually described in the present tense; they state what is going on *now.* However, greater concern often centers on the *potential* effects of those conditions months or years from now if the conditions are ignored. While it is impossible to read the future, we can forecast futures by explicitly identifying factors expected to affect the future, and by using explicitly stated assumptions about the factors we identify.

(e) **Boundaries:** Boundary statements are often included in statements of conditions. They are useful when the facts clearly suggest specific pockets of the target environment or work force are experiencing the conditions we're concerned about. Stating boundaries serves to zero in on the specific parts of the organization, or of the problem we want to address. Stating boundaries is a way of defining and limiting the scope of a program.

Tools for Identifying Conditions

Assessment tools help to inform us about conditions so that we can better determine where to aim the training resource. These tools can provide data which serves as the basis for making the kinds of condition statements listed above. Assessment tools include:

Task Analysis/Standards Development/Performance Analysis

Performance analysis requires that (1) tasks be clearly defined, and (2) clear standard stating the level of expected performance of the tasks be in place. Given these conditions, performance analysis can show whether actual performance meets, exceeds, or falls below performance standards.

Performance analysis enables us to aim training and development at identified performance deficiencies. It is important first, however, to identify the causes of a performance deficiency. Why waste training on a performance deficiency that is not the result of a skill deficiency? Performance can often be improved be addressed with lower cost alternatives. For more on performance analysis I recommend the work of Robert F. Mager and Peter Pipe, *Analyzing Performance Problems or 'You Really Oughta Wanna'* (1974).

Performance analysis produces "cold data" —data that lends itself to rows and columns on a spread sheet and uses numbers—while other methods of conducting needs assessment produce "hot data"—data that comes from inside the organizational member and includes emotion.

Interviews

Skillfully conducted interviews can produce "hot data," providing rich information about conditions in an organization's environment. Effective interviewing requires assuring interviewees of confidentiality, asking of non-leading questions, building trust with interviewees, and recording responses, without editing, exactly as they come from the interviewees' lips.

Group Approaches

Gathering information by engaging small groups of people in interactive focus groups is less costly than individual interviewing; and group interaction itself can produce information and ideas that would not be generated in interviews. Groups, however, tend to produce less candor and less emotional tone than private, confidential interviews. I often use **Nominal Group Technique** and **Delphi** methods conducting needs assessments with groups (Delbecq, Van de Ven, & Gustafson, 1975). (These processes are described in Chapter 9.)

Individual Development Plans

Individual Development Plans (IDPs) are practical, easy to administer, and can form a rationale for determining which people should go to what training. IDPs are developed by individual employees, with the advice and approval of their supervisors. To create the IDP, an employee (1) describes his/her prior work experience, education and training, (2) states his/her long term and short term goals, and (3) proposes an action plan, listing activities, whether they be training events, job rotation, college courses, or, perhaps, working with a mentor, that will lead to goal achievement. Individual IDPs are then approved by management, and used as guides by managers in deciding what training to provide for whom.

Debriefing Critical Incidents

Debriefing (usually in groups) significant incidents (employee or customer deaths, riots, air line crashes, responses to disasters, etc.) can produce rich clues about the performance of organizations and their employees and gaps addressable by training.

Findings from Evaluations, Audits, Inspections, etc.

Virtually all large organizations undergo some form of scrutiny from outside. Frequently inspections, audits, evaluations, or bench marking processes reveal conditions that are addressable by training.

Examination of Personnel or Other Records

Personnel records can provide clues to changing conditions in an organization warranting training. Whether they be absentee records, turnover rates, changes in the character of the workforce, use of sick leave, grievances, bargaining issues, or elements of a memorandum of agreement, information is golden when we truly want to aim the training dollar well.

Informal Approaches

Many less formal approaches to identifying conditions warranting training are used (sometimes intuitively) by organization leaders and members. Observations in staff meetings, walking around, and informal conversations are examples. Any method of learning what's broken, where missed opportunities are, or where are the gaps in an organization, can be a valid needs assessment.

Step 2. Specify Goals and Objectives.

Based upon the needs assessment, decisions can be made about whether and what training to offer. The process of deciding what training to offer begins with establishing the goals and objectives. For statements of goals to fully serve their purpose they must: (a) relate to the conditions identified in the needs assessment, (b) focus on identifying desired results, (c) identify the direction and, when feasible, the amount of desired change, and (d) identify the value of the desired change to the organization.

Development of goals creates a framework for stating objectives. Objectives identify specific changes in the work performance of training participants (or of their team or organization). Training objectives are *not* about what the trainer will *do* or what participants will learn; they are about what changes will occur in work performance as a result of the training. To serve their purpose, training objectives must be measurable and time framed; they must identify a desirable result which can be measured, and they must indicate a time frame within which the result is expected to be achieved (Mager, 1975).

Step 3. Specify Indicators of Outcomes (Outputs)

Goals and objectives identify **outcomes.** Outcomes are the results actually desired. It is often impossible, however, to measure outcomes *directly.* When outcomes cannot be directly measured, it is useful to identify **outputs.** Outputs are measurable conditions that can reasonably serve as *indicators* of the extent to which outcomes have been achieved. Outputs serve as indirect measures of outcomes.

Step 4. Identify Alternatives for Delivering Training

Once we have identified the results we seek to achieve through training (outcomes), and specified how these will be measured (outputs), the next step is to identify the alternative methods available for delivering the training. Our concern here is to find the combination of alternatives mostly likely to meet our goals and objectives at the least cost in time and resources.

There are many alternative ways to engage participants in training. Below is a partial list of training methods:

Lecture:

Presenter speaks to the participants. Lectures can be supported and enhanced by using:

Slides: still photographs projected on a screen.

Videos: video cassettes that sometimes dramatize the information being imparted.

Visual displays: diagrams, maps, layouts germane to the subject matter.

Overheads: transparencies projected on a screen to enhance and enlarge information being presented.

Films: movies or clips from movies demonstrating information or dramatizing subject matter being covered.

Audio Cassettes: tape recordings of information (sometimes dramatized) related to the subject matter being covered is played, reviewed and discussed with participants. Recordings can be of actual situations (interviews of bank customers or wards in a juvenile hall, play back of Air Traffic Control conversations, etc.) or of situations acted out by participants immediately prior to playing the cassettes.

Handouts: Articles, newspaper or magazine clips, custom made narrative or illustrations given to participants and used to memorialize subject matter.

Demonstration:

Presenters act out "the wrong way" and/or "the right way" to do something (sometimes combined with role play, small group exercises, or simulations—i.e. "now you try it.")

Workshops:

Participants are given an assignment to complete a task or build a product related to the subject matter being covered and are expected to complete the task working with others within a prescribed time frame. Workshops usually incorporate one or more other methods (e.g. role plays, hands-on practice, simulations, shared experiences, computer assist, etc.)

Computer Mediation:

Learning tasks at a work station assisted by a computer sometimes combined with on screen tutorials, programmed instruction, branching or decision trees.

Role Plays:

Selected participants are given information on a role (a supervisor, a customer, a customer service representative) and a situation and asked to carry out a transaction the "right" way.

Hands-On Practice:

In a safe training environment, participants practice doing what they've been trained to do; learning can follow error as well as doing it right.

Simulations:

Situations fabricate conditions like those likely to be encountered in the work setting. Participants are asked to perform tasks related to the situations appropriately. Simulations range from the very simple (target practice) to the very elaborate (air line pilot flight simulators, disaster simulations, driver training automobile simulators).

On-The-Job Training (OJT):

Trainees are asked to carry out a task at the work site under the tutelage of a coach and to participate in a debriefing followed by practice. A high percentage of all training occurs on-the-job.

Instruments:

Usually paper-and-pencil devices asking participants to select their favored responses to 10 to 50 questions whereupon responses are cast into profiles characterizing the style, category or world view of the respondent in some framework. Frequently a group norm (anonymous comparison of the profiles of all present) follows.

Program Notes:

Participants in a training session are given outlines of material to be covered and asked to fill in the blanks as subject matter is covered.

Shared Experiences:

Participants are asked to give examples of situations they've been through related to subject matter. Sometimes combined with small groups.

Case Studies:

Given information (sometimes quite detailed) about a situation, participants tell how they think the situation should be handled, how they think it was handled in the real world, or what choices and decisions should be made about the situation.

Fish Bowl:

Selected participants act out behaviors related to the subject matter in front of the other participants (those acting out are in the fish bowl being observed by those watching) who are sometimes asked to take notes or to watch for particular behaviors which differ from observer to observer; observations are later shared and discussion follows. One variation allows for observers to "tap in" after some time has passed and demonstrate how they would prefer to see the performance acted out.

Modeling:

Presenter actually conducts themselves consistent with the conduct about which information is being presented.

Observation:

Participants go to the site of events they will be expected to participate in and watch actual events take place (often followed by a debrief or a discussion). E.g. a court room, an autopsy, or a visiting area in jail.

Recorded Feedback:

Participants are asked to perform a task singly or in groups while being audio or video taped. Playback is then debriefed and used as a learning tool.

Games:

Games are often used as metaphors for events likely to occur in the real world and participants are asked to discover principles from playing of the game to things that could occur on the job. Games are sometimes used with decision making, problem solving, or communication subject matter.

Ice Breakers:

Highly engaging, but brief, exercises to get participants acquainted with one another (usually early in a program) and feeling safe with one another prior to engaging in potentially embarrassing events.

Discussions/Conferences:

Presenter/Trainer evokes dialogue among participants and manages the traffic while ideas and experiences surface.

The above is only a partial list of alternatives currently in wide use. We have now entered the age of electronic information, and training is already beginning to occur over the *Internet.* **Distance Learning** is already available on some subjects, and will no doubt be a widely available alternative method of training delivery in the near future. It is important to recognize that a growing variety of alternatives is available, and to identify select methods and combinations of methods that are available in any given situation so that informed choices can be made concerning how to most effectively and efficiently accomplish training goals and objectives.

Step 5. Analysis of alternatives:

Selecting the best delivery methods from among alternatives requires systematic analysis. There are many different criteria by which people make choices from among competing alternatives: political feasibility, social acceptability, equity of treatment, environmental impact, cost relative to return or impact, etc. Most commonly used criteria have at least some validity. There has been a strong preference, however, in resource conscious organizations to use of **cost/return criteria** to determine which alternatives to pursue. Cost/return criteria answer the question, "Which alternative or which combination of alternatives should be pursued?" with the answer, "Choose the alternative or the combination of alternatives that will result in the greatest favorable impact on the conditions being addressed for the dollars being spent.

Step 6: Selecting the best mix of methods

Systematic analysis enables us to identify the best available mixture of training methods to const/effectively meet the sated goals and objectives of training under existing organizational conditions. Analysis can be done by staff, but *managers* must make decisions to commit training resources. Based on the analysis of alternatives, a decision is made to commit resources to designing and delivering training by those methods. One a decision is made, effort can move to building action plans to implement the training.

Bringing Precision to Action: Steps 7 through 9

Step 7: Building Action Plans, Outlines, Lesson Plans, and Scheduling Plans

The action of developing and delivering training is guided by four types of work plans: Action Plans, Course Outlines, Lesson Plans, and Scheduling Plans. Each type of plan has a specific function.

Action Plans tell "Who" has to "Pursue What Tasks" by "When" and for what amount of "Resources" (often expressed in dollars). Whether the action plan is a simple outline or a complex PERT or CPM chart, or whether it is a Gantt chart, all serve to answer the same who, what, when and for how much money? Action Plans lay out to work process for designing, producing, and delivering the training.

Course Outlines are brief, serve as a thumb nail sketch of the training event, and give and overview of what is to be covered. The purposes of course outlines are to a) get agreement in the management process on the elements of training before building the detail, b) announce the program, c) sell the program, and d) guide design.

Lesson Plans are comprehensive, task specific, highly detailed descriptions of the training to be provided. The purposes of lesson plans are to a) minimize liability potential by documenting what was trained and how, b) ensure consistency of delivery when a program is going to be delivered multiple times and, perhaps with different instructors presenting different offerings, c) guide support personnel expected to have designated materials, supplies equipment and room arrangements in place when participants and trainers show up, and d) guide delivery of the training.

Scheduling Plans deal with the logistics of training delivery. They describe the systems of announcing, assigning, registering or enrolling participants in training programs in a way that guides "go/no-go" decisions along the way if adequate numbers of participants fail to materialize. These systems are also accompanied by rosters and evaluation formats that assist (along with objectives, and lesson plans) with documenting that the training occurred and who received it.

Step 8: Implementation

Carefully developed action plans guide actual delivery of the selected training, and allow flexibility for unanticipated adjustments that must be made along the way. If we have conducted sound needs assessment, stated performance based training objectives, made best choices about which training event will produce the greatest outcome for the organization, carefully selected the "right" methods of delivery and built useful implementation plans, we have laid the groundwork necessary for effective training. But , in order to be effective, training must be delivered well, and delivery depends on excellence in staffing. Selection of the right combination of trainers and facilitators makes an important difference.

Step 9: Evaluation

The primary function of evaluation is to measure the extent to which the conditions (problems, issues, performance deficiencies or missed opportunities), precisely defined in step 1, were improved by training. Evaluation is not primarily concerned with identifying who is at fault when failure occurs. The purpose of evaluation is to identify and solve problems in order to enhance future efforts at accomplishing the objectives and pursuing continual improvement. When Effectiveness Indicators are carefully developed in Step 3, a plan for evaluating the effectiveness of our efforts follows naturally.

There are six primary ways to **evaluate** training. The further down the list we go the greater the expense and the higher their value.

1) Ask participants to rate the training event on a number of factors (quality of instructors, degree to which stated training objectives were met, appropriateness of the training site, appropriateness of materials used, etc.). This method produces subjective impressions of participants, at best, and does not tell us whether conditions in the organization we were trying to impact were impacted or to what degree. This method is expedient, though and minimizes expense of evaluation. It yields valid information at the extremes; that is, when ratings are consistently high or consistently low, we can count on them.

2) Measure change in participants' level of knowledge using a pretest and a post test. Compare the pretest and post test scores of individual participants or construct a comparison of the group norms before and after. Again, this method does not show impact on organizational conditions or performance improvements. It serves as a proximate measure of whether participants will return to

the job site with information presumed to be useful in pursuit of job tasks. Transferability is assumed.

3) Measure the degree to which participants are able to appropriately perform work tasks addressed by the training. Conduct these measures before and after training. This approach is superior to the prior two because it delivers some assurance that transfer can occur to the job site.

4) Measure participants' actual, on-the -job performance of work tasks addressed by the training. Conduct these measurements before and after training. Follow the participants back to the job site. This approach measures whether transference actually has occurred.

5) Replicate data collection methods used during Step #1 of the systems model (measuring of conditions warranting training interventions) through performance analysis, one-to-one interviews, group approaches, findings from inspections or evaluations, examination of Human Resource information, surveys, etc.) to determine if organizational conditions that drove us into the training delivery in the first place have, in fact, changed, and hopefully for the better and to the extent estimated in Step #3 of the systems model. This approach tests whether the organization has actually gained the intended benefits of the training.

6) Evaluation of the training work plans is also important. Evaluation of training's impact on the problem (1 through 5 above) naturally leads to reconsideration and adjustments in our objectives, outputs, and/or training methods.

Notice that evaluation yields new statements of conditions and new identification of problems. In effect, evaluation leads to a new Step 1 in the systems cycle. This is why the nine step systems model is described as a circle rather than as a linear sequence. Notice, too, that when training and development events are selected, designed, delivered and evaluated as outlined above, the training and development is fully integrated the managements overall decision making processes in guiding an organization toward its goals.

Training and organizational development can ensure that leaders and employees are doing right things, and doing them right. The work of training and development is a professional discipline, requiring rigor, systematic analysis, and creativity. When training is selected, designed, and delivered with rigorous professional standards, it can be a powerful communication tool by which an organization can direct its personnel to better performance and better teamwork, and by which management can steer employee efforts toward identified goals.

References

Davis, R. H., Alexander, L. T., and Yelon, S. L. (1974). *Learning system design: An approach to the improvement of Instruction.* New York, NY: McGraw-Hill.

Delbecq, A. L., A. H. Van de Ven, and D. H. Gustafson (1975). *Group Techniques for Program Planning: A Guide to Nominal Group and Delphi Processes.* Glenview, Ill.: Scott, Foresman.

Hager, Olaf (1952). Delphi, Rand Corporation "P", 1952, Santa Monica, CA.

Gagne, R. M., and Briggs, L. J. (1974). *Principles of instructional design.* New York, NY: Holt, Rinehart, & Winston.

Goldstein, I. L. and Buxton, V. M. (1982). Training and human performance. In M. D. Dunnette and E. A. Fleishman (Eds.), *Human performance and productivity.* Hillsdale, NJ: Lawrence Erlbaum and Associates.

Kolb, David A., (1976). *Learning Style Inventory.* McBer and Company, 137 Newbury Street, Boston Mass. 02116.

Mager, Robert F., and Pipe, Peter, (1974). *Analyzing Performance Problems.* Belmont, CA: Fearon Publishers, Inc.

Mager, R. (1975). *Preparing Instructional Objectives* (2nd ed.). Belmont, CA: Pitman Learning, Inc.

Marketing is a communication activity in which all organizations, public as well as private, must engage in order to survive and grow. In this chapter, Dr. Reichert explains the fundamentals of marketing communication and illustrates its importance in organizational communication.

Tom Reichert (Ph.D., Communication, University of Arizona) is Assistant Professor of Advertising in the Department of Advertising and Public Relations at the University of Alabama. Dr. Reichert has extensive experience in teaching and conducting research in the area of marketing communication.

CHAPTER 14

Marketing Communication: How Organizations and Consumers Talk to Each Other

Tom Reichert
University of Alabama

Key Terms

marketing
product concept
marketing concept
marketing communication
promotion
promotion mix
implicit promotion

advertising
personal selling
sales promotion
publicity
public relations
visual merchandizing
internal marketing

VIEW model
marketing communication
AIDA approach
ELM
exposure context
IMC

Objectives

This chapter discusses the importance of marketing communication for organizations and consumers. Its objectives are to:

1. Provide you with a conceptualization of marketing communication
2. Discuss several ways organizations and consumers keep in touch;
3. Identify the five tools organizations can use to get their message out;
4. Introduce a theory of persuasion and show how it relates to marketing communication;
5. Introduce you to future trends in marketing communication; and
6. Present guidelines for effective marketing.

Believe it or not, all of us participate in the process of marketing communication many times every day. Maybe you've been asked a few questions by a telemarketer? Have you participated in a focus group or completed a survey either in person or through the mail? Have you received a credit card offer, seen a promotional message on a website, or clicked on a banner ad? Have you ever redeemed a coupon, read the instructions on a package, or responded to a sale sign in a store window? If you have said no so far, this one will get you: Have you ever watched TV, listened to the radio, seen a billboard, or looked through a newspaper or magazine? Unless you are from another planet—you answered "yes" to some of the questions above. What do all of these activities have in common? You've guessed it: They are all forms of marketing communication. Actually, it's surprising when one considers the massive scope of marketing communication and its prevalence in our lives. Consider the following, for example:

- The average person is exposed to hundreds of advertising messages (Woodside, 1987) and thousands of promotional messages every day (Tynan, 1994).
- Over 322 billion coupons are distributed every year in the U.S. That's more than 1,285 coupons for every man, woman, and child (Whalen, 1994).
- The average adult spends 9 hours and 38 minutes using consumer media each day (Veronis, Suhler & Associates, 1999).
- Almost 13% (15.5 million) of our entire civilian workforce is directly involved in marketing communication (U.S. Bureau of the Census, 1995). This number would surely soar if one considered all the people involved in shipping, producing and financing marketing communication.
- Over $236 billion was spent on advertising in the U.S. in 2000 (Insider's Report 2001).
- The average person watches six hours of commercial messages on TV a week (Comstock, 1991), and by the time children reach their 14th birthday, they've seen over 350,000 TV ads (Wimmer & Dominick, 1994).

As you can see, marketing communication is a powerful force in our society. According to Shimp and DeLozier (1986, p. 3), "the practice of marketing communications is universal." Despite its ubiquity, marketing communication is rarely included in books about organizational communication. Scholarship in this area focuses on communication within the organization (Putnam & Cheney, 1990) as the other chapters in this book will attest (except the chapter on public relations). I find this odd for two reasons.

One, organizations rarely exist in a closed environment. From a systems perspective, a healthy organization must maintain open boundaries with its environment so that information can easily flow between the consumer and the organization. This is especially true in our postmodern world. Organizations must establish and maintain a healthy dialogue with the public to respond to a rapidly shifting marketplace. In the fast changing world of telecommunications, imagine what would happen to Verizon if it simply decided to curtail its marketing efforts. Over time it's likely the company would either lose customers or fail to gain enough customers to exist. Katz and Kahn (1990) argue that understanding how organizations sell their goods is just as important as understanding the communication that takes place within an organization.

Second, I would argue that marketing information is the primary way people become familiar with an organization. For instance, how many of you have had direct experience with Archer Daniels Midland (ADM)? Probably not many of you. However, if you watch its commercials on *CNN* or Sunday morning political talk shows you might know them as the "supermarket to the world." The images and messages we absorb from marketing communication establish an organization's image or reputation. People develop perceptions about a company (sexist, cutting edge, rock-solid, ethical) based on the images they in advertising or the news. What kind of a company is J. Crew or Victoria's Secret? What kind of organizational structure do they have? Whether you realized it or not your attitudes and beliefs about these companies are based almost entirely on the impressions you form of them based on their marketing communication (TV ads, catalogs). Why is this important? Because research has shown that time and again our attitudes and beliefs are directly linked to our behavior.

So far I hope you've come to the realization that marketing communication is pervasive and vital for organizational survival. After reading this chapter, you should be able to define marketing communication and understand how it fits within the organization's overall marketing strategy, appreciate how theory can be used to guide communication efforts, and last, be familiar with the future of marketing communication. Now, let's take a closer look so that we can reach a common understanding of exactly what marketing communication is and how it works.

Definitions

Before explicitly defining communication within a marketing context, it might help us to understand exactly what we mean by marketing. According to the American Marketing Association, **marketing** is defined as:

"The process of planning and executing the conception, pricing, promotion, and distribution of ideas, goods, and services to create exchanges that satisfy individual and organizational goals." (AMA, 1985, p. 1)

If one thinks back to the times of rural markets, marketing literally means "bringing to market" one's goods. Imagine a farmer harvesting some of his carrots (product), rinsing them off and putting them in his wagon for the trip to market (distribution). Once there, he decides on a fair exchange for his carrots (price) which he writes on the sign next to his stand (promotion). We've just seen our farmer complete the four P's of marketing.

Although marketing is more complex for a multi-billion dollar, multinational organization, it still follows a similar process when determining what and how it will market its goods to meet organizational goals. Another relevant question is why the farmer chose carrots to take to market instead of lettuce, eggs, or some of his hogs? If the farmer chose to grow and sell carrots this year because that's what he's grown all these years and he simply likes carrots, it would be safe to say that our farmer is following the **product concept:** Produce what you want and people will buy it. Or maybe, the farmer may have been savvy enough to rely on the **marketing concept.** If this was the case, he may have read in the weekly paper about the need for vegetables in this season's market. He may have talked with some buyers at the local pub and discovered they were looking specifically for carrots. Either way, the farmer discovered the needs and wants of his customers and sought to satisfy them by selling (exchange) his carrots so that he could meet his organizational goals (providing for his family).

What have we learned from the farmer thus far? We know that marketing is about satisfying both consumer and organizational goals and that the marketing concept is integral to this process. All organizations should expend the energy to determine how best to satisfy needs and wants. Are you beginning to see why communication is essential to this process? Organizations must establish a dialogue with customers to survive. As with any dialogue, it is important to note that both the organization and consumers are senders and receivers of messages in this marketing communication process (see Figure 14.1).

Although people think organizations are the only ones doing the talking, marketing communication is a two-way process. Organizations are not the only ones who "do the talking." From conception to post-purchase satisfaction, consumer input is vital throughout the entire marketing odyssey. Methods of encouraging dialogue from consumers come in the form of focus groups, questionnaires, interviews, database management, and telephone surveys.

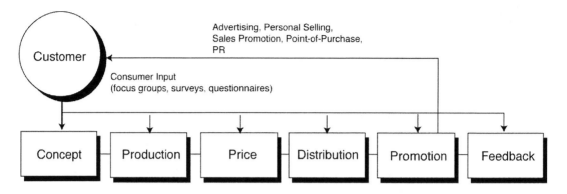

Figure 14.1   The Marketing Communication Process. In this model, the organization establishes dialogue with consumers to maximize mutually satisfying exchanges.

Less sophisticated methods may consist of simply passing complaints from customer service agents to management. Regardless, consumer input not only influences what type of product will be offered, but its shape, its price, where it will be available, what messages will be most effective in delivering customers, why they chose to purchase or not, and any changes that need to be made to enhance post-purchase satisfaction. An effective organization will take advantage of all of these opportunities to provide what the customer wants. Unfortunately, not all companies maintain permeable boundaries to ensure the passage of essential information.

Once the organization has produced, priced, and distributed a product to meet customers' needs, it is time for promotion. Now the organization sends messages to get its needs met (sales). **Promotion** has several functions but its most essential purpose is to motivate customers to action (Shimp & DeLozier, 1986). There are several tools that promotion managers have at their disposal to motivate customers: advertising, personal selling, sales promotion, public relations (or publicity), and point-of-purchase communication. These five tools are generally known as the **promotion mix.**

Let's briefly define these concepts. **Advertising** is defined as the paid placement of messages in any of the mass media by an organization that seeks to inform and/or persuade members of a target market (Anderson & Rubin, 1986; Bennett, 1995; see also Thorson, 1990, 1996). Although ads might attempt to motivate immediate behavior ("Only while supply lasts; Sale ends today"), the most effective use of advertising is to create awareness and teach people about a product. **Personal selling,** on the other hand, is an effective means of persuasion. Salespeople are able to remove psychological barriers to buying by answering objections as they come up. Obviously, personal selling involves delivery of a persuasive message by an agent of the organization (salesperson) to a customer usually in an interpersonal setting. Potential buyers come in contact with the salesperson in two general ways: A sales clerk in a fixed location (e.g., department store) or salesperson-initiated contact (e.g., door-to-door salesperson). The third tool within the promotion mix is **sales promotion.** This element is defined as marketing pressure applied for a predetermined, limited period of time to stimulate trial, increase demand, or improve product availability (Bennett, 1995). Sales promotions can be targeted at the consumer, retailer, or wholesaler by either the manufacturer or the wholesaler. Examples of sales promotion include offering discounts, coupons, sweepstakes, free samples, or special events like Calvin Klein appearing at Bloomingdale's to introduce his new fragrance. **Publicity** (perhaps better known as **public relations**) is also an essential part of the mix. It is generally defined as the generation of nonpaid news or editorials printed or broadcast in the mass media. Two primary functions specific to public relations include overall image management for the organization and increasing or changing the public's awareness or image of the organization or a product it offers. Last, a vital promotion mix element is point-of-purchase or **visual merchandizing.** It is defined as how the product is presented for sale in a store (Anderson & Rubin, 1986). It includes the use of interior and exterior displays, signs, and props—key elements that prompt or reinforce a previous message (in an ad). These elements represent the promotion mix and organizations can utilize all or none of them in a campaign.

When implemented in a coordinated effort these elements serve several important purposes besides those mentioned above. According to Shimp & DeLozier (1986), a variety of marketing communication mechanisms help to accomplish the following functions: (1) Informing customers about the organization's products and services, (2) persuading people to prefer particular products and brands, to shop in certain stores, to attend particular entertainment events, and to perform a variety of other behaviors, and (3) inducing action from customers such that buying behavior is directed toward the marketer's offering and is undertaken immediately rather than delayed. Simply, an integrated marketing communication effort helps both the organization and consumers meet their needs by giving information, persuading, and inducing action.

While promotion is at the heart of marketing communication, other elements of the marketing mix also communicate meaning to the customer (see Figure 2). Other el-

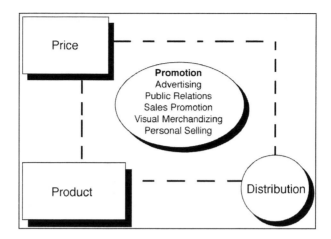

Figure 14.2 Marketing Communication primarily consists of the promotion mix but price, product, and distribution also help to communicate value to the consumer.

ements are often referred to as **"implicit"** promotion. For example, the product itself has indirect communication value. Products communicate to customers via size, shape, brand name, package design, package color, and other features. These features provide the customer with information regarding the total product offering (Dommermuth, 1984). Obviously, marketers want to be sure that the overall package is an effective marketing communication vehicle. Twedt (1968) developed the **VIEW model** which is still widely used today to ensure maximum product communication potential. Is the *visual* appeal of the package sufficient to attract attention at the point of purchase? Does it include essential *information* (usage instructions, claimed benefits, slogans, and supplementary information)? Does the emotional appeal of the package evoke a desired feeling or mood? And last, *workability:* Is the packaging functional (easily stored, protect the contents)?

Price is also a communication mechanism. At minimum, price identifies a rate of exchange, but it also connotes quality. Marketers use price to communicate status, snob appeal, quality, or low purchase risk (Shimp & DeLozier, 1986). As such, price communicates economic and noneconomic factors to consumers.

Last, distribution outlets can have communication value. Stores, like people, possess personalities. Two stores selling similar products can project entirely different product images to prospective customers. Imagine walking into the GAP, or any store for that matter. What is it like? What music is playing? What are the salespeople wearing? How is the merchandise arranged? The point is that a store's image is composed of many dimensions (e.g., architecture and exterior design, interior design, personnel, signs, location, service, displays, reputation, and clientele to name only a few). Store image, in conjunction with the packaging of a product and its price, tell the consumer a lot about the value of the product beyond the explicit messages visible in more traditional promotional activities. Today, nothing is left to chance. All these dimensions (packaging, price, and distribution) are constructed to most effectively fulfill consumer needs and wants. Remember, healthy organizations encourage discussions with customers throughout the marketing process to effectively deliver what people want.

At this point, you should have a good idea of what marketing communication is and what it does. It is much more than ads, press releases, salespeople, and coupons. It also involves "implicit" forms of communication. But more importantly, marketing communication should be thought of as a dialogue between an organization and the consumer. It is through this dialogue that organizations come to understand and subsequently create that which consumers most desire. Also through this dialogue, organizations seek to motivate consumer action by more "explicit" promotional means to get their needs met. This definition of marketing communication is summed up succinctly by Shimp and DeLozier (1986) as, "the collection of all elements in an organization's marketing mix that facilitate exchanges by accomplishing shared meaning with the organization's customers and clients" (p. 4). Next, let's look in more detail at how marketing communication can effectively facilitate consumer motivation.

Theory as it Relates to Marketing Communication

When seeking to understand how marketing communication works, there are a multitude of models and theories upon which to draw. For instance, there are theories that specifically consider personal selling, public relations, advertising, and sales promotion. For the sake of brevity, we will explore a theory that has received a good deal of attention since its inception in the early-1980s as it relates to advertising. Before introducing that theory, it is important to review an approach to marketing communication in use since the 1900s.

Since advertising began, the gospel for doing effective advertising is known as the **AIDA approach.** This model assumes that viewers move in a linear series of steps (from perception to purchase) when exposed to an ad. To most effectively tap that process, an effective ad should grab the viewer's *attention*, get them *interested* in the product, create *desire*, and finally, convince them to purchase the product (*action*). Recently, this model has been criticized because people don't always react in a step-by-step manner. For example, people sometimes buy products because they like them, but occasionally they buy products and then decide whether they like them or not. The AIDA approach doesn't do a good job predicting consumer reaction in these instances. Fortunately, new approaches have been developed to help marketers better understand the full range of consumer responses to advertising. Let's take a closer look at one such theory.

The Elaboration Likelihood Model (ELM) was developed by two social psychologists, Richard Petty and John Cacioppo (1986; see also Petty, Cacioppo, & Schumann, 1983; Petty, Unnava, & Strathman, 1991), to help explain research findings in persuasion studies (see Figure 3). They postulated that people are not able to attend to and think deeply about every persuasive message they are exposed to. People attend to some messages more than others depending on how personally relevant they find the information to be (motivation) and how much ability or opportunity we have to process the message. The theory predicts that persuasion can occur in two different ways depending on motivation and ability to evaluate the central arguments of a persuasive message. Messages that viewers have time to elaborate upon (consider the pros and cons) are processed centrally. Centrally-formed attitudes last longer, are more resistant to change, and are better predictors of behavior. As you know, people don't always have time to read ads or to consider all the reasons why they should or should not buy a product. Or maybe, there isn't even any copy in the ad to consider. In either of these two cases, ELM would predict that persuasion still might occur but attitudes formed in this way are different from centrally-formed attitudes. Attitudes formed through the peripheral route are more temporary, easily changed, and don't do a good job of predicting behavior.

Let's consider two important ways that ELM can help marketers craft effective consumer-oriented messages. First, advertisers can use ELM to help them match their message to the processing strategy of the consumer. For example, research has shown that for certain product categories (e.g., chewing gum, typing paper, pencils) consumers don't have much motivation to read a long list of product benefits. In this instance, the marketer may decide to use flashy visuals, attractive models, or any number of peripheral cues to persuade the audience. On the other hand, certain high involvement product categories like appliances, automobiles, and homes entail a good deal of risk and uncertainty. In these situations, consumers are more likely to search for product information before making a decision. In this case, advertisers may structure their messages to appeal to just such an audience by providing plenty of information (or central arguments) as to why the consumer should purchase the product. In this way the advertiser can match the consumer's level of motivation or involvement by designing messages congruent with those search factors.

The **exposure context** provides another way ELM can inform message construction. This includes consideration of consumers' ability to consider a message. For example, the time someone can spend looking at a billboard varies widely from the time some-

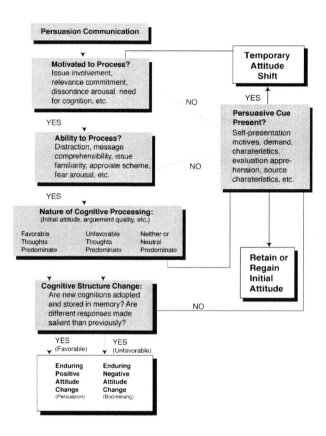

Figure 14.3   The Elaboration Likelihood Model of Persuasion. This theory predicts that persuasion can occur in either a central or peripheral route depending on a receiver's motivation and ability to think about the persuasive arguments within a message.

Source: "Communication and Persuasion: Central and Peripheral Routes to Attitude Change" (p. 4), by R. E. Petty and J. T. Cacioppo, 1986, New York: Springer-Verlag. Copyright 1986 by Springer-Verlag. Reprinted with permission.

one can spend reading a brochure. How can ELM be of assistance? If I'm an appliance dealer, I know that potential customers who enter my store are searching for information. That means that the marketing communication in my store (e.g., brochures, visual merchandising) had better tell them why my washing machines are better than my competition. We already know that motivated consumers are more likely to allocate time thinking about persuasive communication. We also know that if consumers are persuaded by central arguments they aren't as easily swayed by competitive messages, and are more likely to buy from me.

On the other hand, if I wanted to place my message on a billboard to keep my store in people's minds, I would use a simpler message. Maybe we could put an image of a famous celebrity on my billboard. In this instance, people who like the endorser may also come to like products. Likability is a desirable goal, but attitudes formed peripherally don't last as long, are vulnerable to competitors' messages, and don't readily lead to the purchase of a washing machine.

Take a look at an example of a message that was designed to appeal to the central processing route. In Figure 4 we can see that Apple is presenting us with several arguments why a potential computer purchaser (parents in this case) might want to invest in a Macintosh for their child. For most people a computer is a high risk purchase, not only in terms of investment, but also in terms of compatibility with other systems and other users' systems. For people looking to invest a few thousand dollars for the family computer, it is safe to assume that the decision maker will be motivated to consider information to reduce uncertainty related to this high risk purchase. Apple appropriately diagnosed this type of search situation and designed a message that provides many arguments why one should consider a Macintosh. Based on what you know about the ELM, if Apple is able to persuade you that Macintosh is the answer, how receptive will you be to an ad for an IBM personal computer?

The Samsung ad in Figure 5 exemplifies the peripheral approach to persuasion. One obvious difference between this ad and the ad for Macintosh is a lack of copy. There are no strong verbal arguments why you should purchase a Samsung microwave oven. Do they last longer than competitors' products? Are they a better value? The ad doesn't say. What is noticeable in this ad? That's right; an evocative visual. According to ELM, pleasurable visuals in a message provide peripheral cues that may be influential. In this instance, you might come to like Samsung because they have hip ads. What else do we know? According to the ELM, our positive feelings toward Samsung might lead to persuasion via the peripheral route. However, we also know that this type of attitude may not

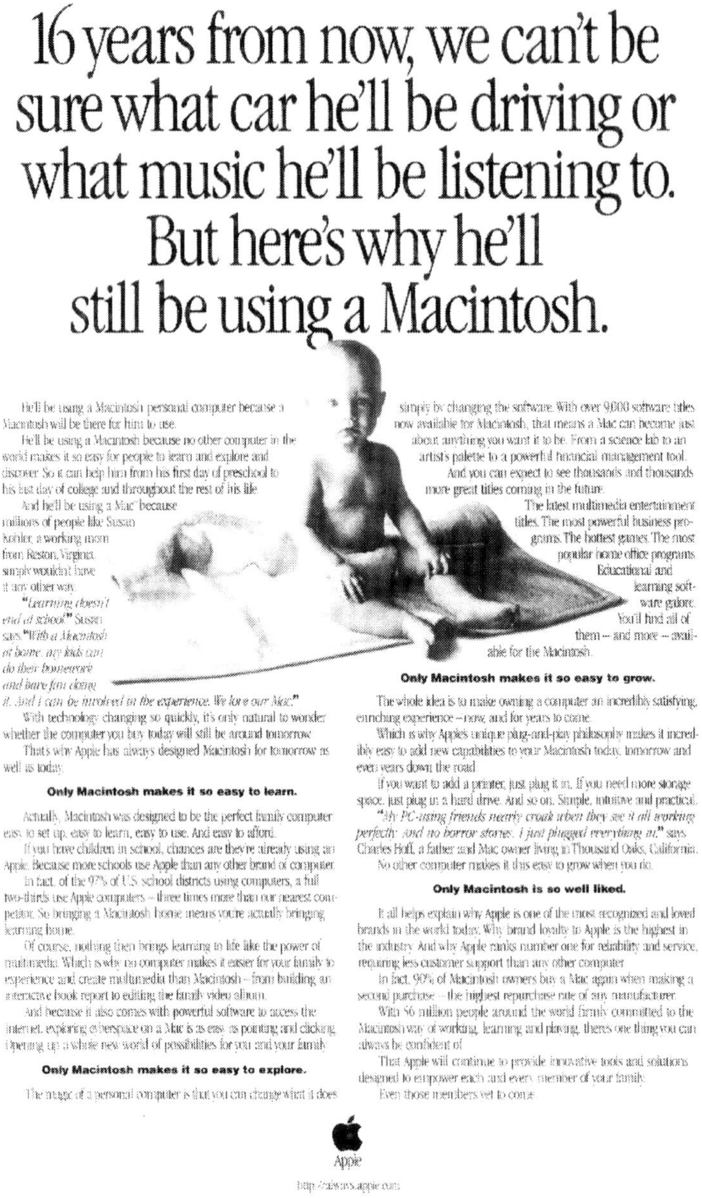

Figure 14.4   The ad from Apple takes a central route to persuasion. Reprinted with permission of Apple.

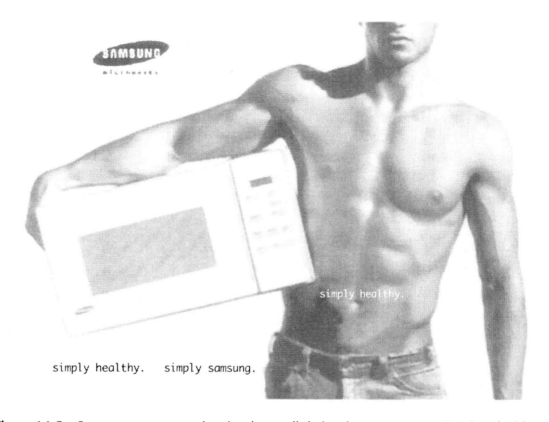

simply healthy.   simply samsung.

Figure 14.5 Samsung uses evocative visuals to sell their microwave opens. Reprinted with permission of Samsung Electronics, USA.

last long or might change in favor of a competitor's ad with even cooler visuals three pages after this one. This is not to suggest that Samsung made a mistake by using this approach. The goal of this campaign may have simply been to change or reinforce the image of Samsung electronics.

The ELM is but one of many ways to model the persuasion process in an advertising context. As you can see, it's helpful to use theory to understand why customers process messages they way that they do and how to craft messages that effectively motivate consumers based on their processing level and the exposure context.

Integrated Marketing Communication

Any discussion of marketing communication would be incomplete without mentioning the concept of Integrated Marketing Communication (**IMC**). This concept represents a new way of thinking "about" and "doing" marketing communication. There is some debate, however, as to whether IMC is new or just a return to a more interpersonally-oriented buyer-seller exchange. Either way, marketing messages are becoming increasingly personal for two reasons: One, technological advances have enhanced the ability of organizations to keep detailed records of their customers in databases. Two, increases in media technology have made it easy to send messages to tightly defined segments of people based on viewing habits. For both of these reasons, it is now relatively simple for companies to send personalized messages targeted directly to customers based on their values, demographics, and past purchasing behavior.

Besides technological advancement, other factors have facilitated this new approach as well. According to both scholars and practitioners, since the 1960s marketing has moved from a mass market production orientation to that of more decentralized niche marketing. Today's consumers are more sophisticated, less tied to tradition, more likely to be single, farther from home, older and more educated than they were immediately after World War II (Schultz, Tannenbaum, & Lauterborn, 1993). This means that consumers are more skeptical of shot gun advertising or promotion approaches. This fact combined with the reality of thousands of new avenues to reach these consumers (e.g., internet, media-rich CDs) has lead to the increased profitability of niche marketing.

Three things differentiate IMC from traditional marketing communication approaches: (1) audience perspective, (2) integration of marketing messages, and (3) evaluation of outcomes (Cathee & Schumann, in press). Schultz et al., (1993), argue that to be successful, marketers must understand what motivates the receiver (audience perspective). An integrated approach also means that maximum results are realized when all the elements of the marketing communication mix are managed together instead of separately. The days when a company goes to an ad agency for their advertising needs, a PR firm for publicity, a direct marketer for sales promotion needs, and a new technology firm for internet commerce needs will soon be a distant reality. Marketing firms are implementing "one-stop-shopping" to ensure messages are consistent across the promotional mix. In addition, promotional activities are called upon to produce measurable results and to show that goals were met (Tynan, 1994).

IMC is structured to result in desirable benefits for the organization such as a stronger brand image. In addition, IMC should also stimulate stronger communication effects resulting in reduced communication costs, increased sales, increased brand equity, and increased brand loyalty (Nowak & Siraj, in press).

Other Marketing Communication Avenues

Before concluding, it is important to realize that this chapter has only considered one approach to marketing communication: the interaction between the organization and the consumer. Communication within the marketing channel is another relevant perspective. For instance, Mohr and Nevin (1990) observed communication strategies between dealers and the manufacturer, and they found that there are optimal ways a manufacturer can communicate with dealers to foster trust, honesty, and satisfaction. These effects have been found to increase efficiency and ultimately sales.

Another perspective is "**internal**" marketing. Quane (1987) argues for the importance of "basic communication skills used to stimulate support among [an organization's] . . . own people for . . . its marketing strategy" (p. 145). He argues that motivating the sales force and staff to implement a marketing strategy can have significant effects upon the success of that marketing strategy.

New media and broadband provide additional opportunities for dialogue between organizations and consumers. Consumers can order products online and voice concerns directly to an organization's website. On the other hand, organizations have new opportunities to reach increasingly fragmented audiences. They can use media-rich CDs, conduct e-commerce, and combine internet advertising with database management to carry out relationship marketing. For example, organizations can send individually tailored promotional e-mails to customers based on past purchasing behavior. The future of new media has opened many opportunities for more personalized interaction between organizations and consumers.

Last, one could be concerned with communication within the coordination of the promotion mix. For instance, client-agency relationships have been a significant area of inquiry. Beard (in press) found that client perceptions of the advertising agency account manager had a profound effect on communication objectives and the attainment of goals. Obviously, there are a number of interesting approaches one could pursue in the arena of marketing communication.

Guidelines to Effective Marketing Communication

1. Understand Your Organization.

According to Robert Denton (1993), organizations frequently get in trouble because they try to offer a product or service that requires skills outside of their area of expertise. Stick to what you know. Be familiar with your organization's strategic goals and honestly assess its culture. "How things have always been done around here," will usually dictate "how things WILL be done around here." Point: Know your organization's strengths and weaknesses and its philosophy of doing business because these considerations must be taken into account when developing a dialogue with consumers.

2. Understand Your Customer.

This includes asking, and subsequently answering, the following questions: Who are your current customers? Who is your ideal customer? How can we describe them demographically, psychographically, by lifestyle, and by reference group membership? Are they decision-makers or decision-influencers? What are their consumption habits? What segments of the population are most receptive to our offering? These questions, and many others will help you develop an audience-centered approach to marketing communication.

3. Understand Your Product, Service, or Idea.

What are the physical and symbolic attributes of your offering that translate into benefits or obstacles for your target market? How is your product positioned in the consumer's mind relative to your competitors' products? Is your product a high-risk, big-ticket item, or one characterized by repetitive, mindless purchases? In addition to insight provided by the ELM, Percy and Rossiter's (1992) advertising strategy model offers suggestions for designing messages according to the consumer's processing strategy. Consider Twedt's (1968) VIEW model to ensure an effective packaging strategy.

4. Understand the Marketplace.

Are you a new kid on the block or an industry leader? Are economic conditions favorable, or not? Who are your competitors? Are they usually aggressive or dormant?

5. Understand the Exposure Environment.

This includes structuring a media plan that matches your audiences' media habits and your product's characteristics. Will you implement a strategy that begins by using advertising and new media to increase awareness and knowledge followed up with a persuasive contact by your sales force? What media vehicles do members of your target market attend to? How can you describe the nature of media exposure? Is it of short or long duration? Will you only have a couple of seconds to grab them with a flashy visual or will the customer have the opportunity and motivation to spend several minutes reading your copy? Should you place your message in the nightly news or *Details* magazine? What are your media alternatives? These are all important considerations related to the delivery of your message.

6. Understand the Purchase Environment.

Should you use a point-of-purchase display to prompt recall of your advertising message? The goal in today's busy world is convenience. Maybe you should put a toll-free number in your ad so they can order it over the phone. How about including your Internet address?

7. Design Your Message.

Based on all the questions you've asked so far, you should be able to determine what you are trying to say, to whom, and in what modality (media vehicle). Remember, your message should be coordinated between all the marketing communication mix so that your message is consistent and that all your messages speak with "one voice."

8. Last (or first), Understand the Post-Purchase Situation.

This means determining why people either bought your product or not. If they did decide to accept your offer, were they satisfied with the outcome? Remember, customer satisfaction is the name of the game. If they are not satisfied next time they will patronize your competitor instead. Use this feedback to reposition your product, service, or message.

Conclusion

We began this discussion by noting how prolific marketing communication is in our lives. Hopefully, the next time you are asked to respond to a telemarketing survey or participate in a focus group you'll know that the sponsoring organization is seeking to establish a dialogue with you and similar others. I'm sure you'll remember that they are seeking to determine exactly what you want, how you want it, how much you want to pay for it, and how best to motivate you to buy it. After internalizing this information, the company should eventually let you know where and how you can obtain the product or service in question. The dialogue you've engaged in (if done effectively) may result in a mutually satisfying exchange for both you and the organization.

For Further Reading

Marketing Communication for Small Businesses

Deran, E. (1987). *Low-cost marketing strategies: Field-tested techniques for tight budgets.* New York: Praeger.

Levinson, J. C. (1989). *Guerrilla marketing attack: New strategies, tactics, and weapons for winning big profits for your small business.* Boston, MA: Houghton Mifflin.

Levinson, J. C. (1990). *Guerrilla marketing weapons: 100 affordable marketing methods for maximizing profits from your small business.* New York: Plume.

Integrated Marketing Communications

Thorson, E., & Moore, J. (editors; 1996). *Integrated communication: Synergy of persuasive voices (advertising and consumer psychology).* Mahway, NJ: Erlbaum.

Schultz, D. E., Tannenbaum, S. I., & Lauterborn, R. F. (1993). *Integrated marketing communications.* Lincolnwood, IL: NTC Business Books.

Business-to-Business Marketing

Chisnall, P. (1995). *Strategic business marketing* (3rd ed.). New York: Prentice Hall.

Block, M. P., & Block, T. S. (1995). *Business-to-business market research: Identifying, qualifying and understanding your customers.* Chicago, IL: Probus.

Social Marketing

Kotler, P., & Roberto, E. L. (1989). *Social marketing: Strategies for changing public behavior.* New York: The Free Press.

Fine, S. H. (1992). *Marketing the public sector: Promoting the causes of public and nonprofit agencies.* New Brunswick, NJ: Transaction Publishers.

E-Marketing

Chase, L. (2001). *Essential business tactics for the net.* New York: John Wiley & Sons.

Strauss, J. & Frost, R. (2001). *E-Marketing.* New York: Prentice-Hall.

References

AMA Board approves new marketing definition (1985, March 1). *Marketing News*, p. 1.

Anderson, P. M., & Rubin, L. G. (1986). *Marketing communications: Advertising, sales promotion, public relations, display, personal selling.* Englewood Cliffs, NJ: Prentice-Hall.

Beard, F. (in press). Marketing clients and their advertising agencies: The antecedents and consequences of client role ambiguity in complex service production. In G. B. Wilcox (ed.), *Proceedings of the 1996 Conference of the American Academy of Advertising.* Austin, TX: American Academy of Advertising.

Bennett, P. D. (Ed.). (1995). *Dictionary of marketing terms* (2nd ed.). Lincolnwood, IL: NTC Books.

Cathee, M. & Schumann, D. (in press). Integrated marketing communications: Construct development and foundations for research. In G. B. Wilcox (ed.), *Proceedings of the 1996 Conference of the American Academy of Advertising.* Austin, TX: American Academy of Advertising.

Comstock, G. (1991). *Television in America* (2nd ed.). Newbury Park, CA: Sage.

Denton, R. J. (1993). *Managing the new product development process: Cases and notes.* New York: Addison-Wesley.

Dommermuth, W. P. (1984). *Promotion: Analysis, creativity, and strategy.* Boston, MA: Kent Publishing.

Goldman, K. (1995, June 14). U.S. ad spending is projected to increase by 7.9% this year. *The Wall Street Journal*, B8.

Insider's Report (2001). Bob Coen's insider's report [onlin], www.mccann.com.

Katz, D., & Kahn, R. L., (1990). Organizations and the systems concept. In S. R. Corman, S. P. Banks, C. R. Bantz, & M. M. Mayer (Eds.), *Foundations of organizational communication: A reader,* (pp. 112–122). New York: Longman.

Mohr, J., & Nevin, J. R. (1990). Communication strategies in marketing channels: A theoretical perspective. *Journal of Marketing, 54,* 36–51.

Nowak, G., & Siraj, K. (in press). Is `integrated marketing communication' really affecting advertising and promotion? An exploratory study of national marketers' promotion practices. In G. B. Wilcox (ed.), *Proceedings of the 1996 Conference of the American Academy of Advertising.* Austin, TX: American Academy of Advertising.

Petty, R. E., & Cacioppo, J. T. (1986). *Communication and persuasion: Central and peripheral routes to attitude change.* New York: Springer-Verlag.

Petty, R. E., Cacioppo, J. T., & Schumann, D. (1983). Central and peripheral routes to advertising effectiveness: The moderating role of involvement. *Journal of Consumer Research, 10,* 135–146.

Petty, R. E., Unnava, R. H., & Strathman, A. J. (1991). Theories of attitude change. In T. S. Robertson and H. H. Kassarjian (Eds.), *Handbook of Consumer Behavior,* 241–280. New York: Prentice Hall.

Percy, L., & Rossiter, J. R. (1992). A model of brand awareness and brand attitude advertising strategies. *Psychology & Marketing, 9*(4), 263–274.

Putnam, L. L., & Cheney, G. (1990). Organizational communication: Historical development and future directions. In S. R. Corman, S. P. Banks, C. R. Bantz, & M. M. Mayer (Eds.), *Foundations of organizational communication: A reader,* (pp. 44–61). New York: Longman.

Quane, M. P. (1987). Internal marketing. In C. Degan (Ed.), *Communicators' guide to marketing,* (pp. 145–158). New York: Longman.

Schultz, D. E., Tannenbaum, S. I., & Lauterborn, R. F. (1993). *Integrated marketing communications.* Lincolnwood, IL: NTC Business Books.

Shimp, T. A., & DeLozier, M. W. (1986). *Promotion marketing and marketing communication.* New York: Dryden Press.

Thorson, E. (1990). Consumer processing of advertising. In J. H. Leigh & C. R. Martin (Eds.), *Current Issues and Research in Advertising* (Vol. 12, pp. 197–230). Ann Arbor, MI: University of Michigan Press.

Thorson, E. (1996). Advertising. In M. B. Salwen & D. W. Stacks (Eds.), *An integrated approach to communication theory and research* (pp. 211–230). Mahwah, NJ: Erlbaum.

Twedt, D. W. (1968). How much value can be added through packaging. *Journal of Marketing, 32,* 61–65.

U.S. Bureau of the Census, *Statistical Abstract of the United States: 1995* (115th edition). Washington, DC, 1995.

Veronis, Suhler & Associates. (1999, November). *The Veronis, Suhler & Associates communication industry forecast.* New York: Author.

Whalen, J. (1994, January 17). Coupon marketers felt chill in '93. *Advertising Age,* p. 26.

Wimmer, R. D., & Dominick, J. R. (1994). *Mass media research: An introduction.* Belmont, CA: Wadsworth.

Woodside, A. G. (1987, June). *Communication briefings,* vol. 10.

Organizations rely on their stakeholders for their survival. Communication with internal and external stakeholders is therefore a key element of successful organizational communication. Through the use of public relations and the other tools of Integrated Marketing Communication (IMC), organizations are able to engage their stakeholders in a dialogue that will hopefully result in a successful organizational image.

Dr. Joseph Eric Massey is Assistant Professor at the University of Texas at San Antonio, where he teaches courses in organizational communication, Integrated Marketing Communication, and Crisis Management.

CHAPTER 15

Managing Organizational Images

Joseph Eric Massey, Ph.D.
The University of Texas at San Antonio

Key Terms

systems theory
organizational image management
public relations
organizational environment
public
integrated marketing communication

functions of public relations
stakeholder
interdependence
crisis management
stakeholder engagement

Objectives

The goal of this chapter is to explain how and why organizations communicate interactively with their environments. The chapter objectives are to:

1. Explain how systems theory helps us understand interactions between organizations and their environments.
2. Explain the theory of organizational image management.
3. Describe the elements of an organizational environment, including publics and stakeholders.
4. Discuss Integrated Marketing Communication (IMC).
5. Describe the functions of public relations.

> 6. Explain organizational crisis management and illustrate with examples the consequences of managing organizational crises well, and of managing them poorly.
> 7. Briefly describe the functions and processes of stakeholder engagement, including the use of communication technologies to develop a dialogue with organizational stakeholders.

This chapter presents a perspective on *how and why* organizations communicate with their internal and external environments. The perspective is based in systems theory, which you learned about in Chapter 2. Systems theory highlights the role of the organization's environment, and provides a model of organization-environment relations. Communication theorists realized the important role of communication in **systems theory** and applied the notion of systems to the study of organizational communication. Systems theory provides the *how* of organizational interaction with the environment.

Organizational image management is a theoretical perspective that will be discussed to provide more understanding of *why* organizations must interact with their environments in order to survive. The underlying argument in this perspective is that an organization must present an effective image of itself to its publics to be successful. What type of image any organization projects for itself depends on a variety of things, including what type of organization it is (public vs. private, non-profit vs. for-profit, etc.), what type of services it provides or what type of products it delivers, what image the organization wants to project, and so on. What is effective for one organization, then, is not necessarily effective for another.

These two theoretical perspectives provide the foundation for the discussion that follows. Additionally, the chapter introduces you to the practice of public relations, since public relations provides much of the organization-environment interaction that is used to successfully position the organization in its environment. First we will provide conceptual definitions of many of the terms in the chapter so that you understand better what is discussed.

Definitional Issues

Since this chapter is concerned with the interaction between organizations and their environments, it makes sense to first define the term environment. Recall from Chapter 2 that systems theory provided a new way of viewing organizational environments. Although many theorists had analyzed the internal organizational environment, systems theory was the first of our modern theories of organizations to consider the *external* organizational environment.

An **organizational environment** is both the internal system of relationships among organizational units, and the external system in which the organization exists. Internally the environment is composed of all the organizational functions, or units, that allow the organization to create its products and/or provide its services. The internal environment is composed primarily of employees, at all levels of the organization. The idea of systems theory is based on a biological/ecological model. We could think of the internal environment of an organization in much the same way we can think of the human body. Internally, the human body consists of organs, like the heart, lungs, brain, and so forth. These internal aspects of the human body work together in a unified system to produce energy, thought, etc.

The external environment is also based on a biological/ecological model. Just like living organisms, the organization exists in a field that is comprised of resources and competitors for those resources. For example, birds in the desert live in an ecological system in which different resources exist. These resources consist of food, water, shelter, mates for procreation, and so forth. To be sure, other birds that co-exist in this ecological environment have needs for these types of resources as well, and therefore competition is a natural condition brought about by multiple organisms with similar needs each attempting to satisfy its own needs.

Now lets consider a for-profit organizational environment applying the same ecological principles. Let us take as our ecological environment the personal computer industry. Apple Computer, Dell Computers, and others all are organisms living within that system, and all organisms within the system are exposed to the same resources and competitors (more or less). Internally, Apple, Dell, and the others all consist of internal environments that allow each organization to produce its products and deliver them to the market (e.g., Research and Development, Accounting, Marketing, Sales, etc.). The external environment consists of customers and potential customers, as well as competitors, regulatory agencies, local and federal governments, and so on. We can therefore see that the external environment consists of both resources and competitors for resources. The resources in the computer industry are consumers, the parts used in making personal computers, capital, and other things in the environment necessary for organizational survival, not the least of which is public support for organizational activities. But of course Dell,

Apple, and others are competitors in this ecological system, each doing all they can to maximize their resources.

A major function of organizational communication is to communicate with the various representatives of the environment. According to Tabris (1984), this function is **public relations,** which is defined as all the communication activities of sending and seeking information between the organization and its environment, with the ultimate goal of public relations being mutual influence between organizations and environments. So, for example, at Apple Computer, public relations means, among other things, communicating on the Internet and through the mass media with consumers they wish to persuade to buy their computers. But an often overlooked function of public relations also includes seeking information from the environment. Not only is it necessary for Apple Computers to send information out, Apple must also find out what kinds of products and services its publics want so that it can remain competitive in its environment. Public relations is seen as having a dual role of organizational communication—both sending and seeking information to and from the organization's environment. This concept will be discussed in more detail later.

Increasingly, public relations is being integrated with other organizational communication functions like advertising and marketing. There are key differences between advertising, public relations, and marketing, but there are also similarities. All three organizational units involve communication with various internal and external publics, and all are involved in the management of the organization's image. As more organizations become transnational, and more technologies exist to communicate with organizational audiences, it is increasingly challenging for organizations to promote a consistent image. Because of this and other reasons, organizations have begun to take an **integrated marketing communication** (IMC) approach. IMC involves the coordination of public relations, advertising, marketing, and other organizational communication units into one organizational function. This evolution in the industry can also be seen in agencies, where public relations, advertising, and marketing are all being handled by single agencies, rather than multiple ones. Bromley Communications, one of the largest and best agencies targeting the Hispanic market is an excellent example of this. Bromley provides an integrated marketing approach for many clients, including Proctor & Gamble and Western Union. Visit their website at http://www.bromcomm.com.

The discussion of interaction with the organization's environment also raises the question of publics. Just what is a public? A **public** can be defined as "any group of people who have a common interest" (Goldhaber, 1986, p. 278). So, for example, external publics include customers, competitors, regulatory agencies, financial representatives, media representatives and so forth. But there is also the internal public as well—the employees of the organization.

Recently, a new term has become popular with most organizational theorists and practitioners that refines our notion of publics, and that is **stakeholder.** A stakeholder is defined as a person or group identified as a(n) employee, customer, competitor, regulator, supplier, lender, shareholder, or representative of the media, government, or society in general (Caillouet, 1991). Think about the word itself. The term stakeholder identifies those who have a stake in the organization in some way. Another way to put it is that stakeholders have a vested interest in the organization and its activities. Research indicates that an organization's survival depends on its ability to satisfy its various stakeholders (Bedeian, 1987), and therefore interaction with stakeholders is one of the most important functions of organizational communication.

This section has defined several key concepts in our discussion of interacting with the organization's environment. First, the nature of the organizational environment was introduced in ecological terms—that, like living organisms, organizations exist in environments comprised of resources and competitors, among other things. Public relations was defined as all the communicative activities that take place between organizations and their publics to develop mutual understanding and influence between organizations and environments. We introduced the notion of IMC as a trend in organizations as they attempt to create a consistent image. Publics include internal and external groups or individuals who have some vested interest in the organization and its activities. The term stakeholder was defined as any individual or group who has a stake in the organization and provides a clearer picture of the nature of publics.

Now that a grounding in the terminology relied on in this chapter has been provided, we will now turn attention to the theoretical grounding—organizational image management theory. You may also want to review Chapter 2 and the discussion there of systems theory before going on.

Image Management

Image management theory has traditionally been applied to individuals as they attempt to manage the impressions that others form of them. We explained in Chapter 4 that as people we all want others to regard us in particular ways, and we engage in strategic communication behavior in order to achieve this. So for example, as a college student you probably want to impress upon your professors that you are a hard-working, dedicated student. To that end, you probably show up to class regularly, turn in assignments on time, and come to class prepared to discuss the material assigned. But not every student is successful at this endeavor. Some students are better than others at managing this kind of impression.

One of the most important people in the development of this kind of theory was Erving Goffman (Goffman, 1959). Recall that we discussed Goffman's "dramaturgical metaphor" in Chapter 4. Goffman argues that people engage in performances for audiences in regions referred to as the stage. There is the front stage, and the backstage. The front stage is where (like the theater) the performance occurs, while the backstage is where actions take place that may somehow contradict the performance in the front stage.

Goffman argues that people should perform in ways audiences expect and desire. In the real theater actors do this by engaging in a particular role. In the real world, actors also engage in performances, and each actor has many different performances that are engaged for different audiences. For example, the performance you might give while with your friends at a party is probably different than the performance you would give while having a meal with your family. A variety of factors determine which role is appropriate, including the audience, the setting, and the actors involved in the performance, among other things.

While Goffman's work on impression management was limited to people, the work can also be applied to organizations, since organizations also enact performances for different audiences (stakeholders), and must determine which particular role(s) should be enacted with each particular audience.

Recently, organizational theorists have begun to apply image management principles to organizations. Research demonstrates that organizations do indeed engage in strategic communication behaviors in an attempt to produce an effective image of themselves to their various stakeholders (Caillouet, 1991; Elsbach & Sutton, 1992; Massey, 2001; Watkins-Allen, & Caillouet, 1994).

Organizational image management has its historical roots in public relations, which began in the late nineteenth century as a response by many organizations to the unfavorable public opinion they were experiencing (Cheney & Vibbert, 1987). The railroads provide a good example of organizations which were faced with the need to foster a more favorable public image. Railroad companies were some of the most influential of the nineteenth century. But the railroads were not unblemished. When workers demanded better pay and better working conditions, the railroads' response was often violent, forcing their workers to work in the conditions and for the wages that the railroads had established (Crable & Vibbert, 1986). William Vanderbilt, railroad owner, once replied, "The public be damned," when asked whether the railroads should be run for the public good. Additionally, the railroads were caught in scandals involving kickbacks and payoffs and other illegitimate activities. The railroads were one of the first organizations to utilize public relations as a response to the unfavorable image they had fostered for themselves.

The initial goal of public relations was to defend the public actions of organizations. But in the 1970's many organizations began to utilize public relations for a quite different purpose. Rather than simply *responding* to public opinion (as the railroads had done), organizations began to *shape* it. Through public relations communication, organizations attempt to control the image internal and external stakeholders develop of the organization (Cheney & Vibbert, 1987). One of the major goals of interacting with the organization's environment, then, is to present an image that is effective and legitimate. In order to know what is considered legitimate to their stakeholders, organizations must engage in public relations activities of seeking information from their relevant publics, and then designing strategic communication to present an image that is appealing to their stakeholders.

Organizational image management is a dynamic and on-going process that involves three stages. First, the organization must *create* an image of itself to its various stakeholders. This is challenging because many people have a negative view of the unknown. If the organization is successful at creating an image for itself, it must then work to *maintain* that image. Image maintenance is an on-going process and is itself challenging, primarily for two reasons. The first is that when an organization is doing something well, that is, when it has created a successful image, it will tend to continue to do what brought about success. In technical terms this is referred to as structural inertia-the tendency to replicate stable structures and processes. Many organizations have learned the hard way that structural inertia can destroy the image that was created, assuming that what was successful yesterday will be successful tomorrow. The second reason image management is challenging is stakeholder heterogeneity. This means that the organization's audiences are varied and changing. Maintaining an image with these diverse and dynamic audiences is difficult at best. Finally, organizations must sometimes face the difficult task of *regaining* their image. Typically, this is brought about because the organization has experienced some type of crisis event. A crisis typically causes stakeholders to question the image of organizations. If an organization has experienced a "spoiled identity" to use Goffman's terms, it must engage in image restoration strategies to regain an effective image in the eyes of its stakeholders. More about crisis communication will be discussed later.

We now have a theoretical foundation for the study of public relations as the management of communication in order to achieve an effective organizational image. Attention is now turned toward the specific activities of public relations.

Interaction with the Organization's Environment as Public Relations

Given the fact that organizations, like living organisms, must interact with their environment in order to survive, it becomes incredibly important for organizations to do this successfully. Through public relations and other IMC activities, organizations enhance their abilities to know their environments, and for their environments to know them. This brings us to the functions of public relations—just what exactly public relations does for an organization. Although not necessarily exhaustive, the four **functions of public relations** listed here highlight the central aspects of public relations activities.

The Functions of Public Relations

The first function of public relations is *providing **publicity** for the organization* (Crable & Vibbert, 1986). Quite simply, organizations must be known to their publics in order to be successful. Of course different organizations have different publics, and so this doesn't mean that every organization must utilize the Internet, television or print media in order to survive. While you may have heard of McDonnell Douglas, a company that builds aircraft for the military and for commercial organizations like American Airlines, you probably wouldn't be familiar with the many organizations that supply parts to McDonnell Douglas so that it can build its planes. These organizations still engage in organizational communication activities designed to publicize themselves to McDonnell Douglas and other companies that buy their products.

Regardless of organization type, an organization must be publicized in order to achieve its goals. Advertising of various sorts (television commercials, magazine advertisements, radio spots, Internet banners, etc.), and the so-called "free media" (stories about the organization that appear in television news and newspapers for-profit organizations, and things like public service announcements for non-profit organizations) are useful tools to provide publicity for an organization. For example, the Old Pueblo Trolley, Incorporated (OPT) operates trolleys in Tucson, Arizona. In the mid-90s, OPT produced a public service announcement (PSA) to help publicize its activities and its presence in the community. A PSA is an advertisement created for non-profit organizations at little or no cost to the organization, and is run on local television and/or radio stations for free. PSAs are an inexpensive way for non-profit organizations to help promote an effective image of themselves. Also, if you watch NFL football, you have no doubt seen the many United Way advertisements in which football players are seen working in the community, with kids, the elderly and so on. These advertisements of course show the work of United Way, but they also project a particular image of the NFL that is effective. The NFL is seen as a caring organization that is involved in community affairs.

The **second function** of public relations is *maintaining relationships with members of the organization's environment*. Recall that we refer to these members as stakeholders. Employees must be kept abreast of past, current, and future organizational activities, and how the organization is doing in general. Consumers must be informed of products and services of organizations, including new product lines, changes in services offered, and so on. Organizations must also maintain relationships with their competitors, so that they know what the competition is doing. Relevant regulatory agencies (like the Food and Drug Administration (FDA) for pharmaceutical companies like Merck and Johnson & Johnson) must be reported to on a regular basis, and organizations must maintain an open relationship with these regulators to know and better abide by the laws governing organizational activity. Suppliers to the organization (the people who supply jet engines to McDonnell Douglas, like Rolls-Royce, for example) must know what the organization needs, what the organization's plans are, and organizations must be aware of any changes on the part of their suppliers. Financial representatives, like lending institutions (banks) must be kept aware of organizational successes and failures, and organizations must know things about these financial institutions as well. Organizational shareholders, the people who have stocks in the organization, must be informed about the performance of the organization in the case of public, for-profit organizations. Relationships must also be maintained with representatives of the media, so that the "free-media" discussed above is favorable to the organization and not antagonistic to it. And finally, society in general may also be part of the organization's environment and therefore, positive relationships with the general public may also be an important function of public relations activities.

One important aspect of relational maintenance to highlight is that this is a dialogic process and not a monologic organizational communication activity. In simpler terms, organizations are not simply sending out information to stakeholders in order to establish and maintain relationships with them, they are also seeking information from stakeholders. Organizations want and need to establish and maintain an on-going dialogue with their stakeholders in order to provide products and services that are desirable. Quite simply, organizations can't give their stakeholders what they want if they don't know what stakeholders want. Domino's Pizza provides a good example of a dialogic approach. Domino's first began operating internationally in the mid-80's and assumed that what was good for Americans was good for anybody. When sales suffered internationally, they began asking customers what they wanted on their pizzas and sales increased dramatically. Who knew that the Japanese wanted squid and mayonnaise on their pizza? Only by engaging stakeholders in a dialogue is Domino's able to be successful internationally.

The **third function** of public relations is *promoting the exchange of understanding and influence between relevant organization functions and members of the organization's environment.* As highlighted in the second function, maintaining relationships with stakeholders, knowledge of environmental activities on the part of organizations, and knowledge of organizational activities on the part of publics is an important aspect of public relations. This third function points to the reasons for maintaining relationships—to promote mutual understanding for organizations and their environments, and to allow for organizations to influence their environments, and vice-versa.

The notion of mutual influence highlights yet another concept from systems theory, and that is the notion of **interdependence.** Interdependence is simply defined as mutual dependence. In the case of for-profit organizations, this is illustrated in the supplier/buyer relationship. An organization, like Nike, makes a product, for example athletic shoes. Nike could not continue to make athletic shoes if there were no consumers to purchase the product. And where would consumers be without companies like Nike to make shoes for them? Barefoot, unless they were to make the shoes for themselves. So Nike and its customers share an interdependent relationship, in which each influences the other. Now it seems obvious how Nike influences its consumers: through the Internet, television and magazine advertisements promoting their products, the promotion of certain sporting events, and so forth. But how is it that consumers influence Nike? By telling Nike (either directly or indirectly) what they like and dislike about their products, and whether they like a product at all. Directly this is done through surveys and other kinds of data collected from consumers. Indirectly it is accomplished when people refuse to buy particular products. When this occurs, Nike realizes people don't like the product and discontinue production. All of this mutual influence is accomplished through public relations activities and other IMC activities.

The **fourth function** of public relations is *image management—the creation, mainte-nance, and in some cases restoration of the organizational image.* I believe that in fact this function underlies all public relations activities and subsumes all public relations func-tions. The reason for creating publicity, maintaining stakeholder relationships, and en-gaging in mutual influence with stakeholders is to manage the organization's image. If an organization is not able to achieve and sustain an effective image of itself, it will not suc-ceed. Through public relations and other IMC activities, organizational image manage-ment is accomplished.

The above discussion of public relations functions illustrates the importance of this organizational communication activity. Let us briefly outline the model of interaction with the organization's environment as it has been presented in this chapter. First, or-ganizations exist in environments. These environments consist of publics, or stakehold-ers, both internally and externally. Effective communication between the organization and its stakeholders is a must for organizational success. Organizations rely on public re-lations and other IMC activities to communicate with stakeholders, and they do this for a variety of reasons, including publicizing the organization, maintaining relationships with stakeholders, promoting mutual understanding and influence, and maintaining an effective organizational image. So public relations is an important part of organizational communication. As mentioned above, public relations involves the giving and taking of information between organizations and their environments. According to Kreps (1990) this dual role of public relations involves:

1) Sending organizational information to representatives of the environment.
2) Seeking pertinent information from the environment for the organization.

Through public relations and other IMC activities, organizations are able to create a dialogue with stakeholders. Recall the Nike example above. Nike performs the first role, sending information, by advertising its products, keeping its stockholders informed, keep-ing pertinent regulatory agencies informed, maintaining positive relationships with em-ployees, and so on. Nike performs the second role—seeking information—by the use of questionnaires, test marketing products before deciding whether to market them nation-ally and internationally, and by following the sales of existing merchandise. All of this is done to ensure survival of the organization. As Goldhaber puts it, "organizations must be able to sense a change in their environment and to meet the change—create and exchange messages internally among relevant departments and units and externally to important publics—or they will not survive" (1990, p. 281). Without IMC organizations would be ill-prepared to cope with the changes that take place within their environments.

Although the advantages public relations provides organizations may be obvious from what we've discussed already, let's spell them out specifically. You have learned in this chapter that public relations isn't just about communication with the external environment, but about communication with the internal environment as well. Internally the advantage of public relations is increased operational efficiency (Zelko & Dance, 1965). Increasingly, workers are demanding more from organizations, like child care centers, fitness centers, flex time, and opportunities for telecommuting. Additionally, organizations have become increasingly diverse, with more gender and ethnic diversity than ever before. Organizations that are not responsive to these changes and that do not effectively communicate with their employees about these changes risk failure. While the myth that "a happy worker is a productive worker" was dispelled decades ago, it is true at least to some extent that efficiency is affected by satisfaction. Employees who are more satisfied with their jobs tend to be more efficient. By engaging in a dialogue with employees about their satisfaction, organizations increase their chances for success.

Externally, the advantage public relations offers is a more effective organizational image. Recall from the previous discussion of organizational image management that enhancing the organization's image was what led to the development of public relations in the first place. Organizations must be perceived as being legitimate in order to survive. If stakeholders don't believe that the organization has a right to continue operations, then the organization, in ecological terms, will most likely die. Many public relations activities are designed to enhance and maintain a legitimate image. While this differs from one organizational type to another, maintaining a legitimate image is important for all organizations.

Organizational Crisis Management

Probably at no time in an organization's life is image management more important than during a crisis situation. An **organizational crisis** is a major, unpredictable event that threatens to harm the organization and its stakeholders. Crises are characterized by three factors: (1) the element of surprise, (2) a short decision time, and (3) a threat to the organization and its image. More organizations are experiencing crisis now than ever before because of increased reliance on technology and other factors. Examples of crises include environmental disasters, product recalls, industrial accidents, and other unanticipated events that lead stakeholders to question the image of the organization.

Recall the discuss of organizational image management, which involves the creation, maintenance and restoration of the organization's image. Organizational crisis management is the systematic attempt to restore the image of the organization. If organizations are successful at crisis management, they will increase their chances for continued success and will restore their image. If organizations are not successful at crisis management, their chances for success will be diminished and their image may remain tarnished indefinitely. Although rare, successful crisis management has in some cases created a better public image for organizations than they had before the crisis, as in the case of Johnson & Johnson's handling of the Tylenol incident (Barton, 1993). In this section we will provide a description of this crisis and also what Johnson & Johnson did that was so successful. Koontas (1988, pp. 12-13) describes Johnson & Johnson's Tylenol crisis as follows:

> At the end of September in 1982, seven Chicago area residents died from taking cyanide laced Tylenol capsules they had purchased over the counter at area stores . . . The cyanide was present in quantities thousands of times a fatal dose. Death occurred within minutes—the victims never had a chance. The next evening, all three major networks carried stories about the contaminated drugs. "The publicity caused a nationwide scare. One Chicago hospital received 700 calls about Tylenol in one day." (Tifft & Griggs, 1982, p. 18). Johnson & Johnson found itself facing a crisis, the kind of nightmare that haunts many pharmaceutical companies . . . At the time of the poisonings . . . "Tylenol commanded 37% of the $1.3 Billion analgesic market" (A Death Blow for Tylenol?", 1982, p. 151). Within days, the demand for all brands of pain relievers dropped 16.7% nationwide. Chicago area sales were down 38%. Johnson & Johnson's stock dropped from 46 1/2 on September 29, to 42 5/8 on October 8. This represented a paper loss of $657 Million . . . In November [of 1982], Dean Witter Reynolds analyst Larry N. Feinberg said, "Tylenol will never again be as profitable as it once was" ("J & J Will Pay Dearly," 1982, p. 37).

But Johnson & Johnson and their main product Tylenol did return to profitability. From the outset, key executives were in charge of the situation. They smartly brought in specialists from other parts of Johnson & Johnson's companies to assist with the crisis. They stopped production of Tylenol capsules immediately. They worked with local and federal law enforcement agencies to assist in the apprehension of the guilty parties. They stopped all advertising campaigns immediately. They used the media to send warnings to the public not to purchase Tylenol capsules until they could find the cause of the problem. A few days after the incident, Johnson & Johnson pulled all Tylenol capsules nationwide. Also, Johnson & Johnson introduced new, tamper-proof packaging. The tamper-proof packaging that now comes with almost anything you buy at drug stores and grocery stores became an industry standard in the wake of the Tylenol crisis.

The efforts by Johnson & Johnson were successful. By the middle of 1983, Johnson & Johnson had regained 85% of Tylenol's former market share. But not only economically was Johnson & Johnson returning to its former status. More importantly, they were regaining their reputation as a legitimate, good, caring organization. By 1987 Johnson & Johnson ranked first in the "responsibility to community and environment" category of all Fortune 500 companies (Koontas, 1988). Most analysts believe that this was due to the outstanding job Johnson & Johnson did in handling the crisis through image management activities. In fact, Johnson & Johnson's handling was so exemplary that they were awarded the Silver Anvil Award from by the Public Relations Society of America (Kreps, 1990). But what was it that Johnson & Johnson did that was so successful? Koontas has identified six steps that Johnson & Johnson took during the Tylenol crisis. These six steps are now industry standard for how to deal with a crisis.

The first step is *senior executives should take immediate action*. In the Tylenol case, executives took immediate action by identifying the problem and presenting a solution. They also immediately discontinued production of Tylenol and pulled Tylenol off all store shelves. They recalled Tylenol capsules.

Next, *the company actions must be perceived to be in the public good*. The perceived motives must be for the public good. The public cannot believe that the true motive, or hidden agenda of the organization is related to the cost or benefit to the company.

Third, *the company should conduct frequent research to assess the target public's perceptions*. A company shouldn't wait for quarterly or annual sales figures. Rather, like Johnson & Johnson did in the aftermath of the Tylenol poisonings, companies should conduct research to determine stakeholder attitudes and establish plans for subsequent actions.

Fourth, *top executives should meet with the press*. Johnson & Johnson's top executives did this by making themselves available for interviews with the press, and the company's chairman even appeared on the *Donahue* show. This kind of activity makes the media (and therefore the public) feel that they are getting the facts from an authority.

Fifth, *the company should keep all publics informed.* This includes all stakeholders, including internal and external customers. This can be challenging, because crises are dynamic events, and information comes more slowly than most stakeholders would like. Because of this, organizations are sometimes compelled to provide information that may not yet be fully confirmed. Although informing internal and external stakeholders should be a priority in crisis management, the organization should be prudent and verify all facts before going public.

And finally, *the company should be up front about its intent to rebuild its image.* Johnson & Johnson straightforwardly asked the public to continue to trust them. They used television and print advertisements to ask for continued trust and support.

Because of the success of Johnson & Johnson in rebuilding its image though crisis management strategies, these strategies have become the expected way for organizations to manage crises. But there are still organizations today that fail to employ crisis management. This failure typically results in a negative image for organizations. If organizations fail to manage crises, several undesirable effects can result. In the next section, we will outline these potential results.

Results of Poor Crisis Management

Johnson & Johnson's handling of the Tylenol crisis is taken as the industry standard for crisis management. Yet many organizations continue to mismanage crisis situations. In the summer of 2000, Bridgestone/Firestone faced a crisis situation when manufacturing defects resulted in over 170 deaths as a result of tire failure. Rather than following the advice of crisis management experts, Bridgestone/Firestone engaged in several misguided communication efforts, including (1) denial of a problem, (2) shifting the blame to individual automobile owners and independent tire dealers, and (3) cover-up of the problem, which they had known about for years. The company's mismanagement of the crisis was so poor that it led Fleishman-Hillard International Communications, the nation's largest public relations firm, to quit, after being hired by Bridgestone/Firestone to help control the damage to its reputation.

The Bridgestone/Firestone case and other cases illustrate what can happen if crises are not managed successfully. Tabris (1984) identifies eight potential results of poor crisis management.

- Damage to the organization's reputation and loss of confidence in the organization and its management by investors, customers, and employees.
- Deterioration of employee morale, which can lead to problems with labor relations and employee recruitment.
- Declines in stock prices and strained relations with investors.
- Preoccupation of management time with crisis issues rather than with important organizational activities.
- Increased scrutiny of organizational affairs by external political agencies, leading to excessive government regulation and punitive measures.
- Costly and time-consuming litigation procedures.
- Threats to organizational autonomy, such as involuntary reorganization or bankruptcy.
- Strained community relations.

Perhaps one of the most discouraging facts regarding crisis management is that most organizations are ill-prepared to handle a crisis if it should occur. Only 57% of major companies have a crisis management plan (CMP), and of those, 13% developed their CMP *after* experiencing a crisis (Barton, 2001; Coombs, 1999). A CMP "consists of a full range of thoughtful processes and steps that anticipate the complex nature of crises real and perceived" (Caywood & Stocker, 1993, p. 411). The development of a CMP represents a proactive approach to crisis management. Rather than simply responding to crises after they occur, organizations anticipate threats to the organization and prepare in case they occur. Many, if not all of the potential results of poor crisis management could be avoided if organizations take a proactive approach to organizational crisis.

This section has highlighted the importance of crisis management. Johnson & Johnson's handling of the Tylenol incident provides an example of successful crisis management, while Bridgestone/Firestone provides an example of what can happen if crisis management efforts fail.

One of the things that has been highlighted throughout this chapter is that successful communication with organizational stakeholders involves the creation of a dialogue between the organization and its environment. An appropriate consideration at this point is how organizations go about achieving a dialogue—specifically, how do organizations interact with representatives of the environment? The next section addresses this issue.

Stakeholder Engagement

One way of thinking about interacting with the organization's environment is as **stakeholder engagement.** Recall that stakeholders are employees, customers, competitors, regulators, suppliers, lenders, shareholders, or representatives of the media, government, or society in general. A stakeholder is any individual, group, or institution that is affected by the organization and, in turn, can affect the organization. A stakeholder thus has a relationship with the organization whether or not it is recognized. Providing these groups with information and soliciting information from them, as has been argued throughout this chapter, is a necessary ingredient for organizational success, and sometimes for organizational survival. This section identifies four of the most commonly used methods to achieve this purpose: written surveys, telephone surveys, public meetings, and focus groups. Also, these four methods are listed in order from least interaction possible to most interaction possible.

Written surveys, while they do not allow for much information to be sent to publics, provide easy-access data from stakeholders. Surveys are one of the easiest ways to obtain information from publics in order to guide organizational behavior. Sometimes written surveys are mailed to stakeholders, and sometimes they are administered in more direct ways. For example, Sears mails consumers written surveys after they have used one of Sears' service centers to determine whether people are satisfied with the service they received. American Airlines, on the other hand, randomly selects flights and seats within flights to administer written surveys on board their aircraft to assess customer satisfaction.

Telephone surveys are much like written surveys, except that they allow for some interaction between interviewer and interviewee. This means that the interviewer can clarify the meaning of questions, engage in dialogue with interviewees about relevant issues, and use the telephone survey to provide interviewees with information about the organization. At Old Pueblo Trolley, for example, telephone surveys were used to determine what percentage of the population of Tucson was aware of the Trolley, and what percentage of the population had ridden the Trolley. In the case where the interviewee had never heard of the Trolley, the opportunity was taken to inform them of the existence of the Trolley, the hours of operation, and the location of the Trolley.

Public meetings allow for much more interaction than either type of survey. They provide a forum for the exchange of information and ideas about organizational activities. Politicians have realized the potential value of these meetings, which are commonly called "town hall meetings" by politicos. In such town hall meetings, political representatives meet with their constituencies face to face to discuss issues that dominate the political landscape. Such meetings enable politicians to know better what issues are facing their publics, and enable their publics to know better what politicians' stand s are on those issues. Most other types of organizations utilize public meetings as well.

More than any of the methods of stakeholder engagement listed so far, the one that creates the most opportunity for interaction between organizational members and stakeholders is the focus group. Focus groups consist of small groups of stakeholders brought together to discuss pertinent organization-environment issues. Typically there is little structure provided, and a "free-flow" of discussion is encouraged. Focus groups are used widely by organizations to assess stakeholders' attitudes regarding current or planned organizational activities. Since little structure is provided by organizational planners, stakeholder involvement is maximized.

Stakeholder Engagement and Communication Technology

Increasingly, organizations are relying on communication technologies to establish and maintain a dialogue with stakeholders. The Internet, Intranets, World Wide Web, E-mail, and Videoconferencing are all examples of communication technologies that have either replaced or augmented traditional communication channels. As recently as 10 years ago, few people had ever "surfed the Net." Now, most of you reading this book have done so countless times. Communication technologies allow both internal and external stakeholders to communicate with organizations in ways that have never been possible before.

Internally, communication technologies like the Internet and Intranets allow the organization and its employees to communicate with one another. Intranets are sometimes preferred because they typically are restricted to employees only, and therefore sensitive and proprietary information can be communicated. E-mail is the number one form of business communication in use today. E-mail has in large part replaced "snail mail" because of its nearly instantaneous delivery and response abilities. Videoconferencing allows employees in different parts of the world to communicate with one another in an environment that mimics face-to-face communication.

Externally, communication technologies like the Internet and E-mail allow external stakeholders to communicate with organizations with more immediacy than ever before. As recently as 10 years ago, most organization-stakeholder communication was done through the mass media, and it was primarily monologic in that there was little opportunity for feedback. Now, you or I can visit the website of an organization and obtain information about the organization, and we can send information back to the organization 24/7.

Recalling the model of organizational image management discussed earlier, organizations work to create, maintain, and in some cases, regain images with their stakeholders. Increasingly, organizational image management is achieved through communication technologies like those listed above. One challenge for organizations is that the increasing reliance on a variety of communication technologies makes the creation and maintenance of a consistent image very difficult. Through Integrated Marketing Communication a consistent image, across diverse stakeholders and around the world, can be achieved.

Conclusion

This chapter has presented a basic grounding in the processes involved with interacting with the organization's environment. Two theoretical perspectives provided a foundation for this discussion—systems theory and organizational image management theory. These theoretical perspectives provided the how and why of organization-environment relations.

In this chapter public relations is viewed as communication management. Through public relations activities organizations send and seek information so that they can successfully compete for resources in their organizational environment. The most successful organizations are the ones that know what their stakeholders and customers want and like, and strategically communicate messages that produce legitimate images.

We also discussed how organizational crises have a potentially negative effect on an organization's image. Johnson & Johnson was used as an example of how to communicate with stakeholders in times of crisis so that a positive image can be maintained. Bridgestone/Firestone, on the other hand, was used as an example of what not to do during crises. Both of these examples highlight the very important role of interaction with the organization's environment in crisis situations.

Finally, specific methods of stakeholder engagement were discussed. These methods allow for the two-way process of communication flow that the model of organizational image management presented here demands. Listening to the customer has become a top priority for organizations of all types, and these methods are those currently employed by organizations as they interact with the environment.

References

Barton, L. (1993). *Crisis in organizations: Managing and communicating in the heat of chaos.* Cincinnati, Ohio: South-Western Publishing.

Barton, L. (2001). *Crisis in organizations II.* Cincinnati: South-Western.

Bedeian, A. G. (1989). *Management.* Chicago: Dryden.

Caillouet, R. H. (1991). *A quest for legitimacy: Impression management strategies used by an organization in crisis.* Unpublished doctoral dissertation.

Caywood, C., & Stocker, K. P., (1993). The ultimate crisis plan. In J. Gottschalk (Ed.), *Crisis-response: Inside stories on managing image under siege* (pp. 409–428). Detroit: Gale Research.

Cheney, G., & Vibbert, S. L. (1987). Corporate discourse: Public relations and issue management. In F. M. Jablin, L. L. Putnam, K. H. Roberts, & L. W. Porter (Eds.), *Handbook of organizational communication: An interdisciplinary perspective.* Newbury Park: Sage.

Coombs, W. T. (1999). *Ongoing crisis communication: Planning, managing, and responding.* Thousand Oaks, CA: Sage.

Crable, R. E., & Vibbert, S. L. (1986). *Public relations as communication management.* Edina, MN: Bellwether Press.

Elsbach, K. D., & Sutton, R. I. (1992). Acquiring organizational legitimacy through illegitimate actions: A marriage of institutional and impression management theories. *Academy of Management Journal, 35,* 699–738.

Goffman, E. (1959). *The presentation of self in everyday life.* Garden City, New York: Doubleday Anchor Books.

Goldhaber, G. M. (1990). *Organizational communication.* Dubuque, IA: Wm. C. Brown Publishers.

Koontas, G. (1988). *Faux pas in the pharmaceutical industry: Specific cases of communication to restore consumer/investor confidence.* Paper presented at the Annual Meeting of the Speech Communication Association, New Orleans.

Kreps, G. L. (1990). *Organizational communication.* White Plains, NY: Longman.

Lynch, P., & Rothchild, J. (1995). *Learn to earn: A beginner's guide to the basics of investing and business.* New York: Fireside.

Massey, J. E. (2001). Managing organizational legitimacy: Communication strategies for organizations in crisis. *Journal of Business Communication, 38*, 153–183.

Nulty, P. (1990, April 23). Exxon's biggest problem: Not what you think. *Fortune, 121,* 202–205.

Tabris, M. D. (1984). Crisis management. In B. Cantor (Ed.), *Experts in action: Inside public relations,* pp. 57–73. White Plains, NY: Longman.

Watkins-Allen, M., & Caillouet, R. H. (1994). Legitimation endeavors: Impression management strategies used by an organization in crisis. *Communication Monographs, 61,* pp. 44–62.

Zelko, H., & Dance, F. (1965). *Business and professional speech communication.* New York: Holt, Rinehart, & Winston.

PART IV

Communicating In the 21st Century

Globalization, economic changes, and information technology are rapidly and fundamentally changing organizational life as we know it at the beginning of the 21st century. What kinds of changes can we expect? What will members of organizations have to do to keep up, and to remain viable in their roles as technology changes the world? Drs. Raymond Koegel and Lawrence Chase conclude our book by addressing these important questions.

Professor Raymond Koegel completed his doctoral work at the University of Texas, Austin and is a professor in the Digital Media Program at California State University, Sacramento. His areas of interest are information science, digital media, and applied organizational communication. As a scholar he conducts research on electronic media and web site design. As a consultant he develops institutional web sites for government agencies as well as corporate clients.

CHAPTER 16

Entering the New Millenium: Collaboration, Globalization and Information Management

Raymond Koegel and Lawrence Chase
California State University, Sacramento

> Where is the wisdom we have lost in knowledge?
> Where is the knowledge we have lost in information?
>
> T.S. Eliot

Key Terms

intranet	knowledge based organization
Internet	technological infrastructure
globalization	personal digital assistants
24-7	matrix organizations
loss of privacy	diversity
information management	emotional intelligence
cultural literacy	web based video conferencing
information overload	contingent workers
netiquette	monitoring and surveillance
high performance teams	Internet addiction

Objectives

This chapter describes three major factors that shape the organizational environment of the 21st century. The objectives are:

1. to describe the effects of economic factors, globalization and new information technologies on today's and tomorrow's organizations, and
2. to identify the kinds of communication challenges organization members will face in the 21st century.

Futurists and management consultants present divergent views of the emerging organization, but all agree the work environment of the future will be shaped by three interrelated factors (Aburdene and Naisbett, 1985). **Economic factors** will continue to place tremendous pressure on companies to be efficient producers of goods and services. Second, **globalization** will reshape the work force so that demographically diverse teams will work on projects and will need to coordinate their work across many time zones. Finally, **communication technology** will provide many of the tools for workers to share information and manage their individual work assignments. Using an array of communication tools many organizations will strive for a global presence with **24/7** accessibility to their customers. Peter Drucker accurately envisioned this new organization, which he describing it as "**knowledge based,** an organization largely composed of specialists who direct and discipline their own performance through organized feedback from colleagues, customers and headquarters" (1987, p. 45). The future belongs to those who can navigate this complex global network and produce tangible results for their company.

These three factors will lead to significant changes in organizational culture. For example, consider the impact of workforce **diversity.** The latest United States census projections indicate that the three fastest growing segments of the work force are workers: 55 and older, Asian workers, and workers of Hispanic origin. And women already make-up 46% of the work force. As the marketplace and workforce become more diverse, interpersonal communication skills such as empathy, or seeing the world from another's perspective, and behavioral flexibility, or the ability to adapt to situations, will become even more essential.

Even CEOs are now being coached to improve their "emotional intelligence." A recent case study in *Fortune Magazine* includes the following glimpse into the struggle for mutual understanding in the organization.

"For illustration, we turn to David Pottruck. He's certainly a successful fellow. The co-CEO of Charles Schwab is a risk taker, a visionary who pushed Schwab into its online strategy. But chances are he wouldn't be where he is today had he not confronted his arrogance back in 1992. He was a rising star, but he was also a know-it-all. He bulldozed into meetings with all the answers. He made people feel small. One day, his boss, then-president Larry Stupski, called Pottruck into his office, sat him down, and slammed him with shocking news. "He told me he and my peers couldn't stand working with me," recalls Pottruck, 52. "He said, 'You're overwhelming. Like a freight train,'" Pottruck was devastated, enough so that he met with Terry Pearce, an ex-IBM executive turned leadership coach. In twice-monthly sessions, Pearce worked with Pottruck on how to empathize, build consensus, lead without dominating, and, most critically, listen. "Listen to understand," Pearce instructs, "rather than to defend your position." Pearce's listening course in three quick steps: (1) Pause ten seconds before answering—try it, it's painful! (2) Ask a question to clarify intent. (3) Respond with feelings as well as facts." (Sellers, p. 76).

You may recognize some if not all of the leadership coach's advice as nothing more than competent interpersonal communication. And that's the point. No matter how task-centered the organization, the management of interpersonal communication is central to organizational survival. James C. Collins and Jerry Porras systematically studied the cultures and structure of 18 companies that have stood the test of time and have successfully adapted to changing social and economic environment for at least 50 years. They called the companies "visionary" and set out to describe their distinguishing characteristics. One of the core values of these organizations is an almost cult-like emphasis on interpersonal skills. Consider how Nordstrom's welcomes its new employees.

"Welcome to Nordstroms. We're glad to have you with our Company. Our number one goal is to provide outstanding customer service. Set both your personal and professional goals high. We have great confidence in your ability to achieve them.

Nordstrom Rules: Rule #1: Use your good judgment in all situations. There will be no additional rules. Please feel free to ask your department manager, store manager, or division general manager any question at any time." (Collins and Porras, p. 117)

Today's companies expect and demand of their workers a high level of emotional intelligence. **Emotional intelligence,** or EQ, is similar to IQ. While IQ tests attempt to reflect your analytical abilities, EQ assessments are designed to portray your ability to manage emotions and your interpersonal relationships. One study tracking 160 people in a variety of industries and job levels revealed that EQ skills were twice as important in contributing to excellence as intellect and expertise alone (Goleman, 1997).

In this book you have studied (and hopefully practiced) a variety of key communication skills. These are essential, because you will need to get along with your co-workers and function effectively in teams. As one organizational consultant put it, "The new game is **high performance teaming.** Workers must be able to work well with a variety of teams. A moderate IQ combined with a high EQ can achieve tremendous success." (Murray, 2000, p. 39).

The New Collaborative Environment

Work assignments are often grouped together as a set of interrelated tasks that produce a pre-determined outcome. These kinds of assignments are called projects and are routinely assigned to teams. College students who have worked on group projects should immediately remember all the wonders and woes of these collaborative efforts. The main differences between work and school is that the workplace offers more resources to complete your projects and imposes more life altering consequences on those who succeed and on those who fail.

Whether your project is the development of a new marketing plan, software package or trade show exhibit, it can always be broken down into critical tasks. These tasks are typically accomplished by a coordinated group in a specified timeframe.

Traditional organizations operated with a functional structure in a shift timeframe. This means that each unit—marketing, finance, research and development, for example—was given certain specified responsibilities. The department was part of an organization that was active during a specified timeframe.

Many new organizations, on the other hand, are characterized by a **matrix structure.** This means that you are often part of a cross-unit team that has its own team leader and scope of work. You may be part of the marketing department but you can be put on a team headed by someone from human resources. As you might imagine, matrix organizations require excellent communication skills. You are essentially working for two people and with differential group responsibilities. In some organizations. CEOs move beyond matrixing to a type of perpetual re-organization so that people are continually forced to form new working groups.

"Bill McGowan understood this. That is why he arbitrarily reorganized MCI every six months, not to solve a specific organization problem, but to quash political structures before they became intractable. This strategy opened the opportunity for new networks. No single reorganization was intended to create the perfect new organization design (planning), but rather to given individuals a chance to self-organize and evolve in reaction to the changes taking place in the business around them (adaptation)@ (Davis & Meyer, 1998, p. 116).

When you combine the fluidity that matrixing injects into the organizational environment with the diversity of the emerging work force, the complexity of modern organizational communication begins to emerge.

Globalization and 24/7

The Need for Intercultural Communication Competence. As Cairncross (1997, p. 143) recently observed, "A company's market is no longer its locality or even its nation. Thanks to global toll-free numbers and the Internet's global reach, electronic commerce offers an inexpensive way to sell to the world." Moreover, in a recent study of more than 1000 international CEOs from 28 countries, Rosen, Digh, Singer and Phillips (2000, p. 50) report that the most successful business leaders are able to communicate effectively in the global marketplace. "**Cultural literacy,** knowing about and leveraging cultural differences," is now a leadership requirement.

Since the majority of organizations are international in scope, a new type of business acumen is required. Beyond basic intercultural awareness and cooperation, new age organizational workers now must engage in more sophisticated communication behaviors such as persuasion and conflict resolution across international boundaries. While the call for intercultural communication competence has been sounded in the past, it is clear that we must go beyond giving "**lip service**" to this practice. In a recent study of one American organization, for example, Amason, Allen and Holmes (1999, p. 310) reported:

> "In one of the plant's break rooms, we noticed a large poster prominently displayed in several locations. It showed a culturally diverse group of employees sitting around a table. Beneath the picture, the caption read, 'We are a culturally diverse workplace' and encouraged employees to value diversity. It was in English only and there were no translations."

While the increased use of the Internet will contribute to the rise of English as the common standard for e-commerce, we must always remember that the best language for business is the language of our customer.

The Twenty-Four/Seven Marketplace.   Communication in the modern organization will not follow the nine-to-five workday so prevalent in the last century. The co-worker whom you are trying to persuade about your new marketing plan might be a Basque living in Spain whose view of the persuasion is quite different than yours and who is living nine time zones away from you. In the push for greater market share and customer retention, 24/7 service options have become the norm for large corporations. Rather than looking to people who sit next to us as potential social companions we will come to see those who work at the same time across the world as our organizational colleagues.

Information Management

The New Technological Infrastructure.   It is a trivial but true observation that technology is merely a tool. The mere fact that a tool exists does not ensure that it will have any social impact. However information tools are what is making the emerging organization possible. It is critical that you understand both the role and the utilization of these tools if you are to succeed in the new organizational environment.

Most organizations make desktop personal computers available to their employees. In some cases laptops are also provided. Employees have access to proprietary email systems and corporate-wide web environments called "**intranets.**" In addition, most employees have access from work to high-speed communication lines so that they can download and view material on the world wide web. For workers who travel, many companies provide local access to their global network and employees communicate with their home office via laptops, PDAs (personal digital assistants) and digital cell phones.

Most of these devices can communicate with each other. As such, the home office can schedule a meeting for you in London while you are in flight, and you can download the meeting agenda on your cell phone as you walk from the airplane to your rental car. After the meeting you may be expected to write a brief report on your laptop and post it to your project group's page on the corporate intranet so that others can instantaneously see the results of your meeting.

There is nothing futurist about this. Workers make use of voice and data grade narrow band circuits which are available to them everywhere around the clock. The newer applications of these techniques utilize "wide band networks." These are networks capable of carrying dense media messages such as video conferencing, streaming audio and massive data bases on a real time basis. Rather than a report, your team may want you to set up a small web-cam at remote sales point in northern Spain and conduct a web-based video conference to discuss your sales strategies with co-workers in London and Phoenix. Aside from the obvious benefits, this high power information flow creates its own communication management issues.

Information Theory. In an often quoted and highly influential set of experiments, psychologist George Miller (1967) demonstrated that human beings short term information capacity is the "weakest link" in the human cycle of cognitive processes. Simply stated we can only deal with an average of 5-7 issues using real short-term memory. In addition, sensory psychology research has consistently reported humans' highly selective perception of data in our environment. The combination of highly selective information processing and limited short-term memory has led to increased stress for the new information workers. We do not notice many important pieces of information in our environment and we have trouble efficiently processing those pieces of information that we do perceive. As the information organization has evolved so has the need for addressing these issues. In fact whole new industries have sprung up which offer us tools to organize our minutes, hours, and days. It is routine to see middle school children carrying **personal digital assistants.** Time management is the keynote skill of our era. Yet despite these efforts, we are bound to be forever behind because computer networks are faster and can carry more data than human cognitive networks.

Information overload, a psychological phenomenon, occurs when information flow exceeds our sensory processing abilities. This can cause very real physical stress. Yet a constant online work environment creates expectations of information processing that not all workers can meet. As students you develop norms concerning e-mail. To whom do you respond? When do you respond?

These norms may not articulate with the norms of your organization. Entire sections of intranets are devoted to Netiquette guidelines for dealing with corporate e-mail accounts. These may not meet or may exceed the norms of your organization. Entire sections of intranets are devoted to Netiquette guidelines for dealing with corporate e-mail accounts. Palloff and Pratt suggest that "**Netiquette** not only covers rules for maintaining civility in interaction but also guidelines unique to the electronic nature of forum messages" (1999, p. 190). The pressure to keep up with electronic communication flow has created a whole new category of computer related stress disorders, from carpal tunnel syndrome to **Internet addiction.** The problems of working in turbulent, highly diverse environments often produce addtional negative consequences.

Loss of Privacy. The type of communication technology necessary to provide instantaneous global access is the ideal environment for surveillance. System operators of organization networks have the ability to statistically monitor e-mail and Internet usage. As we move into the new millennium, consumers are beginning to be concerned about privacy issues. Yet the implications of these issues for organizational work are not yet clearly understood. When you use your organization's Internet gateways you are using the equivalent of a company car, and when you use their intranet, you are essentially moving into a part of their virtual office space. Where you drive in the virtual car and how you use the virtual office space become organizational activities which are subject to monitoring.

Across the world companies have moved to more flexible staffing. Job security has become a phrase no longer has meaning in the organization. In a probing essay detailing the need to "re-engineer the right to privacy," Davies (1998, p. 148) notes that one great barrier to extending consumer protection to the work place is anxiety of the modern worker. "America has entered the age of the **contingent** or temporary worker, of the consultant and just in time work force—fluid , flexible, disposable."

To counter the alienation that this type of employer-employee relationship can engender, many organizations now offer some type of stock option or financial involvement with the future of the company. Working 60–80 hour weeks is common at such new organizations as Amazon.com. When the clock strikes 5:00 P.M., Amazon.com workers are not on overtime, but on "ownertime," working for the financial improvement of their own investments in the company. Because of both the fear of being replaced and the pressure to identify with the company, preserving personal privacy is a substantial challenge in the modern information environment.

Content Management. When information becomes interpreted and formatted into an organizational structure such as a quarterly report or a project proposal, it becomes content. Workers must find processes and mechanisms for keeping track of large volumes of such content. A recent study of technological growth indicated the area of content management will be a 5–6 billion dollar business by 2004 (Trippe, 2001). Consider the way Interwoven Technologies, a leader in developing content infrastructure, describes part of the content management business.

> "End users will be able to locate any content (on the Intranet) to edit, to assign content items as workflow for another employee, to expire, deploy content to a production environment where it can be reformatted as part of a different presentation or report, or to download content for offline editing." (Interwoven, 2001, p. 12)

In the technological jargon of the twenty-first century this excerpt from Interwoven°s description of possibilities portrays an environment in which a modern employee may be asked on quite short notice to prepare a detailed sales report for world wide distribution over the company's intranet. This employee may need to find, access and edit prior reports. In addition it may be necessary to embed edited sections of spreadsheets, Powerpoint presentations and/or sections of previously recorded digital video conferences. This material will need to be re-shaped, augmented and delivered as a unified web accessible document. Ability to use search strategies, and to organize reports, presentations, and other material, will be necessary in tomorrow's organizations.

Entering the new millennium, we encounter new challenges. The organizational environment of the twenty-first century will be highly fluid and will be shaped by those workers and managers who have both the desire to lead and the communication skills necessary to coordinate and motivate. The material presented in this book can help you to acquire these skills. We wish you every success.

References

Amason, P., Allen, M. W., & Holmes, S. A. (1999). Social support and acculturative stress in the multicultural workplace. *Journal of Applied Communication Research. 27,* 310–324.

Cairncross, F. (1997). *The death of distance: How the communications revolution will change our lives.* Boston: Harvard Business School.

Rosen, R., Digh, P., Singer M., & Phillips, C. (2000). *Global literacies: Lessons on business leadership and national cultures.* New York: Simon and Schuster.

Aburdene, P., and Naisbitt, J. (1985). *Reinventing the Corporation.* New York: Warner Books.

Celente, G. (1997). *Trends: How to prepare for and profit from the changes of the 21st century.* New York: Warner Books.

Collins, J. C., Porras, J. I. (1994). *Built to last.* New York: Harper Business.

Davies, S. (1998). Re-engineering the right to privacy. In P. E. Agre & M. Rotenberg (Eds.), *Technology and Privacy: The New Landscape* (pp. 143–165). Cambridge: MIT Press.

Davis, S., & Meyer, C. (1998). *Blur.* New York: Warner Books, 1998.

Deal, T. E., & Kennedy, A. A. (1982). *Corporate Cultures: The Rites and Rituals of Corporate Life*. Massachusetts: Addison-Wesley.

Drucker, P. F. (1987). The Coming of the New Organization. *Harvard Business Review*, 66, 45–53.

Goleman, D. (1997). *Emotional intelligence*. New York: Bantam Books, 1997.

Interwoven. (2001). *Interwoven teamsite: Enterprise class content management*. Sunnyvale, California: Interwoven Inc.

Miller, G. A. (1967). The magical number seven plus or minus two: Some limits on our capacity for processing information. *The psychology of communication: Seven essays*. Baltimore: Penguin Books.

Murray, L. (2000, Mar. 10). High performance teaming basis of EQ vs. IQ training. *Business First, 16* (29), 39–43.

Palloff, R. M, and Pratt, K. (1999). *Building communities in cyberspace: Effective strategies for the online classroom*. San Francisco: Jossey-Bass.

Sellers, P. (2001, April 30). Get Over Yourself. Your ego is out of control. You're screwing up your career. Jack Welch, David Pottruck, and others can help you get control of your huge self. As if you care. *Fortune Magazine*, 76–79.

Trippe, B. (2001, Feb./Mar.). Content management technology: A booming market. *Econtent, 24* (1), 22–28.

INDEX